£27.50

CW01066513

# COGNITION, LANGUAGE and CONSCIOUSNESS: INTEGRATIVE LEVELS

# COGNITION, LANGUAGE
# and CONSCIOUSNESS:
# INTEGRATIVE LEVELS

## The T. C. Schneirla
## Conference Series
## Volume 2

edited by

**Gary Greenberg**
Wichita State University

**Ethel Tobach**
American Museum of Natural History

**LEA** LAWRENCE ERLBAUM ASSOCIATES, PUBLISHERS
1987   Hillsdale, New Jersey                    London

Lawrence Erlbaum Associates, Inc., Publishers
365 Broadway
Hillsdale, New Jersey 07642

**Library of Congress Cataloging-in-Publication Data**

Cognition, language, and consciousness.

(The T. C. Schneirla conference series)
Based on a conference held April 6–8, 1984 at
Wichita State University in Wichita, Kan.
Includes bibliographies and index.
1. Cognition—Congresses. 2. Cognition in animals—Congresses. 3. Psycholinguistics—
Congresses. 4. Animal communication—Congresses. 5. Consciousness—Congresses.
6. Psychology, Comparative—Congresses. I. Greenberg, Gary. II. Tobach, Ethel, 1921–
III. Series. [DNLM: 1. Cognition—Congresses. 2. Consciousness—
congresses. 3. Language—congresses. 4. Psychology. Comparative—congresses. BF 311
C6758 1984]
BF311.C549  1987     153     87-5425
ISBN 0-89859-722-6
Printed in the United States of America
10  9  8  7  6  5  4  3  2  1

# Contents

# Preface

The Second T. C. Schneirla Conference was again held at the Wichita State University campus in Wichita, Kansas (April 6 through 8, 1984). The setting provided a great deal of opportunity for animated and provocative discussion, which, unfortunately, is not reported verbatim herein. However, these discussions were the basis for the three papers by Aronson, Greenberg, and Tobach, and we herewith acknowledge our debt to the conference participants, without making them responsible for the final product.

The sequence in which the chapters appear is guided by the title of the volume, and is not the order in which they were presented at the conference. We were once more fortunate to have the greetings of Gerard Piel, a staunch friend of T. C. Schneirla and of comparative psychology. The presentation by Leo Vroman was the highlight of the conference dinner, and his creative and esthetically beautiful presentation of his own view of the concept of levels did much to stimulate all the participants.

We again gratefully acknowledge the continuing generous financial support of Leslie Rudd.

*Ethel Tobach*
*Gary Greenberg*

# PROLOGUE

# 1 "Each animal in its own psychological setting . . ."

Gerard Piel
*Scientific American, New York*

T. C. Schneirla was more interested in questions than in answers. How one arrived at a conclusion engaged his interest, not the novelty, astonishment or other attraction the conclusion might carry. Schneirla was not, therefore, a member of the fashionable animal-behaviorist, comparative-psychology schools of his time. Missing the tides that led on to fortune, he did not share in the Nobel Prize awarded for the discovery of the gene for aggression. Had he lived, he would have had no part in the celebration of the gene for altruism.

Schneirla would, therefore, have been astonished to find himself invited to consider the evidence to be presented here for animal "consciousness" and "cognition." That sort of thing, he would have thought, was long since behind us.

"Attributing consciousness to any lower animal and speculating as to how it must feel to be that animal," Schneirla wrote, "is a popular tendency which has its formal counterparts in speculative philosophy." He cited the 18th century moral philosopher and critic Michel de Montaigne in this connection as finding "from occurrences such as the starting and barking of dogs in their sleep . . ." that "the brutes must possess the power of imagination." Against such ready leaps to conclusion he summoned the consensus of the 20th century founders of the scientific study of animal behavior. They agreed long ago that introspection and analogy, procedures of sufficiently low validity for human psychology, were inappropriate for the study of lower animals.

Schneirla was such a spoil-sport that he did not consider Dr. Doolittle's talking menagerie fit for the entertainment of children, much less for their introduction to the understanding of animal behavior.

As the students of animal cognition take the center of the stage, it appears that the tide of interest in the ethologists is receding. While obeisance is paid in textbooks—always so careful to cover all topics—the work does not engage the interest of active evolutionary biologists. All those animal stories seem to have contributed nothing to the elucidation of the avian or the mammalian family tree.

As to the operant-conditioners, who shared public attention with the ethologists, it is not clear that they contributed anything to the measurement of the learning capacity of animals. They seem rather to have demonstrated the degree to which the behavior of animals outside their natural settings might be reduced to neurotic compulsion. Thus it was that B. F. Skinner could boast that he and his colleagues had succeeded in demonstrating "surprisingly similar performances, particularly under complex schedules, in organisms as diverse as the pigeon, mouse, rat, dog, cat and monkey."

The failure of what has been the mainstream of publication in animal behavior over the past four decades is betrayed most plainly by the poverty of ideas it has carried along. The ethogram and the releaser have none of the compelling, open-ended power of the conceptual apparatus of physics, which deals with an inherently less engaging realm of experience. The infinite interest of the subject matter and of the living subjects of comparative psychology is reduced to self-referential tautology and dead-end "explanation." What declares the success of work in other fields of science is the questions that arise from the work. In the field at hand, it is often not clear what question, to begin with, the work is about.

The next generation of workers in comparative psychology would be well advised to consult Charles Saunders Peirce on "How to Make Our Ideas Clear." Writing in *Popular Science Monthly,* then published by the American Association for the Advancement of Science, Peirce said, "There is no distinction of meaning so fine as to consist in anything but a possible difference in practice . . . It is clear, then, that the rule of attaining the highest grade of clearness of apprehension is as follows: Consider what effects, which might conceivably have practical bearings, we conceive the object of our conception to have. Then, our conception of these effects is the whole of our conception of the object."

William James urged this sensible advice as antidote to the penchant for finalities that "always hankers after unlawful magic." The truth of an idea, James said, "is not a stagnant property inherent in it. Truth happens to an idea. It becomes true, is made true by events. Its verity is, in fact, a process: the process namely of it verifying itself, its verification." In his words, this is "a program for more work."

For the working scientists, Percy Bridgman restated the Peirce counsel and the James program as a prescription for the design and planning of the work: ". . . the meanings of one's terms are to be found by analysis of the operations which one performs in applying the term in concrete situations or in verifying the truth of statement or in finding answers to questions." Thus the terms *velocity* and *position* ascribed to a particle denote not properties inherent in the particle but experiments or observations to be performed on it. The rule holds, he said, for the "non-physical . . . operations of mathmatics or logic" as well as for conventional operations in the field or laboratory.

Mathematicians are now learning to accept Bridgman's rule. At about the time Bridgman wrote, Kurt Gödel showed that finality is not to be had, even in mathematics and logic. In the words of Willard Quine, what Gödel proved ". . . was that no deductive system, with axioms however arbitrary, is capable of embracing among its theorems all the truths of the elementary arithmetic of positive integers unless it discredits itself by letting slip some falsehoods too." Mathematics is now finding place as an experimental science.

The Gödel proof does not imply, however, that logic and mathematics lose their role in the structuring of the thinking process. On the contrary, any deductive system may be cured of its bankruptcy in paradox by appropriate amendment or expansion of its premises. This stratagem engenders new paradox. But now logic adopts the pragmatic attitude; in the words of William James, it "looks away from first things and forward to last things, results, and consequences."

To the perfection of this method for making our ideas clear, Willard Quine adds the discipline of simplicity "Those [hypotheses] are most welcome which are seen to conduce most simplicity in the overall system," he says. "Predictions, once they have been deduced from the hypotheses, are subject to the discipline of evidence in turn; but the hypotheses have, at the time of hypothesis, only considerations of systematic simplicity to recommend them."

It is apparent that the Spartan virtues implicit in the philosophy of science cannot be conveyed by preaching. They can only be acquired by practice. In Schneirla they found a superlative practitioner. As the centerpiece of his life work he left the most complete description and elucidation of the behavioral repertory that we possess for any animal. That his animal was the army ant— which exhibits the most complex organized behavior outside its homesite observed in any infrahuman animal—testifies to his appetite for hard work under the most trying conditions in the field. His accounts of his observations satisfy the Peirce-James-Bridgman test in that the meanings of his terms are to be found in the operations he performed; he imports no causal or organizing mechanism from outside or beyond. In consequence, the Schneirla elucidation of the army–ant repertory gives us no answers of the sort that won acclaim for his more celebrated contemporaries. On the contrary, it asks questions: questions for the insect physiologist armed with the tools of molecular biology; questions for comparative psychology armed with comparably complete elucidation of the behavioral repertory of other animals.

As a philosopher of science, Schneirla practiced with special grace the virtue of simplicity. ". . . of alternative explanations for a given phenomenon," he wrote, "choose the simplest, that requiring the fewest assumptions." In comparative psychology, as he well understood, choice of "the simplest" must reckon with the biological endowment of the animal at hand. As the rule of simplicity in his line of work he embraced the canon of his forerunner C. L.

Morgan: "In no case may we interpret an action as the outcome of the exercise of a higher physical faculty if it can be interpreted as the outcome of the exercise of one which stands lower in the psychological scale." By "higher" and "lower," neither Morgan nor Schneirla implied any hierarchy of excellence but only comparative complexity in anatomy, physiology and behavior.

In essays that Schneirla wrote to admonish his contemporaries and to caution their admiring public, he developed the useful concept of "levels of integration." As between an aggregation of paramecia and of people, he suggested, comparative psychology would encounter many levels at which behavior would find explanation in the degree of elaboration of anatomy and physiology worked by the 3.5 billion years of the evolution of life. That, in Schneirla's estimation, constituted a sufficiently challenging program for his discipline, as long as its practitioners wished it to be credited as a scientific discipline.

Successive levels of integration present sufficiently familiar and contrasting states of affairs throughout the natural order. Oxygen and hydrogen in their elemental and molecular states, independent of one another, each present a different situation from their compound in water. The difference is not additive, but rather a discontinuous jump from one level of integration to another, broadly speaking from physics to chemistry. The behavior of water in the narrow range of the physical variables of the known universe in which life processes proceed shows that physics and chemistry provide inadequate compartmentation of that natural order. In the cytoplasm of the living cell, which is more than 90 percent water, water serves not merely as the diluent, solvent carrier of the large molecules it contains but, in ways still unresolved, as a kind of liquid-crystal matrix of those molecules and also plays a functional as well as supportive architectural role. So also, in the large molecules that encode genetic information, the sequence of the bases encode information that transcends the quantum electrodynamics that coils up the double helix.

In keeping with the rule of simplicity and choice of the appropriate level of integration, the reproductive behavior of the marine mollusk Aplysia may now be described in the performance of a nervous system composed of some 20,000 cells tied together in five ganglional nodes at which afferent sensory stimuli excite appropriate efferent impulses to the musculature—all without invocation of the maternal instinct. The nervous system of Aplasia presents, obviously, a level of integration of anatomy, physiology and behavior qualitatively distinct from that of the vertebrates in which the nervous system is centrally organized and progressively "cerebralized" in more elaborate brains. In the vertebrate order, qualitative saltations in structure and physiology accompany corresponding saltations in behavioral capacity, from rudimentary learning to the onset of evidence for purposive behavior.

Cognition is not an attribute inherent in living tissue or an explanation to which a behavioral episode may be reduced. It is itself a high-order behavioral function regularly observed in the performance of the most highly organized aggregation of matter in the known universe. Attribution of cognition to the performance of a lower-order aggregation may prove to be not only wrong but almost certainly less interesting than the understanding that would issue from a different hypothesis. So, Schneirla's description of the internally propelled, feedback-regulated life cycle of the army ants holds deeper fascination and wider relevance than the "explanations" his bemused predecessors drew from the martial treatises of von Clausewitz.

Not much is to be learned from episodes of behavior observed in isolation from the total repertory and life history of an animal in its natural setting. The Schneirla insistence that the proper study of comparative psychology is the ontogeny of behavior is a prescription for more work than is usually evidenced in the literature of the field. "More work" William James said, "is necessary to make truth happen to an idea." That is the kind of work required of comparative psychology if it is to contribute to understanding of cognition and consciousness.

# 2 Nomans' Languages

Leo Vroman
*Veterans Administration Medical Center*
*Brooklyn, New York*

It seems to me that we are all thinking, working, and living mostly within a set of amputated levels: a small circle of family and friends, information, introspection and field of study. A group of us may climb a mountain and share a view, or lie in a hospital room and share a set of symptoms and thoughts about a particular organ, but we will fail to find thoughts and words that directly connect the distant views with the near pains. I myself study blood, divorced from the body in which it used to live. How real is this isolated level of organization?

Living among a growing herd of poised nuclear weapons, it has become easy for me to imagine this living world shorn of its highest organized levels, with all of structured humanity and all of its structured humans gone. I imagine myself returning then, where mountains have crushed the crowds of cowering people, cut off the old rapids and instead, released a slowly moving stream of live blood crawling where the Colorado River used to run. The Grand Canyon walls must have protected it against rampant radiation. There is little clotting in shocked blood. A skin of denaturing protein protects the deep networks of monocytes that have become nested among the long dead roots of bygone birches. The blood is still active, now no longer defending us but defending itself. In winter, rafts of fibrin form around blood platelets that were broken by frost; small organisms ride the crimson floats to eat the dead red cells, and are in turn devoured by granulocytes lurking underneath. It is a new world, one that owes nothing but its origin to us and that now serves nothing but itself, by means of the same natural laws that, until such a short time ago, we had served ourselves with.

We could prolong the scene by introducing evolutionary changes within this awful river, to keep it alive, but after all, this is only an exercise intended to give my mind in its study of an isolated system, a concrete example to think about. I am not sure what this Blood River could have proved by surviving, to some other, last surviving biologist observing it. To me, the mere thought of life continuing at any level without the mutual benefits of any higher organization, provides a refreshing look at the consequences of defining too strictly the levels we think we are studying. The more we become involved in any level—subatomic or up—the more detail we find existing within that level, the more words we need to describe it, the more we must concentrate these words in the form of contractions and new words for faster description of more and more fleeting events, and the less we can make ourselves understood by those involved in other levels. And the less we understand those others, and the less we may care. The small candle we walk into the dark with leaves all beyond in even deeper darkness. That way, it is easy to concentrate, and perhaps that is helpful.

I believe there are certain deficiencies in our visual perception that are needed by us to allow cognition.

1. We cannot perceive a thing that never repeats itself in space or time. Only when something seems to return in time or space can we begin to believe that there are certain laws responsible for the thing's reproduceable shape, coherence and behavior, and we can give it a name. I distinguish two ways in which the subunits of a thing can contribute to our perception of the thing as an entity: texture, caused by the subunits to be more or less identical to each other; and structure, caused or expressed by each subunit differing from each other subunit so that it contributes in its own way to the coherent function or appearance of the total thing. Its return and predictability give us the sense that we are perceiving some form of eternity: the evidence of never-changing natural laws. At the same time, we can now start counting in numbers of more than one: believing that some things are equal and unchanging, we can describe their crowd digitally, measure them and become scientists.

2. Physiologically, we become insensitive to a stimulus that continues unchanged. If we want to perceive eternity, we can only do so by perceiving cyclic events, and by concluding that the laws reproducing them are eternal.

3. Distant sounds merge, and thanks to the lenses in our eyes, things at a distance appear small enough to make their detail invisible and their shape simple. We climb mountains in our lust for simplification: looking down, we see little enough of our lower origin to think that down there, life remains uncomplicated.

4. Whatever image we call to mind, fills it. Think of a cell containing a nucleus, granules, mitochondria, and the imaginary cell will appear in front of you as an object of about 10 inches diameter, seen at a comfortable reading distance, like a picture in a nice book. Think of our solar system, or of an atom, as a system of orbits and each will swell or shrink to a comfortable size, allowing us to apply our other deficiencies in our efforts to describe the object as a simple system containing a limited number of subunits (Fig. 2.1).

FIGURE 2.1.   The size of things.

I think these shortcomings or preoccupations of those involved in one level can be demonstrated by performing a transition from one level to the next. Take a sheet of white paper in your hand. It is an entity, a thing because its parts resemble each other and hold on to each other in what appears a uniform way. It has texture, but does it have structure? Crumple the sheet very slowly, gathering it into the palm of your hand until the sheet is now a ball fitting inside your fist. What did the sheet do? It adapted, with each point of its flat body in its own way obeying certain identical laws, to create a structure: a system of which each part cooperated in allowing the entire sheet to adapt to the hollow space formed by your hand. Now, we must believe that each tiny element of the original sheet must have had its individual properties to begin with, and that the non-crumpled sheet already had more than texture: it had its own, hidden, structure.

The ball of paper is a three-dimensional model of a protein molecule arranging its atoms, of an organ in an organism, or of a nation. No structured thing can be divided and maintain its character. And yet we often seem to hope that at least the great mass that our personal object of interest is part of, or else that at least the subunits of our object, are each held together in a simpler way, therefore requiring less study. Thoughts, words, even numbers may fail us when we try to characterize each structured subunit that is involved in creating the larger structure. This impotence forces us to pretend that many subunits are identical to each other as if much of the structure we look at consists of texture. That way we can climb a mountain to look around and relax while taking in the woolly or stickly 'texture' of maple– or fir–covered hills, and use a single word to describe it. Unfortunately, we must soon climb down again. Most of us, I think, feel exposed when realizing that our field of expertise is connected to equally complex fields of others' expertise. I hesitate to try and learn the jargon of others for fear that I may begin to understand them and become involved in complexities to which I can contribute less than to my own world.

Yet, the web of causal relationships that I am caught in building, tends to define the level or system I am studying: the more densely coherent it becomes, the more it appears to create a detached shape that in reality it does not have, and the more it tends to blind me to other, even to intersecting ones (Fig. 2.2).

From this simultaneous role, or task, of spider, web, and fly I see no simple way out. It appears as if our minds and languages must spread apart while falling increasingly behind the entirety that we, collectively, are learning about reality. We can demonstrate this dramatically by trying to understand—that is, read— ourselves at the level of protein function. A protein molecule is a chain of usually hundreds out of a choice of about 20 kinds of subunits (residues). This long linear array markedly resembles a word as spelled in our Western culture—a very long word. We can compute roughly how many of these words we contain, and then how much time we would require to 'read' one second of our own life (see Fig. 2.3). I arrived at a need of 20 million years to read that one second of my self—but even then, the brain I am reading with suffers a turnover of molecules that itself can never follow. And each protein molecule can be regarded as having a choice of meanings depending on context: it should be read, not along its length of residues, but across its various coils, loops, and bends that often bring sequentially distant residues together and exclude many from the

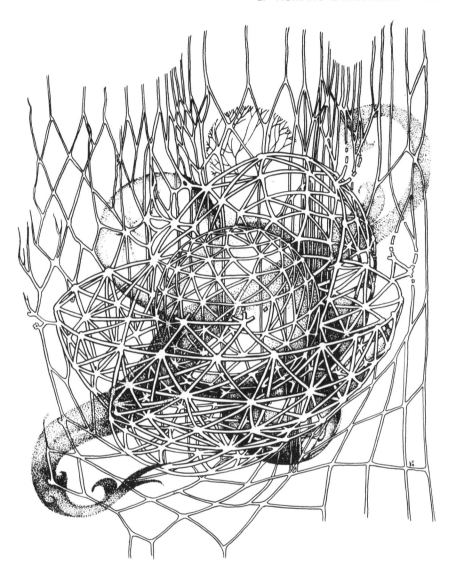

FIGURE 2.2.    Intersecting levels.

molecule's surface that is being read by its environment; so whatever bends the shape of a protein (or other) molecule, changes its meaning.

It is my impression that we usually imagine a hierarchy to exist in life, with subunits serving the parent unit, and the parent unit somehow maintaining an environment in which the subunits can continue to serve. Perhaps our tendency

See our bodies write their news!
And the letters that they use
are our protein residues.

Each body writes the proteins in it
at ten to the sixteenth a minute:
my inside news is near-infinite!

One second of my life would need
twenty million years to read
at a more than human speed—

but what flickering, slanting light
do I shed on what I write?
deep into my body's night!

What fire must illuminate
these facts behind my fears and fate,
seen so early, read so late?

My old words burn to give the flame
that lights the words I just became...
that will be ashes, all the same.

FIGURE 2.3.  Twenty million years to read one second of my life.

to regard the subject or level of our own interest as a master, and its subunits as slaves, alienates and separates our professional languages most thoroughly. I can see my beloved protein molecules then, placed rather low and misunderstood by those describing their master structures. And how vast are the ranges of size and speed in levels both below and above my subject! To see them all, up to an entire live human, I have tried to draw each larger level at such an increased distance

FIGURE 2.4.  Looking up from the atomic to the human body. See text.

that, to the observing eye, the structures at all levels would seem of equal diameter (Fig. 2.4). One can calculate that, if an atomic nucleus were large enough to show us all of its subatomic particles comfortably at reading distance, the atom containing the nucleus would have to be as large as the town hall of Gouda, a molecule containing the atom would be about as large as the

Netherlands containing that city, the pituitary cell containing the molecule would be as large (and drawn as far away) as the moon, the pituitary containing the cell as large as the sun, and the human containing the pituitary would reach to the stars.

Efforts to bring together the scientific data on these very distant levels are, I am sure, a mere reflection of their pre-existing unity, and should know no boundaries within our universe. Neither should we limit our efforts to connect our vastly different languages—from the mathematics describing subnuclear structure to the poetry describing ourselves and our world—even if all we are doing is a recreation of what already exists. Only where structure is recognized will it be respected.

Too often, opposite sides misunderstanding each other's languages meet in battle on a noman's land where their interpreters used to live, and where both vocabularies had merged into a third language: a noman's language, too timid to be heard. That is the way many nations clash, deaf and blind to the common ground they destroy; and that is the way two specialists may clash over a whispering patient. Perhaps we should listen more to those tiny voices speaking Nomanch in various tongues, where the big words shouted around them are understood to be small and often futile.

I must end this chapter confessing that it was written in Nomanch: starting with a more or less poetic description of a scene without scientifically supported content, intended to make a more or less scientific point. And I must confess that I have trouble keeping my own levels apart. When writing scientifically, I am too often tempted to use a word with several meanings that all apply: a poetic device that indicates a science-flavored desire to be sparse and economical. On the other hand, when writing poetry I desire so much to make involvement with scientifically proved truth a part of poetic love for this world's reality, that I tend to lose those readers who do not want to be drawn into a study of blood.

There is a new Dutch textbook of hematology that starts with a rather long and not very recent poem in which I describe an experiment that my assistant and I had just performed at that time. The results were very exciting to me, and they were correct, but my interpretation of them was totally wrong. Fortunately, I wrote the scientific description of our work much more cautiously, so that we did not have to withdraw its publication in Nature.

Now tell me: should I withdraw the poem?

# II COLLOQUIUM

# 3 Reflections on Thinking in Animals

Robert Epstein
*Boston University*
*Cambridge Center for Behavioral Studies*

As recently as two or three years ago, I would have gone to great lengths to try to convince my reader (a) that the utility of the concept of cognition is questionable, and (b) that the mind doesn't even exist. The first claim conceivably falls within the realm of scientific discourse: If someone claims that the concept of cognition has scientific value, then one should examine the available data, see how the concept is employed, and dispute it where more powerful alternatives are at hand. The second topic, the existence of mind, is an issue in the realm of pure philosophy. Scientific inquiry should, I now believe, proceed without paying it any mind.

Instead of arguing against the utility of the concept of mind, I will argue that the original argument is pointless. I will do so by drawing a distinction between the study of behavior and behaviorism, by examining some of the traditional arguments against mentalism in psychology, and by examining some of the ways in which the theory of evolution has been used with respect to thinking in animals.

## BEHAVIORISM VERSUS PRAXICS

The ism that has been most concerned with the utility of the concept of mind is behaviorism. Behaviorism began early in the century as a movement for reform in psychology. Its founder, John B. Watson, like many psychologists of the day, was disillusioned with the progress that had been made in the investigation of mind—psychology's traditional subject matter. He argued that the subject matter of the field should be changed to the behavior of organisms and that all investigations of mind and consciousness should cease (e.g., Watson, 1913). The study of mind held its own, and, with the advent of computers and the various alliances that have been formed between psychologists, philosophers, linguists, and computer scientists, the study of mind has become, once again, the primary subject matter of the field.

Consistent with the dominance of a concern with mind, behaviorism as a movement has died. The few reformers still around today are largely ignored by the field. As I have discussed in detail elsewhere (Epstein, 1984a), however, the movement had substantial outcomes: First, it helped to convince many people that the behavior of organisms was a legitimate subject matter, and second, it produced a school of philosophy, which today is the appropriate referent of the term "behaviorism." Others (e.g., Bergmann, 1956) have argued that the behavioristic movement left an indelible mark on traditional psychology itself: Modern cognitivists are now almost pathologically concerned with objectivity in method and terminology, an outcome, in part, of early behaviorism.

Behaviorism as a movement is dead, but the philosophy survives. And, for a variety of reasons, it is important to distinguish the philosophy from the scientific discipline that the philosophy helped to inspire—to distinguish the *ism* from *the study of behavior*. The latter has been labeled "praxics," a blend of "physics" and the Greek *praxis* for "behavior" or "action" (Epstein, 1984a, 1985c, in press-a). Modern behaviorism makes many controversial claims about the nature of mind, feelings, language, perception, and free will (Zuriff, 1985), but it is not in the nature of science to make such claims.

Note, too, that you can be a behaviorist without being a praxist, and vice versa. You may subscribe to the philosophy but not study behavior. Conversely, you may study behavior and not believe in the philosophy. You may study behavior *and yet believe strongly that feelings are important, that mind exists, and even that people have free will.* There is no contradiction here. One's ability to determine lawful relationships between events in behavior and the environment—to discover how behavior varies as a function of genes, physiology, anatomy, conditioning, sleep deprivation, drugs, evolutionary history, nutrition, and so on—should not be affected at all by such beliefs. Physics has been advanced, and is still advanced, by thousands of individuals who believe in mind, free will, feelings, and, sometimes, even God.

Yet for many years only true believers were allowed to work in behavioral laboratories. Others have made their way in, but they have been known to skulk. What a waste of talent! For the science of behavior to grow and flourish, it must break free of the ism, and the laboratory doors must be opened to all.

Lately, I find I am much less concerned with behaviorism and far more concerned with praxics. I remain relatively convinced by behaviorism, especially by the arguments that behaviorists make regarding mind and cognition. But I have come to regard the arguments, or at least my own participation in them, as unproductive and superfluous for several reasons: First, people's opinions on these issues are very, very hard to change. You can, sometimes, change someone's opinion about the theory of evolution by pointing to a very impressive body of evidence which supports the theory. But no data of which I am aware will convince someone that he or she lacks a mind or free will.

Second, I have found that whenever one debates about free will, mind, or feelings—the traditional triumverate in philosophical psychology and modern behaviorism's triumverate of controversial concerns—emotions turn up. I have seen red faces, I have seen shouting, I have seen spittle, and I have been insulted. On one occasion (and I have this on tape) I was challenged to a duel.

Third, debating these matters now seems to me to be a kind of academic backpedalling. When you backpedal on a modern bicycle, the gears do not engage. You don't go anywhere. It is fun to backpedal—everyone does it—especially when one is coasting down a hill and one's leg muscles are atrophying. When I first started investigating novel behavior in animals, I was invited to debate, to be in symposia—not with praxists, but with cognitive psychologists, some of whom were troubled by my work. As one might expect, I was rarely called on to clairfy my procedures or to defend my theories but rather to defend *behaviorism*! In other words, I was spending a lot of time backpedalling—defending a school of thought which, as I now see it, no datum can defend. And I was being kept from moving forward in my research. That is the point. Science and scientists suffer when philosophy intrudes.

Fourth, the counterarguments to the standard behavioristic positions are not entirely absurd. There is stuff inside the heads of most people, and the nature of the stuff is not yet well understood. Not all behavior is predictable at this point—in fact, a great deal still seems fairly mysterious. The role that genes and physical maturation play in language acquisition and other complex behavioral phenomena is not yet clear. In short, the data are not yet in.

Finally, no one can deny that abstract models, the coin of modern cognitive psychology, have proved useful historically, even models as simplistic as Rutherford's atomic solar system.


## COGNITION


Let me now backpedal by reviewing some of the arguments—mainly behavioristic arguments—against the use of the concept of cognition in the interpretation of animal behavior. I do this reluctantly. It was Hans Reichenbach who said that the history of philosophy would advance ever so much faster "if its progress were not so often delayed by those who have made the history of philosophy the subject of their research" (Reichenbach, 1951, p. 15). I suggest further that our understanding of the behavior of organisms might advance ever so much faster if we spent more time studying it and less time philosophizing about it.

I present five traditional arguments:

1. *The search for variables.* An appeal to mind can obscure the search for the controlling variables of the behavior for which mind is said to be responsible. You see some extraordinary behavior, attribute it to "insight," "reasoning," or "the self-concept," and further inquiry ceases. The contribution of other variables—genes, physiology, anatomy, nutrition, conditioning, sleep deprivation, and so on—is not determined, and, even worse, an illusion of understanding is sometimes created. In attributing the behavior to a "self-concept," we might mistakenly assert that we now understand that behavior.

2. *The reification error.* Sometimes the kinds of concepts that are introduced in discussions of mind or cognition are unjustifiably reified. One commits the so-called "reification error," or "hypostatization," or what Reichenbach (1951) labeled "the substantialization of abstracta." This is often done with "self," "memory," "will," "unconscious," and so on. That is, sometimes people mistakenly use these terms as if they refer to things when they do not. "Will" is more like "love" or "democracy" than like "brain" or "table." That is not to say that such concepts are necessarily useless. But it is a mistake to treat an abstract noun as if it refers to a thing.

3. *Property as explanation.* We sometimes commit an error about which Isaac Newton warned in his *Principia*: We attribute some phenomenon to a property of that phenomenon. For example, we see a child striking other children on a playground—that is, acting "aggressively." Aggressiveness is a property of or description of the behavior. We ask, "Why is the child behaving in this way?" and the answer, sometimes, is "because the child is aggressive." But aggressiveness does not explain the child's behavior, and, at least in this instance, it sheds no light whatsoever on the behavior. We shed more light by identifying variables of which the behavior is a function: The child's parents strike each other or strike their children, the child effectively controls the behavior of other children by striking them, the child lacks sleep or certain nutrients in his or her diet, and so on. To attribute *blank*ful behavior to *blank* tells us nothing about where the behavior comes from.

4. *The teleological error.* In spite of all the caveats and reminders, we all tend, from time to time, to explain current phenomena by referring to *future* events. "Why are you going to the dentist?" *"To have a tooth pulled."* Why did the chicken cross the road? *"To get to the other side."* We excuse ourselves for making such statements by distinguishing between "reasons" and what are sometimes still called "causes." My reason for visiting the dentist was to have the tooth extracted, but there are many possible variables that contributed to the occurrence of the behavior: My tooth was decayed, a nerve was damaged, my wife instructed me to go, in the past under similar circumstances a visit to the dentist removed a source of pain, and so on. Explanations of current events must be in terms of past or concurrent events.

5. *Post hoc ergo propter hoc.* Finally, we tend to rely on sequence to tell us what caused what, but as Hume, Michotte, and many others have noted in various ways, sequence can be misleading. If, on the approach of a tiger, one first feels fear and then runs, one might attribute the running to the fear. James and Lange turned the causal sequence around: Incipient running, they claimed, produces changes in your body that you feel as fear. And indeed most people have had at least a few dramatic experiences in which motor behavior very obviously preceded a rush of emotion. Remember the time you veered your car away from a child in the road and *then* experienced a panic reaction? But to attribute a causal role to either emotion or motor behavior on the basis of such incidents is unnecessary and misleading. Rather, as Skinner has pointed out, the tiger can be said to have produced *both* the emotional and motor behavior. The sequence in which these occurred was presumably determined by other identifiable variables.

To all of these criticisms the cognitive psychologist—that is, *the psychologist*—has answers, and, indeed, I now believe that praxists and behaviorists have been at fault by not listening to the answers more closely. I am not saying that we should be *persuaded* by the answers. Nor am I suggesting that praxists should abandon their concern with the concrete, measurable, and manipulable variables that determine behavior. Rather, I am saying that no psychologist worth his or her salt would deliberately commit any of the five errors I have listed above. Both the methods and theories of many modern experimental psychologists are fairly sophisticated. The sloppy thinking that behaviorists sometimes attribute to cognitivists is, I'm afraid, often in the eye of the beholder.

**The Controlling Variables.**    Many psychologists are simply not interested in the controlling variables of behavior, and why should they be? The key is subject matter. The subject matter of the psychologist is *mind*. The effect that some drug or reinforcement history has on *behavior* is beside the point. Events in behavior and the environment are of interest only to the extent that they shed light on *mental life*. I ask my readers, especially those who have an interest in behavior per se, to pretend that they have a strong and sincere interest in a *science of mental life* (I have to struggle to do this, but it is an invaluable exercise). The determinants of behavior are now beside the point. You are interested in the nature, "structure," and, perhaps, the "function" of *mind*. Does it work like a computer? Is it a serial processor or a parallel processor? Does it have different types of memories? Will one general set of laws account for all of its operations?

The assertion that mind is a legitimate subject matter—or, in other words, that psychology is a legitimate field—leads to "interesting questions." It has "heuristic value." It leads (perhaps serendipitously—but that is the case in all of the sciences) to "interesting discoveries" that often have "practical applications." End of exercise.

The study of behavior can be similarly defended (Epstein, 1984a, 1985c, in press-a).

### Reification and Explanation.

One *can* talk about such things as "memory," "self," and "mind" without committing the reification error. "Self," for example, has been used by people who know enough not to commit this error (e.g., Kagan, 1981) as a hypothetical construct that unifies a variety of apparently unrelated phenomena in early childhood: A variety of "self"-related behaviors all seem to emerge within a few months of each other, suggesting some underlying, possibly causal, process that is common to all (Lewis & Brooks-Gunn, 1979; cf. Epstein & Koerner, 1986). If a variety of self-related behaviors indeed appear in lockstep fashion, and if they prove to be insensitive to variations in the environment, then one may eventually find the actual physical embodiment of "self"—maturational changes in the brain which somehow facilitate the emergence of self-related behaviors. (Note that the mentalist would not be satisfied with the changes in anatomy and physiology alone. "Self" may be correlated with those changes, but it is *not* those changes.)

Cognitive concepts may be abused: They may be reified or used to explain behavior from which they are merely inferred. But they may also be used conservatively and constructively: They may be used to order apparently disorderly data; they may be used as tentative explanations for which, ultimately, some sort of physical instantiation could be found.

### Purpose.

One can also talk about purpose and goals without committing the teleological error. In fact, I have never met a psychologist who believed that the future controls the present, so what is all the fuss about purpose?

Purposeful behavior need not always have a purpose. A little boy may rummage through a box of toys without a goal "in mind." Does a goal make any difference? Is the search behavior any different if he is envisioning a little yellow truck? Is the behavior any different if he says to himself "I want the yellow truck" as he rummages? Very likely it is. But the behavior we speak of as indicative of his goal is just more behavior: It is not in the future; it is current—concurrent with the search behavior (which is also indicative of "a goal"). It demands its own explanation (did his playmate just ask him for the yellow truck?). *It probably also makes a difference in the behavior we observe,* although its sole function may be discriminative—which means, in a sense, that it is a kind of reminder: It helps keep the search behavior from•drifting to other objects or other behaviors. Cognitivists very often mean little more than concurrent behavior of this sort when they speak of purpose.

Sloppy thinking turns up in every discipline, but cognitivists, I now believe, have no special claim on it. Psychologists have, from time to time, committed each of the errors I have just listed, but they may still study what they call "mind" without committing any of them. *Psychologists and praxists are in-*

*terested in different subject matters, not different standards of research or analysis.*

## THE IRRELEVANCE OF EVOLUTON

How, if at all, can the theory of evolution help us to shed some light on "thinking" in animals? Can it tell us whether the notion of cognition in animals is useful?

I regret to say that, unlike other authors in this volume, I believe the theory of evolution cannot help us, for, when it comes to cognition, evolution can easily be twisted to suit one's needs. The theory of evolution has been used in three different ways with respect to the concept of cognition in animals: to support it fully, to support it with reservations, and to reject it entirely (Epstein, 1984b). Moreover, I believe that none of these applications of the theory is unreasonable.

### Support for Cognition

The first pertinent exemplar is the position taken by George J. Romanes (Romanes, 1888), a 19th-century naturalist who, prompted by simple problem-solving behavior or even facial contortions in animal subjects, spoke freely about the mental world of animals; that is, he interpreted animal behavior in traditional human terms, a practice sometimes called "anthropomorphism." Romanes justified this practice by appealing to the theory of evolution, which, after all, drew attention to the fact that species are not quite as separate and diverse as many people had believed. There is continuity among species.

In his new book *Animal Thinking,* Griffin (1983) uses the same approach. From instances of human-like animal behavior he infers the existence of mind, feelings, and intentions in animals: Vultures use stones to break open ostrich eggs. A green heron takes bread from a picnicker's table and strews it on the surface of a nearby creek in order to catch fish that rise for the bait. Polar bears throw large chunks of ice at seals to wound or kill them. I know of no way to discredit the kinds of speculations Griffin makes about such animals, and I see no point in doing so. But—and Griffin does not express interest in this in the book—I think we have come a long way toward understanding and predicting the kind of *behavior* about which he speaks, and an effective understanding of the behavior seems to me to be as valuable an achievement as an effective understanding of "mind."

**Behavior.** Epstein and Medalie (1983), for example, showed that a pigeon with relevant skills could "spontaneously" use a box as an extension of its own beak to reach an object behind a wall. More important, we offered a detailed account of the emergence of the performance in terms of empirically-validated principles of behavior. The pigeon was first taught to push a flat, hexagonal box toward a green spot placed at random positions around the base of a large cylindrical chamber. Then a Plexiglas wall was installed in the bird's chamber. At the base of the wall was a gap, at the center of which was a small metal plate. In the absence of the box, we taught the bird to peck the plate. Then we gradually moved the plate behind the wall, so that the bird had to stretch its head beneath the wall to peck the plate. The box was then added to the chamber on the bird's side of the wall, and we continued to reinforce pecks to the plate while extinguishing behavior with respect to the box.

Finally, after there were no signs of pecks to the box for five consecutive daily sessions, we conducted the following test: With the box still in the chamber on the bird's side of the Plexiglass wall, we moved the plate just out of the bird's reach on the other side of the wall. The resulting performance resembled that of a young child faced with a comparable problem. The bird stretched repeatedly toward the plate, it pushed up against the wall, it scraped its feet on the floor, stretched again, and so on. After about 30 seconds, it approached the box, pecked it weakly, turned and approached the wall again, and then stretched again toward the plate. After 90 seconds, it began, quite suddenly, to push the box directly toward the wall. It pushed the box under the wall, thrust it against the plate and *then began to peck the box repeatedly, which was now in contact with the plate.*

The bird's performance can be accounted for in terms of empirical principles. For example, the bird's first pushes seem to be the result of a phenomenon called *resurgence* (Epstein, 1983, 1985b): When, in a given situation, behavior that was recently effective is no longer effective, other behaviors that were previously effective under similar conditions tend to recur. The bird's stretches toward the plate are ineffective; they are undergoing extinction. Therefore, behavior with respect to the box should become more likely, and, indeed, the frequency of behavior with respect to the box steadily increases, and the bird finally starts to push.

Even more striking were the performances described by Epstein, Kirshnit, Lanza, and Rubin (1984): They showed that pigeons with appropriate training histories could solve one of Köhler's (1925) classic box-and-banana problems in an insightful, human-like fashion. They also showed that different training histories make a difference. To solve the problem insightfully, a bird must have learned (a) not to jump and fly toward the target (a small facsimile of a banana suspended just out of the bird's reach), (b) to push a box toward targets at ground level, and (c) to climb onto a fixed box and to peck a banana overhead. Birds solved the problem clumsily if (a) jumping and flying had not been eliminated before the test or (b) they had learned to push but never to push toward a target. Subjects could not solve the problem at all if they had never learned to push or if they had never learned to climb.

In the test the birds were faced with the banana out of reach and the box elsewhere in the chamber. Birds with appropriate histories at first seemed confused when confronted with this scenario; they oriented toward the banana, turned in circles, oriented toward the box, and so on. Then, in a continuous series of movements, they pushed the box toward the banana, stopped when the box was beneath the banana, climbed, and pecked. More complicated performances have also been generated (e.g., Epstein, 1985a, in press-b), and, in each case, detailed moment-to-moment analyses have been offered (also see Epstein, 1981, 1984c, 1985c, 1986, and Epstein, Lanza, & Skinner, 1981).

Experiments of this sort have led to a formal theory, called Generativity Theory, of the emergence of ongoing behavior in the natural environment, and Epstein (1985c) presented equations and a computer model based on this theory which have proved reasonably successful in predicting ongoing, intelligent performances in human subjects.

## Skepticism

The theory of evolution has been used not only to justify the concept of animal mind but also to question it in various ways. For example, Lloyd Morgan, another naturalist, used evolutionary theory to justify a conservative position. Today we attribute to him a variant of the principle of parsimony, sometimes called Morgan's Canon (Morgan, 1894). Though some speak of it as if it rules out the study of mind, in fact it does not. Morgan said merely that the theory of evolution implies not only continuity among species, but also gradations and differences among species. Humanlike behavior in an animal, he said, must be interpreted economically. When applied to cognition, that means that one must not refer to higher mental processes when lower ones will do. To my knowledge, Morgan never questioned the existence of cognition in animals; he merely raised a question of degree (Epstein, 1984b).

## Rejecting Cognition

The third use of evolutionary theory arose as a result of advances in laboratory research on behavior during the first decades of this century. Thorndike's first puzzle box experiments were published in a monograph in 1898 (Thorndike, 1898) and then in book form in 1911 (Thorndike, 1911), and Pavlov's work came to light during the first decade. A variety of progress was made in accounting for animal behavior, at least under laboratory conditions, in terms of conditioning—in objective, cold, mechanistic terms, without reference to mind.

Once again, the theory of evolution was applied to the question of cognition, and this time, cognition was rejected entirely: If there is continuity among species, the argument went, and if nonhuman animal behavior is explainable by laws of conditioning, then the behavior of *human beings* should also be explainable by laws of conditioning. Thus mind is a spurious concept, even in humans, or, to put the matter crudely, *we err not only by anthropomorphizing with animals but also by anthropomorphizing with people*. This argument is typical of early behaviorism.

All of these views have weaknesses, but I will comment only on the last. The assertion that animal behavior is explainable by laws of conditioning was not supported by data in the 1920s when it was first made with any vigor, and it is still not fully supported today. One also has the extrapolation problem: Though there is continuity, there are also differences and gradations. Thus, even if all nonhuman behavior is explainable this way, it is not necessarily true that all human behavior is explainable this way.

Regrettably, the theory of evolution, which has been so illuminating in our understanding of behavior, sheds no light on the concept of mind.

## CONCLUSIONS

Backpedalling is excusable if you have nowhere to go. But cognitivists seem confident that they are travelling new and exciting roads and that great destinations await. Behaviorists are philosophers, and since philosophers have been known to get airsick simply by detaching themselves from their armchairs, we need not worry about how far they will travel. Finally, laboratory praxics is furthering our understanding of the *behavior* people associate with cognitive processes.

So why backpedal?

## ACKNOWLEDGMENT

I thank D. Kolker for help in the preparation of the manuscript and G. Greenberg and E. Tobach for stimulating discussions and constructive advice.

## REFERENCES

Bergmann, G. (1956). The contribution of John B. Watson. *Psychological Review, 63*, 265–276.

Epstein, R. (1981). On pigeons and people: A preliminary look at the Columban Simulation Project. *The Behavior Analyst, 4*, 43–55.

Epstein, R. (1983). Resurgence of previously reinforced behavior during extinction. *Behaviour Analysis Letters, 3*, 391–397.

Epstein, R. (1984a). The case for praxics. *The Behavior Analyst, 7*, 101–119.

Epstein, R. (1984b). The principal of parsimony and some applications in psychology. *The Journal of Mind and Behavior, 5*, 119–130.

Epstein, R. (1984c). Simulation research in the analysis of behavior. *Behaviorism, 12*, 41–59.

Epstein, R. (1985a). The spontaneous interconnection of three repertoires. *Psychological Record, 35*, 131–141.

Epstein, R. (1985b). Extinction-induced resurgence: Preliminary investigations and possible applications. *Psychological Record, 35*, 143–153.

Epstein, R. (1985c). Animal cognition as the praxist views it. *Neuroscience and Biobehavioral Reviews, 9*, 623–630.

Epstein, R. (1986). Bringing cognition and creativity into the behavioral laboratory. In T. Knapp & L. Robertson (Eds.), *Approaches to cognition: Contrasts and controversies* (pp. 91–109). Hillsdale, NJ: Lawrence Erlbaum Associates.

Epstein, R. (in press-a). Comparative psychology as the praxist views it. *Journal of Comparative Psychology.*

Epstein, R. (in press-b). The spontaneous interconnection of four repertoires of behavior in a pigeon. *Journal of Comparative Psychology.*

Epstein, R., Kirshnit, C., Lanza, R., & Rubin, L. (1984). "Insight" in the pigeon: Antecedents and determinants of an intelligent performance. *Nature, 308*, 61–62.

Epstein, R., & Koerner, J. (1986). The self-concept and other daemons. In J. Suls & A. Greenwald (Eds.), *Psychological perspectives on the self, Vol. 3* (pp. 27–53). Hillsdale, NJ: Lawrence Erlbaum Associates.

Epstein, R., Lanza, R., & Skinner, B. F. (1981). "Self-awareness" in the pigeon. *Science, 212*, 695–696.

Epstein, R., & Medalie, S. (1983). The spontaneous use of a tool by a pigeon. *Behaviour Analysis Letters, 1*, 241–246.

Griffin, D. (1983). *Animal thinking.* Cambridge, MA: Harvard University Press.

Kagan, J. (1981). *The second year: The emergence of self-awareness.* Cambridge, MA: Harvard University Press.

Köhler, W. (1925). *The mentality of apes.* London: Kegan Paul.

Lewis, M., & Brooks-Gunn, J. (1979). *Social cognition and the acquisition of self.* New York: Plenum.

Morgan, C. L. (1894). *An introduction to comparative psychology.* London: Walter Scott.

Reichenbach, H. (1951). *The rise of scientific philosophy.* Berkeley, CA: The University of California Press.

Romanes, G. J. (1888). *Animal intelligence.* New York: D. Appleton.

Thorndike, E. L. (1898). Animal intelligence: An experimental study of the associative processes in animals. *Psychological Review Monograph Supplements, 2*, no. 4; whole no. 8.

Thorndike, E. L. (1911). *Animal intelligence.* New York: Macmillan.

Watson, J. B. (1913). Psychology as the behaviorist views it. *Psychological Review, 20*, 158–177.

Zuriff, G. (1985). *Behaviorism: A conceptual reconstruction.* New York: Columbia University Press.

# 4 Interspecies Communication: A Tool for Assessing Conceptual Abilities in the African Grey Parrot

Irene M. Pepperberg
*Northwestern University*

## INTRODUCTION

The comparative study of behavior is not a new branch of science, but one that began when humans first observed individual differences in the animals that shared their environment. Current interest in comparative work developed as scientists began to examine various capabilities of nonhuman species and to use animals as models for human processes. Comparative investigations enable researchers to determine if a behavior under study reflects an instance of a widespread phenomenon or is specific to a particular subject. Comparative studies thus provide important ideas and data, but agreement rarely exists among scientists as to how such investigations should proceed. Overall goals often become obscured, either by arguments on the degree to which cross-species analogies are valid or by rigid adherence to particular experimental paradigms; contributions from one discipline are rarely appreciated by adherents of others (see Kamil, 1984; Kroodsma et al., 1984; Menzel & Juno, 1982, 1985). Schneirla's importance was not just that he recognized both the significance *and* the inadequacies of comparative studies, but that he perceived (Schneirla, 1950, 1962) that (a) the particular approach chosen by the experimenter could affect the conclusions of a study; (b) research in any discipline, if carried out with appropriate care, could add significantly to the raw data on the problem under study; and (c) integration of data from various approaches might be necessary in order to solve particularly complex comparative problems.

One such problem is that of comparing behaviors involving language, cognition, and consciousness across species. The use of integrative levels as a framework for comparing such behaviors is not entirely new. Although not explicitly dealing with phyletic levels, cognition or consciousness, Hockett and Altmann, using data collected from laboratory and field, devised a series of categories for communication systems that simultaneously defined the implications of membership in these categories (Altmann, 1967; Hockett, 1961; Hockett & Altmann, 1968). Tavolga (1970), in an attempt to clarify the possible effects of phylogeny on such a categorization, explicitly proposed an approach to the study of communication based on Schneirla's levels of integration. Tavolga emphasized that anatomical, physiological, and psychological differences among species allow for discrete classifications; implicit in his writings was the assumption that cognition and consciousness might exist only in conjunction with language, exclusively at the highest level. In this chapter I propose an alternative hypothesis: that certain language-like behaviors—various forms of interspecies communication—are educable skills on more than one of the levels suggested by Tavolga, and that these skills can then be used as tools for assessing relative levels of consciousness and cognitive ability. Underlying my hypothesis is the concept that, until researchers acquire thorough knowledge about the ways in which their subjects act in their natural environments, analyses based on rigid adherence to phyletic constraints may be unwise (see Menzel & Juno, 1982, 1985; Pepperberg, 1985, 1986a, 1986b).

## Problems in Defining the Levels of Analysis

Defining differences between levels of consciousness and cognitive abilities in nonhumans is difficult, especially when judgments are necessarily based on indirect psychological or behavioral evidence and involve cross-phylogenetic comparisons and interactions. And, if we agree with Schneirla that (a) each behavioral level requires its own specific methods of investigation and (b) information learned from the analysis of a lower level will not necessarily predict aspects of the next higher levels (see Tobach, 1970), then we must be certain that we have defined each level correctly if we are to direct our research appropriately. Yet how can we be certain, especially in comparative animal studies, that the similarities and differences for which we are searching are not masked by preconceived notions of a unilinear progressive scale of development? That is, might adherence to phyletic scales lead to an inability to devise appropriate measures against which diverse naturally-occurring systems might be compared? (See, for example, Hodos, 1982). How can we as researchers be certain that we are truly aware of all of the complexities inherent in the natural systems? (see Beer, 1982). Might not the best approach be to devise a set of innovative tools for making these comparisons even if, at the outset, these tools might appear impractical because they ignore phylogenetic differences in our subjects?

I therefore suggest that, despite the clear import of phylogeny on comparative studies, an open-minded "agnosticism" (Griffin, 1981) might be the most fruitful approach for dealing with topics as complex as comparisons between human and nonhuman subjects with respect to behaviors involving language, cognition, and consciousness (see Crook, 1983; Griffin, 1985). To claim that the underlying mechanisms for a behavior must be dissimilar because of dissimilar phylogeny is as narrow-minded as the claim that surface similarities must imply isomorphic mechanisms. Until all the data are in, neither stance can be validated, and the appropriate position probably lies somewhere in between. My purpose in this chapter is not to advocate an approach which ignores species differences, but rather to suggest that cross-phylogenetic analogies and interactions may enable us to (a) develop hypotheses against which to test purported parallels between disparate systems, and (b) thus demonstrate and define the relevant level of analysis. For example, Lenneberg (1969, 1973) argued that cross-species resemblances between human language and any system of animal communication may be spurious unless the correspondences can be shown to be due to a common phylogenetic level; such a stance may be appropriate if one is looking at the two systems from the level of biological origin—but not necessarily if one is looking at the social and ecological constraints that led to development of the behavioral traits. We do not yet know if the apparently comparable proficient natural complex communicative abilities of certain animals represent independent pinnacles of species-typical behaviors or are accidental convergencies: Although there are differences in neurobiology, physiology, and anatomy across phylogenetic levels, similar needs in different species might have led to some equal, convergent evolutionary characteristics. As Schneirla (1946) observed, analogy has an important place in scientific theory, as long as it is taken only as a starting point for a comparative study (see also Hinde, 1982). Bullock (1986), Chevalier-Skolnikoff (1981), Griffin (1981), Nottebohm (1975), and Petrinovich (1972) are a few of the many researchers in disparate fields who suggest how analogies may provide useful insights into the complex (possibly cognitive) behaviors of systems that have no recent common phylogenetic origin. It is possible that, just as Skinnerian techniques (Skinner, 1957) have proved appropriate for examining particular sets of abilities such as sensory discrimination across species, and naturalistic observations have provided suitable schemas for analyzing other behaviors such as imprinting (Hinde, 1982; but note Bateson, 1984), interspecies communication might provide valuable insights and be an innovative approach for solving persistent problems involving the complex relationships between (and among) language, cognition and consciousness (Pepperberg, 1986a).

## Interspecies Communication: A Tool for Assessing Relative Animal Abilities

The ideal tools for assessing qualities such as cognition and consciousness in various nonhuman species would enable researchers to (a) query their subjects in as direct a manner as they now query human participants in related studies; (b) communicate to their subjects, in the most efficient manner possible, the precise nature of the questions that are being asked; (c) take into account the animals' natural predispositions to work in a particular manner or attend to a particular stimulus (i.e., integrate techniques from field and lab; see for example Kamil, 1984; Menzel & Juno, 1982, 1985), and (d) facilitate cross-species comparisons not just between humans and other animals, but between the various animal species.

During the last two decades, diverse projects in interspecies communication have employed exactly such tools. Previously, researchers concentrated on deciphering the natural species-specific signaling systems and other behaviors of their subjects in order to uncover the underlying processes.[1] A few scientists have now instead begun to build onto these natural behaviors so as to teach their subjects, in laboratory situations, various human codes or artificial forms of communication based on rules presumed to underlie human systems (see, for example, von Glasersfeld, 1977). These studies involve primates (chimpanzees: Fouts, 1973; Fouts & Couch, 1976; Fouts et al., 1983; Gardner & Gardner, 1978, 1984; Gillan, 1982; Premack, 1976, 1983; Rumbaugh & Gill, 1976; Savage-Rumbaugh et al., 1980a, 1980b; gorillas: Patterson, 1978; an orangutan: Miles, 1978, 1983); marine mammals (dolphins: Herman, 1980, 1986; Herman, et al., 1984; sea lions: Schusterman & Krieger, 1984); and a psittacid (Pepperberg, 1978, 1979, 1981, 1983a, 1986b, in press-a; Pepperberg & Kozak, 1986). If complex, allospecific communication can be acquired by animals as disparate as these, might not a system based on communicative behaviors be the most efficient scheme for determining levels of cognition and consciousness? In fact, many of the aforementioned projects have employed interspecies communication as a tool for examining the range of intelligent and intentional behaviors of their subjects under the assumption that the mechanisms for these behaviors (a) exist; (b) are used by the animals in question under natural conditions; and (c) can be brought to light under the proper experimental conditions (see Premack, 1983; also Menzel & Juno, 1982, 1985; Marler, 1983, 1985). Although it is probable that the particular combination of numerous behaviors incorporated under the heading "human language" *is* species-typical, it is also probable that comparable (and possibly equivalent) communicative behaviors in nonhumans exist and conform to certain basic principles that cross phylogenetic lines: If human linguistic competence is indeed a reflection of a number of interlocking cognitive skills (see discussions in Atherton & Schwartz, 1983; Rieber & Voyat, 1983), then interspecies communication may help us examine the extent, limits, or even the existence of cognitive behavior and conscious activity in nonhuman subjects across the various levels. [Note: Whereas this chapter has thus far referred

---

[1]For descriptions of studies on possible referential components of communication in the wild see Bauer & Philip, 1983; Beer, 1975, 1976, 1982; Cheney & Seyfarth, 1980, 1982, 1985; Gould & Gould, 1982; Gouzoules et al., 1984; Green, 1975; Griffin, 1981; Krebs & Kroodsma, 1980; Kroodsma, 1981, 1982 (cf. Lein, 1972, 1978); Leger & Owings, 1978; Leger et al., 1979, 1980; Lemon, 1975; Morse, 1967; Owings & Virginia, 1978; Robinson, 1980, 1981; Seyfarth et al., 1980a,b; Sonnenschein & Reyer, 1983; Struhsaker, 1967.

predominantly to aspects of behavior as cognitive or conscious, such a stance need not ignore the behaviorist approach. From that standpoint, work in interspecies communication can be viewed as a tool for effective examination of such capacities as cross-phylogenetic learning ability and problem solving (see, for example, Michael et al., 1983; Salzinger, 1973, 1980; Segal, 1983).]

## INTERSPECIES COMMUNICATION WITH AN AFRICAN GREY PARROT

My own work involves teaching a form of interspecies communication—one based on referential English vocalizations—to an African Grey parrot (*Psittacus erithacus*) in order to examine avian conceptual and communicative abilities. The reasons for the choice of a parrot, particularly a Grey, have been discussed in detail elsewhere (Pepperberg, 1981); the following is a brief review of the techniques used to train this subject and a discussion of the capabilities which have been uncovered as a consequence of his training.

### Training Techniques

This project is not without precedent: Mowrer (1952, 1954, 1958), using standard laboratory techniques, tried to train various avian subjects to understand and produce referential English speech. His lack of success, however, reinforced the popular belief that psittacids were incapable of anything but mindless mimicry (Fromkin & Rodman, 1974; Lenneberg, 1973; see also Grosslight & Zaynor, 1967; Grosslight et al., 1964). But numerous studies, often concurrent with Mowrer's, did demonstrate that avian subjects were capable of the types of behaviors often considered pre- or co-requisites for complex skills, including sophisticated communication (see Geschwind, 1965; Koehler, 1943, 1950; Lögler, 1959; also Thorpe, 1974); avian competence in these tasks often matched that of various primates[2] (Stettner & Matyniak, 1968). These findings suggested, phylogeny notwithstanding, that the previous inability to achieve two-way, func-

---

[2]Comparative examinations of animal intelligence often fail to include avian subjects: Because of the small size of the avian brain, scientists have questioned whether there could be sufficient neural matter to subserve any intelligent behavior. Specifically, birds are known to lack, for the most part, that brain structure which appears to be the mammalian 'organ of intelligence'—a well-developed cerebral cortex (see Jerison, 1973). Recent findings, however, suggest that it is not the absolute size of a brain that is important, but the relative size and presence of certain neural structures and their relationship to other parts of the central nervous system (Hodos, 1982; for discussions with respect to vocal learning, see Kroodsma & Canady, 1982, 1985; Nottebohm, 1981; Nottebohm et al., 1981). The particular areas for avian intelligence appear to be in the striatal regions (Cobb, 1960; Krushinskii, 1960; Nauta & Karten, 1970; Stettner, 1974), and those birds with the highest degree of development in this area—parrots, crows, jays and mynahs—have been shown to exhibit mental capabilities equal to animals with a well-developed cerebral cortex (Hodos, 1982; Kamil & Hunter, 1970; Pepperberg, 1983a, in press; Pepperberg & Kozak, 1986; Stettner & Matyniak, 1968; Zorina, 1982).

tional communication might have been due not to any inherent limitations in the psittacine subjects, but rather to inappropriate training procedures. I therefore decided to see if particular, rather different techniques could facilitate interspecies communication with a nonprimate, nonmammalian subject.

The training techniques that I employ were developed after extensive study of the conditions that affect avian and human learning. The detailed rationale for the procedures are described elsewhere (Pepperberg, 1981, 1986a, in press-b); briefly, the idea was that an animal subject could acquire an allospecific communication code only if the training techniques utilized (a) intense social interaction between the trainers and the subject, and (b) referential, contextually applicable modeling—i.e., demonstrated the functional value of the targeted communicative behaviors under the conditions in which these behaviors would be used.

An important feature of the training procedure, therefore, is that my students and I never employ extrinsic rewards as incentives. Many programs designed to develop communicatory skills, such as those of Mowrer, have relied on extrinsic rewards, generally food, which neither directly relate to the skill being taught nor to the specific task being targeted. For example, all correct identifications of food or nonfood items, or appropriate responses to various specific commands, are rewarded with acquisition of a single food. Such programs are particularly prevalent in the treatment of autistic and echolalic children, yet research has shown that human as well as animal subjects in such programs often fail to acquire the targeted skills, or fail to extrapolate knowledge that has been acquired in such a manner to situations in which the extrinsic reinforcer is absent; e.g., are still unable to communicate in spontaneous and contextually appropriate ways. (See for example Fouts & Couch, 1976; Fulwiler & Fouts, 1976; Richey, 1976; Risely & Wolf, 1968; also Courtright & Courtright, 1979; Lovaas, 1977).

Thus, from the beginning of this project (in June, 1977), the training procedures have focused instead on teaching labels for a selection of objects (e.g., toys) or actions which themselves arouse the interest of the subject so that there is the closest possible association of each object or action and label to be learned (Pepperberg, 1978, 1981). Each correct identification can therefore be rewarded by a relevant, different reinforcer—the object or action to which the label refers, rather than any single extrinsic item. On occasion, the parrot is rewarded with the right to request (vocally) a more desirable item, which may be edible. However, unlike subjects in previous unsuccessful studies (Mowrer, 1952, 1954, 1958; see also Gossette, 1969/1980), this parrot never receives food rewards for correct identification of nonfood items at any time during training, testing, or play periods. Interestingly, studies with severely retarded children provide preliminary evidence that use of a different specific reinforcer for each response to be taught aids children in discriminating among responses to be learned, and that the ease of learning is related to the degree to which the stimulus and reinforcer are related (e.g., these children learned more quickly to "point to X" when the reward was the opportunity to play with X than when the reward was, for example, an invariant food; see Fulwiler & Fouts, 1976; Saunders & Sailor, 1979). Extrinsic food rewards (food for nonfood identification) may actually delay label acquisition by confounding the name of the exemplar to be learned with that of the food reward[3] (Pepperberg, 1978, under review; see also Greenfield, 1978; Miles, 1983).

The primary training procedure is called the model/rival, or M/R technique. It has been adapted from a two-trainer procedure developed by Todt (1975), which in turn is related to the social modeling theory of Bandura (1971a, 1971b, 1977). This technique is described in detail elsewhere (Pepperberg, 1981, in press-b); the scheme can be described briefly as follows: two humans demonstrate to the parrot the types of interactive responses that are desired. One human acts as a trainer of a second human, asking questions, giving praise and reward for correct answers, showing disapproval for incorrect answers (i.e., errors that mimic those being made by the bird at the time: e.g., "wood" for "green wood"). The second human acts both as a model for the bird's response and as a rival for the trainer's attention. Roles of trainer and model are frequently reversed to demonstrate that communication is an interactive process, and the parrot is given the opportunity to participate directly in these vocal exchanges.

## Results

The effect of our training has been significant. Over the course of the experiment, the subject, a parrot named Alex, has acquired a vocabulary consisting of 30 labels for objects: paper, key, grain, chair, grape, wood, cracker, hide (rawhide chips), peg wood (wooden clothes pins), back, knee, cork, corn, nut, gym, carrot, scraper (a metal nail file), walnut, shower, shoulder, banana, water, rock (a lava stone), pasta, chain, wheat, popcorn, banerry (apple), gravel and grate (a nutmeg grater);[4] six color labels: rose (red), green, blue, yellow, orange, and grey; and five phrases for shape: two-corner (football shape), three-corner

---

[3]That is: assume that the experimenter determines that the subject is particularly fond of chocolate, and decides to use chocolate as a reward for all targeted behaviors. The subject is shown X (not chocolate) and receives chocolate whenever the label "X" is emited. Because chocolate is probably of greater interest to the subject than X itself, the subject may connect saying "X" with receiving the chocolate; the presence of X may be considered incidental. Subsequent vocalizations of "X" not in the presence of X would not be rewarded, and the connection between "X" and the chocolate is extinguished. Thus there is successive forming and breaking of the connection between saying "X" and receiving chocolate until the subject comes to realize that X itself must be present. Such a procedure can be successful, but it appears not to be the most straightforward means of teaching the connection between "X" and X.

[4]Labels for food are not tested; however, data from our daily record suggest that these labels do contain referential meaning: e.g.. if Alex requests a "walnut" and is given pasta, he will turn his head, say "no," and reiterate his original request (see Fig. 4.1). If forced to identify the pasta, he will do so, accept it, and then immediately drop it; his requests for food are now generally prefaced with "want."

(triangle), four-corner (square), five-corner (pentagon) and six-corner (hex-agon). He uses the labels "two," "three," "four," "five," and "ssih" (six) to distinguish between appropriate numbers of objects, has acquired functional use of the phrases "come here," and "wanna go X" [X = chair, gym (a construction of wooden dowel rods which he prefers to his cage), knee, shoulder, back (to his cage) and, occasionally, out], the word "no," "want Y" (Y = cork, nut, etc.) and what appears to be functional use of "yeah." He is beginning to use phrases such as "What's this?", "What color?", and "What shape?" to initiate interactions. Alex employs these vocalizations routinely to identify objects which differ somewhat from the training exemplars; e.g., pieces of paper (white, unlined index cards) vary in shape, as do those of hide, wood, and cork. Clothes pins ("peg wood") are correctly identified even though they may be considerably chewed, and the shades of his color objects vary somewhat as they are, with the exception of keys, hand-dyed with food colors.[5]

Alex has averaged scores of about 80% over more than three hundred identification tests (for test procedures and results, see Pepperberg, 1981). For all tests administered, he correctly identified 80.3% of all objects shown to him on the first try; his score is 80.2% when all responses to all presentations are included. For more recent tests, his responses for initial and all presentations were 80.1% and 81.6%, respectively. Alex is considered to have mastered a label by correctly identifying the particular object during testing with an accuracy of 80%.

The following material describes briefly those of Alex's achievements which go beyond object identification: categorization, numerical abilities, functional use of "no", and, finally, limited segmentation and preliminary work with verbs.

## Possible Categorization

The degrees to which a nonhuman subject can perform categorization and comprehend the related concept of same/different have been widely discussed as possible measures of cognitive capacity (Premack, 1976, 1978, 1983; Savage-Rumbaugh et al., 1980b; Thomas, 1980). Determination of Alex's competence in these areas has been a long-standing goal.

We began an investigation into these abilities when, early in the project, we observed a behavior that suggested a possible faculty for categorizing objects: Alex, when he was learning labels for novel exemplars, tended to make "generic" errors. For example, initial identification errors on clothes pins ("peg wood") were to call them "wood," and colored keys were often labeled simply "key."

Our first step in testing this categorical capacity was to examine his ability to

---

[5]Food colors are used because they are ostensibly safe for ingestion; in addition, we can use food colors to dye objects which could not otherwise be obtained in colored form.

classify unfamiliar objects with respect to color or shape: During free (non-testing, non-taping, non-training) periods, Alex was presented with objects whose colors or shapes, but not names, were known (e.g., rose pens, green plastic clips, blue wool, tinted dog biscuits, variously shaped buttons) and queried as to "What color?" or "What shape?" In all cases, he identified correctly, on the first attempt, the colors or shapes of these items. No formal drills or exhaustive discussions preceded such identifications, although the standard tests, which included some colored and shaped objects, had been administered earlier on those days (see Pepperberg, 1981). It is quite possible, however, that correct responses to "What color?" or "What shape?" under such conditions demonstrated only that our subject could extrapolate color or shape markers to unfamiliar items, not that he had necessarily acquired an understanding of the actual words or the relationships implied by the labels "color" and "shape": Alex may not at that time have even attended to the queries, but may have simply viewed the objects and produced all the relevant information.

We have since examined Alex's capacity to learn categorical concepts, and have found that he appears able not only to recognize instances of four different categories (shapes, colors, materials, and numerical quantities) but that he has acquired, through various procedures, a limited understanding of the concept of category; e.g., not just what is or is not green, but that "green" is a particular instance of the category "color"; that, for a particularly colored and shaped piece of wood, "green" and "three-corner" represent different categories of markable attributes of this given exemplar (Table 4.1; see Pepperberg, 1983a). That is, we have been examining his ability to respond to the queries "What color?" or "What shape?" when he is presented with items having both color and shape (e.g., a green wooden triangle, a rose rawhide square) in order to test his actual understanding of the more abstract concepts rather than simply the instances of color and shape.

Alex's tests now include queries of "What shape?" and "What color?" for objects that represent various combinations of six different colors, four different shapes, and three different materials [wood, rawhide, and metal (i.e., tops of keys)]. Alex's scores for such identifications (e.g., queries that require answers of "rose wood" or "three-corner hide") are better than 80% (see Table 4.1). These results suggest that our subject has demonstrated at least the ability to associate labels representing two categorical concepts ("color", "shape") with those labels representing the various instances of these categories (e.g., "blue," "four-corner"); he can view an item that can be described relevantly in more than one way, decode from our question which of two categories is being targeted, and then produce, based on the question posed, the label for the appropriate instance of the category (Pepperberg, 1983a).

The test employed is rather strong, for it actually involves reclassification of objects; that is, our subject is required to classify the same object with respect to shape at one time and with respect to color at another. Reclassification is not only

TABLE 4.1
Test Results for "What Color?" Vs. "What Shape?" Comprehension

Code: C = corner; R = rose; G = green; B = blue; Gy = grey; Y = Yellow; O = orange; W = wood; H = hide; K = key; PW = peg wood (clothes pin)

| Exemplar | What Color? Test Scores[a] | What Color? Frequent Errors | What Shape? Test Scores[a] | What Shape? Frequent Errors |
|---|---|---|---|---|
| 2CBW | 2/2 | | 2/3 | 2CH(1) |
| 2CRW | 1/1 | | 1/1 | |
| 2CRH | 1/1 | | 1/1 | |
| 2CGW | 3/4 | W(1) | 1/2 | 2W(1) |
| 2CGH | 1/1 | | | |
| 2CGyW | 1/1 | | | |
| 2CYW | 1/1 | | | |
| 2CYH | 1/1 | | | |
| 3CBK | 6/8 | K(2) | 8/8 | |
| 3CBW | 4/5 | BCW(1) | 8/10 | 3CH(1), 3W(1) |
| 3CBH | 5/6 | GH(1) | 4/6 | 3H(1), 3BCW(1) |
| 3CGK | 4/4 | | 5/5 | |
| 3CGW | 5/6 | RW(1) | 7/9 | GW(1), 3W(1) |
| 3CGH | 7/10 | BH(2)[b], H(1) | 4/6 | H(2) |
| 3CRK | 5/6 | K(1) | 5/6 | 3K(1) |
| 3CRW | 6/8 | U(1)[c], W(1) | 5/7 | RW(1), CW(1) |
| 3CRH | 4/5 | UH(1)[c] | 4/5 | 2CH(1) |
| 3CGyW | 1/1 | | 2/2 | |
| 3CGyH | 1/1 | | | |
| 3CGyK | 1/2 | K(1) | 1/1 | |
| 3CYW | 1/1 | | | |
| 3CYH | 1/2 | H(1) | | |
| 4CBK | 4/5 | BPW(1) | 7/7 | |
| 4CBW | 8/10 | 4CW(1), BCW(1) | 10/11 | W(1) |
| 4CBH | 5/5 | | 4/5 | UCH(1)[c] |
| 4CGK | 4/4 | | 4/5 | GK(1) |
| 4CGW | 5/6 | 4CW(1) | 5/6 | 4CGW(1) |
| 4CGH | 6/6 | | 6/6 | |
| 4CRK | 5/6 | 4K(1) | 5/7 | UK(1)[c], CK(1) |
| 4CRW | 7/7 | | 4/5 | 4W(1) |
| 4CRH | 5/7 | UH(1)[c], H(1) | 6/6 | |
| 4CYW | | | 2/2 | |
| 4CGyW | | | 1/1 | |
| 4COH | 1/1 | | | |
| 4COW | 1/1 | | | |
| 5CBW | 1/1 | | 1/2 | UCW(1)[c] |
| 5CBH | | | 1/1 | |
| 5CGW | 1/1 | | 1/2 | CW(1) |
| 5CYW | | | 2/2 | |
| 5CYH | | | 1/1 | |
| 5CRW | | | 2/3 | UCW(1)[c] |

[a]Test scores are the number of correct identifications divided by the total number of presentations. Overall, Alex achieved scores of 88.4% (colors) and 83.6% (shapes).

[b]We noticed that one of the exemplars was bluish in tone; after replacing it, these errors ended.

[c]The parrot's production of the marker was unintelligible.

Note: Each test included one such question for a colored and shaped object (e.g., Alex is shown a rose three-cornered piece of wood and asked either "What color?" or "What shape?"). These results are from 189 different tests. (Data from Pepperberg, 1983a) thought to be a more difficult task than simple classification, but flexibility in changing the basis for classification is also thought to indicate the presence of "abstract aptitude" (see Hayes & Nissen, 1956/1971; Pepperberg, 1983a).

Additional studies now in progress demonstrate that, when presented with two objects that vary with respect to color, shape or material, Alex can discriminate and respond with the appropriate vocal label ["color," "shape," or "mahmah" (matter)] to questions as to which of the three variables are same or different (Pepperberg, 1986b). Avian subjects were once thought incapable of performing such a task (Premack, 1978; but see Zentall et al., 1984), which is representative of what Premack (1976) terms "second-order concepts": to comprehend the task, the subject must be able not just to recognize that two independent objects, $A_1$ and $A_2$, are blue, but that there is a single attribute, the category color, that is shared, and that this attribute can be extrapolated not only to two other blue items, but to two novel green items, $B_1$ and $B_2$, that have nothing in common with the original set of A's.

## Numerical abilities

Of all of the so-called intelligent behaviors, some of the more interesting are those that involve a sense of numerical quantity, because many researchers believe that there is a common foundation for both mathematical ability and language: both systems employ abstractions and relational concepts (see, for example, Lenneberg, 1971).

Koehler and his associates performed the first systematic studies of numerical concepts in birds (Koehler, 1943, 1950; Lögler, 1959); they demonstrated that ravens and grey parrots were able to solve match-to-sample problems involving quantities up to eight. That is, their birds were able to match quantities of disparate objects that were assembled in random configurations—for example, six blobs of plasticine with six spots on a box lid. Koehler called this ability "nonnumerical counting" or "thinking in unnamed numbers" because the birds were actually making distinctions between same and different quantities without necessarily being able to count them in the human sense.

Researchers also found that success in these numerical-type problems varied with species—for example, pigeons rarely achieved success on match-to-sample for quantities greater than five, and chickens were limited to two or three. Of particular interest, however, were the results obtained when human subjects were given comparable tests that allowed enough time for groups of figures to be fully observed, but not enough time for actual counting to take place. Koehler found that humans did no better than the parrots, and some, like the pigeons, were limited to five (see also Taves, 1941).

Lögler (1959) carried this work a step further, and demonstrated that nonnumerical counting could be extended across modalities: His parrot eventually responded equally well on match-to-sample problems that employed notes on a flute and flashes of light.

Nevertheless, nonnumerical counting is considered a simpler and possibly different task than the related one of actual verbal labeling of quantity. Numerical labels are, after all, abstract names for conceptualized amounts and, at least in humans, some research indicates that separate areas of the brain may be used for labeling vs. matching tasks (Geschwind, 1979). Therefore, we have begun to examine the sensitivity of our parrot to quantity. The data suggest that Alex can indeed use numerical labels to distinguish quantities of objects: he has learned the vocal labels 2, 3, 4, 5, and 6, and presentation of two pieces of cork or five pieces of wood, for example, elicit the responses, respectively, "two cork" and "five wood" (Pepperberg, 1980, in press-a).

As noted in Table 4.2, Alex is correct about 80% of the time. He most frequently errs by omitting the numerical marker; however, a query as to "How many?" (similar to queries of "What color?" or "What shape?" made when these markers are omitted) generally elicits the correct response.

TABLE 4.2
Data on Numerical Ability

| Object | Quantity | Test Scores | % | Erroneous i.d.[a] (# times error made) |
|--------|----------|-------------|------|----------------------------------------|
| paper | 2 | 9/10 | 90 | paper (1) |
| | 3 | 9/11 | 82 | paper (2) |
| | 4 | 9/11 | 82 | U paper (1), paper (1) |
| | 5 | 7/11 | 64 | paper (2), 4 paper (1), U paper (1) |
| | 6 | 3/3 | 100 | |
| key | 2 | 10/13 | 77 | key (3) |
| | 3 | 9/14 | 64 | U key (1), key (3), 4 key (1) |
| | 4 | 9/11 | 82 | key (2) |
| | 5 | 6/7 | 86 | key (1) |
| | 6 | 3/4 | 75 | key (1) |
| wood | 2 | 11/12 | 92 | wood (1) |
| | 3 | 7/11 | 64 | peg wood (1), 3 peg wood (2), wood (1) |
| | 4 | 9/11 | 82 | U wood (1), 3 wood (1) |
| | 5 | 7/10 | 70 | 3 wood (1), 4 hide (1), 4 wood (1) |
| | 6 | 3/4 | 75 | peg wood (1) |
| peg wood | 2 | 9/10 | 90 | peg wood (1) |
| | 3 | 8/9 | 89 | 4 wood (1) |
| | 4 | 9/12 | 75 | peg wood (2), 3 (1) |
| | 5 | 6/8 | 75 | 4 peg wood (2) |
| | 6 | 3/4 | 75 | [(6 wood, peg wood) as one phrase] |
| cork | 2 | 11/16 | 69 | cork (5) |
| | 3 | 9/10 | 90 | cork (1) |
| | 4 | 10/12 | 83 | 3 cork (1), 4 wood (1) |
| | 5 | 5/5 | 100 | |
| | 6 | 2/3 | 67 | cork (1) |

[a]"U" represents unrecognizable label.
Test scores are the number of correct identifications divided by the total number of presentations. Overall, Alex achieved a score of 78.9%.
Note: One or two numerical questions were included on each identification test, so that these results are from 145 successive tests. This table will be published in Pepperberg, in press, Ethology.

Alex can also label the quantity for collections made of entirely novel items or those presented in random physical arrays. Note that only a single recent study (Matsuzawa, 1985) has demonstrated comparable abilities in a chimpanzee. Moreover, if a collection consists of two different groups of objects (e.g., keys and corks), Alex can, in response to our vocal queries ("How many key?" or "How many cork?") label the quantity of either group (Pepperberg, in press-a).

These are still preliminary results, as we do not know if Alex is limited to the concept of "6." We hope to learn if a parrot, like a human, can recognize quantities beyond eight when taught numerical labels to designate such quantities. Too, there is a significant difference between true counting and recognition of numerical quantity (see Davis & Memmott, 1982; Seibt, 1982; Pepperberg, in press-a); for example, we have yet to test if Alex could listen to a certain number of sequential musical notes and tell us how many he had heard.

### Functional use of "No"

Animals, in much the same way as children who have yet to achieve communicative competence, can be observed to exhibit certain negative behaviors, predominantly those of refusal and rejection. Although such behaviors are necessary before a subject can be considered to have acquired the concept of negation, they alone are not sufficient: negation also encompasses the understanding of nonexistence and denial, and functional use of the forms of negation in all these contexts is rightly considered an advanced stage in linguistic development (Brown, 1973).

From the very beginning of the project, Alex exhibited several types of negative behavior of the form of refusal and rejection: (a) if he didn't want to be handled, he would attempt to bite and emit the noise RAAAKKKKK; (b) he would refuse to identify objects by emitting RAAAKKKK or ignoring people; (c) if he were finished drinking water from a hand-held cup, he would attempt to overturn the container; and (d) unwanted toys were often tossed back at the trainer after identification. Whenever Alex exhibited these undesirable behaviors, he heard the word "No" produced by his trainers in forceful tones. Toward the middle of the second year, we noticed that he was beginning to use a vocalization like "nuh" in situations in which he didn't want to be handled. We wanted to see if we could teach him (a) to use this vocalization in a stable, functional manner, and (b) to extend its use to other relevant situations, particularly those of denial and nonexistence. We employed the M/R technique to demonstrate a functional use of the word "No": refusal of a trainer to relinquish a preferred toy. Within three sessions, Alex began to replace the "nuh" vocalization with a more "no"-like sound in warning/distress situations, and, after only one more session, extended it to all the behaviors just mentioned (Pepperberg, 1981). In many cases, Alex's use of "no" is now accompanied by a turning of his head or body away from the trainer. "No" is also used to refuse small (possibly unacceptable?) pieces of food or exemplars (see also Fig. 4.1).

Although no clear differences have been noted in the order in which denial, rejection, and nonexistence emerge in the development of children's use of "no" (Brown, 1973; cf. Bloom, 1970), Alex has not consistently demonstrated behaviors that would suggest that he can use "no" to deny the truth or falsity of a given statement, or to represent nonexistence in the sense of the childish "Allgone." Unlike children, however (see Snow, 1972), Alex has not yet consistently been exposed to the use of "no" in such contexts. Only after we consciously employed phrases such as "no more cork, cork allgone" in our speech to Alex did he began using "no" just before or just after dropping a toy. Other than by our responses to his errors in identification ("No, that's not an X; it's a Y"), we have not routinely demonstrated to Alex that "no" is a means of commenting upon another's statements; we are presently designing such experiments.

## Segmentation

A critical criterion for the productive use of human codes by a nonhuman subject is the ability of that subject to segment: to view the communication system as being made up of interchangeable units that can be combined in novel ways to describe new situations (Marler, 1975). The ability to segment complete sentences into smaller units that can be re-combined to form novel utterances provides a means of expressing a broad range of meanings—i.e., allows creativity. In the simplest sense, the ability to segment allows a subject that has learned "Polly want a cracker," on subsequently learning the word "dough-nut," to produce spontaneously, "Polly want a doughnut" (Fromkin & Rod-man, 1974). This example, a particular case of segmentation often termed "lex-ical substitution"[6] (see Premack, 1976), has been demonstrated to be an educable skill in nonhuman primates (Premack, 1976; Rumbaugh & Gill, 1976), and our findings suggest that the Grey parrot may also exhibit this ability.

A common argument against the possibility of interspecies communication with parrots has been their supposed inability to attach meaning to individual words in sentences that have been taught as invariant, integral (and not neces-sarily referential) entities; I believe that comparison across species may be partic-ularly relevant here. It is significant that children (unlike most domesticated

---

[6]Segmentation, in a stronger sense, would be the ability of an individual to create a sentence such as "Polly want chocolate doughnut!" after learning "I'm Polly," "I want cookie," "I like choco-late," "That doughnut!" (non-chocolate). Such a "novel" combination would suggest that the individual had a clear understanding of all of the elements in the phrases that had been taught. Lexical substitution, in contrast, implies a somewhat lesser knowledge—i.e., to create "Polly want dough-nut" from "Polly want cracker" + "doughnut," the individual need only segment the original phrase into "objects wanted" (crackers, doughnuts, etc.) and a stock phrase "Polly want." Lexical substitution is non-trivial (see Schuler, 1980) and does require semantic as well as limited syntactic knowledge, but an individual capable of lexical substitution is not necessarily capable of the more rigorous form of segmentation described above (see Ristau & Robbins, 1979).

imitative birds) are not usually taught to imitate sentences that are devoid of referential meaning. In fact, Ruder et al. (1977) has shown that imitation training may delay comprehension in humans (cf. Whitehurst et al., 1974). Parents, instead, tend to adopt the level of speech that corresponds to the child's level of achievement, and only increase the complexity of their utterances as the child develops (Berko-Gleason, 1973; Bohannon & Marquis, 1977; de Villiers & de Villiers, 1978; Snow, 1972). However, parental phrases that are both beyond the child's ability and frequently repeated will become lodged in the child's speech and be retained exactly, as "unassimilated fragments," for long periods of time (Brown & Hanlon, 1970; Cazden, 1972; Clark, 1974; Mattick, 1972). For example, a child will often produce "What's that?" and continue to substitute it for "What are these?" and "Who's that?" for extended periods. The child will have a sense of the usefulness of the phrase, but not what it actually says or that it may be segmented. Adults who learn a second language by exclusively aural methods may exhibit the same behavior (Brown, 1973). Moreover, one of the trio of children in Brown's longitudinal study (1973) of child language acquisition sometimes responded in meaningless, well-practiced routines when she did not know the correct answers to specific questions (Cazden, 1972). Such instances suggest that a parrot could learn to segment if it were exposed to communicatory behaviors in a controlled manner. I present here data that suggests Alex's capacity to form novel combinations of known qualifiers and object labels, and for that form of segmentation known as lexical substitution.

Introduction of color labels provided the first opportunity to examine Alex's ability to generalize from training exemplars. He was taught a single color, green, in connection with two (key and wood) of the five exemplars for which he at the time had labels. After he was reliably using the form "green" + "key" or "wood" to identify these objects, he was shown, for the first time, a piece of green colored hide. Although he initially called it "hide," he attained an accuracy of $\simeq 60\%$ correct for subsequent identification ("green hide") after only 5 min of training with the M/R method. Although even this limited form of segmentation was therefore not spontaneous, it did appear with only minimal instruction—Alex was able to label the object "green hide" correctly four times out of 7 subsequent immediate presentations; he incorrectly labeled it "hide" three times (see Pepperberg, 1981). After his accuracy improved, he was shown, and asked to identify ("What's this?"), a green clothes pin ("peg wood"). He said, and repeated several times, the combination "green wood, peg wood", with no discernible time lapse between the two phrases (see Pepperberg, 1981). Although true segmentation (see Marler, 1975) would have been a response of "green peg wood", the point of interest was that he did attempt to identify this new object by linking phrases that were already in his vocabulary. His subsequent behavior has shown that he can now routinely use the existing words of his vocabulary to identify similar, but novel exemplars: for example, after training on blue key and blue hide, he was able immediately to identify correctly "blue peg wood'' (clothes pin); he reacted similarly with novel yellow items after training on ''yellow wood''; with shaped pieces of paper, rawhide, or wood after training on only one of those materials, and similarly for judgments on quantity (Pepperberg, 1983a, in press-a).

Other data suggest but as yet provide no unequivocal proof for the possible existence of a more advanced form of segmentation (Pepperberg, 1983b). For example: My students and I had begun training Alex on the concepts of ''hard'' and ''soft'' using exemplars of dried and fresh corn. Alex had recently acquired the label ''rock'' as it pertained to a lava-stone beak conditioner. He spontaneously produced ''rock corn'' one afternoon, in the absence of any exemplar, and was give a kernel of dried corn. He ate the dried corn and has since requested dried corn in that manner. We do not know if our subject had actually abstracted the concept of ''hardness'' from the rock and transferred that concept, or if he had merely uttered a fortuitous combination of sounds which, when rewarded, became part of his repertoire. When Alex produced ''rock nut,'' he was rewarded with a Brazil nut; he was unable to crack it, and he lost interest in this item fairly rapidly. Unlike ''rock corn,'' subsequent production of ''rock nut'' has been rare.

We have also investigated lexical substitution in relation to Alex's requests.

''Wanna go X'': When we first acquired Alex, he strongly resisted being placed in unfamiliar locations. There were only two places in the laboratory where he could be situated and still remain calm enough to undergo testing and training: his cage and his gym (a collection of wooden dowel rods and ropes). He had, as a consequence, been exposed to the phrase ''Wanna go gym?'' (and minor variations; e.g., ''Do you wanna go gym?'', ''Guess you wanna go gym'') several times each day for several years; by the Fall of 1979, he would often answer such queries with a squeaky ''yeah'' and, later, occasionally with ''no.'' Alex had often also heard phrases like ''Wanna go back?'' (to the cage), and ''Gotta put you back now,'' but far less frequently: he was not often given a choice about going back to his cage. In late June of 1980, Alex, in the midst of some chatter, emitted the phrase ''Wanna go gym!'' in the presence of a secondary trainer; she immediately placed him on the gym. This interaction was repeated several times over the course of a week, and Alex then began to say ''Wanna go gym'' in the presence of another secondary trainer. If Alex was already on the gym when he emitted this phrase they would respond with 'appropriate' comments (e.g., ''You're already on the gym''). ''Wanna go gym'' began to occur predominantly when Alex was not on the gym, and was often accompanied by a stretching of his body toward the gym. Interestingly, when he was on the gym and appeared not to want to remain there (as signified by physically stretching toward something else), he would say, ''Wanna go gym - no'', or ''Wanna go . . . wanna go . . .'' If then asked by his trainers ''Wanna go back?'' (to the cage), he would generally reply ''yeah.'' Secondary trainers also reported that, if Alex was asked instead, ''Wanna go gym?'' his response was ''no.''

In addition, in July of 1980, Alex began to allow us to situate him elsewhere in the laboratory: on a chair back, on a trainer's knee, on a shelf above the gym. Secondary trainers were told never to say the phrases "Wanna go chair?" or "Wanna go knee?", but were encouraged to devise related sentences, such as "I'm on the chair!", "Let's put you on the shelf!", etc.—we wanted to use Alex's new found desire for mobility to learn if he could spontaneously emit "Wanna go chair!", etc. Although it would be impossible to prove that he had never heard phrases such as "Wanna go knee?", we could be sure that exposure to such phrases would be unlikely (i.e., that any inadvertent exposure he might have would be extremely rare and be due only to an error on the part of a trainer as opposed to, for example, his exposure to "Wanna go gym?" several times each day for more than 3 years) and that he would receive no formal training on such phrases.[7] By October of 1980, Alex began to use "Wanna go X" (X = knee, chair, back) consistently; if we now try to move him somewhere other than the requested location, he refuses to leave our hand. Preliminary data shows that in 3 out of 4 attempts to place him other than where requested, Alex responded with "no", followed by a repetition of his initial request; in the fourth instance, he merely repeated his initial request. He has frequently heard phrases like "I've gotta go out now" when trainers leave (i.e., move behind the curtain that divides the lab) to answer phones, obtain supplies, etc.; he will occasionally say "Wanna go out" to the secondary trainers and has used the phrase once during a taping session when he knew that the PI was "out".

Although acquisition of the verb phrase "Wanna go X" may have suggested that Alex had actually learned two verbs, "want" and "go," we believed that he was using "wanna go" as a single entity; for example, he did not spontaneously extend the portion "wanna" to any other instance. Thus, despite the fact that we have always had substantial contextual data (not unlike that on children in the one-word stage, see Brown, 1973) to support the interpretation that Alex actually "wanted" the objects whose labels he spontaneously emitted (e.g., he used the key to scratch his head, ate the walnut, said "no" to other proffered exemplars) and did not necessarily "want" the exemplar that he identified on a test (he often refused to accept it or immediately dropped it), until recently we had no evidence to support a formal separation in his use of "tacts" and "mands" (Skinner, 1957). In June of 1981, we initiated training designed to teach our subject to preface all requests with the word "want." Thus, in M/R sessions, the bird

[7]We make no attempt to limit our subject's exposure to spoken English. Given that he had been in a pet store for at least six months prior to our experiment, it is impossible for us to determine every phrase to which he may have been exposed. As he has needed at least one intensive training session before he has been able to acquire referential understanding and clear pronunciation of novel targeted vocalizations, we believe that it is unlikely that he could be capable of producing and using, in a contextually relevant manner, words or phrases he may have heard his trainers utter only once or twice and in a casual manner. Note, however, that novel combinations or minor variations of vocalizations already in his repertoire can acquire contextual relevance very quickly.

observed the following interaction: the trainer held two of the bird's favorite toys, e.g., paper and a cork.[8] The model said, "want cork" with the emphasis on the word "want." The trainer gave the cork to the model. This was repeated with the paper, and then the roles of model and trainer were reversed. Alex, who had already learned that the names of the objects had been sufficient for acquisition, often called "paper" or "cork" during these exchanges. Such calls were rewarded at first, as we did not wish to discourage his early associative behavior. However, these one-word calls were later ignored; he now appears to realize that it is the stressed word "want" that causes transfer of the object.

Alex has now begun to use the words "want" and "wanna" to preface requests for foods and some toys: for example, vocalizations such as "wanna nut", "want showah (shower)", "want cork", "want cracker", and "want some water" have all been recorded, with subsequent consumption or manipulation of the requested item. And, while it is extremely difficult to determine intentionality in a parrot, we have performed the following experiment.[9] On several occasions, over the course of several months, when Alex produced "want X", attempts were made by trainers to substitute non-requested items. These substitutions were sometimes made for practical reasons: e.g., we were unable to purchase fresh corn in mid-winter. Such behaviors on our part generally elicited "no" from the parrot (86%), and such refusal was often coupled with a repeat of the initial request (68%). Occasionally, our subject did accept the proffered substitute (9%), possibly the same way a human might accept duck à l'orange in preference to a requested Big Mac (see Fig. 4.1).

## CONCLUSION

In sum, whether or not there are major differences in the capacities of humans and animals, the ability to acquire mutual, explicit representational systems, even if only to a limited extent, allows us most efficiently to define the interspecies similarities and differences that may exist. The surface similarities between human language and animal-human communication are not the issue— not enough information exists to determine if our subjects evince language-like behaviors because they are employing systems similar to those underlying human language, or if they have acquired superficially similar communicative codes because of our use of specific training procedures and transmission modalities (see Malmi, 1976). What is the issue are the abilities these codes enable us to uncover. Tavolga (1970), in his discussion of integrative levels and the develop-

---

[8]Two objects were employed to encourage segmentation; that is, to help the bird realize that the "Want X" phrase contained a variable, X.

[9]The idea for this experiment developed during a discussion with Dr. Donald Griffin during a visit to Rockefeller University in 1981.

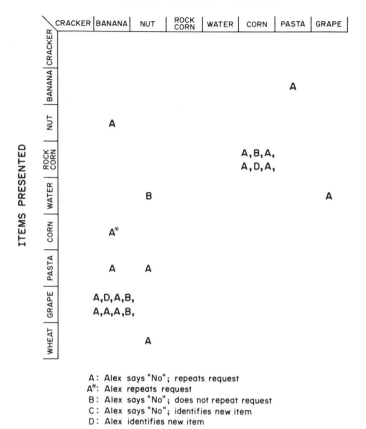

FIGURE 4.1.   Alex's responses to his trainers' presentations of objects different from those he had requested.

ment of human language, states that ". . . . the psychosocial level is reached and surpassed with the use of specific sounds representing objects, classes of objects, physiological and mental states, and finally, abstract ideas. The qualitative differences between human language and other forms of animal communication clearly set this level apart'' (p. 294).   We do not claim that our subject possesses all the qualities that would set him at Tavolga's language level; we merely point out that, using communicative capacities as a diagnostic tool, we have demonstrated in an avian subject several capabilities that were long thought to be exclusively the domain of primates. Does this mean that researchers should ignore phylogeny in cross-species comparisons? The answer is, of course, no: to expect an exact isomorphism between human and non-human communication, cognition and conscious behavior would be unwise. But to ignore the possible insights into both sets of behaviors that may be gained from drawing parallels between them would be equally unwise. What is likely is that the mechanisms that underlie comparable abilities are themselves *comparable* though not necessarily identical. The central issue for all comparative studies, behavioral or cognitive, is in determining whether a given capacity is general or not: Perhaps the time has come to design a truly innovative approach to such studies. Interspecies communication can be a valuable tool for uncovering these abilities and their mechanisms, and for defining levels of achievement.

## ACKNOWLEDGMENT

Preparation supported by a fellowship from the Harry Frank Guggenheim Foundation; research supported by NSF grants BNS 79-12945, 80-14329, 84-14483, and the Harry Frank Guggenheim Foundation.

## REFERENCES

Altmann, S. A. (1967). The structure of primate social communication. In S. A. Altmann (Ed.), *Social communication among primates* (pp. 325–362). Chicago, IL: University of Chicago Press.

Atherton, M., & Schwartz, R. (1983). Talk to the animals. In J. de Luce & H. T. Wilder (Eds.), *Language in primates* (pp. 137–145). NY: Springer-Verlag.

Bandura, A. (1971a). Psychotherapy based upon modeling principles. In A. E. Bergin & S. L. Garfield (Eds.), *Psychotherapy and behavioral change: An empirical analysis* (pp. 653–708). NY: Wiley.

Bandura, A. (1971b). Analysis of modeling processes. In A. Bandura (Ed.), *Psychological modeling* (pp. 1–62). Chicago, IL: Aldine-Atherton.

Bandura, A. (1977). *Social modeling theory*. Chicago, IL: Aldine-Atherton.

Bateson, P. P. G. (1984). The neural basis of imprinting. In P. Marler & H. S. Terrace (Eds.), *The biology of learning* (pp. 325–339). Berlin: Springer-Verlag.

Bauer, H. R., & Philip, M. (1983). Facial and vocal individual recognition in the common chimpanzee. *Psych. Record. 33,* 161–170.

Beer, C. G. (1975). Multiple functions and gull displays. In G. P. Baerends, C. G. Beer, & A. Manning (Eds.), *Function and evolution in behavior: Essays in honour of professor Niko Tinbergen, F. R. S.* (pp. 16–54). London and NY: Oxford University Press.

Beer, C. G. (1976). Some complexities in the communication behavior of gulls. In S. R. Harnad, H. D. Steklis, & J. Lancaster (Eds.), *Origins and evolution of language and speech, Ann. NYAS 280,* 413–432.

Beer, C. G. (1982). Conceptual issues in the study of communication. In D. E. Kroodsma & E. H. Miller (Eds.), *Acoustic communication in birds. Vol. 2: Song learning and its consequences* (pp. 279–310). Orlando, FL: Academic Press.

Berko-Gleason, J. (1973). Code switching in children's language. In T. E. Moore (Ed.), *Cognitive development and the acquisition of language* (pp. 159–167). Orlando, FL: Academic Press.

Bloom, L. (1970). *Language development: Form and function in emerging grammars*. Cambridge, MA: MIT Press.

Bohannon, J. N. III, & Marquis, A. L. (1977). Children's control of adult speech. *Child Devel., 48,* 1002–1008.

Brown, R. (1973). *A first language: The early stages.* Cambridge, MA: Harvard University Press.

Brown, R., & Hanlon, C. (1970). Derivational complexity and order of acquisition in child speech. In J. R. Hayes (Ed.), *Carnegie Mellon symposium on cognition, 4th: Cognition and the development of language* (pp. 155–207). NY: Wiley.

Bullock, T. H. (1986). Suggestions for research on ethological and comparative cognition. In R. J. Schusterman, J. A. Thomas, & F. G. Wood (Eds.), *Dolphin cognition and behavior: A comparative approach* (pp. 207–219). Hillsdale, NJ: Lawrence Erlbaum Associates.

Cazden, C. B. (1972). *Child language and education.* NY: Holt, Rinehart, and Winston.

Cheney, D. L., & Seyfarth, R. M. (1980). Vocal recognition in free ranging vervet monkeys. *Anim. Behav., 28,* 362–367.

Cheney, D. L., & Seyfarth, R. M. (1982). How vervet monkeys perceive their grunts: field playback experiments. *Anim Behav., 30,* 739–751.

Cheney, D. L., & Seyfarth, R. M. (1985). Social and non-social knowledge in vervet monkeys. *Phil. Trans. R. Soc. Lond.,* B *308,* 187–201.

Chevalier-Skolnikoff, S. (1981). The Clever Hans phenomenon, cuing, and ape signing: A Piagetian analysis of methods for instructing animals. In T. A. Sebeok & R. Rosenthal (Eds.), *The Clever Hans phenomenon: Communication with horses, whales, apes, and people.* Ann. NYAS, *364,* 60–93.

Clark, R. (1974). Performing without competence. *J. of Child Lang., 1,* 1–10.

Cobb, S. (1960). Observations in the comparative anatomy of the avian brain. *Perspectives in Biology and Medicine, 3,* Chicago, IL: University of Chicago Press.

Courtright, J. A., & Courtright, I. C. (1979). Imitative modeling as a language intervention strategy: the effects of two mediating variables. *J. Speech and Hearing Res., 22,* 389–402.

Crook, J. H. (1983). On attributing consciousness to animals. *Nature, 303,* 11–14.

Davis, H., & Memmott, J. (1982). Counting behavior in animals: A critical evaluation. *Psych. Bull., 92,* 547–571.

de Villiers, J. G., & de Villiers, P. A. (1978). *Language acquisition* (pp. 270–271). Cambridge, MA: Harvard University Press.

Fouts, R. S. (1973). Acquisition and testing of gestural signs in four young chimpanzees. *Science, 180,* 978–980.

Fouts, R. S., & Couch, T. B. (1976). Cultural evolution of learned language in chimpanzees. In M. E. Hahn & E. C. Simmel (Eds.), *Communicative behavior and evolution* (pp. 141–161). Orlando, FL: Academic Press.

Fouts, R. S., Hirsch, A., & Fouts, D. (1983). Cultural transmission of a human language in a chimpanzee mother/infant relationship. In H. E. Fitzgerald, J. A. Mullins, & P. Page (Eds.), *Psychobiological perspectives: Child nurturance series, Vol III* (pp. 159–193). New York: Plenum Press.

Fromkin, V., & Rodman, P. (1974). *An Introduction to Language.* New York: Holt, Rinehart and Winston.

Fulwiler, R. L., & Fouts, R. S. (1976). Acquisition of American Sign Language by a non-communicating autistic child. *J. Autism Child Schizophrenia, 6,* 43–51.

Gardner, B. T., & Gardner, R. A. (1978). Comparative psychology and language acquisition. *Psychology, the State of the Art.* NYAS, *309,* 37–76.

Gardner, R. A., & Gardner, B. T. (1984). A vocabulary test for chimpanzees. *J. Comp. Psychol., 98,* 381–404.

Geschwind, N. (1965). Disconnexion syndromes in animals and man. Pt 1. *Brain, 88,* 237–294.

Geschwind, N. (1979). Specialization of the human brain. *Sci. Am., 241,* 180–199.

Gillan, D. J. (1982). Ascent of apes. In D. R. Griffin (Ed.), *Animal mind–Human mind* (pp. 177–200). New York: Springer-Verlag.

Gossette, R. L. (1969). In O. H. Mowrer, *Psychology of language and learning* (pp. 105–106). New York: Plenum Press.

Gould, J. L., & Gould, C. G. (1982). The insect mind: physics or metaphysics? In D. R. Griffin (Ed.), *Animal mind–Human mind* (pp. 269–298). New York: Springer-Verlag.

Gouzoules, G., Gouzoules, H., & Marler, P. (1984). Rhesus monkey *(Macaca mulatta)* screams: Representational signalling in the recruitment of agnostic aid. *Anim. Behav., 32,* 182–193.

Green, S. (1975). Communication by a graded vocal system in Japanese monkeys. In L. A. Rosenblum (Ed.), *Primate behavior* (pp. 1–102). Orlando, FL: Academic Press.

Greenfield, P. M. (1978). Developmental processes in the language learning of child and chimp. *Behav. Brain Sci., 4,* 573–574.

Griffin, D. R. (1981). *The question of animal awareness.* New York: Rockefeller University Press.

Griffin, D. R. (1985). The cognitive dimensions of animal communication. In B. Hölldobler & M. Lindauer (Eds.), *Experimental behavioral ecology and sociobiology* (pp. 471–482). New York: Fischer Verlag.

Grosslight, J. H., & Zaynor, W. C. (1967). Verbal behavior in the mynah bird. In K. Salzinger & S. Salzinger, (Eds.), *Research in verbal behavior and some neurophysiological implications* (pp. 5–19), Orlando, FL: Academic Press.

Grosslight, J. H., Zaynor, W. C., & Lively, B. L. (1964). Speech as a stimulus for differential vocal behavior in the mynah bird *(Gracula religiosa). Psychon. Sci., 1,* 7–8.

Hayes, K. J., & Nissen, C. H. (1956/1971). Higher mental functions of a home-raised chimpanzee. In A. Schrier & F. Stollnitz (Eds.), *Behavior of nonhuman primates, Vol. 4.* (pp. 57–115). Orlando, FL: Academic Press.

Herman, L. M. (1980). Cognitive characteristics of dolphins. In L. Herman (Ed.), *Cetacean behavior: Mechanisms and functions* (pp. 363–430). New York: Wiley-Interscience.

Herman, L. M. (1986). Cognition and language competencies of bottlenosed dolphins. In R. J. Schusterman, J. A. Thomas, & F. G. Wood (Eds.), *Dolphin cognition and behavior: A comparative approach* (pp. 221–252). Hillsdale, NJ: Lawrence Erlbaum Associates.

Herman, L., Richards, D., & Wolz, J. (1984). Comprehension of sentences by bottlenosed dolphins. *Cognition, 16,* 129–219.

Hinde, R. A. (1982). *Ethology, its nature and relationship with other sciences.* Oxford: Oxford University Press.

Hockett, C. F. (1961). Logical considerations in the study of animal communication. In W. E. Lanyon & W. N. Tavolga (Eds.), *Animal sounds and communication* (pp. 392–430). Washington, DC: Am. Inst. Biol. Sci., Publ. 7.

Hockett, C. F., & Altmann, S. A. (1968). A note on design features. In T. A. Sebeok (Ed.), *Animal communication* (Ch. 5). Bloomington, IN: Indiana University Press.

Hodos, W. (1982). Some perspectives on the evolution of intelligence and the brain. In D. R. Griffin (Ed.), *Animal mind–Human mind* (pp. 33–56). NY: Springer-Verlag.

Jerison, H. J. (1973). *Evolution of the brain and intelligence.* Orlando, FL: Academic Press.

Kamil, A. C. (1984). Adaptation and cognition: Knowing what comes naturally. In H. L. Roitblat, T. G. Bever, & H. S. Terrace (Eds.), *Animal cognition* (pp. 533–544). Hillsdale, NJ: Lawrence Erlbaum Associates.

Kamil, A. C., & Hunter, M. W. III (1970). Performance on object discrimination learning set by the Indian Hill mynah, *Gracula religiosa. J. comp. Physiol. Psych., 13,* 68–73.

Koehler, O. (1943). 'Zähl'-Versuche an einem Kolkraben und Vergleichsvesuche an Menschen. *Z. Tierpsychol., 5,* 575–712.

Koehler, O. (1950). The ability of birds to 'count'. *Bull. Anim. Behav., 9,* 41–45.

Krebs, J. R., & Kroodsma, D. E. (1980). Repertoires and geographical variation in bird song. In J. S. Rosenblatt, R. A. Hinde, C. Beer, & M-C. Busnel (Eds.), *Advances in the study of behavior, Vol. 11* (pp. 143–177). Orlando, FL: Academic Press.

Kroodsma, D. E. (1981). Geographical variations and functions of song types in warblers *(Parulidae). Auk, 98,* 743–751.

Kroodsma, D. E. (1982). Learning and the ontogeny of sound signals in birds. In D. E. Kroodsma & E. H. Miller (Eds.), *Acoustic communication in birds. Vol. 2: Song learning and its consequences* (pp. 1–23). Orlando, FL: Academic Press.

Kroodsma, D. E., & Canady, R. (1982, October). *Population differences in repertoire size, neuroanatomy, and song development in the long-billed marsh wren.* Paper presented at the American Ornithologists' Union National Meeting (Abst.), Chicago, IL.

Kroodsma, D. E., & Canady, R. (1985). Differences in repertoire size singing behavior, and associated neuroanatomy among marsh wrens have a genetic basis. *Auk, 102,* 439–446.

Kroodsma, D. E. et al. (1984). Biology of learning in nonmammalian vertebrates. In P. Marler & H. S. Terrace (Eds.), *The biology of learning* (pp. 399–418). Berlin: Springer-Verlag.

Krushinskii, L. V. (1960). *Animal behavior: Its normal and abnormal development* (pp. 179–235). New York: Consultants Bureau.

Leger, D. W., & Owings, D. H. (1978). Response to alarm calls by California ground squirrels: Effects of call structure and maternal status. *Behav. Ecol. Sociobiol., 3,* 177–186.

Leger, D. W., Owings, D. H., & Boal, L. M. (1979). Contextual information and differential responses to alarm whistles in California ground squirrels. *Z. Tierpsychol., 49,* 142–155.

Leger, D. W., Owings, D. H., & Gelfand, D. L. (1980). Single-note vocalizations of California ground squirrels: Graded signals and situation-specificity of predator and socially evoked calls. *Z. Tierpsychol., 52,* 227–246.

Lein, M. R. (1972). Territorial and courtship songs of birds. *Nature, 237,* 48–49.

Lein, M. R. (1978). Song variation in a population of chestnut-sided warblers (*Dendroica pensylvanica*): its nature and suggested significance. *Can. J. Zool., 56,* 1266–1283.

Lemon, R. E. (1975). How birds develop song dialects. *Condor., 77,* 385–406.

Lenneberg, E. H. (1969). On explaining language. *Science, 164,* 634–643.

Lenneberg, E. H. (1971). Of language, apes and brains. *J. Psycholing. Res., 1,* 1–29.

Lenneberg, E. H. (1973). Biological aspects of language. In G. A. Miller (Ed.), *Communication, language, and meaning* (pp. 49–60). NY: Basic Books.

Lögler, P. (1959). Versuche zur Frage des 'Zähl'-Vermögens an einen Graupapagei und Vergleichsversuche an Menschen. *Z. Tierpsychol., 16,* 179–217.

Lovaas, O. I. (1977). *The autistic child: Language development through behavior modification.* New York: Irvington.

Malmi, W. A. (1976). Chimpanzees and language evolution. In S. R. Harnad, H. D. Steklis, & J. Lancaster (Eds.), *Origins and evolution of language and speech. Ann. NYAS, 280,* 598–603.

Marler, P. (1975). On the origin of speech from animal sounds. In J. Kavanaugh & J. Cutting (Eds.), *The role of speech in language* (pp. 11–43). Cambridge, MA: MIT Press.

Marler, P. (1983). Monkey calls: How are they perceived and what do they mean? In J. F. Eisenberg & D. G. Kleiman (Eds.), *Advances in the study of mammalian behavior* (pp. 343–356). Special publication No. 7. Amer. Soc. of Mammalogists.

Marler, P. (1985). Representational vocal signals of primates. In B. Hölldobler & M. Lindauer (Eds.), *Experimental behavioral ecology and sociobiology* (pp. 212–221). Stuttgart: G. Fischer Verlag.

Matsuzawa, T. (1985). Use of numbers by a chimpanzee. *Nature, 315,* 57–59.

Mattick, I. (1972). The teacher's role in helping young children develop language competence. In C. B. Cazden (Ed.), *Language in early childhood education* (pp. 107–116). Washington, D.C.: Nat'l Assoc. for Education of Young Children.

Menzel, E. W., & Juno, C. (1982). Marmosets (*Saguinus fuscicollis*): Are learning sets learned? *Science, 217,* 750–752.

Menzel, E. W., & Juno, C. (1985). Social foraging in marmoset monkeys and the question of intelligence. *Phil. Trans. R. Soc. Lond.* B 308, 145–158.

Michael, J., Whitley, P., & Hesse, B. (1983). The pigeon parlance project. *VB News, 2,* 6–9.

Miles, H. L. (1978). Language acquisition in apes and children. In F. C. C. Peng (Ed.), *Sign language and language acquisition in man and ape* (pp. 103–120). Boulder, CO: Westview Press.

Miles, H. L. (1983). Apes and language: the search for communicative competence. In J. de Luce & H. T. Wilder (Eds.), *Language in primates* (pp. 43–61). New York: Springer-Verlag.

Morse, D. H. (1967). The contexts of songs in black-throated green and Blackburnian warblers. *Wilson Bulletin, 79,* 64–74.

Mowrer, O. H. (1952). The autism theory of speech development and some clinical applications. *J. Speech and Hearing Dis., 17,* 263–268.

Mowrer, O. H. (1954). A psychologist looks at language. *Am. Psychol., 9,* 660–694.

Mowrer, O. H. (1958). Hearing and speaking: an analysis of language learning. *J. Speech and Hearing Disord., 23,* 143–152.

Nauta, W. J. H., & Karten, H. J. (1970). A general profile of the vertebrate brain, with sidelights on the ancestry of the cerebral cortex. In F. O. Schmitt (Ed.), *The neurosciences second study program: Evolution of brain and behavior* (pp. 7–26). NY: Rockefeller University Press.

Nottebohm, F. (1975). A zoologist's view of some language phenomena with particular emphasis on vocal learning. In E. H. Lenneberg & E. Lenneberg (Eds.), *Foundations of language development* (pp. 61–104). Orlando, FL: Academic Press.

Nottebohm, F. (1981). A brain for all seasons: cyclic anatomical changes in song control nuclei of the canary brain. *Science, 214,* 1368–1370.

Nottebohm, F., Kasparian, S., & Pandazis, C. (1981). Brain space for a learned task. *Brain Research, 213,* 99–109.

Owings, D. H., & Virginia, R. A. (1978). Alarm calls of California ground squirrels (*Spermophilus beecheyi*). *Z. Tierpsychol., 46,* 58–70.

Patterson, F. (1978). Linguistic capabilities of a lowland gorilla. In F. C. C. Peng (Ed.), *Sign language and language acquisition in man and ape* (pp. 161–202). Boulder, CO: Westview Press.

Pepperberg, I. M. (1978). Paper presented at Midwest Animal Behavior Society Meeting (Abst.), W. Lafayette, IN.

Pepperberg, I. M. (1979, June). *Object identification by an African Grey parrot.* Paper presented at Animal Behavior Society Meeting (Abst.), New Orleans, LA.

Pepperberg, I. M. (1980, June). *Evidence for numerical counting ability in an African Grey parrot.* Paper presented at Animal Behavior Society Meeting (Abst.). Ft. Collins, CO.

Pepperberg, I. M. (1981). Functional vocalizations by an African Grey parrot (*Psittacus erithacus*). *Z. Tierpsychol., 55,* 139–160.

Pepperberg, I. M. (1983a). Cognition in the African Grey parrot: preliminary evidence for auditory/vocal comprehension of the class concept. *Anim. Learn. Behav., 11,* 179–185.

Pepperberg, I. M. (1983b, June). *Interspecies communication: Innovative vocalizations of the African Grey parrot.* Paper presented at Animal Behavior Society Meeting (Abst.). Lewisburg, PA.

Pepperberg, I. M. (1985). Social modeling theory: A possible framework for understanding avian vocal learning. *Auk, 102,* 854–864.

Pepperberg, I. M. (1986a). Acquisition of anomalous communicatory systems: Implications for studies on interspecies communication. In R. J. Schusterman, J. A. Thomas, & F. G. Wood (Eds.), *Dolphin cognition and behavior: A comparative approach* (pp. 289–302). Hillsdale, NJ: Lawrence Erlbaum Associates.

Pepperberg, I. M. (1986b, June). *Communicative competence in the African Grey parrot.* Paper presented at the International Ornithological Congress, Ottawa, Canada.

Pepperberg, I. M. (in press-a). Evidence for conceptual quantitative abilities in the African Grey parrot: Labeling of cardinal sets. *Ethology.*

Pepperberg, I. M. (in press-b). The importance of social interaction and observation in the acquisition of communicative competence: Possible parallels between avian and human learning. In T.

A. Zentall & B. Galef (Eds.), *Social learning: A comparative approach*. Hillsdale, NJ: Lawrence Erlbaum Associates.

Pepperberg, I. M., & Kozak, F. A. (1986). Object permanence in the African Grey parrot (*Psittacus erithacus*). *Anim. Learn. Behav., 14,* 322–330.

Petrinovich, L. (1972). Psychobiological mechanisms in language development. In G. Newton & A. H. Riesen (Eds.), *Advances in psychobiology, Vol. 1* (pp. 259–285). New York: Wiley-Interscience.

Premack, D. (1976). *Intelligence in ape and man*. Hillsdale, NJ: Lawrence Erlbaum Associates.

Premack, D. (1978). On the abstractness of human concepts: why it would be difficult to talk to a pigeon. In S. H. Hulse, H. Fowler, & W. K. Honig (Eds.), *Cognitive processes in animal behavior* (pp. 423–452). Hillsdale, NJ: Lawrence Erlbaum Associates.

Premack, D. (1983). The codes of man and beasts. *Behav. Brain Sci., 6,* 125–167.

Richey, E. (1976). The language program. In E. R. Ritvo, B. J. Freeman, E. M. Ornitz, & P. E. Tanguay (Eds.), *Autism: Diagnosis, current research, and management*. New York: Spectrum Publications.

Rieber, R. W., & Voyat, G. (1983). *Dialogues on the psychology of language and thought*. New York: Plenum Press.

Risley, T., & Wolf, M. (1968). Establishing functional speech in echolalic children. In H. N. Sloane, Jr. & B. D. MacAuley (Eds.), *Operant procedures in remedial speech and language training* (pp. 157–184). Boston, MA: Houghton-Mifflien.

Ristau, C. A., & Robbins, D. (1979). A threat to man's uniqueness? Language and communication in the chimpanzee. *J. Psycholing. Res., 8,* 267–300.

Robinson, S. R. (1980). Antipredator behaviour and predator recognition in Belding's ground squirrels. *Anim. Behav., 28,* 840–852.

Robinson, S. R. (1981). Alarm communication in Belding's ground squirrels. *Z. Tierpsychol., 59,* 150–168.

Ruder, K. F., Hermann, P., & Schiefelbusch, R. L. (1977). Effects of verbal imitiation and comprehension training on verbal production. *J. Psycholing. Res., 6,* 59–72.

Rumbaugh, D. M., & Gill, T. V. (1976). The mastery of language–type skills by the chimpanzee (*Pan*). In S. R. Harnad, H. D. Steklis, & J. Lancaster (Eds.), *Origins and evolution of language and speech, Ann. NYAS, 280,* 562–578.

Salzinger, K. (1973). Animal communication. In D. A. Dewsbury & D. A. Rethlingshafer (Eds.), *Comparative psychology: A modern survey,* (pp. 161–193) New York: McGraw Hill

Salzinger, K. (1980). The concept of the behavioral mechanism in language. In O. H. Mowrer (Ed.), *Psychology of language and learning* (pp. 213–232). New York: Plenum Press.

Saunders, R., & Sailor, W. (1979). A comparison of the strategies of reinforcement in two-choice learning problems with severely retarded children. *AAESPH Rev., 4,* 323–334.

Savage-Rumbaugh, E. S., Rumbaugh, D. M., & Boysen, S. (1980a). Do apes use language? *Am. Scientist, 68,* 49–61.

Savage-Rumbaugh, E. S., Rumbaugh, D. M., Smith, S. T., & Lawson, J. (1980b). Reference: the linguistic essential. *Science, 210,* 922–925.

Schneirla, T. C. (1946). Problems in the biopsychology of social organization. *J. Abnor. Soc. Psychol., 41,* 385–402.

Schneirla, T. C. (1950). The relationship between observation and experimentation in the field study of animal behavior. *Ann. NYAS, 51,* 1022–1044.

Schneirla, T. C. (1962). Psychological comparison of insect and mammal. *Psychol. Beitr., 6,* 509–519.

Schuler, A. L. (1980). A review of intervention techniques. In W. H. Fay & A. L. Schuler (Eds.), *Emerging language in autistic children* (pp. 137–164). Baltimore, MD: University Press.

Schusterman, R., & Krieger, K. (1984). California sea lions are capable of semantic comprehension. *The Psych. Record, 34,* 3–23.

Segal, E. (1983). *Generalized discriminative-response sequences (syntax?) in a Barbary macaque.* Paper presented at Psychonomic Society Meeting, San Diego, CA. (Abst.).

Seibt, U. (1982). Zahlbergriff und Zählverhalten bei Tieren. Neue Versuche und Deutungen. *Z. Tierpsychol., 60,* 325–341.

Seyfarth, R. M., Cheney, D. L., & Marler, P. (1980a). Vervet monkey alarm calls: semantic communication in a free-ranging primate. *Anim. Behav., 28,* 1070–1094.

Seyfarth, R. M., Cheney, D. L., & Marler, P. (1980b). Monkey responses to three different alarms: evidence for predator classification and semantic communication. *Science, 210,* 801–803.

Skinner, B. F. (1957). *Verbal behavior.* New York: Appleton-Century-Crofts.

Snow, C. E. (1972). Mothers' speech to children learning language. *Child Devel., 43,* 549–565.

Sonnenschein, E. & Reyer, H-U. (1983). Mate-guarding and other functions of antiphonal duets in the slate-colored boubou (*Laniarius funebris*). *Z. Tierpsychol., 63,* 112–140.

Stettner, L. J. (1974). Avian discrimination and reversal learning. In I. J. Goodman & M. W. Schein (Eds.), *Birds: Brain and behavior* (pp. 194–201). Orlando, FL: Academic Press.

Stettner, L. J. & Matyniak, K. (1968). The brain of birds. *Sci. Amer., 218,* 64–76.

Struhsaker, T. (1967). *Behavior and ecology of the Red Colobus monkeys.* Chicago, IL: University of Chicago Press.

Taves, E. H. (1941). Two mechanisms for the perception of visual numerousness: *Arch. Psychol., 37,* 1–47.

Tavolga, W. N. (1970). Levels of interaction in animal communication. In L. R. Aronson, E. Tobach, D. S. Lehrman & J. S. Rosenblatt (Eds.), *Development and evolution of behavior* (pp. 281–302). San Francisco, CA: W. H. Freeman.

Thomas, R. (1980). Evolution of intelligence: an approach to its assessment. *Brain Behav. Evol., 17,* 454–472.

Thorpe, W. H. (1974). *Animal and human nature.* New York: Anchor Press, Doubleday.

Tobach, E. (1970). Some guidelines to the study of the evolution and development of emotion. In L. R. Aronson, E. Tobach, D. S. Lehrman, & J. S. Rosenblatt (Eds.), *Development and evolution of behavior* (pp. 238–253). San Francisco, CA: W. H. Freeman.

Todt, D. (1975). Social learning of vocal patterns and modes of their applications in Grey parrots. *Z. Tierpsychol., 39,* 178–188.

von Glasersfeld, E. (1977). Linguistic communication: Theory and definition. In D. M. Rumbaugh (Ed.), *Language learning by a chimpanzee* (pp. 55–72). Orlando, FL: Academic Press.

Whitehurst, G. J., Ironsmith, E. M., & Goldfein, M. (1974). Selective imitation of the passive construction through modeling. *J. Exp. Child Psychol., 17,* 288–302.

Zentall, T., Hogan, D. E., & Edwards, C. A. (1984). Cognitive factors in learning by pigeons. In H. L. Roitblat, T. G. Bever, & H. S. Terrace (Eds.), *Animal cognition* (pp. 389–405). Hillsdale, NJ: Lawrence Erlbaum Associates.

Zorina, Z. A. (1982). Reasoning ability and adaptivity of behaviour in birds. In V. J. A. Novák & J. Mlikovský (Eds.), *Evolution and environment* (pp. 907–912). Praha: CSAV (trans. provided by the author).

# 5 Chimpanzee Signing and Emergent Levels

Roger S. Fouts
*Central Washington University*

In regard to progress in scientific thought, the Cartesian notion of discontinuity has had little, if any positive effect. Gardner and Gardner (1983) state in their discussion of the defeat of vitalism, when organic chemicals were first synthesized, that:

> Truly discontinuous, all or none phenomena are rare in nature. Historically, the great discontinuities have turned out to be conceptual barriers rather than natural phenomena. They have been passed by and abandoned rather than broken through in the course of scientific progress. (p. 1)

This is certainly not only true for vitalism and chemistry but also for some of the more recent attempts in the behavioral sciences to separate *Homo sapien* from nature by devising arm chair conjectures about human uniqueness such as, tool use, tool making, adolescence and so on. The most recent conjecture has to do with language. But this is beginning to be abandoned also. For example Thorpe (1972) states:

> It would no doubt be easy to devise definitions of language such that no examples of animal communication could readily find inclusion therein. There have always been, and no doubt there will continue to be, those who resist with great vigor any conclusions which seem to break down what they regard as one of the most important lines of demarcation between animals and men. We must surely be justified in accepting such preconceived definitions only with the utmost caution. One of the tasks of the scientific student of animal behavior is to attempt to establish whether or not there are such hard and fast dividing lines and if so, what and where they are. Of one thing we can be certain: it is that work such as that of

57

the Gardners' and of Premack is only the beginning of the application of an important and powerful new technique from which we stand to learn much in the years to come. I believe that no one should have anything to fear from its cautious and objective applications. (p. 47)

Thorpe's statement is almost prophetic in its insight when one considers the recent advances in this research. The Gardners' pioneering cross-fostering experiment (1971) was expanded successfully to four other chimpanzees (1978). The research in my laboratory with Washoe has found that her sign language is culturally transmitted to her adopted son (Fouts, Hirsch & Fouts, 1982). Finally, our research is presently examining the spontaneous sign language conversations between five sign language using chimpanzees (Fouts, Fouts, & Schoenfeld, 1984, and D. H. Fouts, 1984).

## THE GARDNER'S CROSS-FOSTERING RESEARCH

In the first half of the 20th century there were several unsuccessful attempts to teach vocal speech to apes. But it wasn't until 1966 that the first successful attempt to teach a chimpanzee sign language was begun by Gardner and Gardner (1969) with Project Washoe.

Washoe was about 11 months old when the project began and by the end of the 51st month of the project she had acquired 132 reliable signs of American Sign Language (Ameslan) (Gardner & Gardner, 1978). Washoe used her signs for classes of referents rather than specific objects or events. As the Gardners (1978) note: "Thus the sign for dog was used to refer to live dogs and pictures of dogs of many breeds, sizes, and colors, and for the sound of barking by an unseen dog as well . . ." (p. 38).

The Gardners (1978) used a systematic program of testing. The resulting record was only a small fraction of Washoe's verbal behavior because she used her sign language spontaneously; to communicate to her human companions, strangers and animals; in other words it occurred throughout each day. The Gardners (1978) state:

> She learned to ask for goods and services, and she also answered questions with verbal descriptions and commentary about the world of objects and events that surrounded her. Washoe's descriptions and comments were not limited to replies to our questions; she initiated many of the conversations with questions and opening statements of her own. (p. 38–89)

Washoe's combinations were comparable to human children's early combinations. The Gardners (1978) note that:

> . . . Roger Brown concluded that "the evidence (from Gardner & Gardner, 1971) that Washoe has Stage I language that is about the same as it is for children."

Project Washoe continued for another 15 months and progress continued to accelerate. In further development of her combinations, in her replies to Wh- questions, in her use of negatives, prepositions, and locatives, Washoe compared favorably with children at Brown's Stage III and beyond. (p. 39)

Washoe's rearing conditions were a very important aspect of the project. As a contrast to later studies by other researchers using chimpanzees, the Gardners assumed that the best language acquisition would be found under the best environmental conditions and that those conditions should be comparable to a child's. This position is in contrast to the position held by certain psycholinguists. For example, Van Cantfort and Rimpau (1982) state that:

Those psycholinguists who were influenced by Chomsky maintained that the acquisition of language was completed quickly and was quite independent of environmental support and intellectual development . . . In contrast there are investigators of child development who argue that language development is dependent on the development of intelligence, which is, in turn, dependent upon an appropriate rearing environment. (p. 17)

The Gardners approach fell into the later position. Even though later chimpanzee researchers ignored this important aspect (Premack, 1971, Terrace, 1979, Rumbaugh, 1977), earlier researchers did not. For example, Kellogg (1968) states: ''Apes as household pets are not uncommon . . . but pet behavior is not child behavior, and pet treatment is not child treatment.'' (p. 423). The Gardners raised Washoe in an environment much like that of a human child's; in Washoe's environment the quality of the behavioral environment was emphasized. Her days were made up of meals, naps, baths, play, schooling, and outings to interesting places. Her living quarters had furniture, toys, tools, a kitchen, a bedroom and bathroom. Compared to a human child's, Washoe's environment was comparable, but compared to other apes in cages or in restricted environments, Washoe's was indeed enriched.

In 1972 the Gardners began a multiple subject project. Now that the ground had been broken by Washoe, a replication was in order. Their multiple subject project not only allowed for replication but it had the advantages of enrichment through older sibling/younger sibling relationships and the fact that signing between chimpanzees could be studied. From November 1972 to August 1976 the Gardners acquired four infant chimpanzees; Moja, Peli, Tatu, and Dar.

In their research with Washoe as well as their later chimpanzee subjects the Gardners (1978) used a strict and conservative criterion before a sign could be placed on one of their chimpanzee's vocabulary lists. They state their criterion as follows:

When a sign had been reported on three independent occasions by three different observers, the day of the third report was entered as the date of introduction of that sign into Washoe's vocabulary. The sign was not listed as a reliable item of vocabulary, however, until it had been reported to occur spontaneously and appropriately at least once on each of 15 consecutive days. (pp. 47–48)

Using the aforementioned criterion for a sign to be considered reliable, the Gardners were able to compare the first signs of Washoe, who was nearly a year old at the beginning of the project, to the four other chimpanzees who began the project just a few days after their births.

In comparing the two projects the Gardners (1978) state:

After seven months of exposure to the conditions of the project, her (Washoe's) vocabulary consisted of the signs, *come-gimme, more, up* and *sweet*. By contrast, both Moja and Peli started to make recognizable signs when they were about three months old. The date of appearance of a new sign is taken as the day that the third of three independent observers reported an appropriate and spontaneous occurrence. By this criterion, Moja's first four signs *(come-gimme, more, go* and *drink)* appeared during her 13th week of life. Peli's first sign appeared during his 14th week, and he had a four sign vocabulary *(drink, come-gimme, more* and *tickle)* by his fifteenth week. Similarly, by 13 weeks Tatu's vocabulary included five signs *(go, drink, more, up* and *come-gimme)* and this was also true for Dar, whose vocabulary at 13 weeks consisted of *more, tickle, come-gimme, up,* and *drink.* (pp. 49–50)

The Gardners (1978) go on to state that even though the acquisition of first signs for chimpanzees may seem early for hearing children, it is not so for deaf children exposed to sign language from birth, in which parental reports indicate that deaf children's first signs appear between the 5th and 6th month.

The Gardners (1978) also compared the five chimpanzees ten-sign and 50-sign vocabulary acquisition to reports in the literature on hearing children's 10-word and 50-word vocabulary acquisition:

The age for a ten-sign vocabulary was 5 months for Moja, Peli, and Tatu, and 6 months for Dar, but 25 months for Washoe; in the case of children, the age at ten words ranged from 13 to 19 months, with a mean of 15 months. (p. 50)

Gardner and Gardner (1983) state that Moja, Peli, Tatu, and Dar reached the 50-sign vocabulary level between 21 and 25 months of age and that in hearing children this 50-word vocabulary is reached between 15 and 24 months of age.

The Gardners found evidence that their chimpanzee subjects used devices in their sign language to modulate the meaning of semantic units. In regard to modulators, Van Cantfort and Rimpau (1982) state:

Spoken languages use devices such as markers, inflections and word order to modulate meaning. Each language uses a unique mixture of these devices. Sign languages use analogous devices, adapted to the needs and advantages of a visual mode of transmission. (p. 35)

The Gardners chimpanzees used the establishment of loci, the use of eye gaze, facial expression and repetition to modulate the semantic meanings of their signs. An example of the establishment of loci is when a chimpanzee signs *tickle* on the hand of the individual by whom they wish to be tickled. In our laboratory we have not only observed instances of this between chimpanzees and humans but also between two or more chimpanzees. The chimpanzees have been reported to sign *tickle* on an object and then give the object to a human who is then expected to tickle the chimpanzee with that object. We have noted in our laboratory that Dar prefers to be tickled with plastic prehistoric dinosaur models.

Eye gaze and facial expression are extremely important as modulators in sign language in order to distinguish between the declarative and interrogative sentence. The Gardners have observed this used by their chimpanzees who acquired their sign language from humans. We have also observed this used in our laboratory by Loulis, who acquired his sign language from chimpanzees. It occurs most frequently during cleaning. Loulis will approach the person cleaning, who is hosing down the floor, and Loulis will look straight into that person's eyes with wide questioning eyes and then hold the sign *drink,* or *that hurry gimme* or *hurry hose* until the person cleaning vocally states "OK" or "Go ahead" and then he will drink from the hose. We have also observed this questioning eye gaze and facial expression between chimpanzees (Tatu and Washoe) during a remote video taping session of their signing interactions.

Repetition in language is often used to modulate the meaning of an utterance in terms of emphasis. For example, anyone who has been to a supermarket or a toy store has observed a child change a question into a demand with the use of repetition. The "Can I have . . ." or "I wanna . . ." repetitive utterances of children are notorious as well as noxious to mothers and other adults alike. Nelson (1980) found in one of her transcripts of a 24 month old girl the repetition of the utterance "Wait John" eleven successive times. Unfortunately some individuals who have not examined the literature carefully, have in an a priori manner assumed that repetitions are meaningless and don't count as elements in the use of language, and have even gone so far as to assume that children do not use repetitions. Nelson (1980) states, in regard to these ignorant individuals, that ". . . anyone who claims children do not repeat has led a sheltered library existence." (p. 1). I personally doubt that these individuals led their sheltered existence in a library because the literature, even on sign language (e.g. Hoffmeister, Moores, and Ellenberger, 1975) is available to someone who bothers to use the library.

We have observed in our laboratory the use of repetition by the chimpanzees in order to modulate the meaning of an utterance. For example, Tatu does this quite often. Just before lunch she will often ask *"Time Eat?"*. If the human response is in the affirmative she will start joyfully hooting. However, if the response is "It's not ready." or "You'll have to wait.", then she will begin to whimper and cry while repeating *"Time Eat"* in a demanding and downright nagging and annoying fashion. We have also observed this use of repetition between chimpanzees signing to each other when a request is ignored or denied by the addressee.

Sign order as a syntactic device to modulate meaning is one device that is dependent on the nature of the particular language being used, as well as the nature of the person using that language. Order or syntax plays an important role in the English language, but in highly inflected languages, such as Russian, it is much less important. Because American Sign Language is a highly inflected language (Klima & Bellugi, 1979) it makes sense that sign order, in terms of syntax, does not play the important role it does in English. The person using the language is also an important determinant in the role of syntax. The use of syntax by a professor of English Composition is very different from that of a two-year-old child, even though both may be using English. Van Cantfort and Rimpau (1982) comment on a study that looked for adult English syntax in the signing of an infant chimpanzee:

> . . . the vast majority of Nim's sign combinations were two or three sign utterances (see Terrace et al, 1979: 894, Tabs. 4 & 5). Such short utterances are likely to be understood no matter how the signs are ordered. In discussing word order in the early stages of child speech, Bollinger noted ". . . a two-word sentence has little need for connective tissue. The elements are of equal rank, and if one knows their meaning it is not even necessary to put them in any particular order—a child is as apt to say *awgone shoe* as to say *shoe awgone,* not to mention his magisterial indifference to "correct" grammatical indications of agreement and subordination." (1975:7). Second, it is questionable that children at the two or three word stage have syntactic structure or produce grammatical sentences. (pp. 41–42)

The main point of this is that the application of syntax or sign order as a criteria for language is inappropriate not only for this particular language (sign language); but also for the age of subjects. Nelson (1980) stated that the apes don't produce grammatical sentences, but when using the same criteria neither do human children who produce two or three word combinations.

Because of the characteristics inherent in sign language as well as the young age of the subjects, the Gardners (1971) were very cautious indeed when inferring anything in regard to syntax relative to Washoe's productions. In fact, they stated that there may be less need to infer syntactic rules rather than semantic. They point out explicitly that they did not feel forced to interpret the non-random features of Washoe's combinations as evidence for syntax. For example, the Gardners (1971) state:

> . . . it may be as misleading to describe nonrandom aspects of the utterances of immature primates (human or nonhuman) in terms of syntax, as it is misleading to refer to nonrandom aspects of the running of rats in mazes in terms of hypotheses. (p. 178)

However, just because order is not important in certain languages and at certain development ages it does not follow that order is beyond the capacity of apes. As Fouts, Shapiro and O'Neil (1978), found: order can be trained. They found that the chimpanzee Ali, when trained on the production of prepositional phrases, was able to produce novel prepositional phrases for objects in a double-blind testing condition. What was particularly interesting in this study was that even though Ali made errors on his labeling of the subject, preposition, or location, he made no order errors. The results of this study has led me to consider the possibility that order, when a constant invariant, may be much easier to acquire than individual vocabulary items. However, in the spontaneous use of language, especially a highly inflected one, the semantic, contextual and social aspects of the language may obviate the necessity for order as a modulator. Judging from the aforementioned studies on human children, it certainly seems that semantic meaning is propaedeutic to syntactic meaning. Indeed, syntax is most necessary in a language when it is written because it is here that the social and contextual aspects of the language are severely reduced if not absent.

Sign order is an inappropriate method of evaluation for sign language and for immature primates. But neither should it be used as a red herring to direct attention away from the important and positive aspects of the accomplishments of Washoe, Moja, Peli, Tatu, Dar, and Loulis.

In addition to the previous findings, the Gardners are also noted for their rigorous testing procedures, which have proven to be an improvement in experimental design and controls as compared to the research that has been done with human children by psycholinguists.

One of the more important innovations in linguistic testing was the Gardners' use of the double-blind procedure in testing the vocabulary of the chimpanzees. This procedure insured that it would be impossible to cue the subject being tested. In other words, the only person present who could see the stimuli was the chimpanzee. The Gardners used slides of particular objects the chimpanzees had not seen before in the double blind test. The use of slides enabled the Gardners to find novel examples to represent the particular signs. This procedure in the vocabulary tests demonstrated that the chimpanzee's signs were not merely a particular response associated with a particular stimuli, as one might find in conditioning or instrumental learning studies; but instead the chimpanzees were able to use their signs to describe conceptually related novel stimuli (Gardner & Gardner, 1974).

The Gardners used two observers in their double-blind slide tests. One observer was with the chimpanzee and could observe the chimpanzee but not the slide and the second observer was in a separate room and able to observe the chimpanzee through a one-way mirror and again they were unable to see the slide stimuli. Using this method, the Gardners were able to use deaf observers who were not a part of the project. They also used the two observers to obtain interobserver reliability. The Gardners (1974) report that the interobserver agreement was about 90% for Washoe (Gardner & Gardner, 1974), and the chimpanzees in the later project had an interobserver agreement of 71% for Moja, 91% for Tatu and 94% for Dar (Van Cantfort & Rimpau, 1982). The importance of this measure demonstrates that the chimpanzee's Ameslan signs were easily recognized as such even though context was absent under these blind conditions.

The Gardners also used subject-paced testing, which meant the subject was not being forced to respond, or was under duress during the testing. With Washoe they used rewards as encouragement for her to participate. With the later multiple-subject project they abandoned this system because the rewards were distracting and had a deleterious effect on the subjects' performance; the chimpanzees would often sign for the reward rather than about the stimuli (Gardner and Gardner, 1984).

The chimpanzees in both projects performed well above chance on these tests. But perhaps more interesting than their correct responses were their errors. Most of the errors fit into two categories. One being *semantic errors* in which a sign of similar meaning was incorrectly used (e.g., *comb* for *brush*). The other noted type of errors were *form errors*. For example, the signs *meat* and *oil* are very different semantically but very similar in their physical form. Initially the Gardners (1971) emphasized the importance of conceptual errors in terms of understanding the chimpanzees use of the signs. The form errors were considered to be uninteresting errors. In a recent discussion with R. Allen Gardner (October, 1983) he stated that this emphasis may have been an oversight and that the form errors are much stronger evidence for the chimpanzees understanding sign language than the conceptual errors. After all, he pointed out, only a chimpanzee that knew sign language would be able to make a form error, by confusing one sign with another sign that was highly similar in its form but not its meaning. A chimpanzee producing a sign language version of a malapropism is strong evidence for being competent in sign language; the irony being that this special type of incompetence demonstrates competence.

Another study of the Gardners (Gardner & Gardner, 1975) examined Washoe's replies to Wh- questions. Using a rigorous experimental design, they were able to produce a detailed statistical analysis of Washoe's replies to 10 different types of Wh- questions, which were answered by Washoe 50 times each over a period of 3 weeks. By using a set of preconceived rules, they avoided the weakness so often found in the use of retrospective analysis. Thus, many of Washoe's replies that would have been accepted by psycholinguists studying human children were scored as errors in the Gardner project. For example, one of Washoe's human companions, Susan, had placed a lollipop in a cupboard and then asked Washoe *"Where lollipop?"* and Washoe's reply was *"Open lollipop please."* Whereas one might retrospectively classify this as a correct response, the Gardners (Gardner & Gardner 1975, p. 252) scored this as an incorrect response because it contained no locatives.

The Gardners (1975) noted that in Roger Brown's study of responses to Wh-questions in human children that Brown (1968) considers:

> The best evidence in the child's spontaneous speech that he has such constituents is his ability to make the right sort of answers to the various Wh- questions addressed to him, giving noun phrases in response to *Who* and *What* questions, locatives to *Where* questions, predictors to *What-do* questions, etc. (p. 28)

The Gardners (1975) go on to point out that:

> The appearance of appropriate words in about half of the replies was sufficient for Brown and Ervin-Tripp to claim that children have grammatical mastery or control of a particular question type. Both agree that Stage III children should be credited with that much mastery of who, what, and where questions. They disagree about the ability of Stage III children to respond appropriately to whose and what do. Neither found evidence for mastery of why, how or when. (p. 255)

The Gardners are true pioneers in a field where much more remains to be explored. One would have assumed that with the Gardners' success that other researchers would have built on their findings by carefully following their procedures. But unfortunately this did not happen that often. Other researchers often ignored the important aspects of the Gardners' approach, as well as how human children acquire language. As a result, they used methods very different from the Gardners. For example, with regard to one of these ill conceived projects, B. T. Gardner (1981) states that:

> Some where in the second or third wave of research in this area Herbert S. Terrace fielded the project he describes in *Nim*. Latecomers often profit from the pioneering work of others, but Terrace's work falls far below the standards set by the earliest workers in the field. (p. 425).

## CULTURAL TRANSMISSION AND CHIMPANZEE CONVERSATIONS

The Gardners research was obviously very threatening to the proponents of Cartesian dichotomies. The Gardners are in the same position that Galleo was in facing a well established dogma, a dogma that is willing to forfeit scientific principles as well as the pursuit of knowledge in order to maintain the status quo. Fortunately for the Gardner's, the "stake" has gone out of fashion. Unfortunately, many of the critics have shed more heat than light on the subject and are better understood in clinical psychology rather than in the objective view of experimental psychology. However, even the unfounded criticisms and confounded experi-

ments can be useful and productive in terms of accenting the important characteristics of a proper experiment. In addition, they can help us to understand what
is important in the same way that a deprivation experiment tells us what is
important in the development of an organism by depriving that organism of
certain important experiences.

Before I integrate these apparent discrepant studies, I present some positive
results from our ongoing research project examining cultural transmission and
chimpanzee-to-chimpanzee conversations. The present research answers many
of the criticisms to arise over the past 10 to 15 years. So that you may better
understand the importance of this research, I state some of the more popular
criticisms: (a) the chimpanzees are cued to make their signs by the humans (the
Clever Hans phenomenon), (b) the chimpanzees do not sign spontaneously, (c)
the chimpanzees only sign for rewards, and (d) you need humans to teach
them—they don't develop it by themselves.

When I answer these criticisms it is not to say that some of the critics did not
find such results from their own research. Indeed they did, but their results were
a direct function of the procedures they used in their studies (Fouts, 1983).

The present research implicitly tests a major difference between the Gardners'
approach, which was one that implicitly assumed that a chimpanzee, like a
human child, would actively acquire the dominant mode of communication in
which they are immersed in their social environment as opposed to the approaches of other researchers that used structured drill sessions to "train" their
subjects how to produce a language. As is evident, these two approaches stem
from very different conceptions of organisms. The Gardners' approach assumes
an "active" organism whereas the projects that failed assumed a "passive"
organism that had to be trained to produce the experimenters' a priori assumptions of what constituted their particular notion of language.

The Loulis experiment addressed these issues in a very parsimonious manner.
If sign language acquisition requires human tutelage, then it would be impossible
for one chimpanzee to acquire it from another. However, if they are active
organisms then a chimpanzee should be able to acquire it without human tutelage
by simple exposure and immersion, as was found by the Gardners.

The Loulis study was arranged as follows: All signing by humans in Loulis'
presence was limited to seven signs: *who, what, want, where, which, name* and
*sign.* Other than these seven signs, vocal English was used to communicate to the
chimpanzees. Washoe had been exposed to vocal English for 9 years and had
good comprehension of that language. The purpose of not signing to Loulis was
to insure that he could not acquire signs from humans, other than those seven
used in his presence. We have used live-observations, video-taping with humans
present, as well as video-taping without humans present in order to control for
cueing and to examine the spontaneous chimpanzee-to-chimpanzee
conversations.

The results of this research is dramatic in that it indicates that human intervention is not necessary for a chimpanzee to acquire a sign language, and in fact cultural transmission between chimpanzees is a robust phenomenon. Not only has Loulis acquired signs from Washoe and the other signing chimps he lives with (Moja, Tatu and Dar), but Washoe and the other chimps have acquired new signs from each other. This has resulted from the chimpanzee-to-chimpanzee signing that is so common within this group of five chimpanzees.

The results from the first 2 years of Loulis' acquisition of signs have been extensively reported (Fouts, Hirsch, & Fouts, 1982). During that period Loulis acquired 22 signs from Washoe and Maoj, and began using two-sign combinations during his 16th month of exposure to signs. To March 1984 he has been observed to use 51 different signs, and he has been with Washoe five years on March 24, 1984 (As of December 1984, Loulis' observed vocabulary is 62 signs.)

We have observed very little tutoring on Washoe's part. However, we have had three reports of observations that occurred very early in their relationship of behavior that included a tutorial component. The first occurred during Loulis' first 8 days with Washoe, and it seemed to focus more on comprehension of a sign than production. For their first 3 days together, Washoe would orient toward Loulis, sign *come* to him, approach him and then grasp his arm and retrieve him. For the next 5 days the sequence remained the same except that the last component of retrieval dropped out. After the first 8 days, then, Washoe reduced it to simply orienting toward Loulis and signing *come* and he would respond to her command. *Come* was the first sign he acquired.

The second observation of tutoring occurred when Washoe was excitedly awaiting some food and was food barking while signing *food* in excited repetition. Loulis was sitting next to her watching her. Washoe stopped signing and took Loulis' hand and molded it into the *food* configuration and touched it to his mouth. He has acquired this sign.

A third type of tutoring was observed when Washoe placed a toy chair in front of Loulis and demonstrated the *chair-sit* sign to him five times. We have never observed Loulis to use this sign. Nor have we observed Washoe to attempt to teach Loulis another sign in this manner. This example is interesting in that it failed, yet Washoe did not continue in this chimpanzee version of a ''drill session.'' Apparently she displayed greater sensitivity to the problems in this approach than some human experimenters who have used drilling as a tutoring method only to find very meager results. Indeed, when comparing Loulis' success with the failures in the literature one can not help but think that the incisive restrictions used by the failures actually had a deleterious effect on their chimpanzee' communication skills.

Perhaps the most important element in Loulis'acquisition of sign language is the enriching social environment where his chimpanzee family use their signs to communicate to him in a spontaneous and contextually meaningful fashion. Fouts, Fouts, and Schoenfeld (1984) note in their study that the introduction of

Dar and Tatu to Washoe, Loulis and Moja had a profound effect on the incidence of signing. Prior to the introduction of Dar and Tatu (5 year old male, 6 year old female) to Washoe (18-year-old female), Loulis (3.75-years-old male) and Moja (10-year-old female) the monthly average of chimpanzee-to-chimpanzee sign conversations ranged from 12 observations to 85 observations, with a mean of 37.75. However, the monthly average of chimpanzee-to-chimpanzee sign conversations for the 13 months following the introduction of Dar and Tatu had a range of 118 to 649 with a mean of 378.15. These results speak to the importance of social enrichment as opposed to incisive restrictions. With Dar and Tatu as peer-playmates for Loulis, this family of five chimpanzee obviously had a lot to talk about.

Another study by D. H. Fouts (1984) examined these chimpanzee-to-chimpanzee conversations using three mounted video cameras to record the chimpanzees when no humans were present. She sampled the chimpanzees for 15 days, video taping three 20 minute sessions randomly distributed throughout each day. Because these were random samples, in some of the sessions the chimpanzees slept or groomed during the entire 20-minute session. However, in many sessions chimpanzee-to-chimpanzee conversations were recorded and in one 20-minute session 29 different chimpanzee-to-chimpanzee conversations were recorded.

We have also compared the live observation reports to the video-tape results and found that to be true over the same period. The video tapes from the D. H. Fouts' (1984) study had 612 occurrences of signs in the chimpanzee-to-chimpanzee interactions; whereas 15 hours of the live-observations from the same period only had 186 signs in the chimpanzee-to-chimpanzee interactions. This not only speaks of the advantages of using video-tape, but it has implications for the Fouts, Fouts, and Schoenfeld (1984) study that reported over 5200 observations of chimpanzee-to-chimpanzee conversations. If video had been used for these the figure could be closer to 17,000 occurrences.

In summary, given the results of these research projects the criticisms mentioned are inappropriate for these chimpanzees. The use of remote video taping prevents the possibilities of humans cueing the chimpanzees. If one chimpanzee is cueing another chimpanzee then it means that the chimpanzees are much more sophisticated about their use of sign language than most humans are about their own language. The criticism that the chimpanzees do not sign spontaneously is also countered by the over 5200 observations of chimpanzee-to-chimpanzee signing in the Fouts, Fouts, and Schoenfeld (1984) study, in addition to D. H. Fouts' (1984) study using 15 hours of video that reported study with the 612 observations of chimpanzee-to-chimpanzee signs. With regard to the criticism that chimpanzees only sign for reward, the Fouts et al, study (1984) also contradicts this criticism in that of the more than 5200 chimpanzee-to-chimpanzee conversations, only 5% dealt with food, whereas 88% occurred in the contexts of play, reassurance, and social interactions. This supports a position that these chimpanzees primarily use their sign language in a social manner. Finally,

Loulis' acquisition of signs from his adopted mother and playmates, as well as the fact that Washoe and the other chimpanzees have acquired new signs from each other, lays to rest the speculation that chimpanzees need to be taught their sign language by humans.

However, it does not make these criticisms invalid for all the ape language projects. These criticisms that have been leveled against all of the projects in reality only apply to a few that developed in the second or third wave of this type of research. As I noted in another article (Fouts, 1983):

> Results from the different ape language projects appear to be contradictory if the differences in individual research procedures are ignored. Some researchers, such as Terrace, Petito, Sanders, and Bever (1979), and Savage-Rumbaugh, Rumbaugh, and Boysen (1980), attribute the failure of their research to produce results that they expected to the biology of the chimpanzee rather than considering other aspects of their projects, such as training procedures, methods of data collection and analysis, and teachers. It is surprising to find this approach in experimental psychology, because a basic assumption of the discipline is that environmental stimuli control behavior. This assumption is translated from the general environmental situation into the laboratory with the approach that different experimental procedures produce different behaviors. What Terrace et al. (1979) and Savage-Rumbaugh et al. (1980) have done is comparable to a Skinnerian who, wishing to produce scalloping in the bar pressing behavior of a rat, uses a variable ratio schedule of reinforcement, instead of the fixed-interval schedule of reinforcement that normally produces a scalloping effect, and then blames the rat's failure to show any scalloping on the mental capacities of the rat rather than looking to the procedures for possible biases (Savage-Rumbaugh et al., 1980; Terrace et al., 1979). (p. 63)

One of the more obvious procedural differences between the different ape language projects is the different approaches to the use of extrinsic rewards. Gardner and Gardner (1984) state in regard to their use of extrinsics rewards:

> Chimpanzees are among the many species that behave as if they have a strong need to communicate (Van Lawick-Goodall, 1968). Captive chimpanzees are similar to wild chimpanzees in this respect (Kellogg, 1968) unless their conditions of captivity are so severe that normal behavior is suppressed. In the Reno laboratory when we did introduce extrinsic rewards for signing as, for example, when we rewarded Tatu and Dar with treats for obedient test-taking behavior, the extrinsic rewards usually interferred and had to be discontinued. (p. 402)

They go on to point out that their approach to extrinsic rewards was very different from some of the other projects and that this difference accounts for the different conclusions drawn by the different investigators:

> Most, if not all, of the techniques used by the Rumbaughs and by Terrace can be described as teaching the chimpanzee elaborate ways of begging for food and other commodities (Essock et al., 1977; Gill & Rumbaugh, 1974; Savage-Rumbaugh et

al., 1983; Terrace, 1979; Terrace et al., 1980). At the same time, working with human children, Lepper, Greene, and Nisbett (1973) and Levine and Fasnacht (1974) demonstrated that the heavy handed application of extrinsic rewards impairs the performance of intrinsically motivated tasks, such as drawing. Heavy reliance on extrinsic rewards probably has a similarly negative effect on the performance of chimpanzees. Characteristically, those who have relied most heavily on extrinsic rewards have been those who most insistently claimed that chimpanzees lack intrinsic motivation to communicate (Savage-Rumbaugh & Rumbaugh, 1978; Savage-Rumbaugh et al., 1983, pp. 462, 485–486; Terrace, 1979, pp. 221–224; Terrace et al., 1980, pp. 438–440). (Gardner & Gardner, 1984, p. 402)

## EMERGENT LEVELS

Prior to my first exposure to T. C. Schneirla's (1972) concept of levels, I had what I would consider the standard theoretical position held by most comparative psychologists: that the difference between different species is one of degree rather than kind. With regard to my own research, I held that chimpanzee sign language was different in degree from comparable behaviors in the human species. It had been my experience that individuals who disagreed with this position were adherents of the Cartesian position of discontinuity: that humans are different in kind from the rest of nature, which sets humans outside of nature while lumping all the "have nots" into one great defective mass.

Because of my background and previous experience I was surprised to find a noted comparative psychologist such as Ethel Tobach (a student of T. C. Schneirla) telling me that language was unique to humans. After several hours of lively discussion I discovered that Ethel not only held that language was unique to humans, but that what our signing chimpanzees were doing was unique to them and that not only were humans and chimpanzees unique species, but so were cockroaches, ticks, ants, and every other species known to science. This is a position that comes from T. C. Schneirla's theory of levels.

T. C. Schneirla's (1972) theory of levels is one in which a contradiction occurs within a species and this contradiction results in the emergence of a new or unique level of species development. The immediate implication of this theory is that it gets one off the two horns of the dilemma of continuity vs. discontinuity and in effect both positions are correct. By removing this either/or dilemma a new system of examining animal behavior emerges that encourages the systematic study of mentality and behavior in relation to the continuities and discontinuities of nature.

I do have one major reservation about T. C. Schneirla's theory; this is his use of the words "higher" and "lower" to describe different levels. He uses these words to present the notion that "higher levels" are more complex than "lower levels." This is unfortunate because implicit within the semantics of these words is the notion of superiority. My position is that the use of these words is an unjustified value judgment that is entirely dependent on an idiosyncratic frame of reference; whether from an individuals' or a species' point of view. For example I could argue that humans are "lower" or "less complex" as compared to bees; because humans lack the innate ability to discern polarized light or to innately determine the trigonometric relation between the sun, a food source and their home. These notions of higher or lower and more or less complex are a function of an individual point of view as well as what characteristics one arbitrarily decides to emphasize. This would be true at a phylogenetic level (the bee example) as well as at an ontogenetic level. The 3 year old toddler is *not* less complex than the mature developmental psychologist. The only true distinction that can be made is that the organisms at different levels of phylogenetic or ontogenetic development are different. I would hold that there are quantitative differences in the interaction of different qualities that would manifest themselves as uniquely different emergent levels in evolutionary as well as the individual developmental processes. Therefore, these two processes would have continuous as well as discontinuous characteristics. In the following section I present a theoretical model to support this position.

## BIOLOGICAL ALCHEMY: A LEVELS MODEL OF EMERGENT DEVELOPMENT

In an earlier article (Fouts, 1983) I presented a theory in which I used a model of a normal curve overlayed by a skewed curve to represent the phylogeny and ontogeny of cognitive development. The normal curve represented the cognitive distribution of human children and animal cognition while the skewed curve represented the cognitive distribution for the adult human along a sequential/simultaneous continuum. As can be seen in Fig. 5.1, I presented cognition as being the result of the interaction of the two poles of the cognitive continuum ranging from sequential processing to simultaneous processing. Sequential processing would be involved in such things as causality, specific discrete motor acts, attentional (focused) acts, temporal organization (e.g., grammar) and so on. The simultaneous processing would be involved in such things as non-causality, gross motor acts, non-attentional acts (e.g. peripheral vision), simultaneous organization (as found in the perception of spatial relations and nonverbal communication), and so on. I stated that these two processes interacted and that neither one could exist without involving some of the other.

I used this model to explain several different aspects of behavior, cognition, physiology, philosophy and psychological research. Regarding the ape language research, I used this model to demonstrate that all the various projects could be placed along the continuum. For example, the natural gestural communication system of the wild chimpanzees in Africa would be heavily loaded with nonverbal communication and would therefore be close to the simultaneous end of the

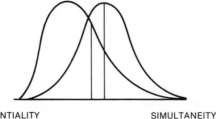

SEQUENTIALITY                    SIMULTANEITY

FIGURE 5.1.  A cognitive continuum representing the distribution of sequential and simultaneous cognitive processing. The hypothetical normal curve with the mean on the right represents the typical pre-laterialized young human and nonhuman distribution which is normally distributed along the continuum between the two processes. The skewed curve with the mean on the left represents the typical adult human distribution of cognition which is skewed toward the sequential end of the continuum.

continuum. On the other hand, the Gardners' (1971, 1975, 1978) cross-fostering research with Washoe, Moja, Peli, Tatu, and Dar would be closer to the middle of the continuum because the sign language used in those projects would interject a great deal of sequentiality. Yet this was balanced by the simultaneity of the enriched social relationships found in the Gardners' method of home-rearing. Finally, those ape-language projects that used highly structured methods such as extensive drilling and tutoring sessions (Premack, 1971; Rumbaugh, 1977; Terrace, 1979) would be placed very near the sequential end of the continuum. My conclusion was that the apparent differences between the various projects were merely a reflection of the environmental influences as well as the very distinctly different experimental procedures. Therefore, these were not contradictory studies at all; but complimentary—just as Gestalt Psychology can be viewed being complimentary to Behaviorism.

I was never completely satisfied with the two-curve model as a proper visual representation of the phylogeny and ontogeny of cognitive development. I next present a new model of this process that supercedes the one in Fig. 5.1, and adds the new component of emergent levels.

I began this new model by taking a clue from the Ionians who were concerned with nature as whole. I used an empty circle to represent the limits of our physical and mental perception of nature. Next, I bisected the circle from left to right with a straight line representing time, in the sense of existence across time. Next, I realized that I needed another symbol that would reflect the variations in time as found in the seasons; or cyclic change over time as in development or evolution. To create this I bisected the circle again with an undulatory wave, as in Fig. 5.2, which is representive of a developing process.

In Figure 5.2 there are two distinct areas in the circle. One above the wave that represents the sequential process and one below that represents the simul-

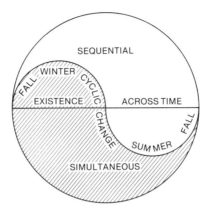

FIGURE 5.2.   A two-dimensional model of the continuity of change and emergent levels of nature. The circle represents the mental and physical limits of human perception. The straight bisecting line represents sequential perception of existence across time. The bisecting wave represents cyclic change over time in nature. The top white area represents the sequential processes in nature and the lower shaded area represents the simultaneous processes in nature. These two processes interact to produce the emergent levels in nature such as Fall, Winter, Spring and Summer; while at the same time producing the continuity of cyclic change.

taneous process. The two areas increase or decrease relative to any point on the straight existence line through the center. These two areas represent the contradictory processes (necessary in T. C. Schneirla's theory) whose interaction would result in the emergence of new levels.

An historical/philosophical exposition at this time might help to clarify the model I propose. Historically, after the Ionians there is a change in focus in our attempts to understand nature. The Ionians were concerned with discovering the essence of nature, in other words, nature as a whole. Later philosophers such as Plato, focused on humans in their attempts to explain nature. What is apparently inherent in nature and particularly disconcerting to many Western philosophers is the co-existence of opposites or contradictory qualities in nature. Most Western philosophers found these apparent paradoxes to be most annoying and in order to find Truth in nature they sought to find the dichotomies; the blacks and whites, the goods and bads, and so on. So rather than attending to the areas of interaction where the contradictory qualities met and created new qualities, it was much more satisfying—and simple minded—to perform the mechanical ritual of dichotomization. This is exactly what Descartes did when faced with the paradox of rationality and emotionality co-occurring and interacting in nature: the rational soul and the brute soul. He assigned the rational soul to man while relegating the brute soul to his conception of nonrational creatures such as women and animals.

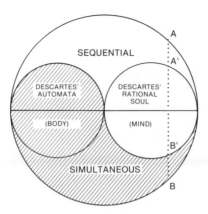

FIGURE 5.3. A representation of Fig. 5.2 that has now been di-chotomized into two smaller circles by Descartes in an attempt to represent his notions of the Brute Soul and the Rational Soul. Line A/B represents the influence of the sequential/simultaneous processes in-teraction at the intersected point on the bisecting straight line. A'/B' represents the incomplete and incorrect view of this interaction.

(This dichotomization is represented in Fig. 5.3). Descartes' approach empha-sizes the importance and study of the rational aspects of man's nature while lumping women and animals together as nonrational brutes. Descartes' *de novo* approach held that the brute soul was not only inferior with its subservience to emotionality, but it was completely without thought and was nothing more than an unfeeling machine. The implications of this Cartesian philosophy are epito-mized by the 17th Century notion that a dog who yelps when it is kicked suffers no more than a bell that rings when it is struck.

Not only does this Cartesian approach limit and de-emphasize the study of simultaneous process, but because it ignores the interaction between the two processes it also limits and distorts the understanding of the sequential process. For example, if a behavior at the rational soul level is examined (represented by the broken line between A and B in Fig. 5.3) then only the part of the behavior on line A/B that will be examined will be between A' and B'. The result will be that the sequentiality of A to A', the simultaneity of B' to B and the *interaction* will be ignored. Therefore not only does this result in an incomplete understanding of the sequentiality (A to B') but the influence of the simultaneity (B' to B) is completely ignored. I propose that this understanding of the behavior would be incomplete and incorrect because it is impossible for anything totally sequential or totally simultaneous to exist in our known universe. Therefore I would hold that the interaction of contradictions is necessary for existence, or in other words, that it is the interaction of contradictions that manifest themselves as empirical events.

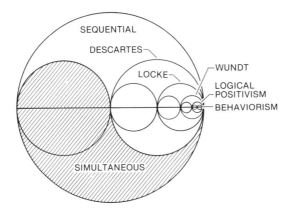

FIGURE 5.4. A representation of the continual dichotomization and myopic focusing of certain scientific approaches ranging historically from Descartes to Behaviorism. This illustrates that these approaches are not incorrect; but just very incomplete in that they only examine smaller and smaller areas of the sequential process while remaining ignorant of the influences of the simultaneous process and the interaction of the two processes.

The behavioral sciences of the United States extended the position held by Descartes and continued to dichotomize and exclude behaviors from study that were considered to be non-empirical or impalpable. Psychology has traditionally separated the two processes and Behaviorism has almost exclusively studied the sequential aspects of behavior while for the most part ignoring the simultaneous process. The Gestalt perceptual psychologists in Europe did study the simultaneous process, but it was never fully accepted in the United States.

After Descartes, this process of dichotomization and exclusion can be seen to continue in the empirical philosophy of Locke and through the Logical Positivists and finally culminating in naive behaviorism of John Watson and the present day Behaviorists. As in Fig. 5.4, I am not proposing that Behaviorism is wrong, just that it is an extremely myopic view of nature. Others have noted this reductionistic development of the behavioral sciences. For example, Donald Griffin (1976) states:

There remains that tendency for what was originally an agnostic position to drift implicitly into a sort of de facto denial that mental states or consciousness exist outside our own species. It is easy for scientists to slip into the passive assumption that phenomena with which their customary methods cannot deal effectively are unimportant or even nonexistent . . . Here I should also like to follow the example of Holloway (1974) . . . : ''The first step is to measure whatever can be easily measured. This is okay as far as it goes. The second step is to disregard that which can't be measured or give it an arbitrary quantative value. This is artificial and misleading. The third step is to presume that what can't be measured easily isn't very important. This is blindness. The fourth step is to say what can't be easily measured doesn't exist. This is suicide.'' (p. 56)

Indeed, some scientists and disciplines did present artificial expositions of behavior, whereas others were blind and some were even suicidal. Yet not all scientists fell victim to this passing phase and instead sought to reinstate some of the parts and processes of nature that others had chosen to ignore or banish.

One example of a scientist who moved away from the myopic focus on one small portion of the sequential process and expanded his scientific perception to include a greater portion of the perceptual circle of nature was Jean Piaget. Rather than taking a baloney slice out of the process of human development, Piaget choose the course of describing the process of cognitive sequential development from birth up to adulthood; but not through adulthood. He focused on the increasing influence of sequential processing on the cognitive development of the human child. He described this process in terms of developmental phases or stages. By interpreting Piaget into the present theory we see that contradiction plays a role in the emergence of new phases of the child's development and that this contradiction is resolved by accommodation after new information, that is incompatible with old schematas, is assimilated. The emergence of a new level (Piagetian phase) would result from the equilibration of the new information. However, as in Fig. 5.5, Piaget does not address the complete developmental process. First, his phases stop around 14 years of age and, secondly he focuses on the sequential aspects of an individuals development. As a result, one can only grasp the changes in the role of the simultaneous process by inferentially noting what simultaneous qualities are being subsumed by the sequential process.

The emergent levels fit nicely into a Piagetian model but if there are levels of Piagetian phases then those levels should also be represented in the neurological development of the brain. In an earlier article (Fouts, 1983) I pointed out how the gray matter of the brain would be the neurological representation of sequential processing and the white matter would be the neurological representation of the simultaneous process. I stated in that article:

. . . the distribution of gray matter (involved in sequential cognitive processing) in relation to the distribution of white matter (involved in simultaneous cognitive processing) in the two cerebral hemispheres has shown that the left hemisphere in right-handed adult human males has more gray matter than white matter (Gur, Packer, Hungerbuhler, Reivich, Obrist, Amarnek, & Sackeim, 1980). The greatest amount of gray matter in the left hemisphere, as well as the greatest interhemispheric difference in the relative amount of gray matter, was found in the region that includes the basal ganglia, which is associated with fine sensory motor control. (pp. 67–78)

It is the fine motor movements of speech that would most influence the development of the gray matter and in this manner play a very important role in

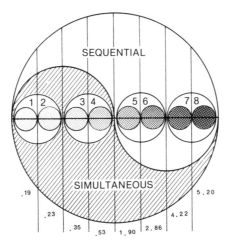

FIGURE 5.5. A representation of the emergence of levels resulting from the changing interaction of the sequential and simultaneous processes. The numbers outside the underside of the large circle are approximate proportions of the light area to the shaded area in each vertical column. The small eight circles across the center represent emergent levels that emerge as a result of the contradiction produced in the sequential/simultaneous interaction. The small circles 1 and 2 together represent the first phase of Piagetian development and circles 3 through 6 represent the final four phases of Piagetian development all of which emphasizes the sequential aspects of human development. All eight of the circles can also be used to represent the eight stages of affective development as proposed by Erik Erikson.

laterialization of the brain. The fine motor movements of gestures would have a similar effect on the development of gray matter, but not on the laterialization process if both hands were used equally. The reason for this difference is because we have only one tongue and two cerebral hemispheres, therefore the control of the fine motor movements of the tongue, as used in speech, would be under the control of the hemisphere that had a predisposition to sequential processing (left or right) and result in the laterialization to that hemisphere.

The aforementioned position would explain lateralization of the brain and the basis for sequential processing in humans, but it does not account for the emergence of levels. As Fodor (1975) pointed out in regard to Piaget's model of phases of intellectual development, it is difficult to understand why a child would move into the next phase. This certainly is a problem if a model of continuous development is used. However, the levels model would handle it nicely if it had neurological evidence that development of the brain occurs in spurts rather than in a gradual continuous process. Such evidence is supplied by Epstein (1974, 1978). Epstein has found that brain growth is periodic and that both the growth periods and the plateau periods are chronologically predictable for 85 to 95% of children (Toepfer, 1980). The growth spurts occur between the ages of 3- to 10-

months-of-age, 2- to 4-years-of-age, 6- to 8-years-of-age, 10- to 12- or 13-years-of-age, and 14- to 16- or 17-years-of-age (Epstein, 1978). Epstein points out that the growth spurts are not due to the development of new cells, but due to the increase in brain weight (This is the same measure used by Gur et al., 1980.) Epstein (1978) states that after the age of two the brain increases in weight by 35% without the development of new cells and that the increase is in the form of:

> . . . (a) more extended and branched axons and dendrites of brain cells, (b) the laying down of the fatty insulation (myelin sheath) of axons, and (c) increased input of energy and materials through an increase in arterial blood supply to the brain. (p. 343)

Epstein then compares these growth spurts to Piaget's phases:

> . . . those experimentally established intervals correlate in time with the classical stages of intellectual development as described by Piaget, except that the fourteen to sixteen brain growth stage has no Piagetian counterpart. We therefore predict a hitherto unknown stage of intellectual development. Very recent work by Arlin [Arlin, 1975] yields the beginning evidence for such a stage, which appears at about the predicted age. (p. 344)

As can be seen in Fig. 5.5, both Piaget's phase model of intellectual development and Epstein's brain growth spurts fit very nicely into a model of levels representing the interaction of sequential and simultaneous processes that result in emergent levels of development. I have represented in Fig. 5.5 the various levels with the eight circles across the middle of the circle. Beneath each of the eight circles and the rim of the largest circle I have placed a number that represents the proportion of sequential area to simultaneous area and represented this proportion visually with dots in each of the eight circles. Circles 1 and 2 would represent Piaget's Sensorimotor phase of 0 to 24 months of age. (Note that the proportionate difference between circles 1 and 2 is very slight and that the proportions increase significantly between all the other circles except between 7 and 8.) The next four circles would represent the rest of Piaget's phases as follows: circle 3 represents the Preconceptual Phase, circle 4 the Intuitive Thought Phase, circle 5 the Concrete Operational Phase and circle 6 the Formal Operational Phase. (Note: The Piagetian phases are from H. W. Maier, 1978, p. 69.) My model would indicate that not only is Epstein probably correct that there is a hitherto unknown stage of Piagetian intellectual development (circle 7), but there is probably one more (circle 8).

Another theorist who recognizes the process of development and the phase (levels) aspect of development is Erik Erikson. However, where Piaget focuses on the sequential aspects of development, Erikson focuses on the simultaneous aspects. In other words Piaget emphasizes the cognitive whereas Erikson emphasizes the affective. Another difference is that Erikson carries out the developmental process throughout an individual's lifetime represented by eight stages of development (Maier, 1978). These two theorists focus on different aspects and do not exclude or deny the others' process. The difference is mainly one of emphasis and not exclusion. Taken together they represent an integrated picture of human development.

I have yet to demonstrate how this model can be used to remove the dichotomy between continuous and discontinuous behavior. Up to now I have shown how it can be used as a model for emergent levels supporting a discontinuous view of nature. However, I have been using a geometric model to present this theory and that when using a geometric model I can theoretically continue to divide each circle with two more circles an infinite number of times. If I did this, the resulting emergent levels would soon, in our perception, turn into a continuous line that would be impossible to discriminate from the original existence line in Fig. 5.2. In this manner the model would represent both a continuous and discontinuous view of nature at the same time.

Another aspect of the model presented in Fig. 5.2 not previously mentioned is the notion of cyclic change. If the top of any circle in Fig. 5.5 is connected to the bottom of any adjoining circle of the same size, then a wave will result. And certainly the notion of rhythms in behavior are well established ranging from circadium rhythms and monthly cycles to our own life cycle. If there is one thing we can say about organisms it is that they are rhythmic.

A theorist of human development who incorporates both the cyclic aspect of human growth and at the same time looks at levels or phases of development in much smaller units than either Piaget or Erikson is Arnold Gesell. For example, Ilg and Ames (1955), with regard to Gesell's stages, state:

> As we describe the succeeding age levels, you will note that the same general kinds of things seem to be happening over and over again. Careful analysis of behavior trends in the first ten years of life—supplemented by later studies of the years from ten to sixteen—make it apparent that a rather distinctive sequence of behavior stages seems to occur repeatedly as the child matures. (p. 10)

They point out that the stages of the child's development alternate between equilibrium and disequilibrium. They characterize this cycle as going from (1) Smooth, consolidated to (2) Breaking up to (3) Rounded balance to (4) Inwardized to (5) Vigorous, expansive to (6) Inwardized-outwardized, troubled, "neurotic" and finally to (7) Smooth, consolidated again. One can almost see the rhythm of the seasons Fall, Winter, Spring and Summer in this cycle. They state that this cycle repeats itself three times. The first time is between 2 and 5 years-of-age, the second is between 5 and 10 years-of-age, and the last one is between 10 and 16. In addition to the cycles, Gesell breaks the child's development up into 25 different stages representing 4, 16, 28, 40, and 52 weeks; 15, 18 and 24 months; and 2½, 3, 3½, 4, 4½, 5, 6, 7, 8, 9, 10, 11, 12, 13, 14, 15 and 16

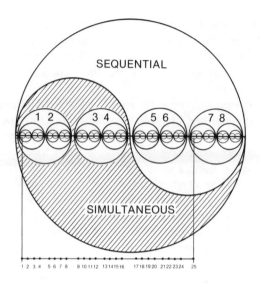

FIGURE 5.6. A representation demonstrating that it is possible to have levels within levels until the levels eventually become undifferentiated from a continuous line and in this manner transcends the dilemma of continuity vs discontinuity by the use of waves and levels. The first 25 of the smallest circles through the center are used to represent the 25 stages in Gesell's model of human development.

years. These stages are represented as levels of development in Fig. 5.6. If the reader holds the page farther and farther away they will note how Gesell's stages begin to appear as a continuous line.

Using Gesell's theory of human development we see how the model presented here incorporates both discontinuity in terms of developmental levels and continuity by examining levels within levels or by the notion of continuous cyclic change. The study of behavior can once again look to physics as a model. For example, just as physics has found that light has the characteristics of a wave and a particle, so too does behavior have both the characteristics of continuous cyclic change and emergent discontinuous levels. This model would serve to resolve the dilemmas that have torn psychology asunder in the past. For example, the nature/nurture controversy can be resolved by viewing the simultaneous process as the representative of nature or non-plasticity and the sequential process as the representative of nurture or placticity. In this manner organisms can be arranged along the time line and those organisms whose behavior has the greatest amount of prewired behavior would be on the left and those with the most plasticity would be placed nearest to the right end. As with the developmental phases, each organism could be viewed as the result of an interaction between the contradictory qualities of simultaneity and sequentiality.

As pointed out earlier, this is not only a model of ontogeny but phylogeny as well. Just as the various phases of Piagetian cognitive development are emergent with unique characteristics for each particular phase or level, so too can individual species be viewed as emergent levels of phylogenetic development within the continuity of the evolutionary process. Species as levels would result from the contradiction that would occur within a species when new genetic information is assimilated by that species. The emergence of a new species' level would result from a process similar to Piaget's concept of equilibration. Maier (1978) defines this concept as follows: ". . . equilibration constitutes feedback and forecasting, . . . a series of active adaptations which are retroactive and also anticipatory of the outcome of more complex (more adaptive) ways of comprehending and managing environmental factors" (p. 23). In this manner the phylogenetic scale can be viewed as a continuity of emergent levels of evolution.

This model of emergent levels of phylogenetic development differs from the traditional model of phylogenetic development that describes the evolutionary process as a gradual monotonically increasing process with man at the top. The notion of gradualism is being discounted as the sole model for phylogenetic development by evidence from the fossil record that indicates that evolution can occur in spurts of rapid change followed by long periods of stability (Gould, 1977).

The contradictory processes, whose interaction results in a new emergent level, should not be seen as opposing forces. Instead, they should be seen as complimentary polarities that exist within the comprehensive whole of nature and it is their natural interaction that results in the emergence of new and unique levels of ontogenetic as well as phylogenetic development. Thus, when these two processes are reconciled, a new creation is brought about. In the empirical world this principle of contradiction allows for the differentiation of things by levels, phases, or qualities. Once the polarity is recognized in the comprehensive whole of nature then the problem of undifferentiated chaos is replaced by order and then continuity as well as discontinuity finds a place in the understanding of nature. Likewise, the simple-minded dualism of Descartes and others is replaced with a continuity of unique levels.

Finally, it can be seen that biological alchemy is possible because it is possible to create a new unique existence from an old one. Not in terms of changing lead into gold, but in terms of creating something truly new. For example, the chimpanzee sign language research can be viewed as a kind of biological alchemy. The chimpanzees who have acquired sign language are different in kind from those that have not. Just as environmental influences have an effect on the physiological and cognitive nature of an individual in creating a type of processing that is absent in those that have not received this experience, so too has the sign language had an effect on the cognitive development of these chimpanzees. They are chimpanzees, but a unique kind of chimpanzee—signing chimpanzees. They are different from feral chimpanzees and yet they are not humans. They are unique.

# REFERENCES

Arlin, P. K. (1975). Cognitive development in adulthood: A fifth stage? *Developmental Psychology, 11*, 602–606.

Bollinger, D. (1975). *Aspects of language.* New York: Harcourt Brace.

Brown, R. (1968). The development of Wh- questions in child speech. *Journal of Verbal Learning and Verbal Behavior, 7*, 279–290.

Epstein, H. T. (1974). Phrenoblysis: Special brain and mind growth periods: II. Human mental development. *Developmental Psychobiology, 7*, 217–224.

Epstein, H. T. (1978). Growth spurts during brain development: Implications for educational policy and practice. In J. S. Chall & A. F. Mirsky (Eds.), *Education and the brain: The seventy-seventh yearbook of the National Society for the Study of Education, part II* (pp. 343–370). Chicago: University of Chicago Press.

Essock, S. M., Gill, T. V., & Rumbaugh, D. M. (1977). Language relevant object- and color-naming tasks. In D. M. Rumbaugh (Ed.), *Language learning by a chimpanzee* (pp. 193–206). Orlando, FL: Academic Press.

Fodor, J. A. (1975). *The language of thought.* New York: Thomas Crowell.

Fouts, D. H. (1984). *Remote video taping of a juvenile chimpanzee's sign language interactions within his social group.* Unpublished master's thesis, Central Washington University, Ellensburg, WA.

Fouts, R. S. (1983). Chimpanzee language and elephant tails: A theoretical synthesis. In H. Wilder & J. de Luce (Eds.), *Language in primates* (pp. 63–75). New York: Springer.

Fouts, R. S., Fouts, D. H. & Schoenfeld, D. (1984). Sign language conversational interactions between chimpanzees. *Sign Language Studies, 34*, 1–12.

Fouts, R. S., Hirsch, A., & Fouts, D. H. (1982). Cultural transmission of a human language in a chimpanzee mother/infant relationship. In H. E. Fitzgerald, J. A. Mullins, & P. Page (Eds.), *Psychobiological perspectives: Child nurturance series Vol. III* (pp. 159–193). New York: Plenum Press.

Fouts, R. S., Shapiro, G., & O'Neil, C. (1978). Studies of linguistic behavior in apes and children. In P. Siple (Ed.), *Understanding language through sign language research* (pp. 163–185). Orlando, FL: Academic Press.

Gardner, B. T. (1981). [Review of *Nim.*] *Contemporary Psychology, 26*, 425–428.

Gardner, R. A., & Gardner, B. T. (1969). Teaching sign language to a chimpanzee. *Science, 165*, 664–672.

Gardner, B. T., & Gardner, R. A. (1971). Two-way communication with an infant chimpanzee. In A. Schrier & F. Stollnitz (Eds.), *Behavior of non-human primates: Vol. 4* (pp. 117–184). Orlando, FL: Academic Press.

Gardner, B. T., & Gardner, R. A. (1974). Comparing the early utterances of child and chimpanzee. In A. Pick (Ed.), *Minnesota symposium on child psychology* (Vol. 8, pp. 3–23). Minneapolis: University of Minnesota Press.

Gardner, R. A., & Gardner, B. T. (1975). Evidence for sentence constituents in early utterances of child and chimpanzee. *Journal of Experimental Psychology, General, 104*, 244–267.

Gardner, R. A., & Gardner, B. T. (1978). Comparative psychology and language acquisition. *Annals of the New York Academy of Sciences, 309*, 37–767.

Gardner, R. A., & Gardner, B. T. (1983). *Early sign of reference in children and chimpanzees.* Unpublished manuscript, University of Nevada, Reno.

Gardner, R. A., & Gardner, B. T. (1984). A vocabulary test for chimpanzees (*Pan troglodytes*). *Journal of Comparative Psychology, 98*, 381–404.

Gill, T. V., & Rumbaugh, D. M. (1974). Mastery of naming skills by a chimpanzee. *Journal of Human Evolution, 3*, 483–492.

Gould, S. J. (1977). Evolutions' erratic pace. *Natural History, 86,* 12–16.

Griffin, D. (1976). *The question of animal awareness.* New York: The Rockefeller University Press.

Gur, R. C., Packer, I. K., Hungerbuhler, J. P., Reivich, M., Obrist, W. D., Amarnek, W. S., & Sackeim, H. A. (1980). Differences in the distribution of gray and white matter in human cerebral hemispheres. *Science, 207,* 1226–1228.

Hoffmeister, R., Moores, D., & Ellenberger, R. (1975). Some procedural guidelines for the study of the acquisition of sign language. *Sign Language Studies, 7,* 121–137.

Holloway, R. L. (1974). [Review of H. J. Jerison, *Evolution of the brain and intelligence.*] *Science, 184,* 677–679.

Ilg, F. L., & Ames, L. B. (1955). *Child behavior.* New York: Harper & Row Publishers.

Kellogg, W. (1968). Communication and language in the home-raised chimpanzee. *Science, 162,* 423–427.

Klima, E., & Bellugi, U. (1979). *The signs of language.* Cambridge, MA: Harvard University Press.

Lepper, M. R., Greene, D., & Nisbett, R. E. (1973). Undermining children's intrinsic interest with extrinsic reward: A case of the ''overjustification'' hypothesis. *Journal of Personality and Social Psychology, 28,* 129–137.

Levine, F., & Fasnacht, G. (1974). Token rewards may lead to token learning. *American Psychologist, 29,* 816–820.

Maier, H. W. (1978). *Three theories of child development.* (3rd ed.). New York: Harper & Row.

Nelson, K. (1980, March). *First words of chimp and child.* Paper presented at the meeting of the Southeastern Psychological Association.

Premack, D. (1971). On the assessment of language competence in the chimpanzee. In A. Schrier & F. Stollnitz (Eds.), *Behavior of non-human primates: Vol. 4* (pp. 183–228). Orlando, FL: Academic Press.

Rumbaugh, D. M. (Ed.). (1977). *Language learning by a chimpanzee: The Lana project.* Orlando, FL: Academic Press.

Savage-Rumbaugh, E. S., Pate, J. L., Lawson, J., Smith, S. T., & Rosenbaum, S. (1983). Can a chimpanzee make a statement? *Journal of Experimental Psychology: General, 112,* 457–492.

Savage-Rumbaugh, E. S., & Rumbaugh, D. M. (1978). Symbolization, language, and chimpanzees: A theoretical re-evaluation based on initial language acquisition processes in four young *Pan troglodytes. Brain and Language, 6,* 265–300.

Savage-Rumbaugh, E., Rumbaugh, D., & Boysen, S. (1980). Do apes use language? *American Scientist, 68,* 49–61.

Schneirla, T. C. (1972). Part III on the concept of integrative levels in the study of behavior. In L. R. Aronson, E. Tobach, J. S. Rosenblatt, & D. S. Lehrman (Eds.), *Selected writings of T. C. Schneirla* (pp. 197–253). San Francisco: W. H. Freeman.

Terrace, H. (1979). *Nim.* New York: Alfred Knopf.

Terrace, H., Petitto, L., Sanders, R., & Bever, T. (1979). Can an ape create a sentence? *Science, 206,* 891–902.

Terrace, H. S., Petitto, L., Sanders, R. J., & Bever, T. G. (1980). On the grammatical capacity of apes. In K. E. Nelson (Ed.), *Children's language* (Vol. 2, pp. 371–495). New York: Gardner Press.

Thorpe, W. (1972). The comparison of vocal communication in animals and man. In R. A. Hinde (Ed.), *Non-verbal communication* (pp. 27–47). Cambridge: Cambridge University Press.

Toepfer, Jr., C. F. (1980). Brain growth periodization data: Some suggestions for re-thinking middle grade education. *The High School Journal,* March, 222–227.

Van Cantfort, T. E., & Rimpau, J.B. (1982). Sign language studies with children and chimpanzees. *Sign Language Studies, 34,* 15–72.

Van Lawick-Goodall, J. (1968). A preliminary report on expressive movements and communication in the Gombe Stream chimpanzees. In P. C. Jay (Ed.), *Primates: Studies in adaptation and variability* (pp. 313–374). New York: Holt, Rinehart & Winston.

# 6 Human Specificity in Language: Sociogenetic Processes in Verbal Communication

Vera John-Steiner
Carolyn P. Panofsky
*University of New Mexico*

> *Language is an intensely immediate exchange between living people in actual historical and social circumstances . . .*
>
> —Holquist, 1983

The study of language provides a focal point for the examination of the issue of human specificity and for the discussions of continuity and discontinuity in evolution. It is appropriate that scholars committed to a levels-of-integration approach examine the implications of current studies of language mastery. While these studies have become a major and fruitful domain of inquiry in the social and biological sciences, efforts to place them into a consistently historical and developmental context are still limited. Novikoff, in 1945, warned of the danger of reducing social phenomena to the biological level, of overemphasizing "similarity of organizational development in evolution to the exclusion of any consideration of the uniqueness of each level" (Novikoff, 1945, p. 213). Nevertheless, such an orientation is still widespread among those who use animal communication as a model for the examination of human language. Novikoff also warned of the dangers of "organicism," an approach that is strongly manifested by those students of language who rely on a nativist, Cartesian framework.

The specificity of language is viewed by these nativist scholars as the result of "wired-in" neurological structure that provides young learners with linguistic universals, with a biological endowment that consists of a universal theory of grammar. Children are seen by Chomsky (1965) and his co-workers as faced with the task of generating specific hypotheses about a particular language that characterizes their own speech community. One set of hypotheses deals with word order: in some languages, such as English and French, the order consists of the subject first, followed by the verb, and then the object (SVO word order); in contrast, in Tagalog (a language spoken in the Philippines) the word order is verb first, followed by object, and lastly by the subject (VOS word order). In attempting to generate correctly produced strings of words, children are not assisted— according to nativist theory—by other aspects of their development. They see syntactical mastery as largely independent of cognitive and social growth.

This concept of a distinctly human, "wired-in" grammar is opposed by behaviorist students of language and by many researchers who work in the field of animal communication. Their focus is on the contexts of learning and on the schedules of reinforcement that they see as critical to any mastery of behavior. In their analyses they do not differentiate between animal and human communication. A major criticism of this reductionist stance is provided by scholars committed to a levels-of-integration approach. One of the contributors to this volume, Charles Tolman, presents an evolutionary account of human specificity: "Human language which uses culturally and historically produced meaning to guide and regulate activity. . . . is qualitatively distinct from animal communication which does not operate on the basis of such systematically produced meanings" (Tolman, this volume).

The central role of culture and history in the construction and uses of language characterizes our own approach as well (for example, John-Steiner & Tatter, 1983), in which we attempt to go beyond nativist and behaviorist accounts. One way to characterize new approaches in the field is to adopt Bruce Bain's (1983) term *sociogenesis,* which he has identified in the following way:

> Sociogenetic ideas are few in number: that of Bertalanffy, that the human is the only member of the animal kingdom that makes and is made by the social signs that constitute its existence; that of Humboldt, that language is not *ergon* but *energia,* and thus should be studied genetically and not as a constant product; that of Marx and Engels, that language is thought made real and is subject to the dynamics of social history; that of Mead, Dewey, Peirce and Bruner, that the earliest and most fundamental function of speech is pragmatic—to direct and control and alter human activities—and thus is inseparable from social relations; that of Sapir, that consciousness is largely verbal in nature. (p. xxii)

Bain also reminds the reader of his collection of works detailing the sociogenetic approach "that language is an evolutionary confluence of biological, psychological, and socio-historical determinants" (1983, p. 5).

Of particular importance to the study of language acquisition is the work of Jerome Bruner. Bain includes Bruner among those who have fashioned the sociogenetic approach. In summarizing his work of the last decade with infants and preschool children, Bruner documents the role of caretaker-learner interactions in providing the necessary "scaffolding" for the linguistic realization of the toddler's communicative intentions. Bruner (1983) proposes that there is:

> a Language Acquisition Support System that frames the interaction of human beings in such a way as to aid the aspirant speaker in mastering the uses of

language. It is this system that provides the functional priming that makes language acquisition not only possible, but makes it proceed in the order and pace in which it ordinarily occurs. (p. 120)

Although children's early years are characterized by dependence on their caretakers, childhood development is not simply shaped by needs and by the reinforcement of behaviors. Children are active participants in patterned social interactions. These activities, and the utterances built upon them, are coordinated with and extended by those who care for the young speaker. The role of "socially and culturally defined events" is stressed by Katherine Nelson (1983). She argues that "scripts" and communicative procedures are central to the acquisition of language. Scripts are "familiar events involving interaction and communication," including such routines in the lives of small children in this country as meal-eating, supermarket-shopping, and saying good-bye to one's mother at the door of the nursery school. Of particular importance to language mastery are such scripted activities as picture book reading with a caretaker; these are settings in which early teaching of reference and labeling take place (Ninio & Bruner, 1978).

The influence of L. S. Vygotsky is apparent in the writings of these language researchers. He was the first to articulate what Bain describes as the leitmotif of sociogenetic thought, "a recognition that behind all mental processes stand real relations among people" (Vygotsky, 1962). In *Thought and Language*, Vygotsky compared the similarities and differences between the communicative means of anthropoids and humans. He also studied the development of speech from early vocalizations to the formation of inner speech and verbal thinking, stressing that "*the nature of the development itself changes*, from biological to socio-historical" (Vygotsky, 1962). He argued that in higher mammals, sounds as communicative means are qualitatively different from the "*functional use of signs* . . . corresponding to that of speech in humans" (1962, p. 38). He saw in the human use of language a necessary unification of speech and action. In his analysis of "Tool and Symbol in Child Development," Vygotsky (1978) wrote,

The specifically human capacity for language enables children to provide for auxiliary tools in the solution of difficult tasks, to overcome impulsive action, to plan a solution to a problem prior to its execution, and to master their own behavior. Signs and words serve children first and foremost as a means of social contact with other people. The cognitive and communicative functions of language then become the basis of a new and superior form of activity in children, distinguishing them from animals. (pp. 28–29)

This emphasis on specifically human and socially patterned ways of acquiring language is now shared by many language researchers in diverse settings. But in spite of the growing importance of a sociogenetic position in this field, the old controversies among nativist, behaviorist and Piagetian scholars continue. A central issue in these debates is the role of language input, especially the way in which adults simplify and clarify their language when they address very young children. Are such modifications in using language with children important? Or is all input language, as the nativists claim, marred by disfluencies and thus lacking qualities of an effective model for the novice? These concerns are central to the sociogenetic theory of language.

## THE ROLE OF INPUT IN LANGUAGE ACQUISITION

One of the central biological universals that shape the acquisition of language is the prolonged dependency of young children on their caretakers. The earliest formats of communicative exchange are those of eye-to-eye contact, smiling, and vocalizing exchanges, which provide the frequently overworked caretakers with signs of mutual recognition and pleasure. Adults usually treat infants as persons with intentions, and they bring to their interactions with young children both their general knowledge of what is meaningful in discourse and their specific familiarity with the young children in their care.

From the first hours after birth, an intersubjective relationship between infant and caretaker begins to develop (Trevarthen, 1980) that evolves into the finely-tuned interactions discovered by researchers in early language acquisition. Early language input is finely-tuned to maximize its communicative success. It includes linguistic features such as simplified syntax, higher pitch, longer duration of words, use of distinctive stress patterns, re-duplication of phonological units, shorter sentences, and simpler vocabulary (e.g., Ferguson, 1977; Cross, 1977; Garnica, 1977; Newport, Gleitman & Gleitman, 1977). Even 4-year-olds have been found to adjust their speech to 2-year-old children (Gelman & Schatz, 1977). In addition, recent research has also begun to document the importance of non-linguistic features such as synchronized gesture and gaze in assisting the communicativeness of the linguistic input (Zukow, Reilly & Greenfield, 1982).

When children's dependency needs are met and they are able to engage in finely-tuned interactions with adults who know them well, they proceed from the conversation of gestures to the joint activity of formatted, communicative games such as the peekaboo routines so well described by Bruner (1983). Such studies document what Bruner has dubbed the "hand-over principle," that over time, through the process of fine-tuning, the caretaker hands over increasing responsibility for the activity to the child, so that the roles of initiator and recipient become reversible. Thus, speakers not only adjust their speech to maximize communication with young children at any given time, but also their adjustments are progressively altered to transfer increasingly more active participation to the learner.

The specific role of language input is still debated by many language researchers, however. Objections to an interactionist or sociogenetic position derive from the failure of some early studies to account for the interrelationships of linguistic as well as non-linguistic stimuli, and of cognitive and socially facilitated development. Thus, some researchers continue to place the major stress on biological factors in their explanations of children's language development. Gleitman (1981) suggests, for example, that language learning is not dependent on external factors or adult-child interactions. Instead, she proposes that "much of the burden of explanation has to be borne by innate capacities and dispositions in the learners, rules and representations specifically relevant to language." Her evidence is that certain syntactic forms appear at similar ages across varied environments. Such a position is challenged by some of the cross-cultural comparisons documented by Slobin and his co-workers (1980). In addition, such a position is challenged by the variability revealed by some recent ethnographic investigations and studies of pre-school environments, to be discussed below. The issue of sociogenetic versus biogenetic determinants requires the separation of many interrelated aspects of growth. Such an effort is difficult to achieve under ordinary circumstances.

An extraordinary circumstance that provides evidence for this debate comes from a recent Japanese study of severely neglected children. Fujinaga (1983) and his staff worked with two children who suffered from extreme parental neglect. Although they were around six years of age at the time of their rescue, they were the height and weight of toddlers. During their early years their parents kept them in a small enclosed space without any adult supervision. Their survival was minimally attended to by older siblings. The researchers found that the children not only suffered from nutritional deprivation, but they were deprived of linguistic, emotional and cognitive interaction and stimulation. These 6-year-old children lacked any linguistic facility and even lacked the more highly biologically programmed process of walking.

Once the rescued children were placed into an adequate caretaking environment, they started to walk only weeks after their placement. Their emotional development was slower, and they showed "weak self-assertion" years after their rescue. The area in which growth occurred at the slowest was their language and cognitive development. Fujinaga emphasizes the role of verbal interaction with "caring, sharing adults" as crucial for the mastery of language, opportunities that these children lacked in their original home environment. Once they were able to form some attachments to their nurses, the communicative aspects of their verbal development progressed. However, it was language used for cognitive purposes that was evidently most vulnerable to the absence of sustained, finely-tuned verbal interaction throughout the developmental span. The importance of language input to the development of the cognitive uses of language is a critical issue to which we will return later.

The story of these unfortunate Japanese children shows that speaking is not accomplished simply by the child's testing of hypotheses about the syntactic rules of his or her speech community. However, one need not turn to examples of such deprivation to find variation in language input and corresponding differences in acquisition. The varied ways in which parents use language with their children is documented in a recent major ethnographic study, Shirley Brice Heath's *Ways With Words* (1983). Heath depicts language socialization in three communities in the Carolinas: a black rural community, a white rural community, and a nearby town were the settings for her work. Heath writes, "There were profound differences across the three communities in the limits and features of these situations in which communication by and to children occurs, and the patterns of choice children can exercise in their uses of oral and written language" (pp. 349–350).

The Bible served as a major source of language stimulation in the two rural communities Heath studied, but parents in these villages did not engage in lengthy periods of reading or writing. The Black children of "Tracton" were frequently held by their elders as they were exposed to prayers and songs based on the Bible: "Tracton children have learned through their long hours in the laps of adults and on the hard church benches, that in the free flow of time there are multiple types of talk and song about the written word" (1983, p. 349). Thus, these young people have an involvement with language but it is not one that prepares them for success in the schools.

Language researchers who question the importance of language input and finely-tuned interaction for acquisition frequently refer to Heath's study. A closer examination of her findings is necessary in order to assess the role of language input, particularly the description of language learning in the Black community of Tracton. Heath provides a detailed account of socialization in this community. During the first year of life, babies "are always held in position so that they can see the face of the caregiver or the person the caregiver is talking to" (1983, p. 350). These are children who are bathed in language; they are seldom separated from the family and community life around them. Their movements are carefully monitored, and many warnings are given to them to insure their safety. These children learn about adults, about their moods and words in the course of the many opportunities they have to observe them closely.

In contrast to the language socialization described by Bruner, however, where adults engage in carefully formatted language games with young speakers, the Tracton children rely more on overheard conversations as the basis of their mastery. Heath describes this process as consisting of repetition: "The ends of adults' utterances in discourse are repeated by young children who play or sit on the floor or sofa nearby. . . . they pick up and repeat chunks (usually the ends) of phrasal and clausal utterances of speakers around them" (1983, p. 75). Then the children start to manipulate the language that they hear, creating monologues and also playing with language forms. Participation in talk with adults is not always easy, but there are more opportunities for boys than for girls to do so. Such opportunity fits the expectation that boys be partners to public teasing and defend themselves by using gestures and utterances—frequently but a single sentence to which they give varying intonations—with which they demonstrate their ability to deal with teasing. Girls receive less attention during their pre-school years, although they too develop facility in a gender-linked speech event, "fussing." In addition, during their early school years girls learn and create many forms of games with songs, such as jump-rope songs, hand-clap songs, and so forth (1983, pp. 95–103).

The young learners of Tracton most fully acquire social and interactional uses of language. They are exposed to a large amount of language input, but it is language as spoken by adults to adults. It lacks the specialized formats and fine-tuning that characterize language interaction between adults and learners in the families of middle-class professionals. Heath's study of language socialization in the Carolinas is important because it provides some insights into patterns that are likely to be practiced in rural communities both within and outside of this country.

The challenge that faces a child raised in a community such as Tracton is to link speech he/she hears to the referential situation, and to accomplish such a matching without much adult assistance. The task is akin to running after a fast moving train. Recurrent situations do provide a scaffold for a child in this situation, as do the many opportunities to observe adults, and the occasional verbal assistance that the child receives from older siblings. Children do acquire language in such a language-rich setting: but without much adult assistance, their processes of acquisition are slower, they are less focussed on the cognitive uses of language, and they are less effectively prepared for school (as it is presently constituted) than is the case with urban, socially-advantaged children. Thus, an important factor in the rate of acquisition, and of the acquisition of various functions and styles of language by children, is the uses of language by their caretakers, particularly the role of language in the work life of adults.

In contrast to Tracton, the influence of adults' work-life language is seen in the cross-generational interactions of the mainstream townspeople. The children of the townspeople are provided with home experiences that prime them for academic achievement. Heath (1983) observes:

> They teach them to label items and events, to describe their features, to read books, and play with educational toys. But beyond these aspects of language socialization, townspeople also immerse their children in an environment of repetitive, redundant, and internally consistent running narratives on items and events. They draw from fantasy books and their own imagination to read, perform, and create stories with their children. They link items in one setting to items in another, naming the points of similarity in labels, attributes, uses and functions. (p. 252)

What are the long-range implications of these differing patterns of language socialization described by Heath, Bruner and others? Heath concludes that children's language socialization varies not only in the amount but also in kinds of talk. For success in school it is the language-linked mastery of symbolic representation and analysis that is most important. Are parents the only source for this kind of growth or are there other caretakers who can also enrich a child's development of the communicative and cognitive uses of language?

Kathleen McCartney's (1984) research in Bermuda provides a perspective on this question. She studied the quality of day-care environments and their impact on the language development of pre-school children. The large majority of the children of Bermuda are placed in day care by the time of their second birthday. The way these children perfect their language skills can offer an important insight in the examination of *extra*-familial influences on development. As McCartney suggests, the usual focus on *intra*-familial influences may have resulted in "genotype-environment confounds." Variations in the learning environments of the children of Bermuda were assessed by trained observers who measured the over-all quality of care in eight day care centers. They also judged the type and amount of verbal stimulation provided for the children in these settings. Of particular interest are McCartney's findings that caregivers' representational utterances—the giving and requesting of information—correlated most highly with the day care children's scores on their language tests. The frequency of the children's own initiation of interactions also correlated positively with measured language achievements, and while verbal interaction was central to their language growth, interaction with peers did not result in similar strong verbal gains.

McCartney's study reveals that a well-planned language environment can indeed contribute to young children's language development, even when parents are at work. Similar findings characterize the work of David Weikart and his colleagues in this country (Weikart, 1974/5; Schweinhart & Weikart, 1980), and the intervention programs reported by Feagan and Farran in the USA and Britain (Feagan & Farran, 1982).

These ethnographic, observational, and interventive studies highlight the importance of language input by adults for the acquisition of the varied forms and functions of language. These findings are of importance both for language acquisition theories and language educational practice. In assessing the role of language input we are reminded by Clark and Hecht (1983) that the "input-becomes-output class of models appears too simple." Rather, researchers studying the role of input language in acquisition must look beyond the typical dependent variable of children's language production. Not only is it important to discover when children begin to produce a particular language form, but it is also essential to account for what children comprehend, and when, since input necessarily has its most immediate effects on comprehension. An additional weakness of the input-becomes-output approach is that it ignores the uneven and frequently hidden processes of acquisition. For instance, while the child is focussing on the relationship between linguistic and non-linguistic features of the environment in order to comprehend, certain features of language input relevant to production may be ignored. The importance of this relationship is stressed by Zukow et al (1983):

if it has previously been difficult to find relations between environmental input and the language acquisition process, this is because the input as considered has been entirely linguistic. [There is] a strong relationship between input and the development of comprehension abilities when sensorimotor input and its relationship to linguistically presented information is also taken into account. (p. 84)

Thus, a sociogenetic model of language acquisition requires a broader view of development than the biogenetic view. It includes the relationship between linguistic and non-linguistic inputs, the social and cognitive aspects of interaction, and a careful examination of language input under varying social and historical conditions.

Rapidly changing, highly industrialized societies require maximally developed language and literacy skills on the part of their citizens. These skills can be transmitted to future generations if the insights gained from acquisition studies are applied to all children. In the future training of day-care-center personnel, the role of adult-child verbal interaction must be stressed further in order to meet the ever increasing demand for highly developed language skills. As McCartney's study has shown, the finely tuned interaction between adults and children is of particular importance in the development of language for thought.

## INPUT LANGUAGE AND THE DEVELOPMENT OF VERBAL THINKING

In the examination of the relationship between input and the development of cognitive functions, research into private speech is of key importance. Private speech refers to speech for the self. The spoken and whispered private speech of children has been investigated as it functions in activity involving planning and problem-solving. In these studies, private speech is seen as an intermediate developmental step between social speech—speech between interlocutors—and inner speech, which is essential for verbal thinking. An underlying notion in this research is that the use of language as a form of mediation between, for example, the presentation of a problem and its solution is not a given human process, but one that develops through the internalization of the external process of dialogue.

Recent studies of private speech and language stimulation are providing some additional insights into the relationship between speech for the self and the growth of verbal thinking. The development of private speech among low-income Appalachian children was examined by Berk and Garvin (1984). The researchers chose to work in Appalachian communities because they were interested in the effects of an adult-centered culture "where communication between adults and children is minimal and tends to be gestural and non-verbal." In addition, these communities interested the researchers because of anticipated different sex-role expectations in language use among males and females: women are seen as the primary talkers, and boys are trained from an early age to prefer silence.

These investigators compared their findings on private speech to those obtained by Kohlberg and his co-workers with children drawn from mainstream urban families (Kohlberg, Yaeger & Hjertholm, 1968). The expected developmental differences were found by Berk and Garvin: Appalachian children showed a slower rate of mastery of private speech than the mainstream children, and the Appalachian boys revealed more immature forms and uses of speech for the self than girls growing up in those mountain communities. Their study confirmed the sociogenetic thesis, that language socialization differs in different historically-patterned environments and that such differences in socialization are matched by correspondingly different developments in cognition.

Thus, verbal interaction across generations is critical for the mastery of private speech—a language form which, once internalized, becomes the basis of verbal thinking. The relationship between external, private and inner speech was first examined by L. S. Vygotsky (1962). He proposed that speech produced by children in the presence of others but directed to the self has the important role of self-regulation. Private speech among pre-schoolers gives voice to task frustration, but it is also a powerful means for planning and problem-solving. Recent studies document in considerable detail the development and functions of speech for self-regulation (see, for example, studies by Fuson, 1979, and Diaz, 1984). The developmental relationship between adult uses of language and children's verbal self-regulation has been described by Vygotsky's co-worker A. R. Luria (1982). The dialogic process of adult-child interaction becomes internalized by the child, developing inner speech:

> Inner speech retains all the analytical, planning and regulative functions found in external speech: *it continues to fulfill the same intellectual role originally performed by the adult's speech addressed to the child* and later carried out by the expanded speech of the child him/herself. (pp. 106) [Emphasis added].

Research just presented has shown that there is considerable cultural variation in the ways in which adults address young children, and the ways they use informative and analytical language. Some studies have documented differences in the larger patterns of input, while other studies have documented presumably corresponding patterns of differences in the development of children's processing strategies. However, research has not yet yielded a fine-grained and thorough understanding of the relationships between these two. One exception is the work of Wertsch and his co-workers (Wertsch, 1979; Hickman & Wertsch, 1978), which examines the directive role of adult speech in children's problem solving activity and documents the process of mastery in which the child's functioning progresses from a dependent process to an independent one, constituting the development of self-regulation.

The work discussed in this article provides a strong argument for the sociogenetic position on language. The sociogenetic position stresses the connections between the social and individual planes of development, between knowledge gained from the experiential world and its elaboration through inner speech, "the language of thought." Most discussions of language acquisition fail to stress this crucial connection between language and thought and between certain kinds of language input and verbal self-regulation.

## CONCLUSION

Humans are biologically prepared to acquire language as our upright stature, skillful hands and cortically specialized areas contribute to the possibility of such mastery. The lengthy period of dependence on caretakers during human infancy provides the developmental framework for language acquisition, a process that, while rooted in biology, becomes transformed into a socio-historical process. As Vygotsky as well as Luria (1982) have proposed, in order to explain the highly complex forms of human consciousness one must go beyond the human organism:

> One must seek the origins of conscious activity and "categorical" behavior not in the recesses of the human brain or in the depths of the spirit, but in the external conditions of life. Above all, . . . one must seek these origins in the external processes of social life, in the social and historical forms of human existence. (p. 25)

The acquisition of language requires that children be exposed to language and interact actively with speakers. It also requires that children use contextual information and non-linguistic input in linking their knowledge of the world and of language into a system of representation. Many children in the world are beneficiaries of conditions of stimulation that permit them to enter into speech communities as increasingly effective participants. Severe verbal deprivation in the lives of young children is rare, but when it does occur, it can have lasting and devastating consequences, as demonstrated by Fujinaga's work. The language functions most susceptible to damage are the cognitive functions, the uses of language for memory, planning, self-regulation and the transmission of knowledge from one generation to the next. Overall, the specific aspects of language socialization vary in terms of societal demands. Cultural variations in language socialization are linked to historically shaped sex roles, economic conditions, and societal resources for informal and formal education. Theoretical approaches that minimize the impact of specific societal conditions on the diverse forms and functions of language, or that equate human language with sophisticated animal communication, fail both in terms of theory and practice. Not only does such theory fail to provide a convincing account of the rich and biologically unique human condition, it also fails to provide the educational practitioner with a foundation capable of lending guidance in the service of achieving equality for all learners.

## REFERENCES

Bain, B. (Ed.). (1983). *The sociogenesis of language and human conduct.* New York: Plenum.

Berk, L. E., & Garvin, R. A. (1984). Development of private speech among low-income Appalachian children. *Developmental Psychology, 20,* 271–286.

Bruner, J. (1983). *Child's talk.* New York: Norton.

Chomsky, N. (1965). *Aspects of the theory of syntax.* Cambridge, MA: MIT Press.

Clark, E. V., & Hecht, B. F. (1983). Comprehension, production and language acquisition. *Annual Review of Psychology, 34,* 325–49.

Cross, T. (1977). Mothers' speech adjustments: the contribution of selected child listener variables. In C. E. Snow & C. A. Ferguson (Eds.), *Talking to children.* Cambridge: Cambridge University Press.

Diaz, R. (1984, September). *The union of thought and language in children's private speech: Recent empirical evidence for Vygotsky's theory.* Paper presented at the International Congress of Psychology, Acapulco, Mexico.

Feagan, L., & Farran, D. C. (Eds.). (1982). *The language of children reared in poverty.* New York: Academic Press.

Ferguson, C. A. (1977). Baby talk as a simplified register. In C. E. Snow & C. A. Ferguson (Eds.), *Talking to children.* Cambridge: Cambridge University Press.

Fujinaga, T. (1983). Some sociogenetic determinants in human development revealed by the study of severely deprived children. In B. Bain (Ed.), *The sociogenesis of language and human conduct.* New York: Plenum.

Fuson, K. (1979). The development of self-regulating aspects of speech: A review. In G. Zivin (Ed.), *The development of self-regulation through private speech.* New York: Wiley.

Garnica, O. (1977). Some prosodic and paralinguistic features of speech to young children. In C. E. Snow & C. A. Ferguson (Eds.), *Talking to children.* Cambridge: Cambridge University Press.

Gelman, R., & Shatz, M. (1977). Appropriate speech adjustments: The operation of conversational constraints on talk to two-year olds. In M. Lewis & L. Rosenblum (Eds.), *Interaction, conversation and the development of language.* New York: Wiley.

Gleitman, L. (1981). Maturational determinants of language growth. *Cognition, 10,* 103–114.

Heath, S. B. (1983). *Ways with words.* Cambridge: Cambridge University Press.

Hickman, M., & Wertsch, J. (1978). Adult-child discourse in problem solving situations. *Papers from the Fourteenth Meeting, Chicago Linguistics Society.* Chicago: Chicago Linguistics Society.

Holquist, M. (1983). The politics of representation. *Quarterly Newsletter of the Laboratory of Comparative Human Cognition, 5,* 6.

John-Steiner, V., & Tatter, P. (1983). An interactionist model of language acquisition. In B. Bain (Ed.), *The sociogenesis of language and human conduct.* New York: Plenum.

Kohlberg, L., Yaeger, J., & Hjertholm, E. (1968). Private speech: Four studies and a review of theories. *Child Development, 39,* 691–736.

Luria, A. R. (1982). *Language and cognition.* New York: Wiley.

McCartney, K. (1984). Effect of quality of day care environment on children's language development. *Developmental Psychology, 20,* 244–260.

Nelson, K. (1983). The conceptual basis of language. In Th. B. Seiler & W. Wannenmacher (Eds.), *Concept development and the development of word meaning*. Berlin: Springer-Verlag.

Newport, E. L., Gleitman, H., & Gleitman, L. (1977). Mother, I'd rather do it myself: Some effects and non-effects of maternal speech style. In C. E. Snow & C. A. Ferguson (Eds.), *Talking to children*. Cambridge: Cambridge University Press.

Ninio, A., & Bruner, J. (1978). The achievement and antecedents of labeling. *Journal of Child Language, 5*, 1–16.

Novikoff, A. (1945). The concept of integrative levels and Biology. *Science, 101*, 209–215.

Schweinhart, L. J., & Weikart, D. P. (1980). Young children grow up: The effects of the Perry Preschool Program on youths through age 15. *Monographs of the High/Scope Educational Research Foundation*.

Slobin, D. I. (1980). Universal and particular in the acquisition of language. In L. R. Gleitman & E. Wanner (Eds.), *Language acquisition: State of the art*. Cambridge: Cambridge University Press.

Trevarthen, C. (1980). The foundations of intersubjectivity: Development of interpersonal and cooperative understanding in infants. In D. R. Olson (Ed.), *The social foundations of language and thought*. New York: Norton.

Vygotsky, L. S. (1962). *Thought and language*. Trans. E. Hanfmann & G. Vakar. Cambridge, MA: MIT Press.

Vygotsky, L. S. (1978). *Mind in society: The development of higher psychological processes*. In M. Cole, V. John-Steiner, S. Scribner, & E. Souberman (Eds.). Cambridge, MA: Harvard University Press.

Weikart, D. P. (1974/1975). Parental involvement through home teaching. *High/Scope Educational Research Foundation Report*, 2–5.

Wertsch, J. V. (1979). The regulation of human action and the given-new organization of private speech. In G. Zivin (Ed.), *The development of self-regulation through private speech*. New York: Wiley.

Zukow, P. G., Reilly, J., & Greenfield, P. M. (1982). Making the absent present: Facilitating the transition from sensorimotor to linguistic communication. In K. E. Nelson (Ed.), *Children's language, Vol. 3*. Hillsdale, NJ: Lawrence Erlbaum Associates.

# 7 Aphasia as a Communicative Disorder: Application of the Levels Concept

Georgine M. Vroman
*Consultant, New York University*
*Medical School*

The questions I asked myself before writing this chapter were: (a) Is it possible to apply the levels concept, (in the sense of interrelated but qualitatively different systems of complexity and integration), to a clinical entity such as aphasia? (b) Will doing so teach us something new about this disorder? (c) Will we also learn something more about the levels concept itself?[1]

Aphasia is a language disorder caused by brain injury. To scientists it has all the fascination of an "experiment of nature," analogous to the procedure where the disruption of a system in balance becomes the wedge that opens it up to scientific investigation. Neurologists have used aphasia to discover how the functions of the brain are localized. Nielsen (1962) is a modern example of a strict localizationist. Head (first published 1926), on the other hand, had little use for the "diagram-makers." At present, the importance of localization in brain functions is generally accepted. This does not mean however, that we can always predict how the injury of specific brain areas will influence function in the individual case. Important were Penfield and Roberts' observations of the results of stimulating areas of the brain during surgery (1959). A further step was the availability of noninvasive and accurate methods of visualizing the living and working brain, (e.g., computerized tomography and evoked potentials). However, research using these methods is far from complete and the realization is growing that the outcome of these tests cannot really predict how the course of aphasia will be in the individual patient.

---

[1]I thank Dr. Ethel Tobach for clarifying the levels concept during our discussions, and Dr. Rosamond Gianutsos for her helpful comments on an earlier version of this paper. The association with both colleagues continues to instruct and inspire me.

Neuropsychologists, by defining and measuring cognitive functions with great sophistication, have further correlated specific behavioral deficits with injury to specific areas of the brain. Luria (1973) may well be one of the most influential workers in the field.

Linguists have studied aphasia to gain insight in the nature of language, in how it develops and how it breaks down. Roman Jakobson's theories linking these two processes, although controversial, have led to new research (Jakobson, 1961, 1971, 1972).

Speech pathologists have accepted the challenge to restore the lost language functions, using whatever methods that gave results. Schuell and her co-workers (1975) have been very influential.

We know a great deal about aphasia, thanks to these specialists. For the patient, however, aphasia can only be a catastrophe. It is a totally unexpected form of excommunication in the midst of life, and one that profoundly affects the lives of many others. There are many accounts by aphasics, who either alone or with some help, tried to describe their experience. Hodgins (1963/1971) and Brodal (1973) give good descriptions of people whose aphasia was very slight, but who nevertheless suffered greatly from their loss. Unfortunately, these auto-biographies are often considered interesting and poignant, but too anecdotal to have much scientific value.

The application of the levels concept to aphasia is appropriate on several counts. In the first place, ever since the publications of Broca, in 1861, and Wernicke, in 1874, the study of this disorder of language functions has focused on matters of hierarchy and on systems of complexity. In the second place, because the language disorder is caused by a brain injury, the rehabilitation of the patient must attempt to restore this patient's functioning on many levels, including the physical, the cognitive and the social.

Anthropologists, such as myself, have an interest in the matter on both counts: because of our long-standing concern with language, cognition and communication, and because we study people within their culture and society. Anthropologists should be particularly interested in the rehabilitation process, since it deals with the available mechanisms that enable a person to return from an anomolous position to being, once again, an acknowledged member of the community. See Van Gennep (1908/1960, English publication) and Victor Turner (1969) on transition rites that prescribe the rituals that make such a return possible. The onset of puberty and childbirth, for instance, are occasions where people leave one stage of life and must be prepared for the next. The curing of certain illnesses may also require rituals of restoration and reintegration. The rehabilitation process bears a marked similarity to transition rites (Vroman, 1980). During it people are helped in the restoration of lost functions and prepared for a return to the community, but they do so as a person different from the one they were. Goffman (1963) called attention to the fact that disability leads to profound changes in identity which may be modified but are never totally undone.

The levels concept can be applied to aphasia in several ways, of which the following two are the most important. (1) From the viewpoint of evolutionary and developmental levels aphasia is a cognitive (language) disorder that may well be exclusively human. According to some aphasia specialists, the term's use is only correct, if it describes the loss of previously intact language functions. The so-called "childhood aphasias" comprise a generally accepted and very intriguing area of study, although some consider the designation aphasia for these disorders to be ambiguous. In any case, the phylogeny and ontogeny of the neurophysiology of the brain and its language functions should be part of any comprehensive study of aphasia. In the past, Hughlings Jackson (republished 1932), Freud (1891/1953, English translation) and more recently, Lenneberg (1967) were among those who devoted considerable attention to the subject. (2) Another levels concept in aphasia studies derives from the fascination, mentioned earlier, which this disorder has always held for many branches of science. The two extreme poles of this continuum are probably neuro-anatomy and psycholinguistics. The latter studies language as part of cognition, i.e., of those processes that help us obtain, integrate, store and share knowledge about ourselves and our environment. Each of these worlds of scientific fact and theory, with its own vocabulary and concepts, has staked out an exclusive territory. There seems to be only intermittent interest in mutual communication across boundaries and in arriving at a working relationship between these domains. Representatives of each field of study appear to rate its particular contributions as the ones most likely to uncover the essence of aphasia, and therefore tend to place it at the top of the ranking order. We are dealing with levels in the sense of systems of integration and complexity. But even where there is some awareness of the interrelatedness between these systems, we find more often than not, several self-imposed hierarchies among them. This chapter deals mainly with this particular form of levels concept.

## DEFINITIONS AND CLASSIFICATIONS OF APHASIA

Benson and Geschwind (1984), in their chapter for Baker and Baker's definitive textbook of Clinical Neurology, favor the following simple definition of aphasia: "Aphasia can best be defined as a disorder of previously intact language abilities secondary to brain damage" (pp. 1). Let us look at this definition more closely. Its virtue is that it focuses on three essential characteristics. (a) The primary cause of aphasia is always brain injury. In other words we must always consider factors such as the cause and nature of this injury, its location and its size, when evaluating the symptoms we observe. Also, we may observe symptoms that are not necessarily aphasic in nature while still being caused by the underlying brain injury.

(b) The disorder is a language disorder. This means that many different functions of language may be impaired. However, Wepman (1951) cautioned that much more than language is involved in aphasia and Halpern (1972) warned that not all language disorders after brain injury are aphasic. Usually we can distinguish a combination of impaired language functions and this allows us to discern patterns, or syndromes, and enables us to draw up a taxonomy of aphasias. Some of these relate syndromes to particular brain functions and to the localizations of the lesions. But this is by no means the case with every classification system. As a matter of fact, there are so many of these systems and there is so little correlation between them that the situation has been called chaotic. The classification system proposed by the Boston School (as described by Benson & Geschwind, 1984, and to be discussed later in this chapter) is an attempt to introduce a more comprehensive and historically justified system, but it does not yet appear to be universally adopted.

(c) Finally, aphasia as defined is the loss of previously intact language functions. This formulation immediately poses at least one obvious question. Can we speak of aphasia in the case of language disorders that children are born with, such as aspects of cerebral palsy or forms of language retardation? The term "developmental aphasia" is used in these cases but, strictly speaking, its use is incorrect, at least within this definition of aphasia. It is even controversial to speak about "acquired" aphasia in children, i.e., those forms that develop when there is at least some language function present. In any case, it is obvious that essential differences can be expected between adult and childhood aphasia. In the latter case language functions are not as yet fully developed and the juvenile brain itself may not yet have fully matured in all its functions and may still have a certain plasticity no longer present in the adult brain.

There is comparatively little literature on childhood aphasia. Lenneberg (1967) was a landmark publication. This author hypothesized on the basis of clinical data that, until the age of puberty, the language centers of the brain are not as strictly localized in the left hemisphere, as is the case in most adults. He noted that the dominance of the left hemisphere over the right and of the right hand over the left hand is not yet firmly established at this age. Consequently, although aphasia in children is not rare, it almost always disappears presumably because the other hemisphere takes over. Satz and Bullard-Bates (in Sarno, 1981) carefully gathered case material from the available literature and concluded that the evidence does not support Lenneberg's hypothesis. They found that hemispheric dominance and handedness, and consequently lateralization, develop within the first few years of life. And, although children's aphasia does tend to dissolve, these children have reportedly not been able to make normal progress in school, and the take-over by the other hemisphere, if it exists, must be considered incomplete. Still, while there appears to be little evidence for the "progressive lateralization" and "equipotentiality of the brain" hypotheses (as proposed by Lenneberg), there remain many unexplained findings. Even among adults we occasionally see aphasia after right-sided brain injury, often, but not always, in left-handed people. Patients, young and old, who start out with similar symptoms, often show a very different degree of recovery. Several authors have called attention to the lack of initiative and general poverty of expression (for speaking, reading and writing) in children with aphasia under the age of 10. See Satz and Bullard-Bates (in Sarno, 1981, p. 413) referring to Alajouanine and Lhermite. After the age of 10, childhood aphasia appears to have more similarities with adult aphasia. Obviously, many questions remain.

The definition of aphasia we discussed mentions the three requirements that must be met before we can use the term. But there are many points left unaddressed. It may have the virtue of simplicity, but it certainly does not give us much information on what we can be expected to find and the impairments responsible for those findings. The text of the chapter in which it was proposed makes clear that the primary purpose of the authors was to go back to basics as they saw them (i.e., to a definition derived from clinical neurology). The contributions of philosophers and many different scientists may have enriched our insight, the authors add, but this interest also has "introduced considerable confusion to the evaluation of aphasia" (ibid).

Even a partial survey of the literature on aphasia demonstrates that many authors have not been satisfied with this kind of definition and have added to it or changed it to suit their own opinions. As a matter of fact, we find that the different definitions reflect not only the discipline but the particular theoretical position of their authors, and frequently their approach to therapy, as well. A rather extreme example is that of the psychologist Wepman (1951): "Differing rather sharply from previously held theories that aphasia is a disorder of speech or a language problem, narrowly conceived, it is held here that aphasia is a disorder affecting the patient's total reaction pattern due to a disturbance of the integrating capacity of the cortex" (p. 85). It is obvious that theory and definition have become interchanged, in this case. This phenomenon should not, I think, be interpreted as an example of inexact terminology or confused ideas. It demonstrates my contention that definitions are never neutral because their authors are not. They reflect and impose a way of thinking, and, in the case of a clinical disorder, dictate the ways the patients will be treated. For instance, Wepman's therapy consisted of re-education and stimulation. His goal was the re-establishment of "the use of neural capacities which are present and functional but which are blocked from use by the pathological condition existing within the cortex" (ibid: 263). It is of some interest to note that Wepman considered the breakdown of language functions in adult aphasia to resemble the stages of language acquisition in children, in reverse order. The linguist Jakobson (1971, 1972) held similar views. Few people agree with this position, but some form of language re-education, starting from a simpler level, is the basis of all successful aphasia rehabilitation. Hughlings Jackson, writing more than a century ago, thought that when the higher brain functions fall out (i.e., those governed by more recently evolved parts of the brain) lower, more ancient, functions would become evident. Freud, writing some decades later, proposed that complex activities such as speaking, reading and writing, that have become automatic in adults, may have to be relearned, much the way children learned them. Lately there has been renewed interest in these viewpoints.

We must realize that a person suffering from aphasia is encountered (experienced) quite differently by the many people he or she meets, including representatives of the different disciplines who study aphasia. As indicated, such a many-sided view can be seen as reflecting a levels approach. Each of the points of view represents a level of integration but the most prominent over-all feature appears to be the lack of integration between these levels. Such a failure is typical for any subject of study in which different disciplines have an interest. But, common as it may be, this lack of interrelation and integration remains a waste in theoretical and practical terms. Worse, it may be a real disservice to the patient. This chapter defends the position that the best, possibly only, hope for a true integration between these levels is a shift of focus from the disorder to the person and situation of the patient. Only in the individual case can the various clinical and theoretical perspectives come together. If this process does not take place, the stress remains on the perceived differences between the disciplines, specifically on the gap between theory and practice, and judgments about their relative worth will be inevitable.

Perhaps it is understandable to find Halpern, a speech pathologist, defining aphasia as follows: "Aphasia can be defined as a multi-modality language disturbance due to a brain injury. It is a linguistic deficit that causes the individual to have difficulty in the comprehension and/or formulation of language symbols. Aphasia is not a generalized intellectual impairment, apraxia of speech, confused language, or dysarthria, although components of any combination of those disorders may accompany aphasic disturbance" (Halpern, 1972, p. 3). The linguistic nature of the disorder is acknowledged, but at least as striking is the (speech) clinician's emphasis on the need for a clear distinction between aphasia proper and certain other specific language or cognitive disorders. This is so, even though aphasia admittedly is often accompanied by these disorders, and all may have to be treated simultaneously. In other words, we see a clinician's preoccupation with differential diagnosis that may benefit the patient only marginally. Contrast this with Wepman (1951) who listed 34 "most frequently observed behavioral manifestations of aphasia," all of them nonlanguage-related (pp. 32–33), and each requiring specific attention. It appears to be a matter of scope and focus, of being able to envision more than one level at once.

Still, students of aphasia owe a great debt to some speech pathologists, who, more than most other specialists, have made significant clinical as well as theoretical contributions. Foremost among them are the late Hildred Schuell and her coworkers (Schuell, 1974; Schuell et al., 1975). She designed the famous Minnesota Test for Differential Diagnosis of Aphasia and was a superb diagnostician and therapist. Martha Sarno, aside from making her own contributions (the Functional Communication Profile, 1965), has set herself the specific task of reviewing the literature on aphasia and providing opportunities for exchange among representatives of many disciplines. The books on aphasia that she edited are among the best examples of how to select and bring together pivotal articles with a wide appeal (Sarno, 1972, 1980, 1981).

An interesting example of total concentration on therapeutic interaction within a social context, with disregard for any other aspect, can be found in Valerie Griffith's book *A Stroke in the Family* (1970). This is the story of the treatment by friends and neighbors of the actress Patricia Neal, who had become almost totally aphasic after a stroke during pregnancy. The only rationale for this very successful approach was that the patient should be kept busy all day and that special interests and remaining strengths should be used as the basis for the exercises. There is no definition of aphasia, no mention of its neuro-anatomical substrate nor of any linguistic or neuropsychological theory or findings. We simply read how aphasia affected this particular person and we get a list of exercises that were found to be successful. Beyond this, the book has no pretensions. But because it shows people how this case of aphasia was treated by lay persons using very simple means and because we can see and hear Patricia Neal acting again in the movies and on television, Griffith's book has had a wide appeal even among professionals.

What are we to make of this success? Should we conclude that the Griffith method is all that is needed? I think not, but it does focus on the need to look for effective means of rehabilitation once the acute phase is over. Patients who are back at home, or in facilities for long-term care, may no longer have access to scarce (and very expensive) speech therapy. Maybe the Griffith method could be of use here. However, an essential aspect was the presence and dedication of Roald Dahl, Patricia's husband. He saw the need for this therapy and recruited their friends and neighbors. He set up the schedule and supervised the work, even though not participating directly himself. This ostensibly ordinary form of therapy may not have been so ordinary after all. In my opinion it has great value as an example of alternate therapy in the later stages of rehabilitation. However, it requires the organization and supervision of several dedicated and imaginative lay persons, well-matched to the individual patients. This method represents an area where the scientists and the professionals involved with aphasia must make room for yet another approach: on the almost exclusively social level.

By now the impression must be quite strong that there are no strict rules on describing aphasia and its many possible manifestations. The different definitions and classification systems have created considerable confusion, and not just in the mind of the interested lay reader. Aphasiology is a recently recognized specialty, as yet poorly defined. Most of its members are speech pathologists and they usually adopt the classification system (and the diagnostic procedures) they feel most comfortable with. One problem may well be that they must cooperate with, and explain their patients' symptoms to, other health professionals in terms that are easy to understand. Therefore, there is some merit in simplification, at least when dealing with outsiders. Even so, aphasia is not always recognized in general medical practice.

The many classification systems that have been proposed are very much the creation of their authors and it is not easy to find a correlation between them. No matter how detailed some of them are, they never incorporate all the distinctions that the ever-increasing number of diagnostic tests now make possible. Moreover, most classifications are based on the ideal, classic, cases and as speech pathologists especially know from experience, there are almost no classic cases of aphasia. To complicate matters even more, there is a great difference between aphasia in the acute stage and in the later stages, to such an extent that some specialists warn not to attempt a precise diagnosis too early.

Clinicians who do not consider a detailed diagnosis essential, often employ a shortcut and only distinguish between expressive or motor (approximately comparable to Broca's), receptive or sensory (comparable to Wernicke's) and global aphasias. In global aphasia there is no or minimal speech. This simplification is unsatisfactory, if only because so many aphasics have both expressive and receptive deficits and the many other important language functions that can be impaired are totally ignored.

The chaotic situation created by all these different classification systems badly needed the introduction of a generally acceptable one, simple enough to be easily understood and detailed enough to incorporate the most important distinctions agreed on by most specialists. The system proposed by the Speech Pathology Section, Aphasia Research Unit, of the Boston Veterans Administration Hospital, appears to meet these requirements. It combines classic terminology with neuroanatomical localization and relates these to specific language deficits. It is, in other words, a system that incorporates several levels. Its growing acceptance indicates its usefulness. It provides a standard for comparison between other classification systems. We could say that it allows for a translation between them. Consequently it should make old studies more relevant for the present. By facilitating understanding and cooperation across disciplines it should lead to further progress in the study of aphasia. A brief summary of the Boston school's classification system follows. In all but the exceptional cases, the lesions are located in the *Left* hemisphere.

1. *Broca's Aphasia.* The lesion is located in the posterior portion of the third frontal gyrus. Speech is non-fluent (telegraph style); reading, writing and naming are impaired. Comprehension is better than expression. Repetition of spoken words is impaired. There is often a right hemiplegia. These patients are often depressed.

2. *Wernicke's Aphasia*. The lesion is located in the posterior part of the superior temporal gyrus. Spontaneous speech is fluent and syntax is correct, but there are paraphasias (substitutions of words or letters). Reading, writing and naming are disturbed; comprehension is defective; repetition is impaired. Right hemiplegia is less common or does not last.

3. *Conduction Aphasia*. The lesion is located in the left perisylvian region and often involves the auditory and insular regions and the supramarginal gyrus. Spontaneous speech is fluent. Reading may contain many paraphasias. Comprehension of spoken words and sentences is largely intact, but typically these are repeated incorrectly. Naming is usually impaired. There may be hemiparesis of the right side of the face and of the right arm, but the prognosis is good.

4. *Transcortical Aphasia*. A sensory and a motor form are distinguished. In the former, the lesions are located mainly in the posterior portion of the middle temporal gyrus. These patients have fluent speech with many paraphasias. Comprehension is intact. Repetition is intact. In transcortical motor aphasia the lesion is located deep in the left frontal lobe, in the white matter, anterior to the area of Broca. Speech is non-fluent, with many paraphasias. Comprehension is usually impaired. Repetition is intact. This last feature is characteristic for transcortical aphasias and it is an important factor in differential diagnosis.

5. *Global Aphasia*. Here we find an almost total loss of the receptive and expressive language capabilities. Typically the lesion involves the whole of the left perisylvian area.

6. *Anomic Aphasia,* with a more or less isolated loss of the ability to name, i.e., to find the words needed. Wordfinding is often impaired in other forms of aphasia, but not in isolation.

For a more detailed discussion of the Boston school's classification system, see Benson and Geschwind's chapter in Baker and Baker (1983, vol. 1). See also the chapters by Hanna Damasio and Antonio Damasio in Sarno (1981), on which most of this summary is based.

Obviously, the widespread acceptance of a uniform classification system for aphasia will lead to greater compatibility between workers in the field. Greater standardization will ensure that everyone knows what everyone else is talking about and less time will be wasted on trying to reconcile (or preserve) different systems of classification. The differential diagnosis of the various forms of aphasia can then be made according to generally accepted rules, even if the fact remains that there are very few "classic" cases of aphasia. Mutual intelligibility should make it possible to formulate clear research goals and to pursue these cooperatively. One possible disadvantage of such a standardized system could well be that its very existence discourages interest in alternative points of view. This would be a great loss; the literature includes many examples of controversial positions that have led to new insights and developments. Jakobson's distinction between syntagmatic and paradigmatic forms of aphasic errors is a good example.

What are the advantages of such a standardized system for the aphasic patients themselves, aside from a greater unanimity among the specialists assigned to their case? Is it enough to have received a diagnosis that all agree on? Does this also imply that the therapy follows established procedures for each kind of aphasia and that the outcome can always be predicted? The answers to these questions cannot be an unqualified "Yes." It is to be expected that an aphasic patient, moving from one facility to another, may now continue to find a well-informed staff with similar ideas. The treatment, also, is likely to follow a course, similar to the one previously experienced. Yet we hear, again and again, that good aphasia therapy is not just a matter of competence, but equally of creative imagination, of good rapport between patient and therapist, and of understanding the specific needs of the particular patient. At the same time, much of the literature remains devoted to the introduction of new tests and methods or to the assessment of old ones. And here the irksome question remains, whether we will ever be able to prove the effectiveness of specific treatments or of treating people at all.

Also we must deal with such ethical issues as how to choose controls and whether we can withhold certain promising (but as yet unproven) procedures from a patient group. One solution to this dilemma is the single case experimental design (Hersen & Barlow, 1976). This method requires the establishment of a baseline for a particular measurement, followed by the introduction of one change at the time (e.g., a specific treatment procedure). The effect of this change is then evaluated until a new baseline has been attained. At this point a new change is introduced and the whole procedure is repeated. The single case experimental design is ideally suited for research-in-depth of clinical cases because most of these are unique and cannot easily be compared or grouped in one category with others. Each case becomes its own control.

We cannot escape the thought that the existence of a universally accepted classification system might not, in itself, be sufficient for the individual aphasic patient. It may not be enough that an accurate, generally accepted diagnosis can be made or even that corresponding therapies of growing sophistication are available. In the first place, not every aphasic patient will have the benefit of receiving both an expert diagnosis and competent treatment. In the second place, the most accurate diagnosis and the most professional treatment have only limited value, if there is not also an investigation of what being aphasic means to the particular patient. We must always ask: "What is the individual's own experience of aphasia and what are his or her specific needs?" For the answers we have to go back to the definition of aphasia.

Aphasia is a language disorder after brain injury. Regardless of some recognizable patterns, it is endlessly varied in its manifestations and even similar losses may affect the individual patients very differently. Aphasia is not just a problem with understanding or producing speech. Reading and writing may be disturbed as well. Some (e.g., Head, 1926, and Schuell et al., 1975) have called it a disorder of the ability to understand and use symbols. We cannot understand what the loss of language means if we do not look more closely at the nature and functions of language itself.

A fascinating discussion on the subject of aphasia is that by Critchley (1970). After stressing the need to define language first, he quotes several definitions from the literature, most of them either "too terse" (and therefore not sufficiently instructive) or "too awkward" (and therefore unworkable). One favorite was given by Thomson in 1860: "a mode of expressing one's thoughts by means of motions of the body; including spoken words, cries, involuntary gestures, even painting and sculpture, together with those contrivances which replace speech in situations where it cannot be employed." Another favorite is Whitney's (1870): "certain instrumentalities whereby men consciously and with intention represent their thought, to the end, chiefly, of making it known to other men: it is expression for the sake of communication." Critchley's own proposed definition is: "the expression and reception of ideas and feelings" (ibid: 2,3).

If we see aphasia as one of the cognitive disorders we call attention to the processes of receiving, processing and sharing information that depend on intact language functions. Consequently, the communicative aspects of the disorder come into perspective. When we look at the quoted definitions of language, a concept of aphasia as a communication disorder gains validity. Such a concept is not without precedent, although this used to be implied rather than specifically stated and there are indications that it is becoming more widely accepted. The main advantage of this formulation is its stress on the social context in which the language disorder takes place. Effective aphasia therapy must address this social context no less than the loss of language functions per se. Several authors such as Sarno (1965) and Holland (1976) have introduced procedures for testing the ways aphasic patients use language in daily life. The realization had been growing that language performance cannot be evaluated adequately by using standard tests within the constraining environment of the office. The functional language tests of these authors are based on simulations of activities that are part of most patients' daily experience.

A competent and sensitive aphasia therapist has always been aware of the importance of social factors in the evaluation of the patients' performance and for meeting their special needs. Wepman (1951) and Eisenson (1973) are good examples. Elsewhere (Vroman, 1980) I have developed the point that a more systematic approach could be attained by using methods from anthropological and sociolinguistics. Important is the work by Hymes (1974) on the analysis of speech events and the ethnography of communicative communities. Labov and Fanshel (1977) analyzed psychotherapy as discourse, as therapy in the form of conversation. The volumes edited by Bauman and Sherzer (1974) and by Gumperz and Hymes (1972), for instance, contain some relevant contributions and there are many other sources. The point is that we do not have to depend solely on the particular interests or sensitivity of the individual therapist. There is a body of literature available that can form a basis for dealing with the social nature of aphasia in a systematic manner that is also scientifically sound. But this work has barely begun.

## APHASIA AND THE LEVELS CONCEPT

What have we learned, up to now, about applying the levels concept to aphasia? First, we briefly looked at the possibility of studying this language disturbance by way of philogenetic and ontogenetic levels. At this time I should like to mention some additional points. Ever since Hughlings Jackson there has been persistent interest in the language functions of both the old and the new portions of the human brain and the specific contributions of each hemisphere. While expressive and receptive speech functions are located in the left hemisphere for the great majority of the people, the right hemisphere appears to fill a role in automatic speech acts, in the ability to perform the appropriate body movements and to monitor one's own speech acts. The frontal lobes are necessary for activating speech and an intact limbic system is needed for the appropriate emotions accompanying speech. The different facets of speech and language functioning are spread out over many areas of the brain. Moreover, other cognitive functions, such as perception, attention, concentration and memory have a significant influence on the capability to use language adequately. The most important characteristic of these many language-related centra and their functions is their interdependence, much more so than a hierarchical relationship between them. See specifically the work of Luria on these matters.

Second, I do not think that we should try to explain the evolution of language on the basis of what animals are capable of. There are instructive similarities and analogies, but we must assume that the evolution of species-specific communication is part of the evolutionary processes that took place within each species. At best, we may gain greater insight in what is exclusively human about human forms of communication. This is not to deny, of course, that communication across species boundaries can take place, and that shared forms can be developed. Language, as we know it, may be limited to the human species, but it is not the only form of communication.

Third, several students of aphasia (e.g., Jakobson and Wepman) believed that the language breakdown in aphasia resembled the developmental stages of language in children, in reverse order. This theory of ontogenetic levels in aphasia has not found many adherents. Nevertheless it is true that, for instance, children's primers have been found quite useful in aphasia therapy, provided form and subject matter were adapted to the specific adult patient's interests. Next we have spent considerable attention on the levels of integration as represented by the different scientific specialties that have made aphasia their subject matter.

While it is not difficult to demonstrate the interrelatedness of these fields of study, each imbedded in their own systems of thought, it was pointed out that their representatives were not always sufficiently aware of this. And worse, that each of these specialists tends to impose a subjective ranking order upon the fields, which places his or her own at or very near the top. Neurologists, even Critchley who is one of the great authorities on aphasia and well aware of the essential contributions of linguistics, rarely yield the supremacy of their field to any other.

Is there, then, no way in which to apply the levels concept to aphasia studies without immediately having to point out its shortcomings? I think the problem results from our using a limited perspective, if we try to see the different disciplines involved as so many levels of integration and complexity. The interrelatedness of these levels or systems is not in question. The problem starts when we focus on any level in particular. For instance, if we concentrate on neuroanatomy, we will distinguish the microscopic and the macroscopic structure, the biochemical and the biophysical processes and all of these in relation to neurological function. If we stay just within this one field, there are already many levels of integration and complexity. Its relation to other fields, such as linguistics, or to the social context in which aphasia takes place, must then appear insignificant by comparison, or of at least secondary importance. A similar point can be made for each of the different disciplines. Within the domain of everyone of them the levels concept has considerable usefulness; taken together, there is bound to be a continuous jostling for position.

I propose a different perspective that could assign the position of prominence to each of the fields of inquiry in turn, at the same time still acknowledging the others. This is a perspective derived from epidemiology, (if we consider aphasia, the pathological condition) and from personal life history, (if we concentrate on the person of the patient). For both points of view, time, its passage and influence, constitutes the mechanism for transition between levels. It is in many ways an anthropologic perspective because its focus is on the individual within the natural, social and historical context.

We can look at each case of aphasia as the outcome of a sequence of that person's life events (but not necessarily the inevitable or final outcome). In each of the stages of life something could happen that would predispose the person for the eventual occurrence of aphasia. A brief sketch of such a life course should illustrate my point. Throughout the focus will be the patient's personal situation and priorities.

The start (at the time of conception) can be a genetic endowment that causes the formation of fragile or abnormal blood vessels in the brain. In later stages, life style and nutritional habits, added to genetic factors, may predispose towards hypertension, heart disease and eventually stroke, one of the major causes of aphasia. In these stages it is often possible to redirect this course of events, and so to prevent this outcome by making certain changes. Sociocultural and economic factors influence the preconditions as well as the capacity for change. Education may provide the necessary information, but not everyone will be able or willing to act on it. Meanwhile, the language development of the individual, the language network he or she becomes part of, all could influence both symptoms and personal priorities, should aphasia occur. For instance, in a person who is left-handed, aphasia is not always linked to left-hemispheric brain injury. If such a person had been trained to write with the right hand (a routine practice in some school systems) this could modify the symptoms of an eventual aphasia (see Hodgins, 1963/1971).

Up to the moment that the brain injury takes place and aphasia results, biological, social and psychological factors all will interact towards this outcome. It depends on the individual person and on the particular time period we are considering, which of these factors will be of most importance. Each stage of life can be seen as a level integrating many factors, that follows from (and incorporates) the previous levels and changes into the next. The essential way in which these levels differ from one another is that the person will have gone through some irrevocable changes and that the course of events can no longer be redirected by earlier and simpler means (see Maussner & Bahn, 1974).

Once brain injury has occurred and the person turns out to be aphasic, we can say that a watershed-like event has taken place. It is followed by the acute illness episode, consisting of subsequent stages of comparatively short duration. After this comes the chronic stage, which we can call the posttraumatic stage of life (and which will drastically alter the "natural" life stages of the individual). During each of these stages one or the other of the disciplines, concerned with aphasia, will be of most importance. Directly after the brain injury, the correct diagnosis, including extent and localization of the lesion, must be determined. Life-saving measures may have to be taken and the first priority is to pull the patient through. The exact diagnosis may even have to wait until the results of swelling and diaschisis have subsided. (*Diaschisis,* a term introduced by von Monakow, describes the influence a brain injury exerts on areas at a distance from its own location.) The patient may be in coma; life processes must be maintained and the neurologist is in over-all charge. Acute cases of stroke or other brain injury are usually admitted to the neurology or neurosurgery ward.

After the patient comes out of the coma and the condition stabilizes, a more exact diagnosis of the injury and its effects can be made. Several invasive and non-invasive techniques are at the disposal of the neurospecialists (of the latter the CAT scan is of utmost importance). Both lost and remaining motor and sensory functions are determined, so that rehabilitation can begin. The determination of speech and language losses is part of this process. At this point the neurologist makes room for the rehabilitation specialists, one of whom should be a speech and language pathologist. The neuropsychologist may also enter the picture to determine detailed and sophisticated neuropsychological functioning. From the patient's point of view, the rehabilitation specialists should now have the most important role. Unfortunately, some patients and families continue to expect their neurologist or neurosurgeon to make all the decisions instead of assuming a secondary role. The aphasia patient will depend especially on the speech pathologist, who should have been specifically trained to deal with aphasia. This training should include a knowledge of speech and language development and performance, in both normal and pathological conditions. Anatomy and physiology of the speech organs and of the related parts of the central nervous system should be part of this background. The speech pathologist should also be familiar with linguistics, the study of language as the "expression and reception of ideas and feelings." The speech and language pathologist now assumes the central role during this stage of the aphasic patient's life. Much will of course depend on the extent of the other disabilities. Is it more important for a stroke victim to be able to talk or to walk? The capacity for effective communication remains one of the highest priorities for the patient and the family. The patient's ability to profit from any form of rehabilitation may well depend on it; and so will the extent to which former roles in the family or on the job can be resumed. But the care for a patient who is not able to move around, or who needs help with all personal needs, could well exceed the material and psychological resources the family or spouse can muster.

At this stage of the illness social factors become important. The treatment must be oriented towards the specific environment the patient came from and to which he or she will return. Old interests and capabilities may provide a starting point for therapy. New ones may have to be developed. The patient's personal resources and those of the home or professional environment should all be taken into account.

Eventually, the time comes that the patient's future must be decided on. Except for very rare cases there will come an end to the intensive care and therapy. New solutions will have to be found. The social aspects of being aphasic will now become the most important. The neurologist, the speech pathologist, the other rehabilitation specialists remain involved, but only distantly or occasionally. In most cases, the patient is now dependent on the resources of whatever arrangements have been made for chronic care. The family, often with advice from a social worker, may have to make the decision for the patient. Failing this, social agencies may take over. Rarely does the patient take an active role. Even in the best of circumstances, when there is a home and family to go back to, rehabilitation may have to be continued for a very long time. And in many instances, the understanding of this need and the willingness to take responsibility for it, fall short of what is required. Priorities may have to be reconsidered.

This was the stage where Roald Dahl and Valerie Griffith took Patricia Neal's rehabilitation in hand and were able to develop their successful method. Although the circumstances of this success story were unusual, it has been an inspiration and encouragement to aphasia patients and their families. It has also become a model in the search for effective treatment by the patient's peers, in instances where professional treatment is not or is no longer available. The basis for this treatment is the realization that each patient should have the opportunity to undergo a daily workout, specific enough to meet his or her needs, but simple enough so that interested lay people can administer it.[2]

## SUMMARY

In the preceding part we have introduced levels as developmental stages in a patient's life history with the focus on the natural history of a specific disease (i.e., aphasia, secondary to brain injury). This provided a conceptual model that allowed us to integrate microscopic and macroscopic physiological and pathological processes with each other, over short and long periods of time. We could further link these processes to the social environment, within and between levels. The historical perspective made us realize that the focus shifts, over time. Each stage (or level), while representing something new, can only be understood in the light of the previous ones.

Once the brain injury has occurred, a new set of stages will be superimposed on the patient's current life stage. Before the crisis took place, there was still a chance of preventing it from happening. After its occurrence, we enter the post-traumatic stages of recovery. Going from the acute to the chronic, each stage of recovery represents another level, requiring treatment, rehabilitation and prevention of future complications or recurrences. Different branches of science and healing are involved in the study of each level's processes and in the care of the patient within each level. But here again, the focus keeps shifting, and with that the relative importance of the role each specialty plays.

The levels concept seen as an historical process of developmental stages, has proven to be useful. It allowed us to interrelate many different simultaneous and subsequent processes, as well as the different branches of science that study these processes. When we look at a disease as part of a patient's personal history, we do not have to assign absolute ranking to the different fields of study that concern themselves with that disease. Everyone of them will assume the position of

[2]Another alternative form of long-term treatment is being developed by cognitive rehabilitation. This rapidly growing field is involved in the restoration of cognitive functions after brain injury (e.g., memory, perception, and thought processes that are part of language). Cognitive rehabilitation can be initiated at any stage of the recovery, but the need for it may outlast that for other forms of rehabilitation by months or even years. Retraining for the job or for other roles in daily life often becomes a goal.

Some years ago the personal computer was introduced to cognitive rehabilitation. Easy to administer computer programs, especially designed or adapted, have already proven their worth. Several programs are well-suited for work with aphasic patients. Many patients acquire their own computer and work daily with a custom-designed set of programs. They require no more than a minimum of help and the therapist remains available for telephone contact and occasional office visits. (See e.g., Gianutsos & Klitzner, 1981; Gianutsos, Vroman, & Matheson, 1983.)

primary importance, depending on the stage of the disease and the specific priorities of the patient during the period under consideration.

In closing, a word of caution. The levels concept is, in the final analysis, no more than a model. Models are cognitive tools that are inspired by perceived relationships and patterns of order, which have the capacity to reveal meanings and unifying principles about the things we are investigating. Each model does this in a different way. One of the most powerful popular and scientific models is the cognitive principle of opposites (dichotomies). Ultimately, this model, familiar to all anthropologists, was inspired by the contrasts that occur so pervasively in nature, such as hot and cold, right and left, black and white, male and female. The levels concept, as I have used it, has borrowed features from the scale of physiological and structural systems that encompass one another within each biological organism. It also contains features resembling the steps of the evolutionary development of a species.

Not only are there different models, but the same model, in its various applications, shows different characteristics and in doing so reveals its many potentials.

The point I am trying to make is that, like any other model, the levels concept is a tool, used for one or more particular purposes (and better suited for some than for others). Next to its usefulness a model has limitations. In each application there will be aspects that do not fit. It is perfectly legitimate to explore the origin and characteristics of a model and to find out how and when it can be applied. What we must guard against is a temptation to use the model as a stereotype of reality. We should never let any model, no matter how useful and attractive, dictate or restrict the ways we allow ourselves to think.

## REFERENCES

Bauman, R., & Sherzer, J. (Eds.). (1974). *Explorations in the ethnography of speaking.* London: Cambridge University Press.

Benson, F. B., & Geschwind, N. (1984). The aphasias and related disturbances. In A. B. Baker & L. H. Baker (Eds.), *Clinical neurology* (Vol. I) Revised Ed. Philadelphia, PA: Harper & Row.

Brodal, A. (1973). Self-observations and neuro-anatomical considerations after a stroke. *Brain, 96,* 675–694.

Critchley, M. (1970). *Aphasiology and other aspects of language.* London: Edward Arnold.

Damasio, A. (1981). The nature of aphasia: Signs and syndromes. In M. T. Sarno (Ed.), *Acquired aphasia* (pp. 51–65). Orlando, FL: Academic Press.

Damasio, H. (1981). Cerebral localization of the aphasias. In M. T. Sarno (Ed.), *Acquired aphasia* (pp. 27–50). Orlando, FL: Academic Press.

Eisenson, J. (1973). *Adult aphasia.* Englewood Cliffs, NJ: Prentice-Hall.

Freud, S. (1891/1953). *On aphasia.* New York: International University Press.

Gianutsos, R., & Klitzner, C. (1981). *Computer programs for cognitive rehabilitation.* Bayport, NY: Life Science Associates.

Gianutsos, R., Vroman, G. S., & Matheson, P. M. (1983). *Computer programs for cognitive rehabilitation, Volume II: Further visual imperception procedures.* Bayport, NY: Life Science Associates.

Goffman, E. (1963). *Stigma. Notes on the management of spoiled identity.* Englewood Cliffs, NJ: Prentice-Hall.

Griffith, V. E. (1970). *A stroke in the family.* Great Britain: Penguin Handbook. (Reprinted 1975. London: Wildwood House.)

Gumperz, J. J., & Hymes, D. (1972). *Directions in sociolinguistics.* New York: Holt, Rinehart & Winston.

Halpern, H. (1972). *Adult aphasia.* Indianapolis, IN: Bobbs-Merrill.

Head, H. (1926). *Aphasia and kindred disorders of speech* (Vol. I). London: Cambridge University Press.

Hersen, M., & Barlow, D. H. (1976). *Single case experimental designs: Strategies for studying behavior change.* New York: Pergamon Press.

Hodgins, E. (1963/1971). *Episode.* New York: Atheneum. (Reprinted 1971. New York: Simon & Schuster.)

Holland, A. (1976). *Communicative adequacy of daily living.* Pittsburgh, PA: University of Pittsburgh.

Hughlings Jackson, J. (1932). *Selected writings* (Vol. II). Edited by J. Taylor. London: Hodder & Stoughton.

Hymes, D. (1974). *Foundations in sociolinguistics.* Philadelphia: University of Pennsylvania Press.

Jakobson, R. (1961). Aphasia as a linguistic problem. In S. Saporta (Ed.), *Psycholinguistics* (pp. 419–427). New York: Holt, Rinehart & Winston.

Jakobson, R. (1971). *Studies of child language and aphasia.* The Hague, Netherlands: Mouton.

Jakobson, R. (1972). *Child language, aphasia and phonological universals.* The Hague, Netherlands: Mouton.

Labov, W., & Fanshel, D. (1977). *Therapeutic discourse. Psychotherapy as conversation.* Orlando, FL: Academic Press.

Lenneberg, E. (1967). *Biological foundations of language.* New York: Wiley.

Luria, A. R. (1973). *The working brain. An introduction to neuropsychology.* New York: Basic Books.

Mausner, J. S., & Bahn, A. K. (1974). *Epidemiology.* Philadelphia, PA: W. B. Saunders.

Nielsen, J. M. (1962). *Agnosia, apraxia, aphasia. Their value in cerebral localization* (2nd Ed.). New York: Hafner. Publ.

Penfield, W., & Roberts, L. (1959). *Speech and brain-mechanisms.* Princeton, NJ: Princeton University Press.

(Sarno), M. L. Taylor. (1965). A measurement of functional communication in aphasia. In *Archives of Physical Medicine and Rehabilitation, 46,* 101–107.

Sarno, M. T. (Ed.). (1972). *Aphasia. Selected readings.* Englewood Cliffs, NJ: Prentice-Hall.

Sarno, M.T., & Höök, O. (Eds.). (1980). *Aphasia. Assessment and treatment.* Stockholm, Sweden: Almqvist & Wilsell International.

Sarno, M. T. (Ed.) 1981. *Acquired aphasia.* Orlando, FL: Academic Press.

Satz, P., & Bullard-Bates, C. (1981). Acquired aphasia in children. In M. T. Sarno (Ed.), *Acquired aphasia.* Orlando, FL: Academic Press.

Schuell, H. (1974). *Aphasia theory and therapy: Selected lectures and papers by Hildred Schuell.* In L. F. Sies (Ed.), London: Macmillan.

Schuell, H., Jenkins, J. J., Jiménez-Pabón, E., Shaw, R., & Sefer, J. W. (1975). *Schuell's Aphasia in adults.* (2nd Ed.) New York: Harper & Row.

Turner, V. W. (1969). *The ritual process. Structure and anti-structure.* Chicago, IL: Aldine.

Van Gennep, A. (1908/1960). *The rites of passage.* Chicago, IL: University of Chicago Press.

Vroman, G. M. S. (1980). The anthropological dimension in the rehabilitation of aphasics. *Dissertation Abstracts International, 41,* 2. (University Microfilms 8017737)

Wepman, J. M. (1951). *Recovery from aphasia.* New York: Ronald Press.

# 8 Language With or Without Consciousness

N. H. Pronko
*Wichita State University*

In this chapter I examine two diametrically opposed theories of language; one relies on the notion of consciousness and the other dispenses with it altogether.

Let no one think that the term *consciousness* is out of fashion. Its prominence in the title of this conference attests to its au courant status. In an article, "The Return of Consciousness," Webb (1981) shows that renewed interest in such variations of consciousness as "sleep and dreams . . . and alterations of consciousness by drugs, various meditation routes, and hypnosis . . . are but signs of a quiet and certain return of consciousness as it creeps slowly back into all of psychology" (p. 133).

In examining ten representative introductory psychology textbooks, Webb, (1981, p. 138) found that only two did not contain a chapter or section on consciousness or altered states of consciousness. Webb (1981) sees this finding as "the beginning of a paradigmatic revolution à la Kuhn" (p. 140). But what is so new about a paradigm that has been with us for several hundred years—ever since Berkeley's and Hume's conversion of soul into consciousness (Kantor, 1969, pp. 92–94)? I would argue that what we are seeing today is not a paradigm switch, but a revival of the consciousness exemplar and its incorporation within mainstream psychology. The point I want to make most emphatically at this juncture is that consciousness, as a construct, should not be listed among the endangered species. Indeed, it is alive and well and is worthy of our consideration as one type of theory, among others, for understanding language and other forms of human behavior. Having established that we are by no means beating a dead horse named Consciousness, we move on to the consideration of a tactic that will be useful in our comparison of the competing linguistic theories in our survey.

## THE ROLE OF PARADIGMS IN THE SCIENCES

In his renowed book, *The Structure of Scientific Revolutions,* Kuhn (1970) dissects scientific communities (groups of physicists, chemists, astronomers) in much the same way that an entomologist studies insects. Kuhn (1970) finds that scientific groups share certain characteristics which, in his earlier work, he labeled "paradigm" but later (Kuhn, 1977, p. 463) changed to "disciplinary matrix," " 'disciplinary' because it is the common possession of the practitioners of a professional discipline; 'matrix' because it is composed of ordered elements of various sorts." One of the ordered elements of a scientific community is a more-or-less common education and apprenticeship. Furthermore, the members of such a group share a specific vocabulary, read the prevailing literature, are committed to certain goals including the training of their successors, and they join the approved professional organizations. Even at this point, one can sense a certain unanimity or homogeneity of thinking and acting such as one finds among the adherents of a religious faith, but there is more to come.

Of greater relevance to our purpose are other constituents of the disciplinary matrix, particularly those that Kuhn (1970, p. 184) says he formerly labeled "metaphysical paradigms." Beliefs in particular models[1] are among such paradigms. For example, mainstream psychology used to be committed to the belief that the brain was a telephone switchboard, a storage house for ideas and memories and, later, that the brain was a tape recorder. Today, the computer serves as a model for the brain (and vice-versa, the brain serves as a model for the computer as when computers are said to "sense" and to have "memories"). In addition to models as ingredients of a disciplinary matrix, there are tacit as well as stated assumptions and theories as well as subsets of theories that constitute the shared commitments of any cohesive scientific group. If new findings contradict the prevailing theory, the faithful may react with "the facts be damned" or they may defend the favored theory by patching it up with ad hoc assumptions. Kuhn enumerated still other components of the disciplinary matrix. For example, a scientific community that has attained universally acknowledged achievements through accepted models, problems, and methods for solving problems will indoctrinate newcomers into adopting such measures as they progress to full status in their profession. Even more important, after a number of such experiences with the group's paradigms and models, neophytes have "assimilated a time-tested and group-licensed way of seeing" (Kuhn, 1970, p. 189). This group-approved way of seeing is an important point to which we shall return later.

Thus far, we have described what Kuhn calls "normal science." But change is inevitable. When the traditional paradigms no longer account for certain findings and cannot be amended by ad hoc assumptions, that discipline is heading for

---

[1]A fuller treatment of models will be introduced at a later point.

a crisis. Eventually, when things come to a head, the old paradigm is rejected and a new one takes its place. We now know that a revolution has occurred. With the adoption of the new paradigm, a radical transformation occurs in the way the group's members see things. The revolution has produced a change in world view. As Kuhn (1970) put it:

*Revolutions as Changes of World View*

Examining the record of past research from the vantage of contemporary historiography, the historian of science may be tempted to exclaim that when paradigms change, the world itself changes with them. Led by a new paradigm, scientists adopt new instruments and look in new places. Even more important, during revolutions scientists see new and different things when looking with familiar instruments in places they have looked before. It is rather as if the professional community had been suddenly transported to another planet where familiar objects are seen in a different light and are joined by unfamiliar ones as well. Of course, nothing of quite that sort does occur; there is no geographical transplantation; outside the laboratory everyday affairs usually continue as before. Nevertheless, paradigm changes do cause scientists to see the world of their research-engagement differently. In so far as their only recourse to that world is through what they see and do, we may want to say that after a revolution scientists are responding to a different world. (p. 111)

Both Kuhn (1970) and Hanson (1958) compare what happens during a paradigm shift to what happens when one looks at such Gestalt configurations as the Rubin drawing in Fig. 8.1. On first inspection, one may see a goblet, which changes into a silhouette of two people staring at each other.

The interesting thing is that, although the stimulus object has not changed, the response has. The viewer of such a drawing is free to alternate between seeing a

FIGURE 8.1.   Rubin's figure. The same geometrical form offers possibilities for two different discriminations, as a goblet or as two people, in silhouette, staring at each other.

goblet and the two faces. But once a scientist has switched the old paradigm for a new one as if by a conversion experience, the new paradigm dominates. With complete abandonment of the old paradigm, The crisis is over, normal science is reinstated, and its practitioners see the world in a new way. Kuhn's analysis of "seeing" demonstrates how our seeings are corrupted by the way we have learned to see things in our past, a fact that warrants our further consideration of this important topic.

## HANSON ON OBSERVATION

According to the common view, scientists observe their raw data in what they think is the "reality out there" and then construct their theories. Hanson (1958) would say that view is wrong. There are no pristine data uncontaminated by our previously acquired beliefs, assumptions, and so forth. All observations are so intertwined with theory that the two cannot be separated. To take an example from Hanson (1958, pp. 5–6), two astronomers, Kepler and Tycho Brahe, are watching the horizon at daybreak. Do they see the same thing when the sun comes up? Consider the fact that Kepler believed the sun to be fixed with the earth rotating around it. But, according to Tycho, the earth was fixed and all the other heavenly bodies rotated around it. Note that their alleged retinal images are the same; yet the two astronomers "see" different things. Therefore, Hanson (1958, p. 7) is justified in saying, "There is more to seeing than meets the eyeball."

Suppose we show Fig. 8.1 to two different observers, one of whom reports seeing only the goblet. The other insists that the only thing to be seen are the two faces staring at each other. Let us ask them to draw what they see. Lo and behold, they produce identical drawings and yet one insists it's a goblet and the other insists that it is two faces staring at each other. Thus, "seeing is a 'theory-laden' undertaking. Observation of x is shaped by prior knowledge of x" (Hanson, 1958, p. 99). If our past experiences did not determine our perceptions, then all we could ever sense would be meaningless splotches of color, light and shade, auditory frequencies and unrecognized odors. Imagine that the two hypothetical viewers of the illustration in Fig. 8.1 should experience a sudden and total amnesia, would they see anything beyond a nonsensical black and white blotch? Apparently, "there is more to seeing than meets the eyeball." In concluding this section, and in anticipation of our projected survey of two competing linguistic theories, we might find it useful to hang on to the following pregnant statement by Hanson (1958): "Why a visual pattern is seen differently is a question for psychology, but that it may be seen differently is important in any examination of the concepts of seeing and observation" (p. 17). Perhaps this pronouncement of Hanson's may help us understand how two observers of people talking to each other can come up with such radically divergent interpretations of what they see.

## OF METAPHORS AND MODELS

"To speak of models in connection with a scientific theory already smacks of the metaphorical" (Max Black, 1962, p. 219).

He's a "tower of strength."                    She's a "wet blanket."
He "pulls his punches."                         Get "a load of this."

### Of Metaphors

According to *The New Columbia Encyclopedia* (Harris & Levey, 1975) a metaphor is "a figure of speech in which one class of things is referred to as if it belonged to another class" (p. 1758). "The ship plows the sea" is a metaphor. Actually, plows plow the land; therefore, the case of the ship moving over the ocean involves make-believe that the action belonging to the plow is also appropriate to the ship's movement.

In everyday discourse, the comparison of a ship to a plow may cause no particular difficulty because, as we say, we know "how to take it" [another metaphor]. But where precise language is called for, as in scientific statement, metaphors may be troublesome. For example, we talk about people being attracted to each other. Right? But when physicists adopt this way of talking about people to talking about bodies in the universe "attracting" each other, we have a metaphor. Now as an aside, when we say that motion and change in nature are due to "attraction" between bodies are we saying any more than that bodies move in a certain way? However, if we overlook that point for the time being and return to the "attraction" metaphor itself, we might speculate that there might not have been any problem if physicists had used a simile instead of a metaphor. Then they would be saying, "You do know how people attract each other, don't you? Well, all bodies in the universe are attracted to each other *like* people are attracted to each other." And we would see in which specific ways two different classes of things are being compared with each other. But, when they omit people with which bodies in the universe are compared, then we forget the comparison class, people. An echo of Turbayne's (1970) troubling statement reminds us that we have been victimized because "the attraction once merely supposed to exist between all bodies in the universe now seems actually there. This metaphor has entered the very marrow of our bones and seems impossible to remove" (p. 103). As Turbayne would say, "At this point, we are not *using* a metaphor. We are *being used* by the metaphor." Make-believe has been transformed into belief.

In sum, then, the uses of metaphor create no problem as long as we know not to take the metaphor literally. The same holds true for the extended metaphor, the model, which we next consider.

## Of Models

The models of airplanes, automobiles or ships that children assemble out of kits, fit the definition of what Black (1962), in his excellent discussion of scientific models and archetypes, calls *scale models*. Usually, they are three-dimensional, more-or-less true to scale miniatures of the original. They are concrete representations of the original, embodying many of its features. Models of the brain, heart, the uterus are common scientific aids in facilitating the understanding of their anatomical counterparts because they imitate the originals. The resemblance between the original and the model is easily established.

Perhaps a still more common scientific model is the type that Black (1962) designates as *analogue models*. The analogue model is more abstract than the scale model. A dissection of this word analogue may help in understanding the term. *Analogue* is defined in dictionaries as something that is similar to something else. Its more familiar sister-term *analogy* is even more helpful by calling attention to the fact that if two things agree with one another in certain respects they will probably agree in others even though they are otherwise unlike. Black (1962) defines an analogue model as "some material object, system or process designed to reproduce as faithfully as possible in some new medium the *structure* or web of relationships in an original" (p. 222).

That the analogue model, just as the scale model, "smacks of the metaphorical" is easily caught from the comparisons that are implied or stated in the foregoing statements. Of course, the class identity of the scale model with its original is missing in the analogue. Nevertheless, the latter must, in some sense, show a point-by-point correspondence with the original, no matter how abstract that correspondence is.

The analogue is the common theoretical model of the sciences. The geneticist's conceptualization of the genes arranged like beads on a string is one convenient example. The double helix is another. The chemist Kekule is said to have dreamed about a snake with its tail in its mouth, which led to his solution of the structure of the benzene molecule in the form of a ring. Another analogue model comes from the physicist's dynamic theory of gases according to which a collection of (plastic) billiard balls in random motion serves as a model for molecules of gas in motion. Note that only the impact and motion of the billiard balls is analogized, not their color, hardness, texture, and so forth. Thus, metaphors exclude, as well as include properties of the thing compared.

## METAPHORS AND MODELS IN PSYCHOLOGY[2]

If metaphors and models are found in physics, chemistry, and biology, why should they not be present in psychology? They are. One of the oldest and most

---

[2]With *model* defined as an *extended metaphor*, my loose usage of the terms is apparent. After all, both are metaphors.

prevalent models incorporated into psychology is the body-mind concept of the human individual. Gilbert Ryle (1949) has done such a thorough job of exposing the concept of "the ghost in the machine" that we need not go into it here. It is only necessary to point out that the body-mind notion is based on the centuries-old view of two worlds, mind and matter. Ryle is most persuasive in his argument that the body-mind concept is only metaphorical and that there are other ways of talking about psychological action.

The body-mind model is not the only use of metaphor in psychology. The term *mental hygiene* suggests that just as there are practices for maintaining bodily health, so there are ways of insuring proper mental health. Much is heard about the medical model that compares such human psychological problems as anxiety, despair, grief, suspicion, and fear as symptoms [sic] of mental illness or mental disease that call for treatment and a mental cure.

The brain is also a rich source of metaphor. At one time the whole nervous system was compared to a hydraulic system of tubes with animal spirits running through them. In a later historical period, as just mentioned, the brain was analogized to a telephone switchboard and a tape recorder, and today it has been understandably metaphorized into a computer with its input and output, storage and retrieval. Metaphors sometimes work both ways as evidenced by the computer's taking on the qualities of a brain. There is a two-way or mutual reinforcement of the metaphor. The brain becomes more and more like a computer and the computer becomes more and more like a brain. Eventually, the brain is not merely *like* a computer; it *is* a computer, at which point we are no longer using a metaphor; we are being used by it.

The use of a metaphor, then, creates no problem as long as we know we are not taking the metaphor literally but only pretend to do so. The same holds for the extended metaphor, the model. As long as we make-believe that a brain is a computer, there may be no problem; but when we mistake the brain *for* a computer, we are in trouble. This happens when we are not aware of presenting the items of one sort in the idioms of another sort. If it is realized that we are representing the facts of one sort as if they belong to another (a ship *plowing* the sea), there is no confusion. The confusion comes, according to Turbayne (1970), when we "mistake, for example, the theory for the fact, the procedure for the process, the myth for history, the model for the thing, and the metaphor for the face of literal truth. Accordingly, to expose a categorical confusion, to explode a myth, to 'undress' a hidden metaphor is . . . to show that these sometimes valuable fusions are actually confusions" (pp. 4–5).

## HOW MODELS MISFIRE

Max Black (1962) draws attention to the mischief that scientific models can cause even in the older sciences. The particular case concerns Maxwell, the renowned 19th century physicist who did pioneering work in the electro-magnetic theory. After deriving precise mathematical formulae, he represented an electrical field in terms of an imaginary incompressible fluid (the ether). He did this only to embellish his mathematical statement as an aid to maintaining contact with the reality, realizing the dangers deriving from premature theory purporting to explain the facts. Here, there is a conservative use of a model (the "ether") with an apparent full awareness of the metaphorical nature of this postulated fluid.

Before long, what happened to Maxwell had happened to many creators of metaphor and model. He gradually got caught up in his own metaphor and came to believe in the literal existence of what had, for him, been previously an imaginary ether. Black tells how Lord Kelvin, a contemporary of Maxwell's, surpassed Maxwell in taking the metaphor of the ether literally, as evidenced by his defining the ether as real matter (Black, 1962, pp. 227–228). Black's comments on the radical switch of both scientists are appropriate:

> There is certainly a vast difference between treating the ether as a mere heuristic convenience as Maxwell's first remarks require, and treating it in Kelvin's fashion as "real matter" having definite—though to be sure, paradoxical—properties independent of our imagination. The difference is between thinking of the electrical field *as if* it were filled with a material medium and thinking of it *as being* such a medium. (p. 228)

Maxwell and Lord Kelvin were gradually victimized by their metaphors. Instead of using metaphors, they were being used by them. Their make-believe was unwittingly transformed into belief. The zealous student of science is likely to suffer a shock reaction when he reads Turbayne's (1970) astounding statement (clothed in the mind-body metaphor): "The metaphysics that still dominates science and enthralls the minds of men is nothing but a metaphor, and a limited one" (p. 6).

## THE LAST WORD ON METAPHORS

Apparently, there is "no way out for us." We must "come to terms" with the "brute" "reality" that the sciences are "shot through" with metaphor. To resort to another metaphor, apparently "the dice are loaded" against "the facts" that scientists deal with. In still another metaphorical sense, in the observation of the subject matter of the sciences, we have "lost our innocence" and can never hope to view the data pristine, with "uncorrupted eyes," because our cultural learnings insist on "following us" to our observations.

One final point on metaphors. How well do metaphors really help us to understand or explain the facts? For example, when we compare brains with computers, do we understand, and can we explain brains more thoroughly than we did before we hit upon that metaphor? Contrariwise, do we really explain computers by means of the brain model? Such questions will be relevant in the ensuing examination and comparison of language with and without consciousness.

## CHOMSKY'S GENERATIVE GRAMMAR

As a prime example of language with consciousness, we turn to the work of one of the most conspicuous and most influential linguists of our time, Noam Chomsky. Unless otherwise specified, the following account of Chomsky's system is confined to his (1975b) *Reflections on Language*. I shall omit reference to Chomsky's technical procedures that he performs as a linguist and focus attention on the psychological underpinnings of his framework. He himself acknowledges a dependency on psychology in the work just referred to (p. 3) and in *Rules and Representations* (Chomsky, 1980, p. 13).

Why study language? Chomsky admits that language may be studied for the elements that make it up, their order and arrangement, their history, function, and so on. But his special interest is in language as "a mirror of mind" (p. 4), hoping thereby to "discover abstract principles that govern its structure and use, principles that are universal by biological necessity and not by mere historical accident, that derive from mental characteristics of the human species" (p. 4).

Elsewhere, Chomsky sees "the language faculty [sic] as a species-specific, genetically-determined property" (p. 79). Again, ". . . we may say that humans are innately endowed with a system of intellectual organization, call it the 'initial state' of the mind." (p. 137). Maturation and "relatively slight exposure" to language, but without specific training permit. . . . a normal child to "effortlessly make use of an intricate structure of specific rules and guiding principles" (p. 4) in speaking to others. Chomsky names this structure represented in the human genotype "universal grammar" (p. 29). The component systems of universal grammar "may be unconscious for the most part and even beyond the reach of conscious introspection" (p. 35). Furthermore, this "abstract cognitive structure, created by an innate faculty of mind, [is] represented in some still-unknown way in the brain" (p. 23). Chomsky admits that "the neural basis of language is pretty much of a mystery, but there can be little doubt that specific neural structures and even gross organization not found in other primates (e.g., lateralization) play a fundamental role" (pp. 40–41). But he believes that "with the progress of science, we may come to know something of the physical representation of the grammar and the language faculty . . ." (p. 36) Until then, the language faculty must be characterized in abstract terms.

Our interest in metaphors and models sensitizes us to a prominent and provocative use of an analogue model that we come upon in Chomsky's (1980, p. 39) *Rules and Representations*. Because its usage throws light on Chomsky's psychological orientation, it deserves our special attention at this point, even though we must consider the topic more fully again later. As background to our examination of his revealing model, note that Chomsky (1980) assumes "the mind to be modular in structure, a system of interacting subsystems that have their own special properties" (p. 89). Also, there are other "faculties of mind" such as the "number faculty." Even facial recognition might be "represented in the initial state, as a biologically determined innate property" (Chomsky, 1980, p. 145). Chomsky frequently refers to the mind as a collection of organs (p. 89) much like the biological organs, such as heart, liver and kidneys. He pushes this metaphor hard as when he argues that the organs composing the mind do not have to learn to function any more than the heart must learn how to beat. According to him, all are pre-programmed to do their job and require only the attainment of the appropriate stage of maturation or the slight triggering of environmental cues to manifest themselves.

## CHOMSKY'S PHILOSOPHICAL LINEAGE

At this juncture, we digress briefly in order to trace Chomsky's intellectual ancestry to its philosophical source. There are two ancient and contradictory schools of philosophy, i.e., empiricism and rationalism. According to empiricists, all knowledge is derived from experience. Empiricists reject the existence of innate ideas. For them, ideas and beliefs have only one source, i.e., experience. According to an eminent empiricist, John Locke (1632–1704) babies are born into the world with a mind like a blank sheet of white paper upon which will be written all the mind's contents and the resulting mind's reflections on those contents. Nothing is innate (Adams, 1975a, p. 63).

From what we already know about Chomsky, we would hardly classify him with empiricists. In fact, he identifies himself with such men as Descartes (1596–1650), and Leibniz (1646–1716), illustrious exponents of rationalism. In contrast to empiricists, rationalists believe that reason alone can come to understand reality. Here is how Chomsky (1975a) states the case for rationalism:

> The general character of knowledge, the categories in which it is expressed or internally represented, and the basic principles that underlie it, are determined by the nature of the mind. . . . The role of experience is only to cause the innate schematism to be activated, and then to be differentiated and specified in a particular manner. (p. 129)

How closely Chomsky's view resembles those of Descartes is brought out by Adams (1975b, p. 76). We think, according to Descartes, that our ideas of external objects are produced by those objects, Not so. The external objects just provide an occasion "to form these ideas, by means of an innate faculty, at this time rather than at another'' (p. 76). The mind, then, innately, ''possesses specific predisposition to form, on appropriate stimulation, all the ideas of sensible qualities which it is capable of having'' (Adams, 1975a, p. 77). Chomsky shares the traditional rationalist attribution of numerous innate powers to the mind. Therefore, for him, stimuli play a trivial role because, from the very start, the mind is set to react in certain definite ways. It comes, as it were, prepackaged with all it will ever need to get on in the world. It should be apparent, too, that Chomsky's approach to language relies on consciousness as well as the unconscious. Finally, the point must be stressed that Chomsky's intellectual heritage can be traced to Descartes. Admittedly, the two views are not identical. For example, Descartes believes in a unified mind whereas Chomsky endows the mind with separate and diverse faculties or powers (Chomsky, 1980, p. 30). Nevertheless, the basic resemblance between the two systems is close enough to deserve Piattelli-Palmarini's (1980, p. xxxii) characterization of Chomsky as a ''Cartesian anachronism.''

## LANGUAGE WITHOUT CONSCIOUSNESS

Here is the scenario: The proverbial man from Mars somehow manages to find himself inside an operating room of an Earthly hospital. He is viewing a surgical operation in progress. The surgeon utters the single word, ''Scalpel''; instantly, a nurse places a shining instrument into the surgeon's hand. Next, as the surgeon probes into the abdomen of her patient, she executes a movement of the head to one side, whereupon we see the nurse applying a towel to the surgeon's sweaty brow. As the operation proceeds, we see the surgeon silently carry out a scissors-like movement of the index and second finger of her hand and, now, the nurse hands the surgeon a pair of suture scissors.

Assume that the visitor from another planet remains in the operating room and observes the (just mentioned) incidents repeated a number of times. At some point, can we imagine his saying, ''By Jupiter, I've got it. I understand what's going on and I can even predict what will happen, under the three different conditions. I've seen it all!''

Now, envision Chomsky's chance presence in that same operating room. He hears the visitor's remarks and protests, ''But, in addition to what you observed, there are unobservable goings-on in the surgeon's and nurse's consciousness and even in their unconscious. This is the way to explain what you observed.''

The visitor from Mars asks: ''Well, if such goings-on are unobservable, how do you know they are there?''

Chomsky: ''We have to infer them.''

Visitor from Mars: ''But, it seems to me that, if you only infer such imaginary happenings from what you did observe, you can't turn right around and use them to explain the observables. Hasn't one of your notable philosophers of science,

Kuhn (1961, p. 177) declared that 'Merely conceivable theories are not among the options open to the practicing scientist'? And where do you get this consciousness stuff?''

Chomsky: "Well, it has been around at least since the time of Descartes over 300 years ago. And to some of us, even today, it seems real."

Martian visitor: "Don't you know that "nothing 'more real' than the observable is secured by using the word 'real' or by peering for something behind or beyond the observable to which to apply the name" (Dewey & Bentley, 1949, p. 87) What I observed in the operating room was all I needed to understand the communication that took place between the surgeon and the nurse."

## AN INTERBEHAVIORAL ACCOUNT OF
## PSYCHOLOGICAL LANGUAGE

The preceding dialogue paves the way for an account of the interbehavioral theory of language, a theory developed by J. R. Kantor (1977). According to the interbehaviorist here is what happened in the operating room. Above all else, we must analyze, separately, the speaker's and hearer's roles in the linguistic event. Beginning with the surgeon's speaking, we note that, when she utters the word "scalpel," she is reacting to two things at the same time: (a) to the assisting nurse and (b) to the requisite scalpel. The nurse also is brought into relationship with two factors: (a) the speaking surgeon and (b) the adjacent scalpel. This is why, for Kantor (1977, pp. 61–62), the action is labeled referential and bistimulational.

How does the incident involving the sweaty brow and suture scissors fit in here? According to Kantor (1977, p. 6), gestures are just as important as verbal utterances when they are referential and bistimulational. In the sweaty brow situation, the surgeon could have said to the assisting nurse, "Please reach for that towel right there and wipe my forehead with it." Instead, with considerable economy, the surgeon made the by-now-familiar head movement and it worked. From her part, the surgeon's head action referred the nurse to the sweaty brow and to the towel nearby. The suture scissors incident fits the same bistimulational referential paradigm.

We must emphasize that gestures make their strongest claim to recognition as referential language when they do the same job as verbal utterances. It is hardly necessary to point out that the sign language of the deaf is a complete substitute for normal spoken language. Also, Farb (1974, pp. 208–209) reports that during the 19th century, a rich sign language flourished among the scattered American Indian tribes of the North American plains. That sign language could handle specific details without true nouns, verbs, or adjectives (to the utter frustration of the structural linguist). This concludes the interbehaviorist's explanation of what happens when people talk. Next, we move on to a report of the traditional analysis of language in terms of mind and consciousness.

FIGURE 8.2.  A scene in a hospital operating room illustrating the traditional theory of language. An idea in the surgeon's mind is said to activate nerves to cause the surgeon's speech organs to utter the word, scalpel. Sound waves impinge on the nurse's ears, which carry the message up into her brain, which in turn, evoke an idea of scalpel in the nurse's mind.

## THE TRADITONAL ACCOUNT OF LANGUAGE

According to a venerable mentalistic theory, language involves a complex chain of events, which may be made clearer by reference to Fig. 8.2. If we take again the incident in the operating room, this is what is alleged to take place. The drama begins with an idea in the surgeon's mind, presumably an idea of how beneficial it would be for her to have a scalpel in her hand. The idea in the mind activates nerves in the surgeon's brain. The nerves direct the vocal organs to form the word "scalpel." Now the air waves enter the picture; they convey the sound pattern to the nurses' ears. From there, the nervous pathways convey a message to the appropriate brain centers that produce the idea that a scalpel is called for. A similar routine is used to explain extended interchanges between nurse and surgeon.

## CRITICISM OF THE TRADITIONAL THEORY

Such a theory is congruent with Chomsky's writings. He talks about language in terms of mind and brain and often identifies one with the other (e.g., Chomsky, 1980, p. 31), although he admits that how they interact has not yet been solved. An important point about the explanation of language represented in Fig. 8.2 is that no one has as yet shown how the transformations of mind, nerve, physical sound, back to nerve and mind take place. They are entirely imaginary, purely conceptual. We already know what scientific standing "purely conceptual" explanations deserve. Dewey's (1929) statement adds additional support to this point in the following quotation: "The more evident and observable is thus 'explained' in terms of the obscure, the obscurity being hidden from view because of habits that have the weight of tradition behind them" (p. 229).

Consider another point concerning theoretical explanations that can be arranged in a spectrum from concrete to abstract. How can one miss the interbehavioral theory's close contact with the linguistic drama occurring in the operating room? It gives full credit to the dynamic, ongoing event.

As for Chomsky's analytic method, his main concern is with words, words, words, as if they had a separate existence of their own. His business is with the order of words that constitutes a grammatical sentence or an ungrammatical one. As such, he deals with the dead husks of the referential action of the speaker-hearer transaction, arranging or rearranging them in patterns that he pronounces as grammatical or ungrammatical.

McCawley (1979, p. 235), realizing Chomsky's arbitrariness in declaring sentences as grammatical or ungrammatical, offers the following sentences that sound like utter nonsense when taken out of contexts, as our scenario of the operating room, but that are acceptable in specific situations. For example, the statement, "Kissinger conjectures poached," sounds like something out of Gertrude Stein, but, as soon as we are told that the statement is in answer to the question: "Does anyone know how President Ford likes his eggs?" the statement, "Kissinger conjectures poached," makes good sense. One must agree with McCawley's (1979) perceptive statement:

> The division of sentences into "grammatical" and "ungrammatical" is not so much a distinction among sentences as a distinction among sources of unacceptability, a distinction which seems to me to tell one more about the linguist than about the language. (p. 281)

Why such polar assessments of a sentence? The answer lies in the different approaches of the two linguists. By including the context or situation in which the preceding odd sentence is embedded, McCawley has included more of the behavioral event in which that sentence worked. But in doing so, McCawley acknowledges the failure of the linguist's strict adherence to analysis of "a string of words," the by-products of speaking-hearing events. There is more to speaking and to hearing speech than a string of words. As for Chomsky, although claiming that linguistics is a branch of cognitive psychology, he deals with it as if it were autonomous. Therefore, handling words torn apart from speaking-hearing organisms, he can easily declare the odd, out-of-context sentence above as "ungrammatical." In such cases, he functions much like the arbiter of etiquette who pronounces which acts are correct and which are incorrect. As an aside, it would be interesting to determine how pervasively ungrammatical sentences, such as, "I ain't got nobody" would be heard in the land, even among the educated.

Once words are split off as if they had a disembodied existence, separate from the speaker-hearer transaction, the problem of meaning rears its ugly head. Chomsky (1980, pp. 61, 109–120) struggles valiantly with the problem. In one place, he refers to two entities, the word or "form," and "meaning," which are presumably brought together by "representations" attributed to the mind's "system of grammatical competence." Obscure? Of course, because these two are among other imaginary entities with which Chomsky populates the mind. By contrast, the interbehavioral theory of language has no special problem with meaning. Note that speaking is always "about something." Therefore, the meaning of the surgeon's "scalpel" is found in the nurse's reaction to the near-by instrument. By keeping the entire speaker-hearer situation intact during analysis, "meaning" can be literally observed as an aspect of the event before us. By splitting off word and meaning and the two from each other, Chomsky creates the problem for himself of gluing the two together again.

## PARADIGMS, METAPHORS, AND MODELS AGAIN

Our earlier, fairly extensive account of paradigms, metaphors, and models requires only a wrap-up at this point. That Chomsky acknowledges a need for models is revealed on page 1 of *Rules and Representations* (Chomsky, 1980). "Mind and Body" as a paradigm is disclosed in the very first chapter's title of the same work. His assumption of "interior mental objects" (Chomsky, 1980, p. 13) to explain language acquisition and use is stated explicitly. On page 14 of the same work, we are introduced to the brain's "images that share fundamental properties with pictorial representations." On the same page, we are introduced to two metaphors, (a) "the brain stores images," and (b) "the brain does computation." In other words, the brain becomes a container for storable objects and a machine for carrying out computations. One wants to protest, But, Professor Chomsky, these are *only* metaphors! It would be a dreary, uneconomical and unnecessary task to track down each of the aforementioned references, and many others scattered throughout Chomsky's works, to their metaphorical correlate.

And, now, in order to examine Chomsky's approach from still another angle, we need to have at our disposal, Dewey and Bentley's terms, *selfaction, interaction* and *transaction*. Chomsky's system is selfactional. What does this mean? According to Dewey and Bentley (1949), selfaction is seen in descriptions or explanations that view behavior as *originating* within the organism or the organism's alleged mind. According to Chomsky, the mind or the modular mind's faculties act under their own powers as a genetic endowment with very little assist from the environment. It is inevitable that such a procedure results in (verbally) endowing the organism with various entities (consciousness, facial recognition faculty, number faculty and so on). This is a theoretical burden that the organism is asked to carry alone.

In my opinion, science moved forward when it saw a gravitating object, not as something that was propelled to earth because of an alleged force or power within it, but as an interaction between earth and object. Stimulus-response psychology left Chomsky behind some time ago. For the most part, main stream psychology fits the interactional paradigm with its interest in studying the two factors, stimulus-response in causal interconnection.

Interbehavioral theory works with a still broader paradigm than that demonstrated in stimulus-response psychology. It does not ignore these two variables, but views them as of only focal interest. They are seen as aspects of events or occurrences that must be viewed as an inseparable whole including setting factors, media of contact, and so on. Events themselves are held together in their historical flow. The term *situation* is useful if it points to the psychological happening in all its fulness or context. Another term, *field,* is compatible with an interbehavioral view by calling attention to the cluster of connected variables as found in inquiry. It refers to the entire complex process of mutually connected things and their relations and includes the observer in the transaction. The term *transaction* is congenial with the interbehavioral approach to language as well as other behaviors.

What are the advantages of such a system? When psychological events are said to be encapsulated within the skin of an organism, the only resort is to imagine mental or hypothetical neurological goings-on that have not been substantiated because only anatomical and physiological processes can be found there. Therefore, one is forced to invent consciousness, and other fictions. There is no room or need for consciousness in the broadened view of the interbehaviorist who localizes psychological occurrences beyond the organism's skin within the total field of participating factors. In such a view the organism is dethroned from its earlier lofty position much as Earth was demoted in the broader view of astronomy achieved by Copernicus. All of the variables together share the explanatory burden, and not the organism solo.

## WHAT IS THE SOLUTION?

There is only one possibility for a modification of Chomsky's viewpoint and that lies in changing an unwavering belief in his "marrow-embedded" metaphors and paradigms for a radically different world-view. First we must point out that he has had no guarantee of seeing linguistic phenomena with vision unadulterated by Cartesian thinking. Only a gestalt switch or paradigm change from a selfactional paradigm can enable one to see the world a new way. And, in line with Hanson's (1958, p. 99) admonition, we all must remind ourselves that "seeing is a theory-laden undertaking. Observation of x is shaped by prior knowledge of x" (p. 99).

As a fitting conclusion to this section, and as a powerful reminder to us all, we should heed the following caution from Hanson (1958):

> Given the *same* world, it might have been construed differently. We might have spoken of it, thought of it, perceived it differently. Perhaps facts are somehow moulded by the logical forms of the fact-stating language. Perhaps these provide a 'mould' in terms of which the world coagulates for us in definite ways. (p. 36)

If the same world coagulates for different investigators in different ways, does that make the situation hopeless? No. There are tests for competing ways of understanding the world. As a suggestion, those theories should get close scrutiny that are comprehensive but which obey the law of parsimony. This is the type of theory that Einstein (Feuer, 1974, p. 356) aimed for with his "faith in the simplicity, i.e., intelligibility of nature." Theories deserve weighty consideration when they don't require patching up with artificial, ad hoc assumptions. Also theories that make sense of the data instead of creating "problems and mysteries" (Chomsky, 1975a, pp. 137ff.) deserve preferential treatment. Finally, as Feuer (1974) points out, the history of science is marked by heroic renunciations such as the "abandonment of the desire for teleological explanations, the 'why' of things, in favor of a modest satisfaction with descriptive uniformities, the 'how' of things" (p. 352). This chapter has attempted to understand the how and not the way of speaking-hearing humans. At least, here are some criteria for choosing between language with, or without, consciousness.

## SCHNEIRLA AND THE CONCEPT OF INTEGRATIVE LEVELS

And now, our final question: How does all the foregoing discussion relate to Schneirla's approach to behavior? As far as selfaction is concerned, Schneirla's concept of integrative levels enabled him to detect and reject selfactional "powers" resident within the organism. As early as 1949, he spurned the use of such hypothetical terms as "mind," "mental faculties," "instinct," and "innate releasing mechanisms," considering each as " 'a little man inside,' endowed a priori with all the properties to be explained" (Schneirla, 1972a, 1972b, p. 225). Schneirla was equally opposed to easy analogies, "reification of concepts into presumed forces," and "fallacies of metaphor" applied across a whole range of species "so loosely that the essential similarities are blurred and the important differences among capacity levels confused or ignored" (Schneirla, 1972a, 1972b, p. 208).

As for hereditary influences on behavior, he did not see behavior as encapsulated within genes ready to spring forth at the right moment; instead, he viewed genes themselves "in intimate association with the developmental context." Schneirla realized that preoccupation with a presumed native predetermination of behavior exposed one to overlook proper controls or significant environmental variables. In facing the problem of the relationship between the molar and molecular levels, Schneirla (1972a, 1972b, p. 259) states that "although the principles for *the molecular* are basic to the molar level, *the molar* requires operations in investigation and theory beyond the specific terms of the molecular." This statement places Schneirla in opposition to reductionistic procedures, although such statements as the following raise questions. In describing the role of the nervous system, Schneirla (1972a, 1972b, p. 285) states "In addition to neural trace effects, or *fixation,* there is the capacity of advanced neural systems for *correlation,* or the organization of trace effects." And, in the same work, why the *two* terms in the phrase, "the behavior and psychology of animals" (p. 259)? Are there two different referents for these terms?

On a matter of closer relevance to the topic of my paper, i.e., language, I find Schneirla largely silent. This is understandable as soon as one realizes that Schneirla is a comparative psychologist. As such, his survey embraces a wide range of animal species and, let's face it, how often does one stumble across linguistic responses in protozoa, fish, birds, or rats? On this score, his apparent neglect must be pardoned, and, therefore, my chapter must stand on its own without support from Schneirla.

## REFERENCES

Adams, R. M. (1975a). The Locke-Leibniz debate. In S. P. Stich (Ed.), *Innate ideas.* Berkeley: University of California Press.

Adams, R. M. (1975b). Where do our ideas come from? In S. P. Stich (Ed.), *Innate ideas.* Berkeley: University of California Press.

Black, M. (1962). *Models and metaphors.* Ithaca, NY: Cornell University Press.

Chomsky, N. (1975a). Recent contributions to the theory of innate ideas. In S. P. Stich (Ed.), *Innate ideas.* Berkeley: University of California Press.

Chomsky, N. (1975b). *Reflections on language.* New York: Pantheon Books.

Chomsky, N. (1980). *Rules and representations.* New York: Columbia University Press.

Dewey, J. (1929). *The Quest for certainty: A study of the relation of knowledge and action.* New York: Milton, Balch & Company.

Dewey, J., & Bentley, A. F. (1949). *Knowing and the known.* Boston, MA: Beacon Press.

Farb, P. (1974). *Word Play: What happens when people talk.* New York: Knopf.

Feuer, L. S. (1974). *Einstein and the generations of science.* New York: Basic Books.

Hanson, N. R. (1958). *Patterns of discovery.* Cambridge, MA: Cambridge University Press.

Harris, W. H., & Levey, J. S. (Eds.). (1975). *The New Columbia Encyclopedia.* New York: Columbia University Press.

Kantor, J. R. (1969). *The scientific evolution of psychology* (Vol. 2). Chicago: Principia Press.

Kantor, J. R. (1977). *Psychological linguistics.* Chicago: Principia Press.

Kuhn, T. S. (1961). The function of measurement in modern physical science. *Isis, 52,* 161–193.

Kuhn, T. S. (1970). *The structure of scientific revolutions* (2nd. Ed. enlarged). Chicago: University of Chicago Press.

Kuhn, T. S. (1977). Second thoughts on paradigms. In F. W. Suppe (Ed.), *The structure of scientific theories* (2nd. Ed.). Urbana: University of Illinois Press.

McCawley, J. D. (1979). *Adverbs, vowels, and other objects of wonder.* Chicago: University of Chicago Press.

Piattelli-Palmarini, M. (1980). *Language and learning. The debate between Jean Piaget and Noam Chomsky.* Cambridge, MA: Harvard University Press.

Ryle, G. (1949). *The concept of mind.* New York: Barnes & Noble.

Schneirla, T. C. (1972a). Levels in the psychological capacities of animals. In L. R. Aranson, E. Tobach, J. S. Rosenblatt & D. S. Lehrman. (Eds.), *Selected writings of T. C. Schneirla* (pp. 199–237). San Francisco: W. H. Freeman. (Originally published in 1949)

Schneirla, T. C. (1972b). The concept of development in comparative psychology. In L. R. Aranson, E. Tobach, J. S. Rosenblatt & D. S. Lehrman (Eds.), *Selected writings of T. C. Schneirla* (pp. 260–294). San Francisco: W. H. Freeman. (Originally published in 1957).

Turbayne, C. M. (1970). *The myth of metaphor* (Rev. Ed.). Columbia, SC: University of South Carolina Press.

Webb, W. B. (1981). The return of consciousness. In L. T. Benjamin, Jr. (Ed.), *The G. Stanley Hall Lecture Series,* Vol. 1. (pp. 133–152). Washington, DC: American Psychological Association.

# 9

# Materialism and Reductionism in the Study of Animal Consciousness

Garland E. Allen
*Washington University*

## INTRODUCTION

When Ethel Tobach and Gary Greenberg first invited me to attend the symposium on which this volume is based, and give an introductory presentation, I accepted with considerable trepidation. The first question I asked myself was what could I, as an historian of science, have to say to a group of psychologists and ethologists. I was handicapped by not knowing first-hand much of the primary literature in contemporary psychology and ethology. I was ignorant of the fact that there was even a controversy at the moment about the issue of animal consciousness, or what the nature of that controversy was. I was prevailed upon, however, and agreed to present a philosophical/historical overview that might provide some focus to problems recurring in these areas for generations. I did not hope to provide any answers, but at least to present some fresh views that might clarify some of the obviously knotty philosophical problems inherent in trying to understand how animals perceive the world, think, and develop consciousness.

To the extent that I have gotten into the literature of the field as a result of this assignment, I have already encountered a number of fascinating issues. For example, there are major philosophical questions: What are the premises on which the investigation of animal consciousness are based? What are the definitions that are used (such as consciousness, awareness, mind, etc.)? What is the fundamental world view which lies behind posing the question at all? These questions all touch on certain philosophical biases that determine the kinds of evidence collected, the kinds of answers expected, and the kinds of answers that are deemed acceptable.

In addition to philosophical, there are also historical and sociological questions: Why is the issue of animal consciousness becoming so prominent in the fields of ethology and psychology today? What are some of the political and social assumptions behind the study of animal consciousness? How can examination of those assumptions and implications help us to avoid the pitfalls that are all too common in any area of scientific research dealing with aspects of human behavior and society? And finally, how is the study of animal awareness related to those currently controversial subjects such as human sociobiology?

It occurred to me that by looking at the philosophical issues on the one hand, and the socio-political issues on the other, I might be able to bring my experience as an historian of science to bear on the topic at hand. I must emphasize, however, that I approach this subject as an outsider to the field of either animal or human behavior. Although a lack of experience can sometimes have a salutary effect in producing a fresh look, it more frequently can lead to an appalling naiveté. I hope 1 am at least moderately aware of when I am about to trespass in ignorance.

We may well ask why it is important to raise philosophical and socio-historical questions about current scientific research. If the history and philosophy of science have anything to contribute to current scientific research, it is that they force us to go back to the very roots of our thought processes. It is all too easy to get involved in new techniques, new methodologies, and highly specific questions, yet fail to ask some of the most basic questions on which any investigation is based. For example, the study of animal behavior has always been marred with problems of anthropomorphism, ethnocentrism, and various sorts of cultural biases. In a similar way, theories of animal behavior have also been guilty of leading to self-fulfilling prophecies. By using the very language of human behavior and human society to describe animal interactions and animal societies, it has then been claimed that animals have similar social organization to humans (for example, the "class" groupings of social insects); in a very circular way this fallacy has led to the argument that a class society is therefore *natural* for human beings. Indeed, the whole notion of "societies" of other organisms has been tinged by the very assumptions we bring from our own special life as social organisms. And yet, the subject of animal consciousness presents a number of exciting questions that *can* be approached in a meaningful historical or philosophical way. However, to make any progress in this area, I argue we must be conscious of where the fruitful directions for investigation might lie, and, conversely, where the philosophical and methodological pitfalls might entrap us.

## THE PHILOSOPHICAL AND METHODOLOGICAL
## PROBLEMS: AN OVERVIEW

In gaining an introduction to the field of animal awareness, I have relied most heavily on Donald Griffin's (1981) *The Question of Animal Awareness*. For alternative views, I have also used review articles by Charles Snowden (1983) and David Premack (1981), as well as papers by Gary Greenberg (1984) and Ethel Tobach (Tobach & Greenberg, 1984). As an example of what seems to be a predominant, or highly influential trend among the various current schools of research in animal consciousness, I begin with a discussion of Griffin's book. Unless I am greatly misinformed, it represents one of the seminal and still mainstream works in the field.

In Griffin's work I have discerned five lines of reasoning on which the argument for animal awareness is based.

1. First, and central to Griffin's book's entire thesis (see the subtitle), is the quantitative continuity argument. This is the idea that because a quantitative gradient in anatomical, physiological, and molecular structure seems to extend from various lower vertebrates to the primates (including humans), a similar gradient must exist in mental terms, including degrees of consciousness, as well. Griffin and others emphasize the fact that because there is less than 1% difference between human DNA and that of several species of great ape, there might also be a similar quantitative continuity in mental characteristics between the other primates and humans. By stressing the importance of continuity, or mere quantitative differences between species, Griffin argues that human beings are only more complex versions of chimpanzees, or chipping sparrows; whereas he recognizes that human thought processes are certainly more complex than those of other species, Griffin makes a strong argument that the rudiments are there in quantitative form in various lower animals.

2. The second argument is really a variation of the first, but occurs in a more specific form. It is what I call the neurological continuity argument. Here, Griffin argues that because of neuroanatomical similarities (brain symmetry/assymmetry, particular neuronal hook-ups, relative sizes of portions of the brain) between lower vertebrates, other primates, and humans, there must also be similarity of function, including cognition and, therefore, conscious awareness. Although in reality a variety of the first assumption, the neurological argument deserves special recognition because it draws heavily on recent advances in neurobiology, especially the increasingly detailed knowledge of synaptic organization in the vertebrate nervous system. At first glance, the neurobiological argument is powerful, inasmuch as the center of conscious awareness in any animal must reside in the nervous system and brain, and, therefore, it would appear that the more structural similarity in nervous systems, the more functional similarity in behavior and cognition, between species.

3. A third line of reasoning is what I refer to as the communication, or linguistic argument. This is a particularly complex subject, technically and philosophically, involving the whole science and history of linguistics. The point is basically this: many animals, from bees with their waggle dances, to birds with their songs and baboon troops with their warning signals, have communication systems that convey different amounts and kinds of information (baboon communication can distinguish, for example, between the presence of a prey and a

predator, or between general emotional states such as anger, pleasure, or pain). In varying quantitative degrees these animal communication systems contain the rudiments of the complex and more versatile language system of human beings. Since, therefore, human language systems have traditionally been taken to imply conscious awareness, by discovering language homologies in lower animals, it is logical to conclude that, to lesser degrees, animals also have conscious awareness.

4. A fourth line of reasoning is implicit in the third: it is what I call the Darwinian, or evolutionary gradualism argument. If conscious awareness in lower animals provides some selective advantage, however minute such (inherited) tendencies toward awareness are, they would have been preserved by natural selection over a long period of animal evolution. By the gradual accumulation of many such minute variations, the high degree of consciousness found in human beings could have evolved from the sorts of rudimentary consciousness found in lower animals today. The evolution of awareness thus might present a phylogenetic pattern much like the evolution of the forelimbs or the molars of the horse from *Eohippus* through *Pliohippus* to modern *Equus*. It is the gradual accumulation of elements contributing to awareness (measured usually through linguistic capabilities), in a Darwinian sense, that produces the quantitative evolutionary continuum stretching between lower animal mental functions and our own.

5. Fifth and last, Griffin invokes what I call the anthropocentrism argument: that is, the notion that it is simply an expression of human conceit to think we are the only beings with mental experiences, awareness of our own existence, and of our past and future. Griffin says that we must shed that bias and look at animals as potentially conscious beings rather than reject the notion out of hand. We as humans might want to look at animals as if they are capable of consciousness in the way we are. While not arguing that human beings are the same as, or only slightly different, from animals in mental quality, Griffin does suggest that anthropocentpism has blinded us to the possible qualities of consciousness that may exist, in whatever rudimentary form, in lower animals.

Although there is some truth in all of these views, I see behind them all a common set of philosophical problems that, in my view, limit significantly the logical position that Griffin tries to maintain.

One of the most prevalent problems seems to be definitions, or the lack thereof, regarding basic terms like "consciousness," or "awareness." Throughout the literature of animal awareness, the terms "consciousness" and "awareness" are used interchangeably, although each term can mean several different things. Because they are central concepts to the pursuit of the field, the lack of clear definition introduces a vast array of confusions into the subject from the outset. For example, in common usage, the term *consciousness* can have at least four different meanings: (a) A state of being conscious and receptive to outside stimuli, in the sense of being awake (as opposed to being asleep or "unconscious"). Clearly, this is the least interesting and significant definition for Griffin and students of animal consciousness because there is little to be gained in knowledge of human and other vertebrate behavior to know that all vertebrates go to sleep, or can be knocked unconscious by a blow on the head. This meaning has one important attribute, however, that should not be overlooked, especially in comparison to the other meanings listed below: it can be relatively easily and objectively measured. (b) A state of awareness of objects and phenomena in the environment—that is, consciousness in the sense that an organism shows it can recognize one object or situation as the same or different from another. This use of "consciousness" is based on the idea of sensory reception and response—humans for example are not conscious of polarized light whereas honeybees are. As with the first definition, this one has the prospects of being measurable, to some degree, and thus amenable to experimental study. (c) A state of recognizing explicitly that one exists as a being separate from other beings, of the same or different kinds. This definition would discriminate between a state of implicit and explicit awareness: for example, two elk may spar in a mating ritual in a way that seems superficially like two men sparring in a boxing match or fistfight; but one would not necessarily deduce from this observation that the two pairs of organisms are aware of their own individual existence in the same way. Unlike definitions (a) and (b), definition (c) becomes almost impossible to investigate experimentally or objectively in any species that does not possess language. And finally, (d) A state of explicit knowledge about one's own past and future in the sense that we might say someone is "conscious" or "aware" of the motivations behind, or consequences of, their behavior. This meaning of the term "consciousness" specifically refers to the ability to abstract from the past or project abstractly toward the future in a conscious or explicit way (for example, when we say someone is "conscious of what they are doing"). Like definition (c), definition (d) is virtually impossible to investigate experimentally or objectively in any species that does not possess complex, syntactical language systems. In addition to the four previous definitions, there is a fifth: (e) the psychological meaning of "conscious" as opposed to "subconscious" (including everything from ESP to Freudian sub-conscious). I have purposely avoided including this definition because it is fearfully elusive. In some ways it might seem to be covered by definition (d), yet there is something hauntingly different about this meaning; it is not simply another form of remembering the past or learning from past experience and projecting onto the future. With all of the different meanings, and with no clear guidelines offered by which to determine which meaning of the word "consciousness" is being used at any one time, it is little wonder that Griffin's basic idea—that animal consciousness exists—cannot be taken as self-evident.

As if defining the central concept of consciousness were not problem enough, Griffin goes on to introduce a series of additional terms for which he also offers no rigorous definitions. For example, how does one define language? Is there a difference between a communication signal (e.g. baboon warning signals) and language? Are communication systems all variations of the same graded pattern or are there real qualitative differences between simple animal communication systems and human languages? Other terms that are equally poorly defined include mind, animal belief and feeling (what does it mean to say that an animal "believes" or "feels"—Griffin uses these terms many times).

Second, there are methodological problems. How do we determine what an animal really thinks or its "intent"? Is there a way to really understand that? How do we communicate with animals at all? Or, how do we communicate with animals without falling into what is called the "Clever Hans" trap[1]—a real experimental artifact, but one that is often difficult for us to either recognize or control? After all, to investigate consciousness we must establish a two-way communication with animals. In addition, there is the question of experimental rigor. For example, how does one design an experiment to discriminate between a hypothesis that explains a mother baboon's protection of her offspring on the basis of conscious intent, as opposed to blind instinct? A third kind of philosophical problem arises out of the peculiar relationship in human beings between language and conscious thought. Can we have thought without language? Have you ever tried to put yourself in the position of never having learned a language? How would your thought processes work? Obviously you would think, respond, be able to cope with the environment, but what would it be like to think without language? Does it make any sense to talk about conscious thought without a language system? This gets dangerously close to Wittgenstein's central problem: what is meaning and how does language acquire meaning? That is something I won't dare get into, but I raise it to show how important such issues are to even asking the larger questions about animal awareness; grappling with sophisticated philosophy cannot be passed off as something scientifically irrelevant. Failure to be more rigorous in my mind vitiates all the rest of the enterprise.

Having raised, but not resolved, these definitional problems, in the remainder of this chapter I would like to focus on what I see as the most basic philosophical and methodological issue underlying the entire study of animal awareness: a prevailing mechanistic materialist and reductionist philosophy. It is precisely the failure of Griffin and others, that they approach the problem from a mechanistic and reductionistic point of view, and do not seem to understand the importance of the concept of levels of organization, and, more fundamentally, of the philosophy of dialectical materialism.

---

[1] "Clever Hans" refers to the example of a horse (named Hans) who was apparently trained to count; when his trainer would say "four plus two" the horse would tap his foot six times, and when the trainer would say six plus eight" Hans would tap his foot fourteen times, and so on. It was finally found that the horse was picking up unconsciously transmitted cues from the trainer and was not really adding in the sense that we learn to add at all.

## MECHANISTIC AND DIALECTICAL MATERIALISM

I start by distinguishing between mechanistic and dialectical materialist philosophy as ways of approaching the question of animal consciousness. I show how the mechanistic approach has historically led, and continues to lead, to reductionist questions (and reductionist answers), while the dialectical approach avoids some of those pitfalls and leads to perhaps more significant questions and answers. I also show how the dialectical approach leads to appreciation of levels of integration as something more than the lip service that is often paid to interactive or "emergent" phenomena, and that, in fact, it might actually be used heuristically to guide research. Since both dialectical and mechanistic materialism as forms of philosophical materialism, are often contrasted with idealism, a brief discussion of the latter will be useful at this point.

Idealism or non-materialism as some philosophers would prefer to call it, is historically the older view. deriving from classical and medieval philosophy (especially Platonism). Idealism in philosophy is basically the notion that ideas are primary, meaning that it is ideas that are the primary movers of human destiny and contribute to development and change within the material world. Material reality usually follows from ideas, whereas ideas follow less generally from material reality. Idealism is essentially metaphysical, that is, it is a belief in some non-material forces beyond human ken (*meta* = beyond, *physics* = the physical); with it is associated the notion that because there are non-material forces that cannot be investigated by the sense perceptions with which humans are equipped, that therefore there are some things that we can never *in principle* know. Most religions ultimately fall back on *idealism:* for example, the idea that the world was created by God, by some metaphysical force, some mystical or occult quality that human beings by definition cannot understand or know. As Plato put it, the ideas of physical reality originated in the mind of God, and were projected onto material reality. The belief that animals have souls or mystical qualities of perception, or the existence of a vital force that is non-material and differentiates living from non-living organisms, are examples of philosophical idealism in the history of western science.

The materialistic position in general differs from idealism in quite striking ways. It emphasizes the primacy of material reality, that is, arguing that in the long run, our contact with the material world fashions our ideas and our mental constructs. We try to perceive and reconstruct in our mind and communicate to each other views of the world based on our contact with that material reality in which we find ourselves living. In a materialist philosophical system, there is no need for metaphysical forces or occult causes. Because there are no mystical, metaphysical forces involved in the operation of the world, human beings can theoretically understand anything. That is, there is nothing that is in itself essentially beyond the possibility of human understanding. It doesn't mean, of course, that human beings can ever expect to know everything there is to know, or that there is any such thing as perfect knowledge; but it does say that there is nothing which is inherently unknowable. The question of how much we can expect to understand has been a particularly important issue, especially in biology over the centuries. The materialist position holds that one can understand the function of organisms by understanding their physical and chemical (i.e. material) properties not by invoking an *élan vital,* a vital force, or some mystical, occult quality that pervades organisms but does not pervade stones. The Darwinian theory of natural selection, as opposed to the theory of Special Creation, is a good example of the difference, respectively, between materialistic and idealistic explanations. Darwinian theory is materialist because it emphasizes that species come from material reality: for example, the material environment acting on variations in organisms, selecting those that are adaptive and rejecting those that are not. Special Creation, on the other hand, is idealistic because it holds that each species came originally from the mind of God: that is, idea first, form later, arising out of metaphysical processes the likes of which do not occur in the everyday world. The history of the western world shows that idealistic explanations have retreated in ever-increasing quantity as science has expanded, although idealism still finds a haven in various claims within religion, the humanities and social sciences.

Materialism, as a philosophical system, exists in two forms: mechanistic and dialectical. Mechanistic materialism is historically the older, having begun to develop systematically during the 17th century, and becoming more codified and sophisticated during the 18th and 19th centuries. There are four basic features of the mechanistic materialist view. (a) First, mechanistic materialists emphasize that the whole of any complex process—organism, ecosystem or machine—consists of a number of separate and separable parts, or components. Mechanistic materialists tend to look at the parts of the whole in an atomistic way, much as one would look at the mechanism of a clock as a collection of distinct gears, levers, and weights. Each part has its own distinct measurable and describable characteristics, and each part interacts with other parts in distinct, separate ways. (b) Therefore, to a mechanistic materialist the proper method of studying a complex entity is to take it apart and study each component separately. It is possible to measure each gear, pendulum or lever in the clock, describe it in all its dimensions, and then, when all those discrete bits of knowledge are compared we will understand the whole. Essentially this is the analytical approach because it involves taking something complicated apart (''lysis''-breaking apart), and then examining it piece by piece. (c) A corollary of the mechanistic view is that the whole is equal to the sum of its parts and no more. That is, there is nothing mystical to be found in the parts of a clock; if one finds all the components and studies them carefully, it will be possible to understand the whole. There are no ''emergent'' properties coming out of the whole that were not there intact in the separate parts. (d) The mechanistic view is a static, or non-developmental one. It does not see that change to any natural system comes from ongoing dynamic processes within the system, but as the result of external forces acting on the system in the same way that a billiard ball is moved on a table by being hit by the cue stick or another ball. Sometimes those outside actions are accidental, sometimes they are more regular (the earth's orbit is the result of a continuously acting external force), but nonetheless they are acting on the system from outside. At the same time mechanists have had to recognize a class of internally-motivated changes, for example, the changes characterizing the organic life cycle—the idea that organisms are born, mature, and eventually die. Those trends however, are described in terms of programmed changes (as opposed to autonomous, dynamic processes), much as a computer runs through its prescribed program (aging is often described in just this sort of computer language). Programmed changes have only a certain number of variations or modifications to a limited number of possible situations. Thus, they have built-in limitations.

Dialectical materialism as a philosophical system is chronologically more recent, having begun to emerge from a variety of sources in the early and middle 19th century, and later developed more fully by Karl Marx and Friedrich Engels from the 1850s onward. While dialectical views have been gaining in prominence in a variety of areas of the social and natural sciences, even today it is still probably much less prominent than mechanistic materialism in the thought processes of most western countries. We are very much heirs to the mechanistic materialist world view of the 17th century. Today, how is dialectical materialism as a philosophical approach different from mechanistic materialism?

First, dialectical materialism is not atomistic. While seeing complex processes as composed of parts, dialectical materialists emphasize the interconnections among those parts. Dialectical materialists argue that the whole consists of more than the sum of its parts, but not as a result of any mystical properties. Examination of any component of a system in isolation omits one of the important characteristics of that component: its mutual interdependence with other components.

Second, dialectical materialists do not expect to understand the whole by studying its parts only in isolation. It is necessary to study the parts in their interdependent processes because it is only in those processes that we see the way in which the components interact. Interdependence is thus not a property of each part, but it is only a property of those parts as they are working together, that is, in the whole. Biologists, I think, have become increasingly aware of the importance of this feature of complex systems, even though not calling it by its philosophical name. In the 19th century it was fashionable to do physiological studies by taking the kidney or the heart out of an experimental animal, putting it into a perfusion chamber where it could be subjected to various drugs, conditions of acidity/alkalinity, temperature or pressure, and the rate or extent of the organ's function measured. Those studies had, and continue to have, some value; however, it is clear to any biologist today that isolation experiments of that sort only provide a partial picture of how an organ functions. Organ functions *in vivo* are highly dependent on other systems, such as neuronal and hormonal control, and must be studied in that context as well as in isolation.

Biochemists have had a similar kind of experience. Most of the classical kinetics of enzyme systems have been done *in vitro,* where the enzymes are extracted from tissues and cells, purified and concentrated, and then presented with their substrates at various concentrations, and the rate of substrate conversion measured. One major difficulty with those studies emerged when it was recognized that the concentration of enzymes in *in vitro* solutions was a hundred, a thousand, or ten-thousand times greater than that found in a living cell. It is now clear that there is a whole different kinetics of enzyme-substrate systems in very dilute, compared to highly concentrated, solutions. To understand their function, one must look at enzymes within the environment of the cell in which they function.

On a more practical level, the idea that the whole is greater than the sum of its parts is very much apparent in the study of human personality. Every individual has his or her own personality, some aspects of which can be determined by various observations on the individual alone (through tests, questionnaires, interviews, etc.). However, an extremely important part of every individual's personality is the way that person interacts with other individuals. This can only be determined by observing the interactions themselves. Hence, the totality of any component part must include an explicit study of its interactions with other components. It is in this sense that the whole is greater than the sum of its parts.

A third feature of dialectical materialism is that all systems—natural, human, individual or societal—pass through developmental stages, that is, they evolve. The development, or evolution, of a system in dialectical terms is quite different from the changes that a system may undergo in mechanistic terms. Dialectical materialists see the major course of any evolutionary process as resulting from internal dynamics within the system itself, as opposed to change simply impressed on the system from outside. The important distinction between change, in the mechanistic sense, and evolution (or development) in the dialectical sense, is crucial to understanding how dialectical differs from mechanistic materialism. In the mechanistic sense, a system may change or it may not—that is, change is not an inherent or necessary characteristic of the system. If all components of a system are in balance (as in the mid-19th century view of the Newtonian universe), then change is minimal, or non-existent. Indeed, in mechanistic terms, it is quite possible to conceive of systems remaining static for long periods of time. When change does occur, it is always more or less accidental, impressed from the outside. By contrast, in a dialectical view, change is an inherent component, a characteristic, of any system. The rates of change may vary from system to system, or time to time, but change is inevitable. That inevitability is a result of the internal workings of the system itself—that is, the processes within it. There are, of course, external factors that come to bear on a system as well, but in dialectical terms the major motive force for change is internal, not external. In the dialectical sense, then, evolutionary change is not mere accident, but has form and development to it. It is not a programmed, or teleological change: that is, there is no final goal, no end to evolutionary change (this is why embryonic development, for example, is not true evolutionary change; it is programmed in distinct directions and is teleological in the true sense of the word). In the dialectical sense every system carries within it the seeds of its own change, the internal workings that produce its own continual, and un-ending evolutionary development.

This latter point is one on which many people incorrectly criticize Marx's theory of historical development. They interpret Marx (and Engels) to have stated that classless (Communist) society is the final stage of historical evolution—which of course is not true. It may be the next higher stage after capitalism, but that does not mean there is no further evolution beyond it. The course of any evolutionary development can be understood a posteriori, but cannot be predicted a priori, that is, from a knowledge of its antecedent events. This is a problem faced as much by biologists as by historians. The inability to make accurate predictions for the future in an evolutionary world is an aspect of evolutionary development that has led to much confusion in both biology and history when approached from a mechanistic point of view (for example, the standard claim that evolutionary theory is not science, that biology has no laws, or that history cannot be approached scientifically).

We come now to the notion of evolutionary change as a result of a dialectical process: the interaction of opposing forces, or contradictory elements within the system itself. This is a particularly knotty problem, leading to all sorts of philosophical issues (from those concerned with why there are two and not three or more opposing forces, why the forces have to be seen as opposed, or whether the dialectical view is merely a convenient method of analysis, as opposed to an inherent characteristic of nature itself). This is not the place to try and sort out all of these questions, but rather to explain briefly now the dialectical view—that is, of two opposing forces, or contradictory tendencies within a system—leads to a more clear understanding of events and processes in the world—in the present context, the nature of historical evolutionary development.

Engels (1940) has provided many examples of dialectical processes in nature: life/death, anabolism/catabolism, stasis/change, attraction/repulsion, positive/negative, matter/energy, to which we can add any number of additional cases from everyday life: light/dark, hot/cold, young/old, good/bad, working class/upper class (bourgeoisie), etc. Whether conveniences of description (a model) or inherent realities of the world is less the point here than the fact that most changes in the natural and social world appear to be understandable in terms of the interaction of such opposing forces. The dialectical view provides a particularly useful way of understanding the dynamics of any process because it sees all processes as constantly in motion—there is no state of stasis, or inactivity; change is not an occasional or periodic process, but something that occurs continually, and is thus inherent in all material entities. The mechanistic view does not see such forces of change as necessarily inherent in the process itself, a feature peculiar to, and characteristic of, the dialectical position. The dialectical view also emphasizes that change is like Time's Arrow—it proceeds in a non-random, uni-directional pathway. Evolutionary processes cannot be reversed—they proceed down a one-way street that is both non-repeatable, yet at the same time has no end.

The process of organic evolution as described in Darwin's theory of natural selection illustrates the main characteristics of the dialectical view with admirable clarity. To Darwin, evolution was the result of two contradictory and opposing forces: the conservative force of heredity, which produces faithful and exact replication, and the radical force of variation, which produces unfaithful, inexact replication. Without both of these opposing tendencies, operating continuously, there could be no evolution. If organisms showed only exact replication, there could be no variation, hence all organisms would be identical. If there was no heredity (but only variation), no trait, however favorable, could be preserved and passed on to the next generation. With both heredity and variation present, however, organic evolution becomes inevitable. This means that the evolutionary process must occur in all organisms. It is not a matter of periodic change, or cyclical processes, but of continual, unidirectional (but not teleological) motion. Organic evolution may be rapid or slow, depending on various conditions of time and place, but it will always occur. Its dynamic originates within organisms themselves, not from changes impressed on organisms from the outside (of course, the outside is involved in the form of environmental selection); it is thus a dialectical change in the truest sense of the word.

People sometimes ask what is gained by describing evolution (or anything else) in dialectical terms. Are not the key concepts of heredity and variation enough? To some extent, of course, the answer is yes. It is quite possible to understand many processes quite accurately without the conscious language of dialectical materialism. Marx, indeed, did not use overtly dialectical language most of the time. But he did think dialectically, and that, of course, is the key. The value of a consciously dialectical description lies in the generality it provides, the interconnection that it affords between a number of seemingly diverse processes. Dialectical thinking represents a world view, a way of looking at phenomena that raises questions often overlooked by idealistic or mechanistic thinkers. For example, to continue the example of organic evolution, consider a truly dialectical view, compared to a mechanistic one, of the interaction between organisms and their environment. Mechanists see the organism as adapting to the environment; if the environment changes, it is as a result of geological and climatic forces, not of organisms themselves (except in special, and usually extreme situations such as over-grazing). By contrast, dialectical materialists see organisms and environment as co-evolving with every new adaptation on the part of the organism producing a change in the environment, exploiting it in some slightly different way (that, after all, is what adaptation is ultimately about: exploitation of environmental resources more effectively). The environment is not a constant "adaptive landscape" (in Sewall Wright's terms) to which the organism adapts. As the environment is changed by the adaptation of a population of organisms, new adaptations become possible, even necessary, because the environment is no longer the same as it once was, two, or more generations previously. As a result, evolution of organisms will never end—an inbuilt feature of the evolutionary process itself. It is this dynamic interaction that mechanistic thinkers often fail to appreciate, or even to see. To a dialectical thinker it is second nature. Thus, a dialectical analysis has more advantage than simply being a uniform or consistent way of viewing and/or describing phenomena. It opens whole new problems and possibilities. It focuses attention on interactions in a way that mechanistic thinking does not. It is indeed a different world view.

A final feature of dialectical materialism is the notion that quantitative changes leads to qualitative changes. The classic example was given by Engels (1940): when a pan of water is heated, its temperature gradually rises, increasing by quantitative increments. Eventually, however, the water boils and an entirely different--a qualitatively different, we might say—state of matter is achieved: water has passed from the liquid to the gaseous state, and by all meanings of the term this represents a qualitative change. Another example could well be the evolutionary divergence of one parental population into two species over time. If a parental population is divided into two by a geographic barrier, and the two populations remain separate for many generations, the gradual accumulation of small quantitative differences (variations) will eventually lead to the production of two separate species, which, if brought back together, cannot interbreed. At this point a qualitative change has occurred, the two groups are no longer interfertile, and can now be regarded as two separate, and thus qualitatively distinct, species. This qualitative difference has been achieved by the gradual accumulation of quantitative differences (i.e., variations or mutations). And here is the important point: Through quantitative change qualitative change inevitably results. It is not a random process, occurring sometimes and not others. It is not true that some quantitative changes lead to qualitative changes whereas others do not. In some cases the period of quantitative change is very slow, in others more rapid. Nonetheless, accumulation of quantitative change inevitably leads at some point in time to the appearance of qualitative changes.

The concept of "levels of organization" is based explicitly on the dialectical notion of quantitative changes leading to qualitative. If we accept this concept, then it follows inevitably that associations among lower-level components, say individual organisms or gears in a clock, must necessarily lead to higher level phenomena (such as communication, or actual recording of time) that are qualitatively different. Quantitative change leads to qualitative change only because the additional quantitative elements are also capable of new, and higher degrees of organization. For example, consider the classical philosophical problem of men trying to move a barge moored in a harbor. One man cannot move the barge, though he pushes against it with all his might. Neither can two men, or five, or ten. Somewhere along the way, as more men are added, it becomes physically possible to move the barge. A threshold is reached after the addition, let us say, or the fifteenth man, where actual movement (maybe slow, but nonetheless movement, as compared to non-movement) can occur. However, the actuality of movement requires something else: the organization of those fifteen components. If all are equally spaced around the barge and all push with equal strength, there will be no movement. Similarly, if all fifteen men push in random directions, or at random moments in time, there will be no movement. However, if all fifteen men push in the same direction at the same time, the barge will move. Organization is thus crucial to producing a qualitatively new phenomenon. This is what we mean by a "levels approach". "Levels" implies not only the notion of quantitative changes leading to qualitative, but also the notion of organization. Quantitative change and organization are inseparable in understanding how new levels are achieved in any real system. Quantity makes new forms of organization possible; organization transforms quantity into quality (that is, the effect of quantity can become actualized). Because a levels approach implies recognition of qualitatively new forms of organization, it becomes an inevitable consequence of the dialectical approach to the world.

Associated with mechanistic materialism throughout much of its history has been the philosophical process known as *reductionism*. Reductionism is a difficult concept to define or to describe accurately. Writers such as Kenneth Schaffner (1967), among others, have attempted to define it in as broad a way as possible. The definition that I include here is somewhat more narrow, but draws on Schaffner's explication. In general, *reductionism* is the tendency to explain higher levels of organization of any system in terms of its lower-level components, that is, the complex in terms of the less complex. Examples of reductionism can be: (a) Viewing the nervous system in terms of electric circuitry, (b) describing the behavior of an organism in terms of its response to physico-chemical stimuli (in the early decades of the century the German-born physiologist Jacques Loeb argued that phototropic insects were "photochemical machines enslaved to the light"), or (c) viewing life as the product of the action of enzyme molecules. Reductionism need not always describe complex systems in terms of their direct, simpler components, but can also describe them in physicochemical models at the same level of organization, for example, the nervous system as electrical circuitry (a reductionistic model, though not necessarily at a lower level of organization of the nervous system itself). Reductionism is a methodological extension of the mechanistic materialist view that the whole is equal to the sum of its parts and no more. Reductionists tend to see only the quantitative changes in a system, and not the qualitative changes. They do not see how lower levels of organization inevitably lead to higher levels, or new properties. They traditionally deny the existence of "emergent" properties, identifying such concepts as "emergence" with mysticism or vitalism. Lacking an explicit and working knowledge of dialectical materialism, mechanistic materialists in the past have often made naive reductionist statements, as the only viable alternative, in their view, to introducing mystical, non-material concepts. Unfortunately, terms or concepts like "emergent properties," or "the whole is greater than the sum of its parts," without the benefit of an explicitly dialetical analysis, have often sounded idealistic and vague. As a result, reductionism has often appeared to be the most scientific view to adopt, in the face of what seemed like the only viable alternative to introducing mystical and idealistic thinking.

Thus, while reductionism is a somewhat separate philosophical issue from mechanistic materialism itself, it is closely allied with the mechanistic approach, and can be viewed in some ways as a subset of mechanistic thinking. Both mechanistic materialism and reductionism have been persistent problems in the history of biology in the last century or century and a half, and still underlie the approach to many biological problems, including especially such difficult ones as the study of animal consciousness.

## MECHANISTIC ERRORS AND DIALECTICAL POTENTIAL IN THE STUDY OF ANIMAL AWARENESS

The study of animal consciousness as illustrated in Griffin's (1981) book, is classically mechanistic and reductionist in its recurrent emphasis on the quantitative continuity between the human species and the rest of the animal kingdom. Griffin describes continuity at a number of levels of biological organization: the neuron and nervous system levels, the level of populations (for example, in seeing a continuity of behavior among vertebrate groups), and at the communication level (in seeing a continuity from communication signals to fully developed language). Continuity emerges as the mere accumulation of many small, almost imperceptible (yet quantitatively different) individual variations, between everything from neurons to brain structure. For example, Griffin quotes approvingly neurophysiologists John and Thatcher, (1977) who write of the mind-body dualism problem:

> Perhaps our philosophical quandry arises from the assumption that organized processes in human brains are *qualitatively* different from organized processes in other nervous systems or even in simpler forms of matter. Perhaps the difference is only quantitative; perhaps we are actually not as unique as we have assumed.

Griffin (1981) goes on to point out that the central point of his book is the degree of similarity between animal and human mental functions:

> The basic question I am trying to answer is the degree of similarity of mental experiences resulting from brain function in our own and other species. Only if one

postulates a major, qualitative difference between psychoneurorelationships across species does this complex area of philosophical concern become directly relevant. (p. 25)

Applying the same principle again to the notion of animal communication and its relation to language, Griffin states:

The available evidence concerning communication behavior in animals suggests that there may be no qualitative dichotomy, but rather a large quantitative difference in complexity of signals and range of intention that separates animal communications from human language. (p. 169)

Arguing still further that neurophysiological processes in animals and man are very much the same, Griffin concludes that conscious thought must also be the same. His chain of reasoning is as follows: behaviorists argue that mental experiences are identical with neurophysiological processes; neurophysiologists have discovered no fundamental differences between neurophysiological processes in humans and other animal brains; humans are aware and have mental experiences; therefore, mental experiences must be the same in other species as in humans. "This, in turn, implies qualitative evolutionary continuity (though not identity) of mental experiences among multicellular animals." (Griffin, p. 170). Despite his misuse in this context of the term qualitative, I think it is clear that Griffin approaches the whole issue of animal behavior in general, and animal consciousness/awareness in particular. in terms of quantitative continuity rather than qualitative discontinuity, between humans and the rest of the animal kingdom.

As a result of this mechanistic bias Griffin fails completely to understand the dialectical principle of emergence. Historically, it is important to understand that Griffin and many animal behaviorists in the early and mid-20th century, were consciously trying to avoid the mysticism and subjectivism inherent in late 19th and early 20th century writings in this field. Despite their admirable desire to avoid this older sort of dilemma, Griffin and others seem to have fallen into a new one: they have conflated the various levels of organization—from neuron to complex language behavior—into one continuous spectrum. Perplexed by the apparently vast differences between human and animal awareness, they solve the problem by minimizing its importance, and emphasizing what they assume to be the underlying, though less visible, quantitative continuity. In other words, they ultimately seem to operate on the principle that humans are just somewhat more complex versions of pigeons and chimps.

In a similar vein, Griffin sees the whole—whether an individual animal or its complex behavior patterns—as the sum of its parts. This is apparent in his underlying assumption that human behavior is just a combination of rudimentary traits present in lower animals. They psychoneural continuity that Griffin sees between other vertebrates and humans is taken to imply a behavioral continuity as well. Hence, the ability of various vertebrates to visualize spatial relationships, for example distances, and then to use their visualization to solve problems (for example, in getting to a piece of food) are seen as rudimentary elements in the process whereby humans, for example, see and visually represent complex three-dimensional perspectives. Griffin here fails completely to take a levels approach and recognize that new combinations produce wholly new (emergent) results at new levels of organization. The fact that a chimp and a human child can both solve a spatial problem such as reaching a bunch of hanging bananas by moving a box across the room to a position underneath them, becomes for Griffin, only a quantitative component in the larger problem-solving behavior of adult humans. Although there is no doubt that the problem-solving behavior of apes or other vertebrates is enormously fascinating in its own right, it is not philosophically justifiable to argue that every behavior in another species that appears similar to one in humans, means that human behavior is just a slightly more complex version of simpler animal prototypes. It is the difference in levels that makes the two cases qualitatively different.

Griffin's view of animal and human behavior is also non-developmental. He fails to understand that behavior—ontogenetically or phylogenetically—has developed in a social context. The individual child during its maturation is the constant recipient of external stimuli, as well as itself providing stimuli to the external world. In a constant feedback loop, human behavior grows by development of ideas or conceptions from reality, and testing those conclusions against the real world. We know ontogeny does not recapitulate phylogeny in the older Haeckelian sense; however, it is nonetheless safe to say that in the evolution of behavioral traits, the social context has been particularly crucial. The recognition of social context bears directly on the definition, and thus understanding, of consciousness itself. Consciousness is not an abstract, absolute entity, but a contextually developed state, meaningful only when the context--the ecological, the social, the phylogenetic, the ontogenetic, and the societal—is known. Thus the development of human consciousness, once we even define the term (which seems difficult enough in its own right), must be viewed in terms of the social evolution of the human species as a whole, and of each individual in its social milieu.

Many of the methodological problems that appear separately in Griffin's treatment of other topics, converge in his discussion of the implication of animal and human communication systems for an understanding of conscious awareness. Through a survey of the literature, Griffin argues that many species have the elements of language, in the form of communication systems (some simple, others more complex). He cites examples ranging from honeybees to primates, suggesting that language is little more than successive build-up of symbolic units (sounds, words, or their groupings) that can be manipulated and rearranged to express new meanings and reflect new situations.

The first problem in this argument is, as always, definitional. Griffin does not really define the terms "communication system" or "language," thus tending to conflate their meanings in the mind of the reader. Is there not a difference between a communication system and a "language"? Is the latter merely a more complex version of the former? The answers to these questions determine, in one sense, the actual outcome; that is, whether one sees continuity or discontinuity: calling them all communication systems suggests continuity, while differentiating between communication system and language suggests discontinuity. Griffin's failure to define either term leaves the issue blurred with regard to inferences about animal awareness. The inevitable result of conflation weights the interpretation toward the continuity that Griffin seeks to demonstrate.

A second problem is more philosophical in nature. Griffin shoves under the rug any direct discussion of the relationship (or lack of it) between consciousness and language. This is, of course, an extremely difficult problem philosophically and is at the heart of Wittgenstein's (1958) lengthy attempts to define meaning and its relationship to language in *Philosophical Investigations*. Although aware of the problem—he discusses communication as some guide to degrees of consciousness—Griffin does not face it directly and in-depth. This result, as with the definitional problem just mentioned, is the promulgation of certain assumptions about which there has been much philosophical discussion, and disagreement, in the past. In humans, thought is obviously possible without language, but what about conscious awareness of one's self, one's existence as a separate human being, and ones' history or future? It is virtually impossible to know—to ask the question it is necessary to use the very language one is trying to find out about. Griffin takes the existence of communication systems to indicate the possible existence of conscious awareness. But if awareness is possible without communication systems, or if communication systems exist without implying any necessary awareness on the part of the individual (bee waggle dances, complex as they are, can hardly be taken as indicating consciousness on the parts of individual insects), then the study of animal communication may have nothing at all to say about animal awareness. Griffin fails to stress this point, hence biasing the reader toward the conclusion that communication systems are related to, and thus indicators of, conscious awareness.

A third problem is methodological—a kind of biological example of the indeterminacy principle in physics. Whether conscious awareness depends on communication systems or not, establishing language-type contact between investigators and the species they are studying is the only way, ultimately, to get at the problem directly. Inferences about an animals' conscious thoughts, intentions, or methods of solving a problem are certainly possible from observation of behavior; but they are only inferences at best. Everyone who has worked at all extensively in this area knows the anthropomorphism inherent in making inferences about an animal's state of conscious awareness from its behavior. Indeed, the difficulty is so great that Griffin largely ignores the issue and proceeds to use the analysis of communication systems as the major avenue for inferring states of awareness. Combined with his lack of definitional distinctions as just outlined, the analysis of animal communication becomes a major stumbling block in the march toward Griffin's ultimate conclusions.

Griffin's reductionism and failure to understand the relationship between quantitative and qualitative change emerges clearly in his consideration of the continuity of animal and human communication systems. As in his other arguments, Griffin searches for rudimentary components of human language in animals, and then claims that because of the similarity of the components, animals must have some of the same mental experiences, although perhaps to a lesser degree, as humans. There is no recognition on Griffin's part of quantitative changes leading to qualitative changes, or of the effect of levels of organization on emergence of new properties. In Griffin's view, then, human language is only a quantitatively more complex association of sounds that appear in rudimentary form in chimps. Griffin often pays homage to the difference (ultimately quite remarkable by any standards) between chimp communication systems and human language, but his whole approach to the awareness, or consciousness problem is to minimize the differences and emphasize the similarities.

It is apparent that Griffin and all of those who argue for some form of animal awareness (understood in some sense as simpler forms of what we experience in human awareness) have adopted a highly physico-chemical reductionism. Ultimately, their reductionistic bias leads them to seek out the basis of language, or behavior, in neuronal connections. They imply that by understanding the complexity of neuronal hookups, they can ultimately explain the difference, say, between human and chimp ability to learn language. Without in any way denigrating the very important advances in neurobiology, especially of the brain, that have occurred in recent years, it is a flagrantly reductionist aspiration to think that higher orders of behavior can be understood by knowledge of all the circuitry implicit in the vertebrate nervous system. Understanding neurophysiological processes provides important insights on which we can build our understanding of the higher levels of organization, including full language behavior itself. But the mechanism of neuronal interaction will not by itself, at that cellular level of organization, ever explain the higher levels of integration that produce a complex (or even a simple) behavior. Neurophysiology is a necessary but not sufficient basis for the investigation of animal behavior.

Here, then, is a crucial fallacy of the reductionist position. Reductionists think that by discovering that the chimp brain has 200,000 neurons in the language center of the cerebrum, or that the human brain has 200 million, they will somehow explain the difference in language ability between the two species. On this line of argument, if species A has 10 neurons, B has 100, C has 1000, D has 10,000, reductionists would predict, from a knowledge of A's behavior repertory, that B could do ten times more complex activities, C 100 times more, and D 1000 times more. But as our example of boiling water indicates, it is impossible, in the real world, to make such predictions based on mere quantitative differences. Levels of organization, as they increase in complexity, yield emergent properties that cannot be predicted from knowledge of the simpler components themselves. Reductionism not only starts with the complex whole and "reduces" it to its component parts, but also encompasses the expectation that the whole can be reproduced by going back up the hierarchical scale from simple to complex. This includes, of course, extrapolation to larger wholes that have not yet been studied in themselves. It would be erroneous to think of reductionism as involving only the downward analysis of wholes into parts, without recognizing the implicit character of the reverse process—synthesizing and/or extrapolating the whole from knowledge of its parts. It is in this latter expectation that the reductionistic fallacy shows up most clearly. The fallacy is the failure to recognize the emergent properties of successive hierarchical levels, a fallacy implicit in the approach of Griffin and those who would investigate animal consciousness as merely a lower order of human consciousness.

How can we translate this analysis into a meaningful method of operation, especially in the area of the subject-matter on which the conference is focused: animal consciousness? Being a novice in the field of ethology generally, let me use a very simple, but I think, instructive example from the work of David Premack on chimpanzee behavior. In a recent paper (Premack, 1983), the author explores the problem of testing animals' (mostly chimps, but including summaries of work with pigeons) response to what are called identity studies. Identity studies seek to discover whether an animal can recognize two objects as the same or different. Premack notes that the literature contains two different operational procedures for making such a determination: (a) When the same object is presented at two different times $t_1$ and $t_2$, and (b) when two objects (say, two apples or an apple and an orange) are presented simultaneously. Premack notes that the existing studies tend to conflate the two procedures, treating them as equivalent aspects of the "same/different" problem. However, he notes that in the real world of animal behavior experiments, the two situations are not equivalent. His own work with chimps, as well as the literature at large, indicates that the first procedure yields far more correct responses than the second. That is, it appears to be easier for an animal to correctly determine that two apples are "the same" when presented in sequence, than when presented simultaneously. "One would suppose," he writes, "that in fact both procedures measure essentially the same competence. But this is not the case" (p. 354). He notes that the only animal subjects that seem to shift successfully from the sequential to the simultaneous procedure are those who either have language training by humans, or are subjected to a "heroic number of training trials."

To a mechanist this observation seems puzzling. Mechanists tend to see the two situations as different only in degree, not in kind, with the simultaneous presentation being only slightly more complex than the sequential. To a dialectical materialist, however, the two situations would not be expected to be the same because, as Premack himself points out, the sequential procedure really tests not for the concept of "same/different" but for "familiar/unfamiliar." By the first procedure, in presenting two apples, or an apple and an orange, in succession, what the animal is being asked to recognize is its own past experience rather than necessarily any properties of the objects per se. If two apples are presented sequentially, what the animal sees is a second object of the sort it is already familiar with, or unfamiliar with, from the first trial. The "same/different" concept, however, involves a higher order (more complex) process, namely distinguishing between the essential similarity, or dissimilarity between the objects presented. For example, presenting an apple and an orange simultaneously might produce the response "different" if the animal thought of colored objects or "same" if the animal thought of edible objects. Thus, both responses could be considered correct because there is no immediate way of determining on which type of categorization the animal is basing its choice. Extrapolating from the sequential to the simultaneous procedure is not valid because, in the simultaneous case, at least two sets of possible categories are involved, whereas in the sequential case (it appears) only one category is involved.

For a dialectical materialist as well as for a mechanistic materialist, the discovery of the difference between the sequential and simultaneous testing procedures might not be predicted ahead of time. The dialectical method does not allow researchers to prejudge all new situations. What it does, in a case of this sort, is to alter the kinds of expectations, and therefore, perhaps, short-cut some steps in formulating questions and experimental procedures. For both dialecticians and mechanists, there may be many surprises from experimental work. It is always easier to reconstruct explanations a posteriori than a priori. However, the key lies in expectations. The dialectical method may help make our expectations more realistic (not necessarily more modest), and thus reduce the amount of time involved in fruitless lines of investigation. Thus, I would argue, much time might have been saved, and more meaningful directions for research established in the field of animal consciousness, had Griffin and some of the early formulators been less mechanistic and reductionistic, and more dialectical (especially about levels of organization) in their outlook. Their approach has, I believe, led to a serious mis-formulation of the basic questions of animal consciousness and to lines of research (let us say into neurobiology) that will never yield the answers that are expected from them.

## THE SOCIO-POLITICAL CONTEXT OF RECENT
## STUDIES OF ANIMAL CONSCIOUSNESS

It is not irrelevant to ask why the study of animal consciousness has emerged as such a prominent field of research in recent years. Is this merely accidental, a new fad among biologists that appeals to popular imagination and journalistic sensationalism? Or, is there some significance to the flourishing of such ideas at the present time?

I see the concept of animal awareness conceptually to be the reverse side of the coin of modern sociobiology, and perhaps nourished by the same political concerns and social forces that have given the sociobiologists so much exposure. Sociobiologists and students of animal awareness, though coming from different directions, arrive at the same end: they blur the distinction between animals and humans by setting up an evolutionary continuum from protozoa to human being. Sociobiologists claim that we (humans) are like them (animals); students of animal awareness claim the converse: they (animals) are like us (humans). Phrased differently, animals and humans have varying degrees of similarity in anatomy, physiology and behavior, so therefore they must have similarities in emotions and consciousness as well. Sociobiologists see rudimentary behavior in animals as leading to the fully developed form of that behavior in humans; students of animal awareness see fully developed human awareness existing in rudimentary form in lower animals. The point is the same in the end: there is no sharp dividing line between human and sub-human.

Blurring the distinction between humans and other animals has serious social and political ramifications that deserve close analysis. While I do not want to indulge in anthropocentrism, and appear to claim that humans are in some sense specially created beings, to argue that we are also animals does not mean we are merely animals. There is a qualitative difference between ourselves and other animals that is not merely a result of conceit; it is part of a biological, social and cultural reality. We do not need to be arrogant about this difference to recognize that it exists. To blur the distinction between animal and human, especially by distorting the biological reality (or by claiming for the biological reality more than it can offer), is to play into the hands of a political mood that leads ultimately to fascism. This sounds like a strong and rather extreme claim, so let me explain what I mean.

Fascism is defined as a later stage in the development of capitalism, typified by a highly centralized and autocratic government ruling by force. It is also typified by the imposition of severe cutbacks in availability and/or distribution of resources, aimed at shoring up sagging rates of profit. Fascism is accompanied by the cheapening of many aspects of human life, especially those people deemed to be inferior by virtue of ethnic or social-class background. In Nazi Germany fascists referred to the aged, the physically or mentally ill, the crippled and retarded—in short, those who were not productive for the profit system—as "lives not worth living." Harsh treatment of such individuals (concentration camps, euthanasia, or human experimentation) could only be justified if somehow they were considered less than fully human, or, to put it another way, more like animals. In Germany this was accomplished with the aid of genetics (the German Eugenik and Rassenhygiene movements). Using methodologies as questionable or downright unscientific as the sociobiologists and students of animal awareness use today, eugenicists in the past claimed that persons with certain genetic (and congenital) traits were burdens on the state by virtue of their biological make-up, and should (at the very least) be sterilized, and ultimately eradicated. Extended to various ethnic and/or racial groups, the eugenics argument called essentially for genocide against those "inferior races" and classes that were "polluting" the blood stream of pure-bred and productive. The fascist movement developed in Germany for real economic reasons—it was not motivated primarily by racist ideology—but did succeed in part because it encompassed racist principles disguised as biological reality. After all, it is easier to condone such extreme practices as sterilization or euthenasis, if it can be claimed to the public at large that the affected individuals are less than human, and that, because of this they are a burden on the rest.

What are the present social and political conditions that make both sociobiology and the study of animal awareness part of an evolutionary movement toward fascism? The present era (in the capitalist west, at least) is one of major cutbacks in social services, in care for the infirm, the aged, the physically and mentally handicapped, indeed, for all those unfortunate enough not to be fully useful in the productive process. These cut-backs may not be quite as directly fascistic as putting people in concentration camps, or killing the aged, but they are nonetheless murderous in their own way (how many older people, or mentally handicapped, for example, die as a result of lack of first-rate medical care, not to mention such basic requirements as sufficient heat in the winter, or proper food)? Few people in our society actually like to face cut-backs to the less fortunate. Yet, when money is short, and those who can be denied services are pictured as inherently (that is, biologically) less-that-human, it becomes a little more possible to make the necessary cut-backs without enormous protest and moral outrage from the public at large. Blurring the distinction between humans and other animals, whether by evolutionary, genetic, or neurobiological arguments, paves the way for relegating some people to the sub-human category on the basis of their biology. Once there, the usual moral restraints and considerations cease to apply, and fascism has arrived.

It is in this vein that I think both sociobiology and the study of animal awareness can be seen as part of an evolutionary development of present-day capitalism toward fascism. In the abstract there is nothing inherently fascistic about asking whether animals "think" or have an awareness of their own existence. It is the asking of this question under the present social and economic conditions, and with no procedures for arriving at a rigorous or scientific answer that makes the whole enterprise part and parcel of a fascistic (albeit at this stage a protofascistic) social development.

In making the above argument, I do not mean to imply that (a) Sociobiologists or students of animal awareness are overtly, or consciously fascists, or even see their work as having any connection to one or another political ideology; (b) Nor do I mean that sociobiologists and students of animal awareness are conscious puppets of politicians, or the rich, and are being instructed to blur the distinction between humans and animals. There is, in short, no conspiracy. However, I do suggest that the funds for research into these areas are being made available by those with political and economic power, and that these funds are allocated with some ends in view. The availability of funds for this kind of research is not a matter of fad, or caprice, but has a multitude of purposes, an important one being, I think, the blurring of the animal-human distinction. The purpose for trying to place the study of animal awareness in this much larger (and I am sure, controversial) context, is not so much to accuse and lay blame, but to make investigators in this field today aware of both the methodological and socio-political problems they may be facing. It may well behoove those with sincere concerns to examine the degree to which they participate in this movement— however well-meaning their motives, or how genuine their interest in problems of human and/or animal behavior. Given the methodological problems inherent in the field of animal consciousness (as well as with sociobiology), pursuit of the problem in the ways exemplified by investigators such as Griffin, can only lead to the sort of confusion and false understanding of the biological nature of human beings, on which the future of fascism can be built.

## REFERENCES

Engels, F. (1940). *The dialectics of nature.* New York: International Publishers. (6th printing, 1971).

Feibleman, J. K. (1954). Theory of integrative levels. *British Journal for the Philosophy of Science, 5,* 59–66.

Greenberg, G. (1984). T. C. Schneirla's impact on comparative psychology. In G. Greenberg & E. Tobach (Eds.), *Behavioral evolution and integrative levels* (pp. 49–56). Hillsdale, NJ: Lawrence Erlbaum Associates.

Griffin, D. R. (1981). *The question of animal awareness. Evolutionary continuity of mental experience.* New York: Rockefeller University Press.

Premack, D. (1983). Animal cognition. *Annual Review of Psychology, 34,* 351–361.

Schaffner, K. F. (1967). Approaches to reduction. *Philosophy of Science, 34,* 137–147.

Snowden, C. T. (1983). Ethology, comparative psychology, and animal behavior. *Annual Review of Psychology, 34,* 63–94.

Thatcher, R. W., & John, E. R. (1977). *Foundations of cognitive processes* (pp. 294–304). Hillsdale, NJ: Lawrence Erlbaum Associates.

Tobach, E., & Greenberg, G. (1984). The significance of T. C. Schneirla's contribution to the concept of levels of integration. In G. Greenberg & E. Tobach (Eds.), *Behavioral evolution and integrative levels* (pp. 45–56). Hillsdale, NJ: Lawrence Erlbaum Associates.

Wittgenstein, L. (1958). *Philosophical investigations.* New York: Macmillan. (Third edition).

# 10 Folk-Models, Reductionism, and Emergent Patterns in Human Behavioral Evolution

Alexander Alland, Jr.
*Columbia University*

Allow me to make it clear at the beginning how I intend to use the concept of integrative levels in this paper. In what follows I shall suggest, following the model for linguistic evolution developed by Noam Chomsky (1975), that different evolutionary changes in cerebral evolution, occurring uniquely in the human species, provided the neurological basis for true language and aesthetic behavior. I depart specifically from Chomsky in my thinking, however, because I believe that any evolutionary model constructed to account for these species specific traits must include the social system as the dynamic context in which both language and art evolved. What I am saying is that neurological mechanisms of the complexity, specificity, and cultural quality of language and art could only have evolved as part of a social process within the species Homo sapiens. To put it another way, language and art are both creative systems that could only have originated, and can only be manifested, in the context of cultural life. In this they differ from the traits typically discussed by sociobiologists and that are assumed by them to have arisen on the level of individual organisms. The long criticism of sociobiology, that follows as well as my attempt to locate its theories in European folk-lore rather than in science, is meant to highlight the differences between two distinct kinds of thinking about the role of biology in human behavior. I submit that one is reductive, and that the other involves taking into account human sociality as a major level of integration in our species.

In 1976, I debated a young sociobiologist who was convinced that behavioral genetic models developed for lower animals could be applied without change to humans. Because, like the sociobiologists, I am wedded to a Darwinian view of evolution I did not attack the basic assumptions of behavioral biology. I did attempt to show that my opponent's application of Darwinian principles was theoretically, mathematically, and empirically weak. Although the arguments I offered were simple and clear-cut, the audience, which included lay people and biologists, remained resistant to my views. The reason for this, of course, could have been my lack of debating skills, or a degree of self delusion about the strength of my position, but I am convinced that the problem lay elsewhere.

It is unfortunately the case that poor reasoning by a minority of biologists and even pseudo-biological arguments offered by non-scientists are readily accepted by lay people. Racism, for example, has been scientifically discredited over and over again, yet it has not lost its appeal among a certain public. Sexism is another persistent pseudo-biological argument frequently accepted in the face of hard science. I will readily admit that sociobiology falls into a different category because, properly applied to non human species, it offers powerful explanations for certain behavioral observations. Sociobiology has, in fact, contributed major insights into our understanding of altruism in lower animals. Unfortunately its theory has been frequently misapplied, particularly to questions about human behavior that are best answered through cultural and historical analysis. These misapplications are often seized upon by the press as fact and are then offered as strong evidence for new and supposedly correct ways to put human behavior into biological perspective.

There seems to be something about humans that makes them want simple biological answers to what are very complex and, in most cases, socio-cultural questions. One is almost tempted to suggest a biological cause for this tendency—it is, after all, widespread, perhaps even universal, and, therefore, open to such speculation—but I believe that such an explanation would be wide of the mark. I will, however, admit that the reason we speculate about ourselves the way we do is rooted, at least, in part, in our basic biological equipment. We are highly intelligent, social creatures by birthright. We use our minds to think symbolically about ourselves and our species place in nature. No other animal can do this. When we reflect on existence and describe ourselves, our thinking is based by default on what we know and intuit about the world. Logically we compare ourselves to others, our social group to other social groups, and humans to other animal species. We even borrow from the inanimate world for certain metaphors about behavior. Thus we say that this person is a ''rock'' and that person a ''volcano.'' Such metaphorical descriptions and playful speculation about existence antedate science by however long we have had thinking minds. These patterns are hard to break. It is also true that what are basically metaphorical reflections about ourselves and our social identity have great value, but only as long as they are taken as literary rather than as scientific truth. Unless this precaution is followed we risk disaster. Pseudo-science is capable, as we all should know at least since the holocaust, of destroying human life and along with it the social order built on equity and justice.

This is not merely an abstract problem. When the ''Jensen Report,'' a highly flawed document suggesting that I.Q. differences between blacks and whites was largely genetic, was first published, it appeared on President Nixon's desk the same week. The president was advised that the report had immediate and nega- tive implications for such educational programs as Project Head Start. If I.Q. really was genetic and if blacks were biologically inferior to whites, then such programs were a waste of tax dollars. Although E. O. Wilson, the founder of sociobiology, has been fairly consistent in his attempt to divorce his theory from its political implications, the implications are there. Because sociobiology pre- tends to explain such ideologies as sexism, racism, and xenophobia by appealing to natural selection and behavioral genetics, it can only divert attention from the purely sociocultural processes that underlie them. The notion—deeply imbedded in sociobiology—that these truly antisocial ideologies are the result of positive biological selection proves that 19th century Social Darwinism is not dead; this is the same Social Darwinism that supported the laissez-faire politics of the late 19th and early 20th centuries. The basic tenet of these politics is: leave well enough alone and every thing will take care of itself. A corollary to this is the assumption that under these conditions the stronger and wiser members of soci- ety will replace the weaker and less intelligent members.

Biologizing is a diversionary tactic, and it blocks our understanding of the social process. Wilson's claim that the "true facts" of biology will help us focus our attention on the real causes of social evil so that we can rid ourselves of them has a hollow ring in the light of the role biological determinism has actually played in politics and history. As the anthropologist, Marshall Sahlins, (1976) has pointed out, sociobiology is a misapplication of the principles of natural selection to the notion of maximization. In biology, only the "least worst" can be selected and not the "most best." Therefore, natural selection is not, as is so widely believed, a relentless march towards the best solution to any given biolog- ical problem. Sahlins goes on to show how the attribution of maximization to evolutionary theory is a perfect reflection of a kind of utilitarianism that has pervaded social and economic thought since the middle of the 17th century.

Beyond this, and just as important to our understanding of the appeal so- ciobiology has among the lay public as well as some scientists, is the fact that sociobiology is yet another version of a deeply ingrained means of thinking about the world (in particular, how we define society, ourselves, and others) that has pervaded western thought at least since the Greeks. This is the application to such thought of metaphors that cross natural boundaries—for example the divi- sion between humans and animals or between the living and the dead—to an understanding of the human condition. These metaphors are then combined in powerful myths that come to be accepted as explanations for the state of things. Before the rise of western science, these myths were the only means of dealing with major existential problems. Perhaps because they exercise the imagination creatively and deal, in many cases, with scientifically unanswerable questions, these myths have continued to exist, sometimes in disguised form, into the so called "scientific age." As such, they continue to pervade our unconscious definitions of reality and surface from time to time in what we uncritically call "scientific thinking." Biological determinism, including its latest mutation, sociobiology, is tremendously satisfying to a public inclined to mythological thinking and with a preference for simple as well as inexpensive answers to difficult problems concerning the social order.

So that we might construct a truly scientific theory of human behavior and mind—one that takes biology into account but does not exaggerate or misplace its function—we must clarify the powerful roles metaphorical and mythical thinking have played in the construction of both folk and scientific theories. Such a clarification will allow us to avoid old errors and will provide insight into why basically poor theories—like sociobiology—receive public acceptance so readily.

Myths are explanatory tales, yet they are loaded with imaginary creatures and often describe unlikely events. In the past, they were transmitted from generation to generation by story tellers. Although myths are still told and modern literature often treats mythical themes, it is the modern technology of film and television that provides a new and marvelous way to materialize improbable creatures and events. By examining contemporary and historical folk models and comparing them to what has been offered as scientific truth, we can begin to think clearly about our species. Let us, therefore, immediately plunge into that modern vehicle for myth: contemporary commercial television.

Among the dramatic programs of the 1983 television season were two that crossed the boundary between the human and animal worlds. One, "Mr. Smith," was plotted around the adventures of an ape blessed with superhuman intelligence. The other, "Manimal," followed the adventures of a scientist-crime-fighter who used his intellect to change himself into an animal at will.

Mr. Smith, an ordinary orangutan and passive subject of human scientists in a Washington D.C. think tank, escapes from his keepers. Accidently finding his way into a laboratory he randomly mixes a series of chemicals in a beaker. Upon drinking the mixture he finds himself endowed with instant speech and an I.Q. that reads off the scale. With his new capacities he becomes the perfect foil for a satire on those who govern our lives from politicians to the gurus of high technology.

Mr. Smith in his new role is allowed to "ape" humans. He dresses in pinstripes, lives in a suburban mansion where he is tended, and attended to, by his former trainer (a youth of uncertain intelligence) and a sophisticated gentleman's gentleman. He goes to work in a chauffeured limousine. Mr. Smith wears glasses when he reads and spouts such lines as: "Darwin invented the theory of deterioration." About to assist a famous brain surgeon in a delicate operation he says gleefully, "with your skill and my brains there should be no difficulty."

The plot of "Manimal" contrasts with the plot of "Mr. Smith" as if the programs were opposite aspects of the same story. Jonathan Chase, the hero of

"Manimal" (could his initials be mere accident?) has, through his own intellect, and a supreme act of self-will, discovered a way to transform himself into various animals. For a bird's-eye view of the world, he becomes a hawk. When caught in tight situations requiring agility or frightening power, he becomes a sleek black panther. Chase, a man of independent means (he needs no keeper), lives and works out of his own luxurious town house in New York that is filled with high-tech objects and a private zoo. While Mr. Smith is a super intellectual, given to passive reflection, Jonathan Chase, although highly intelligent, is a man of action. Mr. Smith's new role in life is to create order in the world of the mind. Jonathan Chase's role is to fight disorder in the real world of the urban jungle.

Although both shows were technologically innovative in different ways (one hanging on the gimmick of a real ape that looks and acts as if it can talk; the other, on the expertise of the makeup artist and stop-action filming) both dealt with old and universal concerns. Animals with human capacities, including speech, and humans who are beast-like appear with temporal and geographic regularity in world mythology. These range from fairy tales full of friendly, as well as not so friendly, creatures that talk and are sometimes meant to scare as well as amuse children, to myths containing similar themes but that are generally believed by their adult audiences. The space between animals and humans is inhabited by half-way creatures such as: abominable snowmen, lycanthropes, wily foxes, Jiminy Crickets, and even the centaurs and satyrs of Greek mythology.

Such creatures strike a chord in us because they raise, if only in disguised form, concerns about self and social identity. They allow us playfully (if not always amusingly) to bridge the great divide between ourselves and other species; to explore animal feelings in ourselves as well as the limits of our physical and intellectual powers. Breaking down the human-animal boundary also allows us to experiment with contrasting views of human nature: to model ourselves on, or distance ourselves from, a chosen species. We allow animals to instruct us, and even to make fun of us, but usually with the tacit knowledge that both the instruction and the derision come from within and not beyond human kind.

The age of computers has added another dimension to the question of self-identity, particularly as it concerns speech, mind, and intellect. The boundary between the living and the mechanical has been breached, and intelligence has been given to machines. An old game can now be played with new rules. The word "robot" was invented by the Czech playwright, Karl Kapek, and robots of various kinds have been around at least since the first part of the 20th century. Their success in the entertainment media reached its zenith with "Star Wars." But it is computers that have really sparked the imagination of the public. As they have moved from science to the reality of the home, particularly in the form of games, computers have reinforced the idea that machines can be animated and made to think. Is it surprising that both "Mr. Smith" and "Manimal" were preceded on NBC television by "Knight Rider," a program that stars a robotic, computerized car whose strength, intelligence, and emotional sensitivity are more than a match for any human?

Looking backward to the pretelevision age we find a whole class of films that provided a mythic content similar to that of the newer television programs. Most of these were horror movies, however, and tended, therefore, to lack the humor or the empathy displayed towards the nonhuman on recent television. Such films as the various versions of "Dracula," beginning with Murnau's classic masterpiece, "Nosferatu," and the "Wolf Man" series depict a cyclic change from human to animal that is both involuntary and malign. On another level these films deal with a regression from a civilized *ego* to an animal *id*.

Still another version of boundary breaking between the human and the nonhuman world can be seen on a somewhat more abstract level in films that deal with mad scientists. Here the break is not between human and animal, but rather between human and the uncanny or the supernatural. The use of the mind for "unnatural" or supernatural ends—directing the mind and creative efforts toward the domaines of God or the devil, rather than towards animals—gives us a Dr. Jekyll and a Mr. Hyde or a Dr. Frankenstein. In these films a scientist (either mad or with a mad ambition) attempts to reenter the Garden of Eden by way of the forbidden apple. The results are always monstrous in a quite literal sense. Monsters also appear in stories in which the boundary between the living and the dead is breached. This yields such creatures as zombies and vampires. While the former are dead humans brought to life, the latter cross the divide between human and animal as well as between the living and the dead. The science fiction genre, a favorite subject for films, has also provided a series of strange living forms often endowed with speech or some other type of communication. In most cases these beings live in, or come from, other parts of the universe. Such a device serves as a convenient explanation for their anomalous qualities.

If humans tend to use other animals and the supernatural as categories against which they define themselves as a species, they also identify as members of a particular human, social group and as individuals within that group. If, as is so often the case in modern society, we move between different social groups, we change certain characteristics of our behavior, but at the same time we maintain a core personality: our specific ego. We may not be able to define the latter for ourselves (real self-knowledge is elusive), but others will always define us as we are or, at least, as they think we are. Certain individuals tend to be perceived as having weak egos because they project no self-image or because they adopt the personality characteristics of those with whom they happen to be interacting. People who accommodate to different social groups are generally perceived in a negative light, as social chameleons. World mythology is full of tales dealing with self-loss or, as it is frequently characterized, soul-loss. A particularly powerful and common version of self loss found in myth, literature, and ritual is the theme of the double. Interestingly the ultimate double theme in scientific research is the use—now we know misuse—of data from identical twins reared apart for studies that proport to demonstrate the genetic component in I.Q.

When a person's double appears he or she is threatened with rejection or even replacement. Perhaps the most devastating version of this theme in Western literature is Dostoyevsky's "The Double." The protagonist, Yakov Petrovich Golyadkin, a middle level bureaucrat, leads an unsatisfying and dull life. When people take notice of him at all it is to deride his rather unpredictable and socially inept behavior. Even his servant, Petrushka, is rude to him. We first meet Golyadkin in the midst of a manic crisis. His extravagant comportment magnifies the negative aspects of his personality and increases his isolation from a rejecting social world. At the end of a particularly trying day he meets his exact double who, he discovers, even shares his name. Although terrified at first of the apparition, Golyadkin attempts to befriend him. As the story progresses it becomes clear that the double is a malign presence out to destroy Golyadkin and take his place in society. His success is as much the result of the protagonist's social ineptness as the double's ability to ingratiate himself with Golyadkin's colleagues and enemies. The power of this short novel comes, at least partially, from the ambiguity of the double himself. We can never be sure whether he is a projection of one side of Golyadkin's own personality or a real, if malignant, individual. He could even be the projection of a cruel social world. In any case Golyadkin's downfall is complete. At the end of the story he is led off to the mad house.

The double theme is also found with different twists and degrees of seriousness in Bellow's *The Victim,* Mark Twain's, *The Prince and the Pauper,* and Conrad's, *The Secret Sharer,* to mention only a few authors who have used it. It was also recently exploited, but in a cleverly reversed form, by the Japanese film maker, Kurosawa. His film, "Kagemusha," deals with a complex set of doubles and double like characters. In it a thief, already condemned to death, who strongly resembles the Shogen, is brought to court. He is given the chance to live if he agrees to learn the Shogen's role. Although unwilling, at first, he realizes his untenable position and eventually gives in, becoming quite adroit at court behavior. When the Shogen is killed in battle the double takes his place. Although there are some doubters in the enemy camp he is successful in convincing both friends and foes that he is the actual Shogen. Kept away from the women of the court, who knew the Shogen most intimately, his fraudulent nature is revealed only when. thrown from the Shogen's horse he was warned not to ride, a group of courtiers notice that he lacks an identifying scar on his back. No longer useful, he is cast out. Interestingly, his unmasking comes about only when he overplays the double role. It is pride that fools him into believing that he really is the Shogen. This pride also destroys him but, in dying, he reveals within himself, the heroism of the Shogen. He has, in fact, become a true double. He is killed in battle as he attempts to rally the Shogen's forces in the face of certain defeat. In "Kagemusha" the undoing of the protagonist, but also his real transformation into a heroic figure, come about through his doubling someone rather than having himself doubled. The theme of ego-loss common to double stories is maintained, however—the Shogen is, after all, replaced by his double—but in

"Kagemusha" the focus is switched largely to the development of the usurper's personality as he learns to play the role of the double that has been foisted on him. A man who begins as a thief and a cynic becomes a heroic character. This is more of an "ego gain" than a loss but it is still a case of transformation through the doubling process. But "Kagemusha" is even more complex than this. Kurosawa is not content with a single double. The son and the brother of the Shogen are also his doubles: each in different ways. The brother, rather than constituting a threat to the Shogen's existence, is an extension of his ego and a wise counselor. The Shogen's son, on the other hand, is a more typical double: an evil and voluntary usurper who wishes literally to take his father's place. He is the Japanese Oedipus, but is not Oedipus his father's double?

When people are doubled, from the outside, so to speak, they are passive victims. When they copy others in order to establish their social identity, they run the self-created risk of losing themselves in a shifting social reality. This theme was most recently exploited by Woody Allen in his outstanding film, "Zelig." The character, Zelig, lacking any center, transforms himself physically and behaviorally into whom ever he happens to be with at any given moment. When the public first discovers his gifts he becomes a celebrity, but only as a freak. Even his status as a human is questioned and he is advertised as a "human chameleon." The facts of social life catch up to Zelig when several women whom he has married during one or the other of his various roles accuse him of bigamy and fatherhood. Zelig falls into disgrace. He is later able to redeem himself in the eyes of the world, but only by using his gift to perform a super-human act. (He escapes from Nazi Germany by transforming himself into an expert pilot and flying a plane across the Atlantic—upside down.) In this desperate moment, he uses his strange power to save his own and his companion's life. Thus his transformation is no longer motivated by self-rejection. He has gained confidence in his own feelings through establishing, at last, a genuine relationship of love and understanding with his companion. He is free to be just himself: a rather ordinary person.

The role of Louise Fletcher, the woman psychiatrist who helps Zelig in the process of self discovery and ego development should, therefore, not be underestimated. Where Zelig is weak Dr. Fletcher is strong. Her tenacious involvement with this troubled human being elicits an authentic emotional response that leads to the final cure: the regaining of Zelig's social identity. Furthermore, as a doctor in the late 1920s, she works in a thoroughly masculine world. Thus, like Zelig, and in spite of her personal strength, she is an outsider constantly threatened by her male colleagues who refuse to take her work seriously. Dr. Fletcher's predicament in the film reflects another major boundary in self-definition: that between male and female. This is a particularly sensitive area for it touches on both social and biological differences; on the definitions of both sex and gender.

So far we have been looking at contemporary, or at least modern, television programs and movies of a particular kind: those that contain mythic and fantastic elements and that, I contend, are all concerned with some form of self-or-species-definition. Certainly most films and plays, as well as literature in general, touch on what is a major concern to all of us, but there is a certain special quality in art forms that deal with transformations from one category to another. These transformations are particularly powerful for us when we can actually see them. Like ancient myths, they deal with unreal, often fantastic situations, but in a realistic way. Films and television take the place of myths for most of us, because we live in a secular era as well as one in which we understand a great deal about the natural world. With a few possible exceptions such as the Loch Ness monster or the abominable snowman (and few of us believe even in these), we know that the biological world is divided into rather neat categories in which every species "has its place." When new species are discovered by scientists we are confident that a slot will be found for them in the existing category system: our biological taxonomy. When a peculiar form is discovered, like a bizarrely shaped deep-sea fish, our curiosity is aroused, but we still know that it fits into the fish category. Because we also know that it comes from a particular environment, one that is exceptionally different from that of normal sea dwellers, we are able to assimilate its bizarre nature to its habitat that we have also learned contains other "peculiar" species. When such deep-sea dwellers occasionally wash up on shore or turn up in fishermen's nets, they tend to cause a momentary stir, but we still expect a scientific explanation for both the event and the type of specimen found.

Our knowledge of the natural world has not always been based on science, and our category systems have not always been as neat as they are today. Even well after writing was invented and we were able to keep track of nature in books, humans lived in a world full of creatures that spanned one or another category. In addition, the whole category system was different. For example, the world of vertebrates was divided into land-dwelling mammals and sea-dwelling fish. Among vertebrates the air was inhabited exclusively by birds. Thus, whales were peculiar fish, and bats, peculiar birds because both have characteristics that do not normally fit into their environmentally defined group. Whales have warm blood whereas other fish do not, and bats have fur rather than feathers, the latter being the normal condition for the bird category. Because category systems of this type are full of anomalous creatures (all systems including our own, contain some) the notion of anomaly was easy to accept and, along with it, a biological world that contained creatures that breached the established but highly permeable boundaries.

The medieval conceptual world was loaded with creatures that were antomical mixtures of different animals. Griffins, to take a well-known example, are half eagle, half lion. One of the central characters of medieval belief was the wild man, a creature of mixed human and animal traits. Wild men lived in untamed nature: the forests and mountains of Europe or in those parts of the world that were only dimly known to people at that time. They were generally quite human in physical form, except for an overabundance of hair on the body. In most depicitions, the males of this fictional species are bearded but the rest of the face is clearly visible. Females lack all facial hair but are as hirsute as their male counterparts over the rest of their bodies. Wild men are often depicted with clubs and staffs, but this is usually the limit of their tools. Both sexes went naked.

Beliefs about the behavior of wild men are described, as follows, by Timothy Husband (1980):

> By every account the wild man's behavior matched his primitive surroundings. Strong enough to uproot trees, he was violent and aggressive, not only against wild animals but also against his own kind. His brutish, contentious nature expressed itself in a natural combativeness against which neither beast nor man was equal, though his club—and sometimes only his bare hands—was his only weapon. With his instinctive knowledge of the ways of wild beasts, the wild man was a skilled hunter, but, in spite of his physical supremacy, shrank from contact with humans and frequently even with his own kind. Indeed, his inept social abilities apparently limited him to only that cooperative union required for procreation. Lacking agriculture he was forced to eke out a subsistence from hunting and gathering. Thought to crawl around on all fours, he scratched tubers and roots from the ground, picked berries, and gnawed on verdure. When he killed game he ate it completely raw. . . . By many accounts, the wild man also indulged in cannibalism. . . . The wild man was innately irrational, a condition that was compounded by his limited powers to reason and articulate. . . . In less irrational, but equally abandoned, moods, he gave full rein to sensual desire. Although the wild man could hardly be suspected of overweaning faith, medieval authors stressed not that the wild man was without belief in God, but that he was utterly without knowledge of him. (pp. 3–4)

In the medieval period, the wild man embodied all that was negative about the untamed wilderness. This is not surprising, since during that time, people lived protected behind the ramparts of small cities or beneath the walls of fortified castles. The spaces between settlements—forest, plain, or mountain—were frightening places. They were inhabited by wild animals, some of which were at least believed to be dangerous, and, more importantly, by thieves and cutthroats who preyed upon travelers. The latter had some of the putative qualities of the wild man. The wild man himself was classified among the beasts because no proper human could live as he did. He stood as a mythical contrast to the proper human who lived in society and knew both his place and God.

If the wild man was a cannibal and a threat to human flesh in the literal sense, his woman was a threat to human flesh in the carnal sense. Although exceedingly ugly, she was capable of transforming herself into a beautiful maiden in order to seduce unsuspecting human victims. Her ugliness would be revealed only during intercourse, in the height of passion. The wild man was a cunning thief; the wild woman was a cunning taker-of-men whose sexual pleasure included a need to prove her mastery over those whom she seduced. White (1972) writes:

> In the Christian Middle Ages, then, the Wild Man is the distillation of the specific anxieties underlying the three securities supposedly provided by the specifically Christian institutions of civilized life: the securities of *sex* (as organized by the institutions of the family), *sustenance* as provided by the political, social, and economic institutions), and *salvation* (as provided by the church). The Wild Man enjoys none of the advantages of civilized sex, regularized social existence, or institutionalized grace. But, it must be stressed, neither does he—in the imagination of medieval man—suffer any of the restraints imposed by membership in these institutions. His desire is incarnate, possessing the strength, wit, and cunning to give full expression to all his lusts. (p. 21)

Long-distance commerce was a major characteristic of the Renaissance. As movement increased and communications among towns and cities improved, the wild man was pushed to the antipodes. Newly discovered peoples in exotic parts of the world were often taken as scientific proof for the existence of the wild man. At the same time, at least partially accurate descriptions of natives led to a reassessment of the wild man's physical characteristics, his technological prowess, and his social morality. Debates arose over whether or not the natives had souls and, if so, whether or not they could morally be enslaved. Back in Europe, the taming of nature produced a new attitude towards the countryside which, in many cases, took on a bucolic aspect. Life in the burgeoning cities produced evident problems of sanitation, crime and other forms of social disorganization that are still with us. Under these circumstances, the image of the wild man changed. While, for many, his negative characteristics never completely disappeared, attitudes towards him became, at the very least, ambivalent. For some, the wild man became a convenient means for the criticism of modern life. Thus, Montaigne used the exotic cannibal to parody his own culture, and Rousseau talked of better, simpler times when natural man lived in harmony with the environment. The wild man who through contrast had served to support a positive image of Christian society now became a vehicle for its rejection or, at least, its correction. The problem of the "native" was complicated, however. The beginning of colonial expansion in Africa and the New World, and, later in Asia, brought exploitation. This has been justified to the present day by characterizations of indigenous populations as either racially inferior, culturally inferior, or both. Racial inferiority is used as a permanent excuse for domination; cultural inferiority is used as an excuse to impose change on foreign cultures in order to "bring them into the modern world."

The interpretation of the wild man as native was complicated by the somewhat contradictory desire to encourage immigration to new worlds, on the one hand, and the need to exploit the people of these worlds, on the other. The unconscious use of the wild man image to define self and society was confounded with the conscious need to create a coherent ideology of domination. In his *The Image of the Indian in the Southern Colonial Mind,* Nash (1972) tells us that:

> . . . Men like Gilbert and Raleigh were likely to derive a split image of the natives of North America. On the one hand they had reason to believe that the Indians were savage, hostile, beastlike men, whose proximity in appearance and behavior was closer to the animal kingdom than to the kingdom of men, as western Europeans employed that term to describe themselves . . .
>
> But another vision of the native was simultaneously entering the English consciousness. Columbus had written of the 'great amity towards us' which he encountered in San Salvador in 1492 and described a generous pastoral people living in childlike innocence . . . (pp. 56–57)

Nash goes on to describe how these two attitudes were combined to produce a formula for colonialization that included the notion of goodwill on both sides, the benefits the two cultures could bring to each other, and an admitted premonition of justified violence if the native were to refuse the gift of civilization. Nash (1972) continues:

> Having explained how he hoped the English *might* act, and how the natives *might* respond, Peckham (writing in the 16 century) went on to reveal what he must have considered the more likely course of events: 'But if after these good and fayre means used, the Savages nevertheless will not be heerewithall satisfied, but barbarously wyll goe about to practice violence either in repelling the Christians from theyr Portes and safe Landinges or in withstanding them afterwards to enjoye the rights for which both painfully and lawfully they have adventured themselves thether; then in such a case I holde it no breache of equitye for the Christians to defende themselves, . . . For it is allowable by all Lawes in such distresses, to resist violence with violence.'
>
> With earlier statements of the gentle and receptive qualities of the Indians almost beyond recall, Peckham reminded his countrymen of their responsibility to employ all necessary means to bring the natives 'from falsehood to truth, from darkness to lyght, from the hieway of death, to the path of life, from superstitious idolatry, to sincere Christianity, from the devil to Christ, from hell to Heaven.' (pp. 59–60)

It is this mixture of conscious and unconscious ideology, this self-definition drawn against a mythological other, combined with the practical need to find a justification for domination, that produces a set of highly persistent ideological constructs. These constructs draw their power from both deep-seated psychological processes and real social forces. Even today these constructs pervade much of mythological thinking and provide simplistic explanations for what are really complex questions about such subjects as sex and race. What is less understood is that these same constructs also pervade much of what we are accustomed to call scientific thinking.

Before I move on to specify what kind of scientific thinking I mean, let us take stock of where we are at this point in the argument. I have suggested that a major problem for humans as rational animals is the need to find adequate definitions of self and social group. I have also suggested that we tend to use various real and mythological sets of nonhuman beings and things against which we define our own boundaries and essential qualities. Thus, we compare and contrast ourselves to beasts as humans. We break the boundary in order to better establish it, but not without the possibility of modifying the categories on both sides of the frontier. In the contemporary world where "thinking" machines have become a reality, we play the same game with real and imagined mechanical objects. In another direction, we invent situations in which humans attempt to usurp supernatural powers. These violations of natural law always produce tragic results as in the cases of Frankenstein and Dr. Jekyll. In stories such as these, we play at violating the boundary between ourselves and the gods or other supernatural forces.

In order to define ourselves, we need to establish fixed boundaries around our egos in the face of the somewhat contradictory requirement that we must vary our personal behavior and affect in different social situations. Double myths and double stories of various types are cautionary tales about the fragility of our egos in the world of interaction with others.

The final devastating threat to the self is death. Of course, most religions contain beliefs about afterlife, but, in spite of this, the thought of death remains frightening to many. This is particularly the case among westerners for whom modern science has often undermined religious conviction that, in any case, separates the world of the dead from that of the living. In a host of nonwestern societies, the dead continue on as part of the social system. They are asked for advice and protection, are sacrificed to, and are sometimes blamed for ill fortune. A constant sense of their presence provides the living with a feeling of personal continuity with the dead. In some eastern religions, death is seen as a great release from worldly suffering. In such systems, the loss of self is turned into a gain because it means that the ego has become one with the universe. Whatever the beliefs about death, it is not a subject to be ignored in any society.

Western culture, however, has never been able to leave the dead entirely alone. Although there is supposed to be a break between heaven and earth, between the living and the dead, beliefs about ghosts and ghouls appear in folklore and myth with regularity. In addition, there are many who really believe that the living and the dead can communicate. Another common theme, often found in horror stories and transposed into film, deals with the "living dead." These are the zombies who are brought back to a kind of semi-life through the actions of individuals perverted by the idea of personal gain.

Just as our fear of death is a fear of self-loss, our fascination with animals, and the boundary between animals and humans, reflects a need to understand and preserve that which is specifically human about ourselves and our species. Imaginative play with the human animal dichotomy is particularly common. It is found in historical and ethnographic materials from all over the world and can be seen in contemporary society in a range of manifestations. It is common in myths and folk tales and also appears in literature, theatre, films, and television. Play with this dichotomy is also concretized in a range of settings. Thus, for example, we clothe circus animals and train them to imitate human actions. We teach our dogs tricks and can be caught talking to them as well as to our pet cats and birds. Some of us believe that when parrots "talk" they also understand what they are saying, and few would deny that canaries "sing." Lately, some psychologists have made what is much too much of the ability of apes to use what appears to be human language. On the other side of the equation, sideshow freaks allow us to marvel at the mistakes nature can sometimes make while, at the same time, we distance ourselves from them and reaffirm the integrity of our own normality. Freaks, because they are somehow not human, are frequently put into the animal category.

In nonliterate, traditional societies, tales about talking bears or wolves are more easily accepted than in our own. Anthropomorphism (giving human traits to animals) is a common feature of many nonwestern religions. In our own culture, examples of anthropomorphism, if not readily believed can still fascinate us. However, the contemporary individual wants to be overwhelmed by convincing detail. The appeal of a program like "Mr. Smith," therefore, comes not only from what the ape does on screen. Its producers know that, for maximum effect, such an animal must also be assumed to have a private life. In order not to disappoint the public, its keepers have invented one. The Oct 22, 1983 issue of *T.V. Guide* featured Mr. Smith on its cover with the caption: "Mr. Smith (sh)apes up Hollywood and Washington." The article begins:

> No question who held the power here. Squeezing hands and kissing cheeks, the star of the series had arrived last for the luncheon meeting and now lounged on a pillowed sofa, flanked by two attentive aides. While others ate from a platter of cold delicatessen, the star commanded a special order—hot chicken, fried crisp and brown. Others were offered no dessert. He was served a banana split—three flavors of ice cream, whipped cream, chocolate sauce. Others drank soda from cans. He sipped apple juice from a glass.

So even the ape who plays Mr. Smith has power. He arrives last and lounges on a pillowed sofa. He is served a special menu of cooked food and a complicated dessert while the humans present are given only cold cuts to eat. The humans drink soda out of cans while the ape sips apple juice from a glass. In addition, the article tells us that Mr. Smith's dressing room is in a motor home bigger than Leonard Nimoy's and that following a routine similar to that of any star, he showers every morning and watches T.V. at night.

To maintain the illusion of Mr. Smith's humanity going on the show, itself, the producers admit that certain technical touch-ups are necessary, but:

People on the show are reluctant to discuss details of these touch-ups. They fear such facts will somehow destroy an illusion, will lower Mr. Smith to the level of assorted talking parrots and performing chimps, will reduce him to simply another animal act.

I have already suggested that in order to define our own place in nature it is common practice for us to experiment with the boundary between humans and animals. We do this by playing, in the imagination, with situations in which animals are given human traits or humans, animal traits. I have also suggested that this play is frequently incorporated into folklore and literature. It is also the case that western society has, for a long time, emphasized the great divide between humans and all other animal species. It is part of Judeo-Christian doctrine that only humans have souls. It was this belief, combined with the notion that human-*like* animals existed, that made it possible to argue over the question of whether or not American Indians had souls and, therefore, whether or not they could be enslaved.

It is absolutely correct to say that the theory of evolution as developed by Charles Darwin was an important threat to the central doctrines of organized religion. Darwin's theory challenged both the notion of special creation and the uniqueness of the human species. Evolution was, however, rapidly accepted by the scientific community, and by the end of the 19th century the majority of biologists agreed that it was the most satisfactory way to account for a vast array of data from geology, biology and paleontology. Acceptance by the lay public was much slower to come. Nevertheless, at the present time, even among religious people—with the strong exception of fundamentalists—the evolution of the human species from lower forms is no longer questioned.

We are still able to distance ourselves from the rest of the animal kingdom, however. This is accomplished among believers by continuing to accept the doctrine that humans are the only species to be granted souls by God. Among non-believers, the situation is somewhat more complicated. Many non-religious social scientists and biologists recognize the tremendous role that learning plays in the development of individuals and social groups. They see this, plus language behavior, as special characteristics limited to our species. Others see the theory of evolution as having forever removed humans from a unique and special place in the universe. They accept the possibility of major continuities between ourselves and other animals. Many lay people have an ambivalent and changing attitude towards these questions. For some, it is possible to imagine that certain people (particularly members of different ethnic or racial groups) are somehow not quite human. For others, the notion that we are all animals is readily accepted as an explanation for a whole series of psychological and social problems that plague modern society. The former are racists, but the latter, because they see themselves and members of their own social groups as subject to the same biological laws as everyone else, should not be accused of this error. Instead, they have what, I argue, is a too hasty tendency to confuse a metaphoric use of biology with "scientific" explanation.

Because the categories and problems we have been talking about are emotionally charged and complicated by a mixture of mythological, scientific, and theological ideas, it is difficult for anyone to think clearly about them. Even scientists, not to mention lay people, tend to confuse deep seated feelings about humanity with objective criteria. More often than not, it is this that leads to naive solutions to what are, in fact, very complex problems. Because these problems often concern the well-being of individuals and groups, this is a very serious matter indeed. Not only is racism, whether it is of the "scientific" or the garden variety, dangerous but so is the simple biological reductionism of the type that attributes the causes of aggression and war directly to genes.

Much of biological determinism, particularly in its most recent form, sociobiology, is unable to explain human behavior adequately, however, there is a strong and valid place for biology in the understanding of our species' unique capacity for creative thought. Thus far, we have examined the way humans think about themselves in various dramatic and literary forms and how this relates to the real questions about the biological foundations of human behavior. As a confirmed Darwinian, but also as an anthropologist trained in culture as well as biology, I believe that it is necessary to develop a bio-cultural theory that is able to account for creativity in its many forms, but particularly as it is manifested in language and art. These capacities are characteristic of our species and make us unique in the animal kingdom of which we are an integral part.

As a member of the animal kingdom, the human species shares a wide range of biological traits with all other members of that kingdom. On the other hand, human beings are, like each individual species, endowed with a set of unique characters that set them apart from the rest of the animal world. In the case of humans, the most spectacular of these species specific characters are, undoubtedly, the brain-based capacities for linguistic and artistic behavior. While both of these capacities are the product of evolution, it must not be forgotten that selection for them occurred because we are a social species. Neither language nor art make any sense as behavioral products except in the context of social activity among highly intelligent and flexible creatures.

We know that both physical and behavioral traits make up a species' particular "biogram." Lay people are familiar with many of the physical characteristics that are common to mammals including humans. The most widely known are: warm blood, live birth, and the nurturing of the young with mother's milk. They are also generally aware that humans differ from other mammals in such traits as true bipedalism. Lay people commonly realize that such behavioral traits as language and complex intellectual activity are specifically human. Many also suppose that we share such relatively simple instincts as aggression and territoriality with other mammals. This belief has been reinforced by some behavioral biologists, particularly Konrad Lorenz, who concentrated in his work on the putative similarities between humans and other animals rather than investigate our species' unique behavioral characteristics. Of course, Lorenz and other ethologists were trained to study lower animals. They came to speculations about human behavior late in their lives when their thinking had already been molded by field studies of birds and fish. Thus, much of the work (most of it speculative) that sees a strong continuity between human and nonhuman animal behavior is based on simple analogies between what are frequently *genetic* patters in nonhuman species, but *learned* (cultural) patterns in humans. The fact that humans are sometimes aggressive, can own property, including land, and display patriotic attachments to their nation state does not mean that these patterns are coded into our genome. In fact, the two latter traits are relatively recent additions to the repertoire of human culture. Actually the human species, for the very reason that it is highly flexible in behavior, is one of the most widely distributed and successful of animals. Humans adapt to a wide range of geographic and social environments through culture, which is learned, not programed into our genes. Under certain historically determined conditions we can act aggressively or be totally nonviolent, accumulate property, give it away, or even lack any conception of private ownership, much less display loyalty to a territory. This flexibility, is, itself, a biological characteristic of our species, but is an emergent characteristic dependent on the particular kind of and level of social integration that marks *Homo sapiens.* It has developed in the context of a unique set of interactions between brain development and social activity. Thus it has its own genetic base, but rather than representing continuity with other species, it sets us apart from them.

It is common wisdom among members of my own discipline, anthropology, that, because culture and language are learned, the only thing genetic about them is this overall learning capacity. It is a short step from this reasoning to the conclusion that our ability to learn is only quantitatively different from that of other animals. If we take this to be the case, then the discontinuity between lower animals and ourselves is only one of degree, rather than one of kind. This is the position taken by behaviorists in psychology. I believe the error here comes from the notion that experiments proving that animals can, under specific and highly controlled conditions, be taught to mimic the behavior (and ''intelligence'') of other species, including humans, also proves that all species learn the same way and with the same sort of mental equipment. There is, however, a big difference between cleverly teaching animals clever tricks and explaining the mechanisms that go into the behavior underlying these tricks. For the latter a scientific theory is required. One theory that separates human capacities from that of lower animals is that of the great German philosopher Emmanuel Kant. Modern versions of this theory suggest that there is much in culture, specifically how humans organize and manipulate their perceptual world, that is coded in the brain. These theories can easily be distanced from strict biological determinism for they provide a biological basis for creativity in both language and the arts rather than for such "fixed action patterns" as territoriality and aggression. The name most prominently associated with the modern version of this theory is Noam Chomsky whose ideas should be clearly distinguished from the general run of biological determinism and sociobiology. The latter schools dictate, with different degrees of insistence, that biology is destiny. The Chomskian position is that a specific, biologically determined, brain-coded trait (a genetically programmed universal grammar), provides the basis for creativity in human discourse. This is taken to be the case for language because it is a recursive system, that is, with a finite set of rules, it allow for an infinite number (and kind) of messages. The idea of brain based coding systems has recently been expanded by Jerry Fodor in his book, *The Modularity of Mind* (1983). I am convinced that the theoretical principles advanced by Chomsky and Fodor hold true for aesthetics.

As an anthropologist I differ from Chomsky because of his exclusive theoretical focus on the code as a fixed entity. I want to know how such a code (or codes) evolved, as well as how it (they) operate(s) on the level of real social life. My position (concerning the arts) is that, not only is the capacity for artistic behavior part of our species genetic heritage, but that there are certain underlying and universal aesthetic principles coded in the brains of all normal humans. It is these principles, along with specific sets of sociohistorical factors that allow us to produce and appreciate the arts of our own culture as well as appreciate the art of other cultures. In addition, I believe that these principles contribute to the adaptive power of empathy, which is the means of relating emotionally to others, even to those who might otherwise be strange to us. In order to avoid confusion concerning my position, I must hasten to add that any mechanisms underlying and setting limits around the successful content (as opposed to form) of aesthetic production has to be culturally and historically determined. All of the arts, in their material manifestations, are the result of historical and cultural forces that include: previously established, specific formal-patterns, culturally and personally determined taste, and the individuals' learned capacities to make and or appreciate art. If there is a grammar of aesthetics, it too must be recursive and generative; the content of its messages must be cultural. Aesthetic behavior as behavior is manifested on a higher level of integration than the underlying grammar of that behavior.

I must also emphasize that art is not exactly like language, although it has been assimilated into language by some authors. This error probably occurs because art is often used like language or has been made to carry linguistic messages (in advertising, for example). Art is, certainly, a communications device. I would suggest, therefore, that art, like language, is a member of a family of communication systems rather than a kind of language. Other members of this family, which are neither language nor art, include the set of chemical signals used by bees and ants, and the visual signals used in the mating dances of several species of birds. I am also uncomfortable with any equation between art and language because humans must have language to communicate adequately, but they do not need art to communicate at all. I believe this to be the case even though it is true that art may communicate emotions better than language in the latter's banal, everyday aspect. I am, of course, not talking about poetry that is language used in the service of art.

The important thing to realize here is that the capacity for language behavior, because it is highly adaptive for a behaviorally flexible and intelligent social animal such as we, was undoubtedly selected for directly in that evolutionary process that led from our primate ancestors to the modern human species *Homo sapiens*. It is highly probable that artistic behavior, although it shares many characteristics with language, is only an artifact of evolution: the byproduct of selection for other more directly adaptive traits. Not all genetically based behavior need be the result of natural selection. Such behavior may emerge from the random proliferation of selectively neutral traits or from selection favoring unrelated traits that, together, give rise to some new complex that may itself have some selective value. In my book, *The Artistic Animal* (Alland, 1977) I argued that art resulted from the interaction of at least four behavioral systems, each of which was probably selected for independently. These are: *exploration* and *play,* which foster the understanding and manipulation of the environment; *response to form,* which increases awareness of the environment and subtle changes that may occur in it; *fine grain perceptual discrimination* coupled to *excellent memory,* which increases the capacity to deal with environmental variation and to exploit existing resources; and, finally, what I call *transformation-representation.* The latter involves the means of expressing ideas, feelings, and images in formal ways that make new connections between them, as in metaphors. This capacity is one of the most important elements of language, but lies at the roots of art as well. The ability to manipulate symbols in both language and art provides the basis for free creativity in which previously untapped relationships among unconnected elements are used to add interest and density to spoken and visual messages. (Music must also work this way too.) New metaphors and suggestive combinations of visual symbols provide part of the richness that we associate with all successful works of art. Ezra Pound, the well known 20th century poet, is said to have remarked that ''literature is language charged with meaning, and great literature is language charged with meaning to the utmost.'' This is certainly the case but Pound forgot to add that the elation we get from a successful work of art is also due to the interplay of formal elements in it, and the relationship of these formal elements to the network of multiple meanings present in a great work. This applies just as much to the visual arts and music as it does to literature.

It must be stressed again that any genetic element implicated in the generation of art will affect only its formal aspects rather than its meaning, for the latter depends strictly on free creativity, limited only by individual experience and historically defined culture. Thus, for example, it must be the capacity for transformation-representation that is inherited by all normal humans rather than any specific set of transformation-representations. On the other hand, formal rules for good transformations may be brain coded. Thus, I believe that successful art may be governed by certain universal formal rules affecting structure, but not content. What I am suggesting here is that there is some kind of universal grammar (UG) for aesthetic form. This UG may determine, along with absolutely nogenetic cultural and individual conventions, what is and is not a successful work. Here I must admit that the evidence for such a UG is problematical at the present time. Such an idea is highly speculative, but in full accordance with theories of modular thinking. What scant evidence there is for such an aesthetic UG comes from two sources: cross-cultural regularities of aesthetic preference in individuals connected in some way with the arts; and anecdotes about cross-cultural regularities in aesthetic choices, again among individuals connected in some way with the arts. Thus it is assumed that the phenotype for "tuned aesthetic judgment" emerges only from its putative genetic background when an individual has personal and social experiences with art.

In *The Artistic Animal* I reviewed a series of studies designed to reveal regularities in aesthetic judgment. The first of these were the works of three English psychologists: Dewar, Bert, and Eysenck. Clearly all of these studies were all marred by a lack of control for cultural factors: the subjects tested were all English. Monica Lawlor (1955), also an English psychologist, was among the first to undertake a cross-cultural test of aesthetic preference. She used a set of designs based on common patterns found in West African carving, weaving, and metal work. These designs were shown to groups of English and West African subjects who were asked to rank them in order of preference. Lawlor then compared the results from the two groups to see if there was any agreement between them. Her results were negative. Although there was considerable agreement within each group of subjects, there was no agreement between the English and African groups. The agreement within groups must, of course, be attributed to shared cultural factors suggesting that culture shapes aesthetic choice.

More recently, another approach to this problem was taken by Irvin Child of Yale's Psychology Department. Working first with American subjects, Child found that if the art preferences of a sample drawn from the general public is compared to the preferences of a group of art experts, there is no correlation between them. Aesthetic judgment (as measured by agreement with experts) turns out to be correlated with the amount of formal education in art as well as with experience in looking at art in museums, galleries, books, and magazines. Strangely, it is correlated, but less so, with art-related activities such as sketching, sculpting, or photography. Such results, of course, once again tend to confirm an educational and, therefore, a cultural role in the formation of aesthetic judgment.

Fortunately for the theory expounded here, Child went beyond his original experiments and decided to test art experts in different cultures to see if any transcultural regularities exist among these groups. Child and Leon Siroto (1965), an anthropologist who did field work among the Bakwele of the Congo (now Zaire), showed a sample of photographs of Bakwele masks to a group of Bakwele sculptors and to a group of art history students at Yale who were not familiar with African art. Each subject was asked to rank the photos in the sample according to aesthetic value. While the ranking of the two groups were not identical, agreement was significantly high, suggesting for the first time that aesthetic judgment, at least among art experts, could be transcultural.

In another similar study, Child, Clellan Ford, and Edwin Prothro compared aesthetic judgment among Yale University graduate students in art history, Figian artists, and Greek crafts people living in the Cyclade Islands. Again the aesthetic judgment within and among the different groups was in statistically significant agreement. Then Sumiko Iwao (Iwao & Child, 1966), a Japanese psychologist and colleague of Child, compared New Haven experts with a large group of Japanese potters. The largest sample of 36 potters was from Tanba, a village where pottery has been made for several centuries. The second group of 14 potters was from Izushi, a less traditional village. The smallest group, of 10 potters, was from the city of Kyoto and probably had the greatest familiarity with Western art.

Sets of black and white and colored photos of matched pairs of art works from different media were shown to the subjects who were asked to state their preference for one picture in each pair. Once again, the percentage of agreement between the Japanese and American samples was statistically significant. Furthermore, Iwao also tested the judgments of Japanese experts against American experts and nonexperts and the latter against each other. The average agreement between nonexpert American and American experts was only 47% while the agreement between Japanese and American experts was 63%. Thus, in this case, the factor of culture appeared to be less important than interest and familiarity with art even when the art in question came from two different cultures. And it must be emphasized that the expertise in question does not extend, in the experimental group (the Japanese potters) to knowledge about the sample of art used in the experiment.

Let me now end this discussion with a tantalizing look at some anecdotal evidence for aesthetic universals. These cases all suggest that there is some underlying set of principles that govern aesthetic judgment among individuals in different cultures who are interested in and sensitive to one or more of the arts.

My first case concerns a painter of shields from the Maring area of Papua-New Guinea. In precontact times, this painter, Akus, was famous among his own people as a skilled artist and innovator. Although Maring traditional art consists of abstract designs, after contact with Westerners, Akus began to paint and draw schematized, but realistic pictures on large paper sheets. These were taken to the capital, Port Morsby, to be sold to European collectors. Recently, some of Akus' work has found its way onto the New York art market. In the 1960s Akus, who has essentially born in the stone age (the Maring used stone axes and adzes before contact in the 1950s), was taken to Port Morsby by Rafe Bulmer, an anthropologist. Given the run of Bulmer's apartment, Akus soon learned how to use the record player. After only a few weeks he was heard, as he walked around town, humming themes from Beethoven and Mozart, two composers he had chosen himself from among the many in Bulmer's collection.

In the mid 1970s I began a design analysis of Maring shields using a large collection of photographs taken by Cherry lowman, a Columbia University trained anthropologist who had done her field work among the Maring in the 1960s. Knowing little about Maring culture, and nothing about their art, I picked out a set of shields that seemed to me to be the most aesthetically successful of the lot. They all turned out to have been made by Akus or his cousin, who was also known among the Maring themselves as one of their best artists.

While in Bali in 1977 on a research trip connected with children's art, my wife Sonia took a series of dance lessons with a Balinese teacher. We became quite friendly with him and attended many ceremonies together. The core of much Balinese religious ritual is dancing. While there are many famous dancers in Bali, most ceremonies are performed by dancers of varying degrees of skill. During our visit we also witnessed dance performances by children who were learning the elaborate Balinese choreographic patterns but who were not yet fully formed dancers. Comparing notes on various performers with my wife's teacher, we found that our judgments about the best and the worst dancers in these two different contexts coincided almost perfectly. This was the case even though the rules of Balinese dance are, in many ways, the opposite of the rules for Western Ballet, the classical dance form with which we were both most familiar. Body position and carriage are particularly different in the two cultures. Our judgments were based on kinesthetic elements in performance rather than on the specific choreographic patterns and body positions, which are, of course, strictly cultural in nature.

I could relate many other stories of this type. As interesting and provocative as they are, they cannot be substituted for rigorous scientific research. If universal aesthetic patterns exist, they still need to be demonstrated empirically. Examples of agreement in aesthetic judgment among experts from different cultures looking at the same works of art are not sufficient. We must find out what aesthetic principles, if any, operate in these judgments and what role they play in combination with cultural conventions in the production and appreciation of art in different historically determined cultures.

## CONCLUSION

In this paper I have attempted to demonstrate that a strong folk tradition exists in Western culture that preconditions the public, and even some scientists, to accept such reductionistic theories as biological determinism in its many forms. This tradition involves imaginary play with the human-animal and related dichotomies, often with the effect of either blurring the differences between humans and other species, or of overemphasizing the role biology plays in determining contemporary human behavior. My intention, however, is not to reject all forms of theorizing about the role of biology in the determination and direction of human behavior. Rather than focus on simple analogies between fixed behavioral genetic patterns in lower animals and what is best explained as learned cultural behavior in humans, I have instead suggested that we should construct integrated bio-behavioral theories that make room for learned and historically determined socio-cultural patterns. These can then be used to account for behavioral complexes that are particular to our species and its known level of biological and social integration. Taking Chomsky's theory of language and universal grammar as a point of departure, but expanding it to include the notion of social forces in human evolution, I have presented a tentative and partial explanation of the role behavioral genetic evolution may have played in the emergence of artistic behavior in humans. I realize that these ideas are controversial, but a growing number of psychologists have begun to give them serious attention. I believe that anthropologists and biologists must begin to pay attention to them as well. Whether or not these ideas prove ultimately to be right or wrong they will certainly stimulate the further development of theory construction and the empirical testing of integrated notions about our species specific behaviors.

## REFERENCES

Alland, A. (1977). *The artistic animal*. New York: Anchor Press.

Child, I., & Siroto, L. (1965). Bakwele and American esthetic evaluation. *Ethnology, 4*, 349–369.

Chomsky, N. (1965). *Aspects of a theory of grammar*. Cambridge, MA: MIT Press.

Chomsky, N. (1975). *Reflections on language*. New York: Pantheon.

Fodor, J. (1983). *The modularity of mind*. Cambridge, MA: Bradford/MIT Press.

Husband, T. (1980). *The wild man: Medieval myth and symbolism*. New York: The Metropolitan Museum of Art.

Iwao, S., & Child, I. (1966). Comparison of esthetic judgment by American experts and by Japanese potters. *Journal of Social Psychology, 68*, 27–33.

Lawlor, M. (1955). Cultural influence on preference for design. *Journal of Abnormal and Social Psychology, 61*, 680–692.

Nash, G. (1972). The image of the indian in the Southern colonial mind. In D. Edward & T. Novak (Eds.), *The wild man within*. Pennsylvania: University of Pittsburgh Press.

Sahlius, M. (1976). *The Use and Abuse of Biology*. Ann Arbor: University of Michigan Press.

White, H. (1972). The forms of wildness: archeology of an idea. In D. Edward & T. Novak (Eds.), *The wild man within*. Pennsylvania: University of Pittsburgh Press.

# 11 Human Evolution and the Comparative Psychology of Levels

Charles W. Tolman
*University of Victoria*

## INTRODUCTION

In notes written in the 1870s and 1880s, and published posthumously some 60 years later under the title *Dialectics of Nature,* Frederick Engels wrote: "One day we shall certainly 'reduce' thought experimentally to molecular and chemical motions in the brain; but does that exhaust the essence of thought?" (Engels, 1972, p. 248). He apparently considered the answer to be so obvious that he did not bother to provide it. That Engels took the answer to be negative is obvious from the context of the question, as indeed from the book as a whole and from every thought that he committed elsewhere to paper.

The dialectical view of the world as expressed in the work of Engels is fundamentally, vigorously, and self-consciously anti-reductionist, as is evident in the following comment on heat: "The discovery that heat is molecular motion was epoch-making. But if I have nothing more to say of heat than that it is a certain displacement of molecules, I should best be silent" (Engels, 1972, p. 253).

Engels's anti-reductionism was expressed positively by a consistent dialectical theory and methodology of levels, not unlike those later advocated by Dobzhansky (1941), Novikoff (1945), and Schneirla (1949; see also Aronson, Tobach, Rosenblatt, and Lehrman, 1972). An essential aspect of Engels's approach to levels was its materialism, an important implication of which had to do with explanation and the relations between levels. For example, regarding chemistry and organic life Engels wrote ". . . chemistry leads to organic life, and it has gone far enough to assure us that *it alone* will explain to us the dialectical transition to the organism" (Engels, 1972, p. 249).

A higher level is not reducible to the lower level, but it is explained by it. For Engels, it cannot be otherwise. If it is not the matter of chemistry that explains life, then we open the door to anti-materialist, and thus also anti-scientific, accounts such as vitalism. But the explanation for Engels was not a mechanical one; it was rather one of "dialectical transition." Only a transformational, an evolutionary account of the development of the higher level from the lower one can preserve simultaneously the irreducible distinctness and the unity of the two levels. Engels (1972) wrote that it was the logic of Hegel brought to bear on the evolutionary ideas of Darwin:

> When Hegel makes the transition from life to cognition by means of propagation. . . , there is to be found in this the germ of the theory of evolution, that, organic life once given, it must evolve by the development of the generations to a genus of thinking beings. (p. 309)

In another place Engels (1972) wrote:

> What a beautiful confirmation of Hegel's thesis that the inductive conclusion is essentially a problematic one! Indeed, owing to the theory of evolution, even the whole classification of organisms has been taken away from induction and brought back to "deduction", to descent—one species being literally *deduced* from another by descent—and it is impossible to prove the theory of evolution by induction alone, since it is quite anti-inductive. (p. 227)

Explanation is deductive, but it is a specific kind of "organic" deduction, based on the transformational, evolutionary process by which a higher species, category or level emerges from a lower one. Thus, returning to the question of thought and molecular motion, the explanation of thought will ultimately require both an account of the properties of thought that distinguish it from molecular motion and an account of the process by which thought has evolved from non-thinking matter. In brief, an Engelsian account of the human psyche is necessarily a comparative, evolutionary one.

## ENGELS ON THE TRANSITION FROM APE TO MAN

Not surprisingly, considering the immense intellectual energy of the man, Engels outlined such an approach to the study of human psyche in 1876. Also not surprisingly, Engels (1972) took labour as his point of departure.

> Labour is the source of all wealth, the political economists assert. And it really is the source—next to nature, which supplies it with the material that it converts into wealth. But it is even infinitely more than this. It is the prime basic condition for all

human existence, and this to such an extent that, in a sense, we have to say that labour created man himself. (p. 170)

Owing to the centrality of Labour in Engels's theory, the concept itself merits some attention. Marx (1974) wrote the following well-known definition:

Labour is, in the first place, a process in which both man and Nature participate, and in which man of his own accord starts, regulates and controls the material reactions between himself and Nature. He opposes himself to Nature as one of her own forces, setting in motion arms and legs, head and hands, the natural forces of the body, in order to appropriate Nature's production in a form adapted to his own wants. By thus acting on the external world and changing it, he at the same time changes his own nature. (p. 173)

The main points here are that labour is a human activity directed against our natural environment and which transforms that environment in accordance with our wants. In so doing, we, the actors, change ourselves, or as Engels put it: "Labour created man himself." Marx and Engels intended that these claims be taken primarily as applying to the collective of social humanity. The "change," the "creation," refer first and foremost to human social history. It is this historical character of human labour that most distinguishes it from similar animal activities. Elsewhere in *Capital,* Marx (1974) wrote:

[Is it not true that] . . . human history differs from natural history in this, that we have made the former, but not the latter? Technology discloses man's mode of dealing with Nature, the process of production by which he sustains his life, and thereby also lays bare the mode of formation of his social reations, and of the mental conceptions that flow from them. (p. 352)

The tool is the essential ingredient in human labour. What, then, is a tool? According to Marx (1974):

An instrument of labour is a thing, or a complex of things which the labourer interposes, between himself and the subject of his labour, and which serves as the conductor of his activity. . . . As the earth is his original larder, so too it is his original tool house. It supplies him, for instance, with stones for throwing, grinding, pressing, cutting etc. . . . No sooner does labour undergo the least development, than it requires especially prepared instruments. . . . For use and fabrication of instruments of labour, although existing in germ among certain species of animals, is specifically characteristic of human labour-process. . . (pp. 174–175)

Labour, the systematic, planned transformation of Nature by the manufacture and use of special tools, is the basis of all human history, which is the movement of culture, a "mode of dealing with Nature" which is unique and qualitatively distinct from all animal modes of adaptation, though derived from them.

Engels's (1972) concern was to give an account of how this qualitatively new level was produced, i.e. how it evolved. The initial, decisive step, according to his account, was bipedalism.

> Climbing assigns different functions to the hands and the feet, and when their mode of life involved locomotion on level ground, these apes gradually got out of the habit of using their hands (in walking) and adopted a more and more erect posture. This was *the decisive step in the transition from ape to man.* (p. 170)

Engels recognized the necessary preparation for this step in our primate ancestors. He considered at some length the "different functions of the hands and the feet" in contemporary apes and lists their accomplishments, ". . . but the hand of the lowest savage can perform hundreds of operations that no simian hand can imitate—no simian hand has ever fashioned even the crudest stone knife" (Engels, 1972, p. 171). The difference was the "decisive step" by which the hand of the prehominid had become free to adapt itself to uses other than locomotion. Such use encouraged further structural change and therefore also further refinement of use. "Thus," according to Engels, "the hand is not only the organ of labour, it is also the product of labour" (Engels, 1972, p. 172).

This development, combined with certain other considerations such as the natural gregariousness of our primate ancestors, led to the beginnings of what Engels (1972) called "mastery over nature."

> Mastery over nature began with the development of the hand, with labour, and widened man's horizon at every new advance. He was continually discovering new, hitherto unknown properties in natural objects. On the other hand, the development of labour necessarily helped to bring the members of society closer together by increasing cases of mutual support and joint activity, and by making clear the advantage of this joint activity to each individual. In short, men in the making arrived at the point where *they had something to say* to each other. Necessity created the organ; the undeveloped larynx of the ape was slowly but surely transformed by modulation, and the organs of the mouth gradually learned to pronounce one articulate sound after another. (p. 173)

From the developing process of labour emerged both the possibility and necessity of social organization and joint activity, and simultaneously, the possibility and necessity of spoken language. This, in turn, put pressure on other organs of the body. Engels (1972) wrote:

> First labour, after it and then with it speech—these were the two most essential stimuli under the influence of which the brain of the ape gradually changed into that of the man. . . . The reaction on labour and speech of the development of the brain and its attendant senses, of the increasing clarity of the consciousness, power of abstaction and of conclusion, gave both labour and speech an ever-renewed impulse to further development. (p. 174)

But this development did not take place in a social vacuum.

> This further development has been strongly urged forward, on the one hand, and guided along more definite directions, on the other, by a new element which came into play with the appearance of fully-fledged man, namely, *society*. (p. 175)

The three essential interrelated elements in human evolution, then, were labour, speech and joint activity.

> By the combined functioning of hands, speech organs and brain, not only in each individual but also in society, men become capable of executing more and more complicated operations, and were able to set themselves, and achieve, higher and higher aims. (p. 177)

The result was a "mode of dealing with Nature" that was qualitatively distinct from that of animals: "The further removed men are from animals, however, the more their effect on nature assumes the character of premeditated, planned action directed towards definite preconceived ends" (p. 178). Thus the psychological aspect, the self-organizing function of consciousness becomes central to the distinction. Engels did not imagine, however, that this appeared at the human, cultural level of evolution entirely *de novo*.

> On the contrary, a planned mode of action exists in embryo wherever protoplasm . . . exists and reacts . . . But all the planned action of all animals has never succeeded in impressing the stamp of their will upon the earth. That was left for man. . . the animal merely *uses* its environment, and brings about changes in it simply by its presence; man by his changes makes it serve his ends, *masters* it. This is the final, essential distinction between man nd other animals, and once again it is labour that brings about this distinction. (pp. 179–180)

Here, as elsewhere, the dialectical concept of levels is evident. It is not a theory, like traditional emergentism or holism, that achieves its emphasis on discontinuity by scarificing continuity. On the contrary, it utilizes the internal relations of continuity and discontinuity to reveal the concrete process of transformation by which new qualities are produced. In this way the new qualities are not mystified and a consistently materialist account is sustained.

## THE EVIDENCE OF HUMAN EVOLUTION

A comparative psychology of the human and animal (or prehuman) levels, then, is one that takes into account the physical evidence of human evolution. It is a psychology that is consistent with that evidence and draws from it what implications it can.

It should be noted from the outset that the hard data of anthropogenesis, although increasing enormously in recent years, are still few and precious. Furthermore, what data do exist are not entirely unambiguous. We are as yet far from a general theory of human evolution that is widely and confidently held. There are, however, certain broad aspects of the process on which considerable agreement has been achieved, not the least of which is that the process did in fact occur and that its course and dynamics are in principle discoverable. Regarding such fundamental claims, the available data are sufficient to offer overwhelming evidence. But certain characteristics of the process are also clear such as anatomical changes and the evolution of tool use and manufacture. It is on characteristics of this sort that we shall focus here.

## Evolution of the Brain

The traditional view of human evolution has been diametrically opposed to the materialist theory of Engels. This idealist view, known as the ''brain primacy'' theory, is clearly stated in the following passage from Elliot Grafton Smith, written in 1924 and quoted in Gould (1980):

> The outstanding interest of the Piltdown skull is in the confirmation it affords of the view that in the evolution of Man the brain led the way. It is the veriest truism that man has emerged from the simian state in virtue of the enrichment of the structure of his mind. . . . The brain attained what may be termed the human rank at a time when the jaws and face, and no doubt the body also, still retained much of the uncouthness of Man's simian ancestors. In other words, Man at first . . . was merely an Ape with an overgrown brain. The importance of the Piltdown skull lies in the fact that it affords tangible confirmation of these inferences. (p. 117)

We now know of course that the Piltdown skull was a forgery, which may well have been perpetrated with the express intent of lending the appearance of scientific support to an idealist prejudice. It is worth noting *en passant* that the same prejudice is still widely manifest in contemporary psychology, nowhere more so than in the claims of Jensen, Herrenstein, Shockley and company that intelligence is biologically fixed at conception. The alternative, Engelsian view is that intelligence is ontogenetically, as phylogenetically, the result, not the cause of cultural activity.

The paleoanthropological evidence clearly opposes the traditional brain centered view of human evolution, but there can be no question of the brain's importance, and to begin our considerations with the brain does provide a convenient chronological framework within which our other considerations can usefully be placed. Let us then begin with a graphic illustration of the evolutionary increase in brain size. Figure 11.1 shows the brain size in $cm^3$ of various representative species in the hominid lineage (based on Olivier, 1973; Schurig, 1976; and Foerster, 1981).

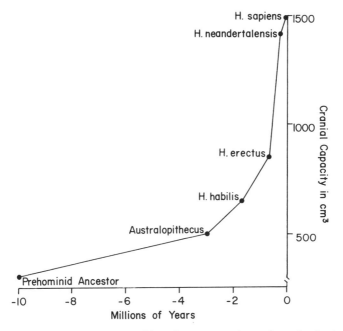

FIGURE 11.1. Cranial capacities of representatives of species in the hominid lineage.

We should first dispose of certain problems associated with the starting point. There are, roughly speaking, two major views represented in the pertinent literature. The first is that the pre-*Australopithecus* period is occupied by an even more primitive homonid known as *Ramapithecus* (Woolfson, 1982, pp. 11 ff.). Remnants of this presumed hominid have been found in India, Pakistan, Turkey, Greece, and Hungary, and are dated between −14 and −7 million years, leaving a so-called "fossil gap" of 3 or 4 million years between *Ramapithecus* and *Australopithecus*. Cranial capacity for the former has been estimated at 300 $cm^3$.

The second view is that what existed prior to *Australopithecus* was our primate ancestor, the one in fact that we have in common with the present day gorilla and chimpanzee. The grounds for this view are findings on differences between amino acid sequences in these apes and humans which indicate, according to the so-called "molecular clock," a lapse of approximately 5 million years since our common ancestor (Gould, 1980, p. 130; see also Pilbeam, 1984).

Fortunately we need not be bothered by this controversy. Both *Ramapithecus* and the primate ancestor would have had similar cranial capacities (the present day chimpanzee, which is similar in size to the presumed ancestor has an average cranial capacity of 300 $cm^3$) and other differences would be so minor as to have little bearing on whatever conclusion we need to draw from this graph.

It might be argued that the increase in brain size has been produced simply by increasing body size. There are two important responses to this. The first is purely quantitative. The correlation of brain size and body size for all pongids yields a regression coefficient of .34. Interestingly enough the same correlation for Australopithecines yields a regression coefficient of .33. The coefficient for the hominid lineage, however, is 1.73, according to Gould, "the highest ever calculated for an evolutionary sequence" (Gould, 1977, p. 184; see also Pilbeam and Gould, 1974). Clearly, much more is required to account for this growth in the brain than mere increase in body size.

The second response is qualitative. What is developing in human evolution is not mere size but a differentiation of structure and function to support what we might at this point loosely term intelligent behaviour. Endocasts of hominid skulls confirm the expected changes (Kochetkova, 1978). The relatively small brains of *Homo habilis* and of *Pithecanthropus* (*Homo erectus*) were already anatomically distinct from similar sized gorilla brains.

We may conclude that from the first hominid or last prehominid in our lineage to *Australopithecus* there was little change in either size or complexity of the brain. From *Australopithecus,* and particularly from *Homo habilis,* however, there was, by normal evolutionary standards a dramatically rapid rise in both size and complexity.

## Bipedalism

Our primate ancestor or *Ramapithecus* was probably at least partially bipedal, much as the apes are now. It is argued by some, on the basis of rather indirect evidence that *Ramapithecus* had begun adaptation to a savannah or ground existence and that he was already advancing toward bipedalism (Woolfson, 1982, pp. 11ff.) We can, however, as mentioned before, remain comfortably neutral on this issue.

What is undeniable since the mid-1970s is that the earliest known Australopithecines were fully bipedal. Two decisive finds can be mentioned here. The first is the group of remains found between 1972 and 1977 in the Afar region of Ethiopia. Among these was the 40 percent complete skeleton of a young female known as Lucy dated at between −3.3 and −2.9 million years. Lucy's pelvis and leg bones, indicate that she stood and walked as fully erect as a modern human (Woolfson, 1982, p. 20).

The second important find occurred in Tanzania, near Olduvai. This was the discovery of fossilized Australopithecine footprints in an ancient riverbed at Laetoli. These have been dated at −3.75 to −3.5 million years. Various analyses of these footprints have all confirmed the conclusion that *Australopithecus* was fully bipedal ((Woolfson, 1982, p. 19; Hay and Leakey, 1983).

The unavoidable conclusion is that full bipedalism had been achieved by our homonid ancestors at least 4 million years ago. It must also be concluded that full bipedalism preceded by a considerable period the development of a fully distinct hominid brain. According to Gould (1980): "Upright posture is the surprise, the difficult event, the rapid and fundamental reconstruction of our anatomy. The subsequent enlargement of our brain is, in anatomical terms, a secondary epiphenomenon, an easy transformation embedded in a general pattern of human evolution" (p. 132).

## Teeth and Hands

The evolution of teeth and that of hands necessarily go together. The development of a more precise grip in newly freed hands represents a shift of functions like seizing, holding, and tearing from the mouth to the hands. As Washburn has said: "Small canines and incisors are biological symbols of a changed way of life; their primitive functions are replaced by hand and tool" (quoted in Woolfson 1982, p. 11).

In human evolution the principal changes in the teeth are the shift from a U-shaped arrangement to one that is more uniformly curved, the reduction in the size of the canines, and an increase in the size ratio of front and back teeth. Most of these changes reflect the shift in function just mentioned, but the altered curvature of the arrangement of teeth also reflects the foreshortened face that accompanied upright posture, and eventually encephalization as well.

It is not certain that *Ramapithecus* had begun the evolution toward more human teeth. It could, however, represent a beginning at most. Certainly *Australopithecus* showed very distinct hominization in its dentition. Comparisons of upper palate and dentition with modern apes and humans show clearly that the curvature has begun, the canines have been reduced, and the size ratio of front and back teeth is clearly approaching that of a modern human (Gould, 1980, p. 127; Clark, 1955, p. 142).

We have no hand bones for *Ramapithecus,* but enough are available for *Australopithecus* to form a fairly accurate picture of it. As with its dentition, the hand of *Australopithecus* is intermediate in form. It has many distinctly human features, but significantly still lacked the fully opposed thumb. While capable of a powerful grip and of a dexterity distinctly above that of the ape, *Australopithecus* would have had difficulty with very precise use of its hands (Woolfson, 1982, p. 20; Lewis, 1974, p. 68). The hands and teeth of *Homo habilis* appear to be more fully modern, and associated tools are often interpreted to mean that this hominid was capable of a precision grip (Leakey, 1979, p. 171).

## Use and Manufacture of Tools

It has been a well established fact for a long time that a wide range of animals from birds to primates use tools of some sort. Recent studies of tool use by chimpanzees are particularly interesting because they clearly show the continuity between animal tool-behaviour and that of humans. Goodall's observations of chimpanzees have even revealed clear cases of rudimentary preparation of natural materials for tool use. According to Goodall et al. (1976):

> In addition to using objects around them . . . , the chimpanzees sometimes modify the material to make it more suitable for the purpose in hand. Thus, during termite fishing, leaves may be stripped from a twig, a strip of bark may be shredded, or the blades may be stripped from a wide length of grass. When drinking from a hollow, the chimpanzee almost always crumples . . . leaves by chewing them briefly before using them as a sponge, thus increasing their water-carrying capacity considerably. These simple modifications may be considered the primitive beginnings of tool-making. (Quoted in Woolfson, 1982, p. 38)

It seems reasonable to assume that our primate ancestor may have been equally advanced. What is of interest for the purpose of illuminating human evolution, however, is not so much the continuities but the discontinuities. Some experiments on chimpanzees by Khrustov are important for what they reveal about the limits of chimpanzee tool-making ability and thus also about how chimpanzees differ from humans. In the first experiment chimpanzees were able to pull a strip off a piece of soft wood in order to retrieve a lure in a manner similar to that of Goodall's free-living animals. A second experiment made the task more difficult by replacing the soft with hard wood. An appropriate stone cutting tool was made available and in further experiments every effort was made, including demonstration, to encourage use of the tool, but in this the chimpanzees failed. According to Khrustov, ". . . *none of them* attempted to fashion the unyielding material with the stone tool offered along with it, or with any other object than their own natural body organs" (Khrustov, 1970).

This inability to use a tool to make a tool undoubtedly constitutes a significant difference between the chimpanzee and human, but there are other related differences worth noting. According to Woolfson (1982):

> No chimpanzee has ever been observed employing weapons as hunting aids in the killing of living mammal prey, nor have any cutting or butchering tools been seen to be used to divide up the carcass. . . . branches may be waved during agonistic displays and occasionally sticks or stones were aimed and hurled both underarm and overarm, sometimes playfully, but on a few occasions as part of threatening displays. Interestingly, when a real fight begins, chimpanzees drop the sticks they may be holding and rely on teeth and hands much as they do when hunting. . . . (pp. 36–37)

In addition, chimpanzees seldom transport tool material for use in another place, and once used, a tool is never saved for use another time. Chimpanzees have nothing resembling a tool-kit that they prepare beforehand, carry around with them, and retain for multiple future use.

We cannot, however, leave the topic of primate tool-making without mentioning a remarkable set of experiments by Wright (1972) using an orangutan. A five-and-a-half year old male orangutan with no previous "scientific" experience succeeded in learning by imitation from the investigator to use a hammerstone to strike flakes from a flint core, which it then used to cut a string, releasing a hinged box top so that food in the box could be retrieved. Although no orangutan is known to have accomplished such a feat on its own in captivity or in the natural environment, these experiments dramatically demonstrate what an ape—and here one less closely related to the hominid lineage than chimpanzees—can do given optimal conditions.

Intending no discredit to the orangutan or chimpanzee, however, these findings still leave a wide gap between the tool related capacities of apes and those of the most primitive humans. When and how did our hominid ancestors overcome—to use Khrustov's term—these "implemental frontiers?"

An important consideration in trying to answer this question is that our evidence will necessarily have mainly to do with stone tools. It is an entirely reasonable assumption that long before our hominid ancestors knew how to manufacture stone tools, they were fashioning implements of more easily worked materials such as wood, bone, and animal skins. Thus the earliest evidence of deliberately fashioned stone tools should probably be taken to represent a fairly advanced stage of tool-related evolution.

A second consideration that overlaps and supports the first is that the economy of the earliest hominids was probably concerned mainly with gathering of vegetable foods and only occasionally with scavenging meat or taking small game. Such an economy does not require much in the way of stone tools. Implements like baskets, carrying bags of leather, and digging sticks would be quite adequate for the job. It is interesting to note that where the predominance of gathering exists in modern hunter-gatherer societies gathering provides up to 71 percent of the calories consumed, and gathering is approximately 67 percent more productive per person-hour than hunting (Woolfson, 1982, p. 29). This means that a hominid society could survive and develop for a very long time on gathering and opportunistic game taking without experiencing the kinds of pressures that require the production of archaeologically durable tools.

Until very recently the best evidence for stone tool manufacture dated back to about 2 million years. This was from the lower strata of the Olduvai Gorge.

In 1959 the Leakeys found fragments of the skull of an early small-brained man ape in rock which was laid down about 1.75 million years ago. What was remarkable about this specimen . . . was that it was found in clear association with stone tools including a hammerstone and waste flakes, indicating a manufacture process, the first evidence of tool-making by early humans. (Woolfson, 1982, pp. 14–15)

Also from Olduvai,

. . . in deposits about 1.6 million years old, comes evidence of a further type of work-camp site, the MNK chert 'factory' site to which stone materials were also imported, in this case for initial preparation as tools. These in turn seem to have been taken to living sites where they were utilized or transformed into shaped tools. Besides a very large number of chert specimens, two hammerstones and working anvil stones were identified. It is suggested that the chert stone materials were brought to the site from sources of no more than 1 km. distance and that the absence of bones or other remains normally associated with living sites suggests its specific function as a factory site. (Woolfson, 1982, pp. 16–17)

Thus by the time of late *Homo habilis* or early *Homo erectus,* an advanced, socially organized, stone tool industry had developed.

More recent evidence pushes the advent of stone tool manufacture back even farther (Lewin, 1981). Numerous flake tools and the cores from which they had been struck were found at Hadar in Ethiopia in 1976 and 1977. These have been dated at between −2.7 and −2.5 million years. No hominid remains have been found in direct association with these tools, so it cannot be stated with any certainty whether they were produced by *Australopithecus* or by *Homo habilis.* One investigator, however, was quite emphatic that, as a result of these finds, ". . . you can't rule out the possibility that *Australopithecus* made and used crude (stone) tools" (Lewin, 1981).

A cautious reconstruction of the development of tool manufacture on the basis of available evidence has been made by Foerster (1981, Schema 4). According to her, *Australopithecus* engaged in the systematic use of unaltered natural objects and some altered by their own body organs, e.g. hands and teeth. Such tools were probably limited to immediate use. *Homo habilis,* according to Foerster, was the probable first maker of pebble tools. These required the systematic use of a natural object to assist in their making. These tools were made in advance of their use, carried with the user, and probably retained for multiple use. The full-scale tool industry involving the systematic manufacture of tools to make tools is reserved for *Homo erectus.*

It is interesting to note here what may be an instance of a version of the old "brain primacy" prejudice. Very often it appears that *Homo habilis* is credited with tool making while *Australopithecus* is not, simply because the brain and hands of the former were more developed. Wright's (1972) experiment with the orangutan clearly shows, however, that advanced hands and brain are not required to produce the kinds of flake tools often attributed to *Homo habilis.* *Australopithecus* was markedly advanced over the orangutan, sufficiently advanced, one might surmise, to make tools on his own and under less than optimal conditions.

It appears, then, that even the cautious account assigns systematic tool use and the beginnings of tool preparation to the stage at which fully erect posture had come about, full development of the hand had not yet occurred, and before any conspicuously dramatic development of the brain.

## Conclusion

The overall picture provided by both the hard evidence and most reasonable presumptions is very much the one anticipated by Engels. Bipedalism is the decisive step by any currently acceptable account. Tool use and manufacture precede development of the hand, which appears to form a reciprocal, positive feedback relation with the former. And growth of both size and complexity of the brain follow the development of tool use and manufacture, again, it may be presumed, in a reciprocal, positive feedback relationship.

The most important implication to flow from this sequence is that in the evolution of the human species it was not so much the action of the environment on the organism that created the evolutionary pressures, but the interaction of the two. Moreover, in this interaction the activity of our early ancestors on their environments gradually assumed the leading role in its own evolution.

A corollary of this implication is that consciousness and intelligence, the complex thinking apparatus so distinctively characteristic of the human, have been not the cause, but the result of hominization. The opposite view, still existing in various forms as a strong idealist prejudice among many Western intellectuals, was expressed phylogenetically as the hypothesis of brain primacy. This idealist theory is now clearly refuted by the evidence of actual human evolution. By contrast, the materialist view of Engels has been upheld.

Understanding why this is so has a direct bearing on our conception of levels. Engels, being a philosophical materialist, knew that something does not come from nothing, that the concrete does not originate in the abstract. Idealist theories like traditional emergentism and the brain primacy theory always leave the key events unexplained. The emergence of a large brain explains nothing if it is itself not explained. Moreover, for Engels environmental pressures alone were insufficient. It could only have been the concrete activity of the prehominid that assumed the key role in its development. Engels thus surmised that by his own concrete labour, man created himself. A new level evolved in a continuous process of interaction from the old, a new level marked by the discontinuity of distinct qualities that are explained by, but not reducible to the qualities of the old.

## PSYCHOLOGICAL IMPLICATIONS

The psychological implications come mainly from a recognition that in the course of human evolution a cultural mode of existence has evolved out of a strictly biotic mode; that in this development labour, that is, human activity on the environment with the aid of tools, has played a leading role both in the development of culture itself and of the organs, e.g. the hands and brain, required to support it; and that as a result qualitative differences between humans and animals have been brought about, the comparative study of which can inform us about the uniquely human qualities and their genesis.

It is not possible here to explore all implications of human evolution for psychology, let alone work out the details of a consistently evolutionary psychology. Fortunately much of this work has been done by others. I propose to offer here a sampling from the work of L. S. Vygotsky (1978), A. N. Leontyev (1981), and the American philosopher, James Lawler (1978).

## The Unit of Psychological Investigation

Introductory textbooks inform us that psychology is the study of behaviour. Earlier they told us it was mental life or conscious elements. Each of these definitions represents an attempt to specify a unit of investigation. The ideal unit is one that implies neither too much nor too little, or that contains most of the qualities that really interest us. For psychology, the muscle twitch clearly is "too little," whereas migrations of populations are "too much." For many psychologists, behaviour has seemed just right—unless you are looking for an account of consciousness, in which case it will seem a bit less than ideal.

An evolutionary approach to psychology also must judge behaviour as "too little." When we begin to see that what interests psychology are precisely those evolving capacities that ultimately account for the distinction between biotic and cultural modes of existence, then surely the unit must be something that plays an essential part within the evolutionary process. Behaviour is "too little" because it is one-sided and abstract. This is evident from the fact that entities as diverse as liver cells and stock markets are spoken of as behaving. Moreover, understanding behaviour as a specific response, it can be said that humans, rats, and even cockroaches press levers. Behaviour, in short, is a unit in which the essential results of evolution are obscured or lost, and is therefore suited to the intentions only of reductionist theory.

It would probably be quite unfair to attribute, without qualification, such abstractness to the thinking of Skinner and other behaviorists, but their writings provide exceptionally unambiguous examples of behaviors or responses as abstract units. For example, Skinner (1956) displays three cumulative curves side by side, and then informs us that ". . . one of them was made by a *pigeon*. . . , one was made by a *rat*. . . , and the third was made by a *monkey*. . . . Pigeon, rat, monkey, which is which? It doesn't matter." In another place (Skinner, 1972, p. 139), he advises the reader that such statements as "there is nothing he wants to do or enjoys doing well, he has no feeling of craftsmanship, no sense of leading a purposeful life, no sense of accomplishment" would be better expressed as "he is rarely reinforced for doing anything." Pigeon, rat, monkey, which is which? Once again, it appears not to matter.

As we have already seen, labour exemplifies the sort of unit required by an evolutionary theory. Labour contains all the necessary qualities; it is both essential and central to the evolutionary process, and it implies or is implied by all the capacities (e.g. consciousness) that interest psychology. Labour will not do as the unit itself, however, because it is part of what psychologists need to explain. Labour is a special and advanced form of the unit we are looking for. The more general form has been called "activity." According to Leontyev (1979):

> Activity is the nonadditive, molar unit of life for the material corporeal subject. . . The real function of this unit is to orient the subject in the world of objects. In other words, activity is not a reaction or aggregate of reactions, but a system with its own structure, its own internal transformations, and its own development. (p. 46)
> The basic characteristic of activity is its *object orientation*. The expression "objectless activity" is devoid of sense. Activity may *seem* to be without object orientation, but scientific investigation of it necessarily requires discovery of its object. . . (p. 48) [The translation has been corrected to read "objectless" in place of "nonobjective," based on the original Russian, Leontyev, 1977b. The German translation, Leontyev, 1979a, confirms the appropriateness of this correction.]

Being an evolutionary unit, it has its own evolutionary history.

> The prehistory of human activities begins with the life process' acquiring object-orientation. . . . . The subsequent behavioural and mental evolution of animals can be adequately understood as the history of the *development of the object content of activity*. (p. 48)

## Activity as a Form of Reflection

The development of the object content of activity is the evolution of processes that accomplish a progressively more adequate or complete reflection of the material world. Leontyev traced this development through five distinct phylogenetic stages (levels) that he called irritability, sensitivity, perceptivity, animal intellect, and human consciousness, the last four of which he identifies as psyche.

In the simplest organisms, irritability is closely tied to metabolism. At the very least an organism must assimilate that which it can metabolize, and expel or reject that which it cannot. This is a very simple form of activity yet it contains all the important ingredients; viz., action by the organism on an object possessing particular properties, which affects both the object and the organism. Unlike simple chemical reactions (of which this is an advanced form), one of the interacting bodies, the organism, is qualitatively preserved. Thus it can be meaningfully claimed that one acts on the other, that we observe here the beginnings of a true subject-object relationship. In this relationship it is the properties of objects that are reflected by the organism, i.e. that form the object content of irritability.

The appearance of psyche occurs with the evolution of irritability into sensitivity. This involves a complication of irritability such that the organism responds not merely to properties that are assimilable, but to other properties that act as signals of assimilable objects. The organism now, for instance, responds to light because it is thereby led to food, because there is an objective association between light and food. Objective properties and relations of properties are reflected in this process, i.e. form the object content of sensitivity.

A more complex stage has evolved when the organism becomes active with respect not merely to properties and their relations, but to things. This is the stage Leontyev calls perceptivity.

In the next stage, which is designated as "animal intellect," further complications evolve whereby activity begins to develop an internal, differentiated structure. This is a two-phase structure normally consisting of preparatory and consummatory phases: the chimpanzee stacks boxes in order to get a banana. It is this differentiation that allows rudimentary problem solving and, in the chimpanzee, the beginnings of tool use and preparation, all of which implies an increasingly more adequate reflection of the properties, things, and interrelations of things existing in the material environment of the animal.

Each of these stages represents a level in the dialectical materialist sense. Each is nonreducible to the lower, but is derived from it by an orderly and discoverable process. And each successive stage is marked by an object content representing an increase in the capacity to reflect the complexities of the surrounding material world and therefore also to deal with them adaptively.

## Labour and Human Activity

The most advanced differentiation of activity is found in the human species. The two phase activity of the advanced primate has now evolved into two or more separable actions, each with its distinct goal, which is, though distinct, still subordinated to the overall motive or object of the activity. This can be seen in the box and banana problem. It is conceivable that a human would practice stacking boxes for the sake of some potential future banana. Chimpanzees are unlikely to do this because stacking boxes for them is still too closely tied to the objective presence of the object of activity. It is also conceivable that humans would cooperate such that one stacks the boxes while another retrieves the fruit, a kind of joint activity seldom if ever seen in subhuman primates. What is responsible for these species differences is a *disarticulation of the phases* of activity for the human. [The Kopylova translation, Leontyev, 1981, p. 211, uses the word "exarticulation." The German translation uses "herausgliedern," Leontyev, 1975, p. 169. The present author assumes responsibility for "disarticulation."] The disarticulation is made possible by a more evolved differentiation of the object content of activity, whereby the relationship between things has become itself a distinct and separable component of the content. This further implies a consciousness in which the final object of the activity is "kept in mind" although it is absent. Such a development is obviously implied in the systematic manufacture of tools. Indeed from an evolutionary point of view, such a development would have had to occurred prior to systematic tool-making. In this regard, it is significant that in working out a model of early hominid social existence, Isaac (1983) concluded:

> . . . the first question that the model must confront is why early hominid social groups departed from the norm among living subhuman primates, whose social groups feed as they range. To put it another way, what ecological and evolutionary advantages are there in postponing some food consumption and transporting the food. (p. 66)

It is entirely plausible that the pressures that led to transporting food and postponing its consumption were the pressures that first led to the disarticulation of phases of activity which later came to distinguish the human psyche and to be exemplified in labour.

The disarticulation of phases, now called actions, within activity is integral to advanced cooperative social organization. Human labour can be said to have begun as the division of labour. The provision of food is more efficient when done jointly. A hunt is more effective when beaters drive the animals toward others who are prepared for the kill. The implications for social consciousness are obvious. The beater, frightening his quarry away must know that what he is doing will lead to his getting the meat that he needs, and therefore that the activity will be completed by others and that the others will share the meat (Leontyev, 1981, p. 210). Systematic cooperation and sharing, we may remind ourselves, are only poorly developed at best in the most advanced subhuman primates.

The systematic manufacture of tools, cooperative social organization and consciousness, all key elements of human cultural historical existence, then, originate in a separation of the phases of activity, based on an evolutionary advance in reflective capacity of the organism, i.e. in the object content of activity.

## Language and Thought

The disarticulation of actions immediately implies both abstraction and meaning. It should be apparent that to make a tool for future use requires the capacity to abstract the tool-making action from the activity, e.g. food getting, of which it is a part. But, once abstracted, it must be kept in relation to the larger activity. This is achieved by meaning. Just as in use, i.e. in labour, the tool itself mediates between the human and the object, meaning now mediates for the tool-maker between the manufacture and the use of the tool. The tool therefore becomes the embodiment of meaning, a meaning that must be understood by the tool-maker so that he or she can know, can think about and be guided by, its eventual use.

Anthropologists have, like Engels, long maintained the view that the development of human language is intimately connected to tool use and making (e.g. Montagu, 1983). It is interesting that recent research on chimpanzees appears to be converging on the same conclusion. For example, Savage-Rumbaugh, Pate, Lawson, Smith and Rosenbaum (1983) conclude:

> The fact that we [humans] are highly motivated to do all manner of things with and to objects, to keep and possess objects, and to carry them from place to place cannot be separated from our equally prepotent tendency to communicate about objects. . . . We are uniquely adapted to act on objects in an interindividual, coordinated manner, and language enables us to do this more effectively and to do it even when things are removed in space and time. Apes do not share this ability. . .
> (p. 485)

It should be evident by now that human labour is social labour. Thus as the tool comes to embody meaning, so too does the gesture and finally the utterance. Likewise, as the tool is understood by others, so too are the gestures and utterances understood. The necessity for human language stems from the need to organize actions socially. Language mediates between individuals just as the tool mediates between the individual and the object.

But language is not only possible and necessary in the sphere of social control. When internalized, it comes to mediate between the individual and his or her own actions. It becomes the basis for planning and conscious control of activity, and therefore for much of what is recognized as "cognition."

Human language that uses culturally and historically produced meanings to guide and regulate activity is qualitatively distinct from animal communication that does not operate on the basis of such systematically produced meanings. This distinction, once again, can be seen to derive from the full separation of the phases of activity in humans.

## Memory

Memory, no less than any other human quality, reveals what might now be regarded as the "logic" of the tool. Animals have memory, but it is a non-mediated memory and is therefore confined within the limits of the biological organism. By contrast, human memory is mediated and can in principle transcend these limits. As Vygotsky (1978) has observed (See also Leontyev, 1981, pp. 327–365):

> The use of notched sticks and knots, the beginning of writing and simple memory aids all demonstrate that even at early stages of historical development humans went beyond the limits of the psychological functions given to them by nature and

proceeded to a new culturally-elaborated organization of their behaviour. Comparative analysis shows that such activity is absent in even the highest species of animals; we believe that these sign operations are the product of specific conditions of *social* development.

Even such comparatively simple operations as tying a knot or notching a stick as a reminder change the psychological structure of memory beyond the biological dimensions of the human nervous system and permit it to incorporate artificial, or self-generated, stimuli, which we call *signs*. (p. 39)

We have already noted how meaning must arise with the tool. The tool is therefore also a reminder. But distinctly human memory emerges when reminders are purposefully created for that end, just as tools are created with special ends in view. The knot is an example. It is an instrument, but as such, is directed at the control not of external objects, but of one's own activity. This control of one's own activity through the production of an external stimulus is carried to a higher stage when the sign itself is internalized. The result, in Vygotsky's words is that "in the elementary forms (of memory) something is remembered; in the higher form humans remember something" (Vygotsky, 1978, p. 51). Remembering becomes active and deliberate: it is the logic of the tool that is evident throughout this development, which accounts for the irreducible qualitative difference between animal and human memory processes.

## Consciousness

We have seen that it is an evolutionary complication in the object content of activity leading to the disarticulation of goal-directed actions within activity that leads to the systematic use and making of tools. This, in turn, generates meanings that are used to guide and control activity. The development of specifically human memory provides an instructive instance of this process in which things, and then signs, are produced with the express intent of organizing one's activity. This deliberate use of things and signs for the purpose of remembering, organizing, planning, and controlling activity *is* consciousness.

Subhuman animals are surely "aware" in some sense of the word, and it may indeed be quite meaningful to assert that chimpanzees are "more aware" than goldfish in that they possess evolutionarily more advanced means of reflecting the reality about them. But there is more to human consciousness than mere animal awareness, and this qualitative difference, as just outlined, is traceable to the full disarticulation of actions found only in humans. This means that human activity, unlike that of other animals (although clear anticipations are to be found in the activity of the nonhuman primates) is regulated by mental images, meanings, signs, and language that are deliberately produced in human activity for that purpose. Thus mediation in human activity, and consciousness—as distinct from awareness—are intimately connected (cf. Leontyev, 1977a; Holzkamp, 1983, p. 237).

## Intelligence

Nowhere has the failure to take the lessons of anthropogenesis into account been more detrimental to the advance of psychological science than in the case of intelligence. The concept of "culture-free" or "culture fair" tests provides but the most blatant manifestation of the prevailing view of intelligence in psychology as the raw, unmediated potential of the biological human organism. But this is the intelligence of the ape, not of the human being. Human intelligence, like memory, is mediated and it is social. It is mediated in that it has more to do with the tools available to the individual than with the limitations of the bodily organs. A child with the use of a hand calculator represents more intelligence than all the ancient geniuses put together. It is social, another way of being mediated, in several ways. Just as the tool embodies meaning, it also embodies the accumulated social wisdom that led to its development. The child need not re-invent the tool. By learning, often in a very short time, to master its use, the child also acquires the social-historical intelligence that it represents. It is social also because no one can claim to have mastered all tools. There is no need for this with a rational division of labour. The intelligence to which each social individual has access and guides his or her choices is seldom his or her intelligence alone. It is the collective intelligence of society. It is also social because whatever its form, it is mediated for the individual by language. A chimpanzee must be *taught how* to do something, a child with the mastery of language can be *told*. The human ability to learn, often identified with intelligence, is qualitatively different from that of the animal owing to language. If this were not the case, then the accumulated intelligence of thousands of generations could not be imparted to the child in a few short school years as it obviously can be. As Lawler (1978) has commented: "Because human learning takes place through the instrumentality of language its capacity for growth is *unlimited*" (p. 95).

An important aspect that is frequently overlooked in the psychology literature is what children learn must be taught, and as the intelligence required becomes more complex, as it obviously is becoming, the instruments and techniques of teaching must be sharpened to meet the demand. Just as we must learn how better to produce the things we need and want, we must also learn how best to pass the collective intelligence on to succeeding generations. This is not likely to be achieved with an IQ test or with a biologistic concept of intelligence.

## Appropriation versus Adaptation

All of our considerations of the psychological implications of human evolution culminate in Engels's (1972) concept of mastery. "The animal merely *uses* its environment," he said, whereas ". . . man . . . makes it serve his ends, *masters* it" (p. 179).

This important distinction between mastery and use has been developed in a more modern form by A. N. Leontyev (1981) as the distinction between appropriation and adaptation.

Even the most elementary tools, implements, or objects of everyday use that a child first encounters, must be actively discovered by it in their specific quality. In other words, a child must perform practical or cognitive activity in relation to them such as would be *adequate*. . . to the human activity embodied in them. It is another question how adequate the child's activity will be and consequently how fully the meaning of an object or phenomenon will be disclosed to it, *but there must always be this activity.*

That is why, when objects of human material culture are put into a cage with animals, they do not lose any of their physical properties, but cannot exhibit those specific properties that they have for man; they appear only as objects for adaptation and adjustment, i.e. objects just become part of the animals' natural environment.

The activity of animals realizes acts of adaptation to the environment, but never acts of mastering the advances of phylogenetic evolution. These advances *are given* to the animal in its natural inherited traits, whereas they are *posed* to man in the objective phenomena of the world about him. To realize these advances in his ontogenetic development man must master them; only as a result of this always active process can the individual express a truly human nature in himself, i.e. those characteristics and abilities that are the product of man's socio-historical development. (p. 294) [The translation has been corrected to read "adjustment" in place of "compensation," based on the German translation, Leontyev, 1975.]

Therefore, Leontyev (1981) continues:

. . . the cognitive, mental development of individual men is thus the product of a quite special process, that of appropriation, which does not exist at all in animals. . . The difference between this process and that of individual adaptation to the natural environment must be specially stressed (p. 25). Can we, for instance, treat man's activity in response to his cognitive need in relation to knowledge.. . in terms of adaptation or adjustment? Man, in satisfying his need for knowledge, may make the corresponding concept *his own* concept, i.e. grasp its significance, but this is not at all like the process of adaptation or adjustment proper. 'Adaptation to a concept', 'adjustment to a concept' are phrases devoid of any sense. (p. 295) [See comment after P. 294 citation]

Space prohibits further development of the concept of appropriation here. It should be sufficiently clear at this point, however, that a psychology, which for over a century has been dominated by the biologistic concepts of adaptation and adjustment, cannot afford much longer to ignore the qualitatively distinct "mode of dealing with nature" which has been the outcome of human evolution.

## CONCLUSION

An anti-reductionist levels theory of human psychological functioning is one in which both the continuity and discontinuity of the human and animal (prehuman) levels are dialectically affirmed. This means that although the qualitative distinction of human functioning is maintained, it is necessary to provide an account of how this level was formed in a process of evolutionary transformation from the lower level. This is perforce an account of hominization.

The evidence of human evolution unequivocally supports a theory that asserts the leading role of activity, specifically the development of labour activity. It is activity with its object content, not behaviour as such, that evolves. This indicates that activity, which alters both its subject and its object, must be taken as the focal unit for psychological study. In the case of human functioning, activity is distinguished by its internal disarticulable structure and by the fact that it is mediated. The logic of the tool, or of mediation, is found to characterize all distinctly human capacities and provides the only sure basis for a theoretical understanding of human language, human cognition, and human consciousness.

It is biologistic reductionism in psychology that insists on ignoring the mediated, distinctly cultural nature of human capacities. This has been very detrimental to the development of adequate psychological theory. The only remedy is the rejection of reductionistic theories and the adoption of a truly comparative, evolutionary approach that actively seeks to understand the real similarities and differences between humans and animals.

## ACKNOWLEDGMENTS

This paper owes a great deal to Charles Woolfson's book, *The Labour Theory of Culture* (Woolfson, 1982). Although the present interpretation of Engels is my own, I have used some anthropological evidence that he did not use, and I have drawn psychological implications somewhat different from his (though the two are, I believe, compatible), my indebtedness to Woolfson remains significant, and one that I wish hereby gratefully to acknowledge.

I have also benefitted from discussions with my anthropologist colleague, Nicolas Rolland, whose patience and erudition contributed importantly to the present effort.

## REFERENCES

Aronson, L. R., Tobach, E., Rosenblatt, J. S., & Lehrman, D. S. (Eds). (1972). *Selected writings of T. C. Schneirla*. San Francisco: W. H. Freeman.
Clark. W. E. LeG. (1955). *The fossil evidence of human evolution*. Chicago: University of Chicago Press.

Dobzhansky, T. (1941). *Genetics and the origin of species.* New York: Columbia University Press.

Engels, F. (1972). *Dialectics of nature* (C. Dutt, Trans.). Moscow: Progress Publishers. (Original work published 1925, first English translation 1935)

Foerster, I. (1981). *Anthropogenese und materialistische Dialektik.* Jena: VEB Gustav Fischer Verlag.

Goodall, J. (1976). Continuities between chimpanzee and human behavior. In G. L. Isaac & E. R. McCown (Eds.), *Human origins* (pp. 81–95). San Francisco: W. A. Benjamin.

Gould, S. J. (1977). *Ever since Darwin.* New York: Norton

Gould, S. J. (1980). *The panda's thumb.* New York: Norton

Hay, R. L., & Leakey, M. D. (1983). The fossil footprints of Laetoli. In B. M. Fagan (Ed.), *Prehistoric times* (pp. 48–55). San Francisco: W. H. Freeman.

Holzkamp, K. (1983). *Grundlegung der Psychologie.* Frankfurt: Campus Verlag.

Isaac, G. (1983). The food-sharing of protohuman hominids. In B. M. Fagan (Ed.), *Prehistoric times* (pp. 56–69). San Francisco: W. H. Freeman.

Khrustov, G. F. (1970). The problem of the origin of man. *Soviet Psychology, 9,* 6–31.

Kochetkova, V. I. (1978). *Paleoneurology* (H. J. Jerison & I. Jerison, Trans.). New York: Wiley.

Lawler, J. M. (1978). *IQ, heritability and racism.* New York: International Publishers.

Leakey, M. D. (1979). *Olduvai Gorge: My search for early man.* London: Collins.

Leontyev, A. N. (1975). *Probleme der Entwicklung des Psychischen* (5. Auflag). Berlin: Volk und Wissen.

Leontyev, A. N. (1977a). Activity and consciousness. In *Philosophy in the USSR: Problems of dialectial materialism* (pp. 180–202). Moscow: Progress Publishers.

Leontyev, A. N. (1977b). *Deyatelnost' soznanie lichnost'.* Moskva: Politisdat.

Leontyev, A. N. (1979). *Taetigkeit, Bewusstsein, Persoenlichkeit.* Berlin: Volk und Wissen.

Leontyev, A. N. (1981). *Problems of the development of the mind* (M. Kopylova, Trans.). Moscow: Progress Publishers.

Lewin, R. (1981). Ethiopian stone tools are world's oldest. *Science, 211,* 806–807.

Lewis, J. (1974). *The uniqueness of man.* London: Lawrence & Wishart.

Marx, K. (1974). *Capital* (Vol. 1). (S. Moore & E. Aveling, Trans.). Moscow: Progress Publishers. (Original work published in 1867)

Montagu, A. (1983). Toolmaking, hunting, and the origin of language. In Bain, B., *The sociogenesis of language and human conduct* (pp. 13–14). New York: Plenum Press.

Novikoff, A. B. (1945). The concept of integrative levels and biology. *Science, 101,* 209–215.

Olivier, G. (1973). Hominization and cranial capacity. In M. H. Day (Ed.), *Human evolution* (pp. 87–101). London: Taylor & Francis Ltd.

Pilbeam, D. (1984, April). The descent of hominoids and hominids. *Scientific American,* pp. 84–96.

Pilbeam, D., & Gould, S. J. (1974). Size and scaling in human evolution. *Science, 186,* 892–901.

Savage-Rumbaugh, E. S., Pate, J. L., Lawson, J., Smith, S. T., & Rosenbaum, S. (1983). Can a chimpanzee make a statement? *Journal of Experimental Psychology: General, 112,* 457–492.

Schneirla, T. C. (1949). Levels in the psychological capacities of animals. In R. W. Sellars, V. J. McGill, & M. Farber (Eds.), *Philosophy for the future: The quest of modern materialism* (pp. 243–286). New York: Macmillan.

Schurig, V. (1976). *Die Entstehung des Bewusstseins.* Frankfurt: Campus Verlag.

Skinner, B. F. (1956). A case history in scientific method. *American Psychologist, 11,* 221–233.

Skinner, B. F. (1972). *Beyond freedom and dignity.* New York: Bantam/Vintage.

Vygotsky, L. S. (1978). In *Mind in society* (M. Cole, V. John-Steiner, S. Scribner, & E. Souberman, Trans. and Eds.). Cambridge MA: Harvard University Press.

Woolfson, C. (1982). *The labour theory of culture.* London: Routledge and Kegan Paul.

Wright, R. V. S. (1972). Imitative learning of a flaked stone technology: The case of an orangutan. *Mankind, 8,* 296–306.

# 12

# Biological Implications of a Global-Workspace Theory of Consciousness: Evidence, Theory, and Some Phylogenetic Speculations

Bernard J. Baars
*Langley Porter Neuropsychiatric Institute,*
*University of California, San Francisco*
*and*
*The Wright Institute,*
*Berkeley, California*

> *It looks as if consciousness is effects of sufficient perfection of organization.*
>
> —Charles Darwin (1838)

## INTRODUCTION

Consciousness is increasingly seen both by cognitive psychologists and psychobiologists as a plain fact that simply cannot be ignored if we are to have any adequate conception of human and animal functioning. Trying to understand consciousness is not a scientific luxury, but a necessity. We cannot evade it, any more than a physicist could evade the fact of gravity (see, for example, Griffin, 1981; Thatcher & John, 1977; Norman, 1981; Mandler, 1975, 1983). Conscious processes are pervasive and central, and as we will see in some detail later, large parts of the brain are clearly involved in conscious processes.

A second defense might appeal to Schneirla's concept of integrative levels of organization, and suggest that no matter how remote the issue of consciousness might seem from the neurochemistry of single cells, or the behavior of ants, these apparently remote orders of biological organization must nevertheless be accomodated in any coherent phylogeny of nervous tissue (Aronson, this volume; Tobach & Greenberg, this volume).

There may be yet a better defense, having to do with an emerging cognitive perspective on consciousness and its functions, based on both experimental and theoretical work in the past few years (e.g. Baars, 1983; Marcel, 1983a, 1983b; Mandler, 1975, 1983; Shallice, 1972, 1976; Shevrin & Dickman, 1980; Posner, 1982; and others). A small number of basic ideas are used again and again to explain a very large number of psychological facts, and these same ideas make sense of much of the neurophysiological literature as well. Whether the great literature on these phenomena makes sense or not is very much dependent on how we approach it: if we approach it with a few good ideas, the apparent complexity may yet reveal surprising underlying simplicity.

The first order of business, then, is to sketch a basic theoretical approach to consciousness from a broad information-processing point of view (elaborated in Baars, 1983, 1985, in press-a,b,c). Second, we examine the extensive neurophysiological literature on the reticular-thalamic system of the brain stem and forebrain and its connections with the cerebral cortex, and show close parallels to our theoretical expectations. Third, we briefly discuss what is known of the phylogeny of these structures. And finally we suggest a way in which, over the course of vertebrate evolution, more and more sophisticated functions appear to be "overlaid" on the same enduring reticulo-thalamic system that seems to underlie conscious experience.

## CONTRASTIVE ANALYSIS OF TABLE 12.1

Table 12.1 shows a set of contrasting pairs of facts about conscious and unconscious events, providing us with the basic psychological evidence we will use in this chapter. We discuss each contrastive pair in turn, both in terms of psycho-

TABLE 12.1
Capabilities of Comparable Conscious and Unconscious Events

| Capabilities of Conscious Processes | Capabilities of Unconscious Processors |
|---|---|
| 1. Computationally inefficient. | Unconscious specialists are highly efficient in their own tasks. |
| (High errors, low speed, and mutual interference between conscious computations.) | (Low errors, high speed, and little mutual interference.) |
| 2. Great range of different contents over time; | Each specialized processor has limited range over time, and is relatively isolated and autonomous. |
| Great ability to relate different conscious contents to each other; | |
| Great ability to relate conscious events to their unconscious contexts. | |
| Internal consistency, seriality, and limited capacity. | Specialists are highly diverse, can operate in parallel, and together have great capacity. |

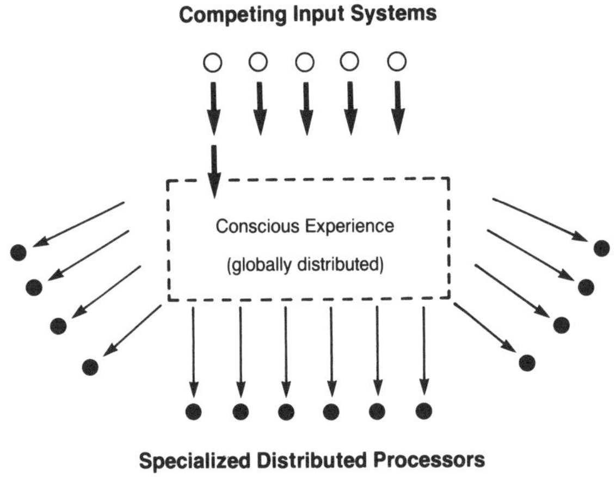

**Competing Input Systems**

FIGURE 12.1.   Model 1. A first-approximation model of the nervous system as a distributed collection of specialized processors, in which specialists can cooperate or compete with each other to gain access to an integrative domain called a "global workspace." The global workspace appears to be closely associated with conscious functioning, while the specialized processors are unconscious.

logical and neurphysiological evidence. Next we show how this set of empirical constraints fits a kind of system architecture called a "global workspace in a parallel distributed information processing system" (Fig. 12.1). This analysis can be carried out in more detail using other sets of contrastive phenomena, and the resulting model becomes a good deal more sophisticated (Baars, 1983); but for our current purposes Table 12.1 will suffice.

## Conscious Processes are Computationally Inefficient, While Unconscious Processors are Highly Efficient in Their Special Tasks

If by "computational efficiency" we mean the ability to perform some abstract or symbolic algorithm, such as the syntactic parsing of a sentence, in a way that is quick, error-free, and without interference from other tasks, conscious processes are not at all computationally efficient. Consider how long it would take to parse this very sentence (assuming the reader could bring the rules of parsing to consciousness), or consider the time needed to perform a visual analysis of this scene, or to carry out the task of reading in a way that was completely conscious. Clearly, if consciousness has an adaptive function, it is *not* the carrying out of efficient symbolic computations. And it is obvious that unconscious capabilities

TABLE 12.2
Some Human Neural Specializations

| |
|---|
| Visual: color, overlapping visual fields, eye contact |
| Auditory: speech-related frequency domain. |
| Smell and taste: less acute than other mammals, though this may be plastic. |
| Manual specialization: fineness of manipulation. |
| Locomotion: bipedal, balance, posture control. |
| Speech and language: specialized vocal control, syntax, learning of arbitrary vocabulary. |
| Social signals: voice and face recognition, perhaps music, sexual signals, pair bonding, in-group loyalty, out-group aggression, social hierarchies. |
| Learning ability: plasticity, ability to override some biological functions. |
| Anatomical specialization in size and frontal growth of cerebral cortex. |
| Ability to create metaphors: selecting similarities between known and unknown information. |

are quite the opposite: unconsciously we control our complex movements, our reading with its thousands of English spelling rules, our recognition of faces in a crowd, our homeostatic regulation, and apparently even some immune control functions, to name but a few examples.

In this contrastive analysis we will routinely refer to conscious *processes* but unconscious *processors*. The reason is that both cognitive psychologists and neurophysiologists are increasingly persuaded that a great many unconscious events in the nervous system are subserved by specialized "modules," defined both anatomically and functionally (e.g. Fodor, 1983; Mountcastle, 1978; Geschwind, 1979). Table 12.2 shows a sample of specialized functions that have been associated with particular brain areas through brain damage and electrophysiological studies in humans, and through a variety animal studies. They include a variety of language functions, affect, music, face recognition, sensory-motor loci, planning and decision-making processes, processes associated with mental imagery, and so on. It is well-known that memory and learning processes are far more elusive in terms of localization, and, of course, anatomical specialization does not necessarily imply functional specialization.

Here, we are primarily concerned with establishing the plausibility of the claim that "unconscious processors are highly efficient in their special tasks." The evidence cited above, plus the fact that we are able to do so many highly complex tasks with little conscious involvement, seems to provide ample evidence.

If consciousness is not very effective in complex symbolic "computations," what is it good for? The next contrastive pair suggests an answer.

### Conscious Processes have Great Range, Relational Capacity, and Context-Sensitivity, While Unconscious Processors have Limited Range and are Relatively Autonomous

The terms here are defined quite precisely. *Range* refers to the number of different contents that can become conscious. In a limited sense this includes anything that can be perceived in any sensory modality, and anything that can be imaged. In a broader sense, it also includes "conscious," or rapidly available beliefs, meanings, knowledge, expectations, and intentions. Thus the range of conscious contents is quite awesome.

Not so for individual unconscious processors. It is most unlikely that areas of the cortex that are specialized for syntactic analysis are any good at visual analysis, homeostatic control, or fine motor control. Specialization implies limitation of range.

*Relational Capacity* is defined as the ability to relate two conscious contents to each other, as in classical conditioning, perceptual learning, the learning of analogies, or the comprehension of a string of words. It is clear that people and animals are rather good at this; while there are biological limits about the stimuli that can be related to each other in non-human animals, numerous relationships can be established that have no plausible counterparts in the natural world. And in the case of human beings, there seem to be no limits at all in the range of stimuli that can be related to each other.

*Context-sensitivity* is defined as the way in which conscious contents are shaped by unconscious processes. It is well-known that visual percepts can be entirely changed depending on one's unconscious "assumptions" about the character and position of the incoming light, about the carpentered space in which the objects are perceived, about distance and depth, and the orientation of the viewer (Rock, 1983). Similarly, perception of the words in a sentence is controlled by our assumptions about the voice and dialect of the speaker, and about the lexical, morphemic, syntactic, and semantic information we use to disambiguate the words. In general we can say that conscious contents are always shaped by numerous unconscious constraints.

What is the evidence that unconscious processors are relatively *autonomous* compared to conscious ones? One source of evidence is the observation that automatic processes tend to take on a life of their own, especially when we are consciously distracted (Shiffrin & Schneider, 1977). Thus numerous errors happen when we are "mindless," which would not happen otherwise. Indeed, the very occurrence of errors suggests a momentary dissociation between the rule-system that is violated and the action planning process (Baars, in press-b; Baars & Kramer, 1982).

*Conscious Processes Appear to have Internal
Consistency, are Serial, and Show Limited Capacity;
While Unconscious Processors are Highly Diverse and
Mutually Inconsistent, can Operate in Parallel, and
Together have Very Great Capacity*

*Internal consistency* of conscious processes can be shown by our experience
of perceptual ambiguities, such as figure-ground ambiguities or the Necker
cube—we can in fact experience only one interpretation of these stimuli at any
time. And the so-called impossible figures (Gregory, 1966) show that we cannot
experience internally contradictory stimuli as a whole. On the other hand, unconsciously we appear to process both mutually contradictory interpretations of
ambiguities (e.g. Swinney, 1979).

Conscious processes tend to be *serial*—or better, perhaps, we can say that the
more conscious and the less automatic some process becomes. the more it tends
to be carried out serially (Newell & Simon, 1972; LaBerge, 1974). Conversely,
unconscious processes can be carried out in *parallel*, if the task can be processed
that way (Shiffrin & Schneider, 1977). As for the neurophysiology, numerous
observers have suggested that "the organization of the brain implies parallel
processing" (Thompson, 1976)—though we would claim here, of course, that
this parallel processing is limited to unconscious functions.

Finally, conscious processes are well-known to have *limited capacity*. The
limits on short-term memory (which is associated with consciousness) are quite
procrustean (Baddeley, 1976). And because conscious contents compete with
other conscious contents, we can consciously monitor only one stream of information at a time (Broadbent, 1958; Neisser, 1976). In contrast, to get a sense of
the processing capacity of unconscious processors taken together, we need only
look at the brain. Recent estimates suggest that the human cerebral cortex alone
contains on the order of 55 billion neurons (Mountcastle, 1978). Each neuron
fires on the average 40 times per second, up to 1000 Hz. Each neuron is also
connected with perhaps 10,000 other neurons, and one can trace an anatomical
path from any neuron in the nervous system to any other by crossing only seven
synapses! To all appearances this is a system that has *great processing capacity*.

## A THEORETICAL INTERPRETATION OF THE EVIDENCE
## OF TABLE 12.1

What sense can we make of these facts? Fortunately, there is a very simple
interpretation. Computer scientists have for some time worked with system configurations that have properties very much like the ones described above: these
systems consist of multiple specialized processors, which are by themselves

quite active and independent—they are referred to as "parallel distributed processors" (PDPs) (McClelland & Rumelhart, 1985). Together, they create a "society" of specialized systems, each able to handle some predetermined type of problem.

The trouble with a PDP is that, although it can handle routine tasks just by assigning such tasks to the appropriate specialist, it has great difficulty in adapting to new problems, which may require a joining of different specialties. To permit interaction between the distributed specialists, various researchers have added a *global workspace* to the PDP, a memory whose contents are broadcast to all processors in the system (e.g. Reddy & Newell, 1974; Erman & Lesser, 1975). This global workspace (also sometimes called a blackboard or a bulletin board) is really a publicity organ for the distributed system. In principle, it allows any processor that can gain access to the global workspace to pose a problem to be solved by all the other processors. Global messages are available to all processors, but can only be interpreted by those specialists which are relevant to the content of the message. Figure 12.1 presents a very simple diagram of this situation. (The functional pros and cons of this kind of system, and its mode of operation, are discussed in detail in Baars, 1983.)

## THE FIT BETWEEN THE MODEL AND FACTS OF TABLE 12.1

Now we can go back to the contrastive analysis of the facts shown in Table 12.1, and see if these facts fit our expectations, if the nervous system were a parallel distributed processing system (PDP) equipped with a global workspace. For present purposes we will pretend that information displayed in the global workspace is conscious, while the specialized processors are unconscious. (Things are probably a little more complex than this. Baars (1983) argues that conscious contents require two other properties besides global representation, namely coherence and informativeness. But for present purposes, just global representation will do.)

Why would information processed in the global workspace be computationally inefficient? The answer to this is very simple: because all processes in the global workspace require at least the passive cooperation of all other processors in the system. In principle, any processor in the "audience" has potential access to the global workspace; thus any global process may encounter interference from other processors, which can interrupt its period of residence in the global workspace. Typically, a coalition of processors must be able to exclude other processors in order to permit exclusively global computations to take place. Thus, computation in the global workspace is inefficient: slow, error-prone, and sensitive to interference from other processes, for much the same reasons that a committee made up of humans is often slow to make decisions;

that is, because any decision requires at least the passive consensus of all participants, who may have very different properties and goals. By contrast, unconscious processors by themselves are highly efficient in their specialized tasks.

Why would the contents of the global workspace have great range, relational capacity, and context-sensitivity? The answer to this is also obvious. Great range, because in principle any processor can place a message on the global workspace; so that the total range of possible contents is equal to the total number of messages which all processors are capable of, plus all those messages resulting from novel combinations of processors. Why relational capacity (defined as the establishment of relationships between two conscious contents)? Because processors that receive information from two contiguous global events may be able to specify some connection between them. And why context-sensitivity (defined as the case where conscious events are shaped by unconscious factors)? Because global messages that violate the requirements of other processors may encounter destructive competition from those other processors, which will quickly remove them from the global workspace.

On the unconscious side, specialized processors have limited domains and relative autonomy—which is indeed, practically a defining property of parallel distributed systems. So far, therefore, all the properties of Table 12.1 fit the model.

What about the third set of contrastive pairs? Why would the contents of the global workspace be internally consistent? The answer to that is very clear: because internally inconsistent contents would trigger destructive competition between different processors responding to different aspects of the stimulus. Why seriality? Presumably for much the same reason: if any single global content must be internally consistent, the only way to display different contents would have to be serially, and not simultaneously. And why limited capacity? Again, for the same presumed reason. If global contents must be internally consistent at any one time, other contents are excluded at that time. Thus two different streams of speech could not be globally represented at the same time, because they would tend to contradict each other.

On the unconscious side, distributed processors are diverse, can operate in parallel, and together have very great capacity—largely by definition of a parallel distributed processing system (PDP).

It seems, therefore, that the model suggested here fits the empirical constraints shown in Table 12.1 in a very natural way. In Baars (1983) and Baars (in press-a,b,c). I pursue the implications of this theoretical metaphor so that it can now encompass a number of other empirical constraints, including facts about habituation of awareness, phenomena such as pre-perceptual processes, spontaneous problem-solving, and conscious control of action.

What evidence is there that the human nervous system is like this? So far, the argument has been psychological and functional. Having defined a theoretical approach, we can now begin to ask more meaningful questions about various domains of evidence, including the neurophysiological domain.

## THE NERVOUS SYSTEM AS A PARALLEL DISTRIBUTED SYSTEM

Most components of the nervous system seem to operate at the same time as other components, and to a degree independently of other components (Thompson, 1976). Further, there is reliable evidence that most anatomical structures in the brain subserve very specific functions (Table 12.2). Under these circumstances it is natural to view the brain as a parallel distributed system, and at least two well-known interpreters of brain function have done so. Arbib has for some years argued that motor systems should be viewed as collections of multiple specialized processors, operating independently of each other to a considerable degree (e.g. Arbib, 1980). And recently Mountcastle (1978) has interpreted the columnar organization of the cerebral cortex in terms of distributed "unit modules."

Recently progress has been made in understanding the nature of parallel distributed systems, and this knowledge has been applied to numerous psychological and neural findings (Hinton & Anderson, 1981; McClelland & Rumelhart, 1985; Grossberg, 1982). Along similar lines, Rozin (1976) has discussed the evolution of intelligence in terms of an increase in the accessibility of specialized functions, which originally developed as very specific evolutionary adaptations. In more advanced nervous systems, he suggests, those specialized functions can become available for new adaptive purposes. All these contributions seem to support the plausibility of viewing the nervous system as a parallel distributed system. Thus Mountcastle (1978) writes:

"The general proposition is that the large entities of the nervous system which we know as the dorsal horn, reticular formation, dorsal thalamus, neocortex, and so forth, are themselves composed of local circuits. These circuits form modules which vary from place to place. . . but which are at the first level of analysis similar within any large entity. . . . The closely linked subsets of several different large entities thus form precisely connected, distributed systems; these distributed systems are conceived as serving distributed functions" (p. 36).

Mountcastle now interprets the cerebral neocortex as such a collection of specialized distributed processors. The cortex is really a huge layered sheet stuffed into the upper half of the cranium. At the microscopic level this sheet consists of a great number of columns of cells:

"The basic unit of operation in the neocortex is a vertically arranged group of cells heavily interconnected in the vertical axis . . .and sparsely connected horizontally.

"I define the basic modular unit of the neocortex as a minicolumn. It is a vertically oriented cord of cells . . .(which) contains about 110 cells. This figure is almost invariant between different neocortical areas and different species of mammals, except for the striate cortex of primates, where it is 260. Such a cord of cells occupies a gently curving, nearly vertical cylinder of cortical space with a diameter of about 30 microns . . . the neocortex of the human brain . . . contains about 600 million minicolumns and on the order of 50 billion neurons."

Next, Mountcastle suggests that these minicolumns of cells are gathered together into *cortical columns,* which constitute the basic "unit modules" of the cerebral cortex:

". . . it is possible to identify within the neocortex a much larger processing unit than the minicolumn. The diameters or widths of this larger unit have been given as 500 microns to 1,000 microns for different areas. . . . this larger unit may vary in its cross-sectional form, being round, or oval, or slablike in shape. . . . one can estimate that the human neocortex contains about 600,000 of these larger (cortical columns), each packaging several hundred minicolumns. The calculations . . . are given to indicate order of magnitude only.

". . . Thus a major problem for understanding the function of the neocortex . . . is to unravel the intrinsic structural and functional organization of the neocortical module.

"That module is, I propose, what has come to be called the *cortical column.*"

Unlike Mountcastle, who defines a module anatomically, I would like to view the basic units as functional rather than anatomical. These approaches are not contradictory of course, because functional units must ultimately utilize anatomical units. But there is a difference of emphasis. To mark the difference, I call these specialized distributed units "processors" rather than "modules."

What constitutes a processor? Can a particular anatomical area like Broca's area underlie a single functional processor? Suppose we speak of a "language processor"--do we need a separate functional processor for syntax, for the lexicon, or for a particular part of the lexicon? After all, different brain lesions seem to attack different aspects of language processing. These questions point out that a processor must be organized recursively. That is, a processor will often be part of a structured coalition of processors, as when a language processor is controlled by a certain goal we want to attain, along with other action systems; this coalition of processors is then also a processor. And of course, the language processor is decomposable into many components, which are in turn decomposable, etc.

This kind of recursive organization does not make life simpler from a theoretical point of view, but it is exactly what we would expect on the basis of artificial intelligence systems that simulate complex human functions (e.g. Boden, 1977). It is also what one finds from a careful analysis of cases of brain damage, as in aphasia or amusia: in some cases large components seem to "drop out," while in others, only subunits within the larger components are affected (e.g. Geschwind, 1979). Thus, functionally separable processors can only be defined momentarily, within the context of a single task—in some other task or context, processors may be re-arranged in some other way; perhaps in a different organization they are functionally inseparable from a superordinate processor.

## EVIDENCE FOR A GLOBAL WORKSPACE (OR ITS FUNCTIONAL EQUIVALENT)

Assuming that we can plausibly speak of the central nervous system as a parallel distributed system, is there evidence for anything like a "global workspace" as well? First, it is important to realize that a functional global workspace may be realized in several different ways. Suppose we view a global workspace as a blackboard in an auditorium full of experts, working so that one expert can come up to the blackboard and write a "global" message which could be received by any other expert. This is functionally equivalent to the system discussed here.

Alternatively, the auditorium could be equipped with a set of portable megaphones, which each expert could use to communicate with all the other experts, with one limitation: only one megaphone may be used at one time, lest the global messages interfere with each other. This, too, is a functional equivalent of the same basic system, even though it is realized in a somewhat different form. The important thing is that different processors should be able to compete for access to some "broadcasting system" that only one processor (or one coherent coalition of processors) can use at a time. One access is gained to the broadcasting facility, however, all processors in the "audience" that can understand the broadcast can receive it.

We can therefore look for two different aspects of a global workspace or its equivalent: input and output. On the input side we expect competition for access between mutually incompatible contents. The psychological evidence for this is very strong. Conscious contents compete with all other incompatible conscious contents, and with all effortful actions as well (Kahneman, 1973). In the case of skills which can become automatic, there is less and less competition as the task becomes more and more practiced, requiring less and less conscious processing and mental effort (e.g. Norman, 1976).

On the output side of a global workspace we expect to find that a message will be available across many different subsystems. In computer science, the term *global* simply means "defined for more than one system." Thus variables may be defined just for one program (locally), or across several programs within the same overall system (globally). But if we think of the brain as a gigantic mosaic of different modules and processors (e.g. Mountcastle, 1978; Arbib, 1980; Geschwind, 1979), the implication is that globally broadcast information should be available literally everywhere in the system.

## HOW GLOBAL IS GLOBAL?

The question then is, how global is global? Several sources of evidence that bear directly on this question:

1. Any conscious or effortful process competes with any other.

If the brain equivalent of a "global workspace" is truly global, then it should be true that any brain event that is conscious or under conscious control can compete with any other event, no matter how different. One could explain the fact that visual processes interfere with other visual processes, or linguistic ones with other linguistic events. But how to explain that conscious involvement with balance mechanisms interfere with conscious involvement with abstract thought? Or language with hunger? Recall that there is little or no mutual interference when these processes are unconscious (which they are, of course, most of the time). It would seem very difficult to explain this remarkable fact of universal mutual interference without something like a truly global workspace.

2. Apparently any neural event can come under conscious control, using conscious biofeedback techniques, at least temporarily.

It is not generally emphasized enough that biofeedback always involves conscious information. To gain control over alpha-waves in the EEG, we sound a tone or turn on a light whenever the alpha-waves appear; to gain control over muscular activity we may play back to the subject the sound of his or her electrical activity in the relevant muscle, down to the control of a single muscle fiber; and so on. In terms of the global-workspace theory, to establish biofeedback control over previously uncontrolled activity in the body, we must broadcast the feedback in some way.

Under these conditions, people can gain at least temporary control over an extremely wide range of physiological activities with surprising speed. Biofeedback control in animals has been established in single neurons in the hippocampus, thalamus, hypothalamus, ventral reticular formation, and preoptic nuclei. Large populations of neurons can also be controlled, including alpha-waves in the EEG, activity in the sensory-motor cortex, evoked potentials, and the lateral geniculate nucleus (Chase, 1974). In the muscle system, single motor units can come under conscious control with half an hour or so of training, and with further biofeedback training subjects can learn to play drumrolls on single spinal motor units! (Spinal motor units involve loops consisting of only two neurons.) Autonomic functions can come under temporary control—more permanent changes in autonomic functions are unlikely, because these functions are typically controlled by interlocking negative feedback loops, producing a system that tends to resist any change. But in the Central Nervous System (CNS), as Buchwald (1974) has written, "There is no question that operant conditioning if CNS activity occurs—in fact, it is so ubiquitous a phenomenon that there seems to be no form of CSN activity (single-unit, evoked potential, or EEG) or part of the brain that is immune to it.''

This is what we would expect if conscious feedback were made available throughout the brain, and local distributed processes decided whether or not to respond to it. We may draw an analogy between biofeedback training and trying to locate a child lost in a very large city. It makes sense initially to search for the lost child around home or school, in a local and systematic fashion. But if he or she cannot be found, it may be effective to broadcast a message to all the inhabitants of the city, to which only those citizens who considered it relevant would respond. The message is global, but only the appropriate experts respond to the global message. Indeed, it is difficult to imagine an account of the power and generality of biofeedback training without some notion of global broadcasting.

3. Evidence from Event-Related Potential (ERP) studies shows that prior to habituation, conscious perceptual input is available everywhere in the brain.

There is some direct neurphysiological evidence for global broadcasting associated with consciousness. E. R. John has published a series of experiments using Event-Related Potentials (ERPs) to trace the neural activity evoked by a repeated visual or auditory train of stimulation—that is, a series of bright flashes or loud clicks (Thatcher & John, 1977). Thus a cat may have a number of recording electrodes implanted throughout its brain, and a series of light-flashes are presented to the cat (which is awake during the experiment). Electrical activity is monitored by the implanted electrodes, and averaged in a way that is time-locked to the stimuli, to remove essentially random activity. In this way, remarkably simple and ''clean'' averaged electrical traces are found amid the noise and complexity of ordinary EEG.

John's major finding of interest to us was that electrical activity due to the visual flashes can initially be found everywhere in the brain, far beyond the specialized visual pathways. At this point we can assume that the cat is conscious of the light flashes, since the stimulus is new. But as the same stimuli are repeated, habituation takes place. The electrical activity never disappears completely, as long as the stimuli are presented, but it becomes more and more localized—until finally it is limited only to the classical visual pathways. These results are strikingly in accord with our expectations. According to Model 1, prior to habituation, the information is conscious and globally distributed. But after habituation, it ceases to be conscious and becomes limited only to those parts of the brain that are limited to visual functions. Only the specialized input processor is now involved in analyzing the stimulus.

4. The Orienting Response, closely associated with conscious surprise at novelty, is known to involve every major division of the nervous system.

We know that any novel stimulus is likely to be conscious, and that it will elicit an Orienting Response (OR) (e.g. Sokolov, 1963). The OR is probably the most widespread ''reflexive'' response of all. It disrupts alpha-activity in the

EEG, it dilates or contracts blood vessels all over the head and body, it changes the conductivity of the skin, it causes orienting of eyes, ears, and nose to the source of novel stimulation, triggers changes in autonomic functions such as heart-rate and peristalsis, it causes very rapid pupillary dilation, and so on. All these changes need not be produced by a globally broadcast message, but the fact that they are so widespread, both anatomically and functionally, suggests that something of that sort may be going on.

5. The reticular-thalamic system of the brain stem and forebrain is closely associated with conscious functions. It is known to involve all input and output systems, virtually all subcortical structures, and it projects diffusely through the thalamus to all parts of the cortex.

There is a network-like structure in the brainstem and forebrain, consisting of numerous specific and non-specific neuronal circuits, in which most of the neurons have very short axons (Fig. 12.2). It is closely related to conscious functions: waking and sleeping, focal attention, the Orienting Response, sensory control processes, and the like. The reticular-thalamic looks anatomically as if it might involve global broadcasting—it takes inputs from all sensory and motor channels, projects upward through the thalamus to all parts of the cortex, and is known to be able to arouse and focus activity in the cortex. It connects as well with all major subcortical structures and the spinal cord. This is exactly the kind of structure that the nervous system might use to broadcast information to all parts of the system.

6. All aspects of a conscious event seem to be monitored by unconscious rule-systems, as suggested by the fact that errors at any level can be caught if only we become conscious of the event in question.

This is a phenomenon that may seem obvious until we try to explain it. Take a single sentence, for example, spoken by a normal speaker. We very quickly detect errors or anomalies in pronunciation, voice-quality, perceived location of the voice, acoustics, vocabulary, syllable stress, intonation, phonology, morphology, syntax, semantics, stylistics, discourse relations, conversational norms, communicative effectiveness, or pragmatic intentions of the speaker. Each of these aspects corresponds to a very complex and highly developed rule-system, which we as skilled speakers of the language have developed to a high level of proficiency. The complexity of this capability is simply enormous. Yet as long as we are conscious of the spoken sentence we are bringing all these rule-systems to bear on it—we can automatically detect violations of any of these rule-system, implying that the sentence is somehow available to all of them. If we are not conscious of a sentence we have just spoken, we do not even detect our own errors. Again, there is a natural role for "global broadcasting" in this kind of situation.

In sum, how global is global? On the basis of the facts previously discussed, we would answer: "very global indeed." It would not be surprising to find that in principle, any neuron in the nervous system can have potential access to conscious information. This is suggested especially by the biofeedback literature, and by the widespread activity found in Event-Related Potentials prior to habituation. This is a strong claim to make, of course, but not one that is inconceivable, especially in view of the anatomy and function of the reticular-thalamic system which appears to underlie this ability. We will discuss this neural system next.

### The Reticular-thalamic System Appears to be the Neural Substrate of the System Described by the Model

What part of the brain could carry out the functions described by Model 1? We can specify some of its properties:

First, it should be associated with conscious functions like wakefulness, focal attention, habituation, and indeed all the facts described in the contrastive analyses in Table 12.1.

Second, it should fit our theoretical model: we should be able to interpret some parts of the brain as specialized unconscious processors, able to act in a distributed way; these processors should be able to cooperate and compete through some central information exchange, like a "blackboard"; and the resulting information should be able to be broadcast throughout the nervous system.

There is an anatomical and functional system in the brain stem and forebrain that is known to have close relationships with consciousness (Magoun, 1963; Scheibel & Scheibel, 1967; Dixon, 1971; Hobson & Brazier, 1982). This structure includes the classic Reticular Formation discovered by Moruzzi and Magoun (1949), which receives nerve branches from all major structures within the brain including all sensory and motor tracts, and permits very close interaction between all these sources of information. It extends well upward to include the nonspecific nuclei of the thalamus, and it makes functional sense to include in this larger system the "diffuse thalamic projection system," which sends numerous fibers to all parts of the cortex (Fig. 12.2). We refer to this whole set of anatomical structures as the *reticular-thalamic system*. It is described by one of its co-discoverers (Magoun, 1963) as follows:

"Within the brain, a central transactional core has been identified between the strictly sensory or motor systems of classical neurology. This central reticular mechanism has been found *capable of grading the activity of most other parts of the brain* . . . it is proposed to be subdivided into a grosser and more tonically operating component in the lower brain stem, subserving global alterations in excitability, as distinguished from a more cephalic, thalamic component with greater capacities for fractionated, shifting influences upon focal regions of the brain.

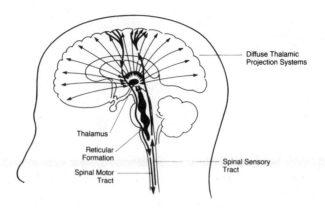

FIGURE 11.2. A schematic diagram of the reticular-thalamic system, which incorporates the classical brain-stem reticular formation, the non-specific nuclei of the thalamus (nucleus reticularis thalami), and the fibers that project diffusely upward from the thalamus, and which are involved in both specific and nonspecific "activation" of the cortex. In many ways, this broad reticular-thalamic system behaves like a global workspace in a parallel distributed system.

"In its ascending and descending relations with the cerebral cortex, the reticular system is *intimately bound up with and contributes to most areas of nervous activity.* It has to do significantly with the *initiation and maintenance of wakefulness;* with the *orienting reflex* and *focus of attention;* with *sensory control processes* including habituation . . . ; with *conditional learning;* through its functional relations with the hippocampus and temporal cortex, with *memory functions;* and through its relations with the midline thalamus and pontile tegmentum, with the cortex and *most of the central integrative processes* of the brain." [Italics added]

The fact that the reticular-thalamic system involves wakefulness, the orienting response, focus of attention, and "most of the central integrative processes of the brain" certainly suggests that it may be what we are looking for. Other neurophysiologists associate parts of this system with the capability of altering the content of consciousness and with general alerting and focused attention. The overall reticular-thalamic system thus easily meets our first criterion, that our neuronal candidate should be closely associated with conscious experience.

What about the second criterion, the idea that the brain structure in question should fit Model 1? There are three parts to this claim: First, we should be able to view parts of the nervous system as consisting of specialized distributed processors; second, these processors should be able to cooperate and compete for access to our anatomical candidate for a global workspace, ultimately resulting in a single coherent representation; third, that this coherent representation could then be broadcast globally throughout the nervous system.

Let us take these points one by one.

**Neurophysiological Evidence for Distributed Specialists.**    We have already discussed evidence for specialized unconscious processors. In recent years several prominent brain scientists have specifically suggested that the major structures of the brain can be interpreted as a collections of distributed processors (Szentagotai & Arbib, 1974; Arbib, 1980; Edelman & Mountcastle, 1978; Grossberg, 1982).

This meets our first requirement: there is evidence that many neural structures, specifically the cortex, consist of collections of specialized distributed modules. Presumably the reticular-thalamic system is to the cortex as a global workspace is to its specialized processors.

**Neurophysiological Evidence that Specialists can Cooperate and Compete for Access to a Central Integrative "Blackboard".**    The caudal component of the reticular-thalamic system is called ''reticular'' (i.e. network-like) because the neural axons in this system are usually very short, suggesting a great amount of interaction between adjacent neurons. Further, it receives collateral branches from all sensory and motor systems, as well as from other major structures in the brain. Through its connections with the thalamus, it can send and receive information from all areas of the cortex. If the reticular-thalamic system corresponds to our ''blackboard,'' different specialized systems can have access to it.

Aristotle's common sense was supposed to be a domain of integration between the different senses. In fact anatomists who have studied the reticular-thalamic system (RTS) have pointed to its resemblance to Aristotle's concept. Scheibel and Scheibel (1967) point out that ''Anatomical studies of Kohnstamm and Quensel, which suggested pooling of a number of afferent and efferent systems upon the reticular core, led them to propose this area as a 'centrum receptorium', or 'sensorium commune'—a common sensory pool for the neuraxis.''

Moreover, these authors note that ''. . . the reticular core mediates specific delimitation of the focus of consciousness with concordant suppression of those sensory inputs that have been temporarily relegated to a sensory role'' (p. 579). Thus different sensory contents can suppress each other, as we would indeed expect from the ''internal consistency'' constraint on conscious contents. This competition is represented in Model 1 by the idea that mutually inconsistent groups of processors can compete with each other for access to the global workspace.

This meets our second requirement, that the reticular-thalamic system can be viewed as the domain of competition and cooperation between different specialized processors.

**Neurophysiological Evidence that Integrated, Coherent Information can be Broadcast from the Reticular-Thalamic System to all Parts of the Nervous System.**    As we just noted, we are including in the term *re-*

*ticular-thalamic system* the diffuse thalamic projection system, a bundle of neurons which project outward like a fountain from the thalamus to all parts of the cortex. It contains both specific and non-specific projections, and the specific ones usually contain feedback loops going in the opposite direction as well. This system may work to "broadcast" information from the lower levels of the reticular system to all parts of the cortex.

What is the relationship between the reticular-thalamic system and the cortex, especially the sensory-motor cortex? Information and control seem to flow in both directions. Based on Model 1, we suggest that the reticular-thalamic system underlies the "global broadcasting" function of consciousness, while the cortex supplies the particular contents of consciousness that are to be broadcast. (These are typically perceptual contents, because the reticular system receives collateral pathways from all sensory tracts.) These perceptual contents, in turn, when they are broadcast, can trigger both motor and associative activities.

There is independent evidence that activity in the sensory-motor cortex by itself does not become conscious (Libet, 1977; Shevrin & Dickman, 1980; Posner, Klein, Summers, & Buggie, 1983). We would suggest that this sensory-motor activity must trigger reticular "support," perhaps in a circulating flow of information, before it can be broadcast globally and become conscious (e.g. Shevrin & Dickman, 1982). Dixon (1971) has also argued that a circulating loop of information flow between the reticular formation and the sensory areas of the cortex is required before the sensory input becomes conscious. This view adds something to our model, namely circulating control from some of the "receiving processors" which tend to keep the "broadcasting processors" broadcasting as long as the receivers are interested in this information.

Presumably in the process of being broadcast globally, the perceptual information also reaches language processors which can carry out voluntary reports of the conscious experience.

In sum, there is considerable neurophysiological evidence to suggest that the reticular-thalamic system is the major substrate of conscious experience, while the cortex and perhaps other parts of the brain may provide the content of conscious experience. Contributions from both the RTS and cortex are presumably required to create a stable conscious content. The evidence comes from numerous studies showing a direct relationship between the RTS and known conscious functions like sleep and waking, alertness, the Orienting Response, focal attention, sharpening of perceptual discriminations, habituation of orienting, conditioning, and perceptual learning (see references just cited). Further, there is evidence consistent with the three major properties of Model 1: first, that major brain structures, especially the cortex, can be viewed as collections of distributed specialized modules; second, that some of these modules can cooperate and compete through the RTS; and third, the anatomy and physiology of the RTS suggests that its information may be broadcast globally to other parts of the nervous system, especially the huge cortical mantle of the brain.

The evidence from neurophysiology seems to support Model 1, with one addition: there seem to be feedback loops coming from cortical modules back to the "blackboard," suggesting that a circulating flow of information may be necessary to keep some content in consciousness.

Let us review where we have been. First, a contrastive analysis of conscious vs. unconscious phenomena yielded a set of empirical constraints on theory (Table 12.1), and suggested a certain systems architecture technically called "a global workspace in a parallel distributed processing system" (Fig. 12.1). Next, we argued that several established facts about the nervous system suggest that we may take the notion of global broadcasting quite literally. A brief review of the large research literature on the reticular system of the brain stem and forebrain showed it to bear out our theoretical expectations regarding a system that can take input from specialized modules in the brain, and broadcast this information globally to the nervous system as a whole (Fig. 12.2). Thus the story seems fairly tidy. Assuming that this convergent pattern of evidence and theory is not leading us astray, what does all this mean about the evolutionary development of conscious processes?

First, it is quite clear that there is no simple "ladder" of evolutionary development with regard to intelligence or consciousness (Aronson, 1983; Tobach & Greenberg, 1984; Rozin, 1976). Many animals have better vision, hearing, or olfactory sense than humans. Any migratory animal is better at finding its way than humans. The difference between humans and other organisms is clearly not a matter of increased intelligence in some single well-defined domain.

**Phylogeny of the Reticular-Thalamic System.**   If we can associate conscious processes with the reticular formation, we may be able to make some inferences about the evolutionary development of the structures that underlie consciousness in humans. This evidence clearly points to very great antiquity of these structures. Thus Bishop (1969) writes of "A chain of structures extending from the spinal cord level through various levels to the cerebral cortex has been recognized in as primitive a form as amblystoma, where Herrick designated one region of the alba as the precursor of the reticular formation. These structures may therefore be looked for in the early development of the vertebrates" (pp. 128).

**Phylogeny of the neocortex.**   Although many brain structures can be viewed as collections of distributed specialized modules, we will focus on the neocortex. Its evolutionary development is discussed by Mountcastle (Edelman & Mountcastle, 1978):

> The avalanching enlargement of the neocortex is a major aspect of mammalian evolution and, in its degree, distinguishes primates from other mammals and man from other primates . . . the new and old world monkeys, diverged from the line leading to man (and from each other) more than 30 million years ago. However,

detailed measurements of the total brain and of the relative sizes of different brain parts in insectivores, prosimians, and simians do provide an ordinal ranking of species in terms of brain development, and the degree of brain development provides the best available correlation with the evolutionary level of achievement. Moreover, the careful measurements of Stephan and his colleagues . . . in more that 60 species have revealed that, of all cerebral parts, it is the absolute and relative development of the neocortex that correlates best with evolutionary achievement. (p. 9)

The living basal insectivores are thought to have evolved very little from their ancestors, from which man's line also arose. Stephan has used this fact to establish an index of the evolutionary development of brain structure as the ratio of its observed volume to that expected in a basal insectivore of the same body weight. The progression index for neocortex is 156 for man, 60 for chimpanzee, and 40 for Cercopithecidae . . . The degree of differential development of the neocortex is emphasized by the progression indices for different brain parts: neocortex, 165; striatum, 17; hippocampus, 4; cerebellum, 5; dorsal thalamus, 5; basal olfactory structures and olfactory bulb, 1 or less.

[However] the enlargement of the neocortex in primates has been accomplished by a great expansion of its surface area, without striking changes in vertical organization. Indeed, Powell and his colleagues have shown that the number of neurons in a vertical line across the thickness of the cortex—that is, in a 30-micron-diameter circle—is remarkably constant at about 110 . . . The counts are virtually identical for the five areas studies in five species: the motor, somatic sensory, and frontal, parietal, and temporal homotypical cortices in the mouse, cat, rat, macaque monkey, and man.

. . . a cortical area may be defined both by its intrinsic structure and as the zone of projection of a specific thalamic nucleus. This generality has since been confirmed in a large number of species, including primates . . . both the static and the dynamic functional properties of cortical neurons can be correlated with the cytoarchitectural area in which they are located. . . (p. 14)

In summary, I conclude that cytoarchitectural differences between areas of neocortex reflect differences in their patterns of *extrinsic* connections. [italics added] These patterns are in no way accidental. They are detailed and precise for each area; indeed, they define it. The traditional . . . "functions" of different areas also reflect these differences in extrinsic connections; they provide no evidence whatsoever for differences in *intrinsic* structure or function. This suggests that neocortex is everywhere functionally much more uniform than hitherto supposed and that its avalanching enlargement in mammals and particularly in primates has been accomplished by replication of a basic neural module, without the appearance of wholly new neuron types or of qualitatively different modes of intrinsic organization.

To be quite simplistic: it seems that the reticular-thalamic system has changed relatively little during vertebrate evolution, whereas the neocortex has ballooned at increasing rates of change in the development from early vertebrates to mammals to primates to man. In terms of our model, again speaking simplistically, it seems as if the global workspace has remained much the same while the number of specialized distributed modules has increased geometrically.

The question is, of course, whether we can attribute to ancestral forms of the human reticular system the same functions it appears to have in humans. The discussion thus becomes inevitably more speculative at this point. We can get some guidance, however.

First, we note that evolutionary developments are typically accretive rather than entirely novel. As Darwin noted in the last century (Gould, 1980):

> . . . if a man were to make a machine for some special purpose, but were to use old wheels, springs, and pulleys, only slightly altered, the whole mechanism, with all its parts, might be said to be contrived for that purpose. Thus throughout nature almost every part of each living being has probably served, in a slightly modified condition, for diverse purposes, and has acted in the living machinery of many ancient and specific forms.

If this is so, then early forms of the reticular system may have carried out more "primitive" versions of similar functions. If we can assume that the basic function of the reticular system is to combine information from multiple specialized systems (which have, of course, existed from the beginning of nervous systems), and to broadcast that information to the system as a whole, then we can suggest a fairly convincing set of functions for such a system, some of which would seem to presuppose others. Those functions that are presupposed by other functions may well be the ones that have existed longest. For example, one of the first functions of this kind of system may be to serve as a "common sense" in Aristotle's sense, to combine information from several sensory sources in one coherent package. Human beings need this capability, but so do many other organisms. Further, it is essential for an organism to combine multiple sources of information in deciding on a single course of action. Arbib (1980) calls this the "mode consensus" constraint on action, and again, our global workspace would seem like a natural candidate for this function.

On the other hand, the use of conscious and voluntary speech to control various mental and physical activities is clearly limited to human beings, speech being one of our special adaptations (Lenneberg, 1977). But this use of speech is based on, and presupposes the functions just listed—the ability to combine multiple sources of perceptual information, and the ability to combine multiple considerations in deciding on a coherent course of action. With this kind of reasoning we can tentatively suggest an ordered expansion of the functions of the same fundamental structure, with some implications for phylogenetic development. Table 12.3 presents a hypothetical ordered set of functions associated with consciousness, and thus presumably with the reticular system. going from the most basic to the most "advanced."

TABLE 12.3
A Speculative Phylogeny of a Conscious Global Workspace

1. unimodal input
2. S-R reflexes

The Following May Characterize Vertebrates

3. perceptual integration within and between modalities (*)
4. integration of sensory input with its broader context (*)
5. perceptual constancies
6. object permanence: representing absent perceptual events

The Following May Characterize Mammals

7. using percepts to trigger novel actions in a context-
   sensitive way (*)
8. using images to trigger novel actions in a context-
   sensitive way (ideo-motor control) (*)
9. imitation: learning actions by observations of other
   animals (*)
10. re-experiencing images of earlier percepts (*)
11. re-experiencing images of earlier images (*)

The Following Seem to Characterize Humans Uniquely

12. gaining ideo-motor control over mental images (*)
13. development of outer and inner speech (*)
14. arbitrary sign-referent relationships (*)
15. syntactic tools for propositional referring (*)
14. rapid cultural evolution using propositional use of
    social speech (*)
14. establishing novel analogies between known and unknown
    information (*)
15. propositional referring in the presence of the referent (*)
16. propositional referring in the absence of the referent (*)
18. propositional evocation of a referential context (*)
19. propositionally referring to one's own mental contents (*)
20. propositional use of inner speech in problem-solving (*)
21. Short-term memory functions (rehersal, etc.) (*)
20. Metacognitive control of consciousness (voluntary attention,
    voluntary recall(*)

Note: (*) These properties suggest the use of a global workspace.

# A SPECULATIVE PHYLOGENY OF CONSCIOUS FUNCTIONS

Specialization of neural function must surely be very ancient, and in a sense, a primitive collection of specialized neurons and small neural circuits is already a "parallel distributed system." Integration between and within sensory modalities evolves early as well, and it seems likely that specialized integrative circuits develop to handle predictable kinds of integration: spatial integration between the both sound and light senses, for example. None of these applications require a "global workspace" or its equivalent until we arrive at the ability to combine previously unpredictable combinations of stimuli and responses, for which specialized integrative systems do not exist. Thus the earliest organisms capable of being classically conditioned with a range of arbitrary stimuli that do not occur naturally in their biological niches, might give us a candidate for the beginnings of a functional global workspace. Alternatively, we can look for organisms that display competition between novel stimuli in different modalities. This, too, suggests the existence of a limited central capacity, such as a global workspace.

Table 12.3 also suggests that actions are frequently initiated by globally distributed percepts or images. This is a variant of James' "ideomotor control" concept (1890), which suggests that actions are often directed and initiated by conscious images of a goal-state. The ideo-motor notion fits perfectly into a global workspace conception of consciousness, suggesting that goal images are broadcast globally, and that the appropriate distributed effector systems are thus recruited to carry out the action (providing the goal image does not encounter competition from other executive processors) (Baars, in press-b; Baars & Kramer, 1982; Arbib, 1980). There is evidence that images involve internally generated activity in the same sensory modality which the image appears to reflect subjectively (Finke, 1980). If images are indeed self-generated quasi-percepts, the ability to use images for self-control may be rather old. Again, the distinctive feature suggesting the involvement of a global workspace is the ability for arbitrary percepts or images to be related to arbitrary actions (essentially operant conditioning). A further step is taken when the activity controlled by a percept or image is itself internal—that is, when an unconscious process or a conscious image is triggered by another image or percept. With this extension, the ideomotor notion can be used to account for internal control of abstract representations such as ideas, beliefs, intentions and the like.

It is ironic that we are taking the existence of classical and operant conditioning with arbitrary S-S and S-R relationships as a cue to the early existence of consciousness—quite the opposite of our behavioristic forerunners, who tended historically to take classical and operant conditioning as a reduction of complex learning to reflex action! But it is also a sign of our renewed respect for the complexity and sophistication of animal nervous systems.

Rozin (1976) presents an interesting approach that is very compatible with the present one, viewing the evolution of intelligence in terms of access to the cognitive unconscious:

> Intelligent functions should be organized out of component 'subprograms' . . . that are called adaptive specializations. [These correspond to what we have earlier called specialized modules or processors.] Adaptive specializations, by their nature as solutions of specific problems, tend to maintain themselves only in the narrow set of circumstances related to the problems that directed their evolution . . . Since all reasonably complex animals have quite a few sophisticated circuits or programs (adaptive specializations) in their brains, I suggest that a major route to increasing flexibility and power over the environment, surely hallmarks of intelligence, would be to make these more generally available or accessible. [Rozin continues by suggesting that] . . . in the course of evolution these programs become more *accessible* to other systems, and, in the extreme, may rise to the level of consciousness and be applied over the full realm of behavior and mental function. . . .

the notion of . . . *levels of accessibility* is useful in understanding the development and dissolution of intelligence . . . It is suggested that part of the process of learning and education can be considered as bringing to consciousness some of the limited-access programs, the cognitive unconscious, already in the head.

Obviously we have a ready mechanism to carry out this function of creating more and more accessibility, which Rozin associates with consciousness— namely, the global workspace. Rozin's argument seems to suggest then that specialized functions in more complex nervous systems may be more "portable" from one application to another. One noteworthy function of the global workspace in this respect is the ability to facilitate analogies between the global representation and other processors that can respond to the global message. Another important function is the ability to learn a complex skill slowly, one component at a time, and then to integrate the new skill into a new, automatic module. Both of these abilities exist in a developed form in humans and perhaps other primates, but the ability to do these things in a relatively arbitrary fashion probably increases sharply in humans when compared to other mammals.

Complex learning in predictable biological contexts is much more widespread, of course—again, the distinction rests on the issue of biological arbitrariness. Thus, the ability of humans to associate smells with voluntary actions, and visual stimuli with getting ill, suggests that the limitations of the Garcia Effect with other mammals does not apply to humans. Nevertheless, humans do not have total "portability" of specialized functions from one context to another. Many of our cultural inventions are in fact adaptations of biological capabilities—thus, the ability to read is facilitated by our existing language capability.

From this point of view, the invention of language as a tool for cultural transmission is a critical event in the functional development of consciousness. In a sense, the development of arbitrary sign-referent relationships allows the social group to program the individual through the manipulation of social symbols, supplemented by mental images and inner speech. Finally, the development of syntax as a rule system that permits arbitrary propositional descriptions to be shared between members of a group, makes it possible for us to share the contents of our consciousness in a flexible way. It is plausible to think that the social use of such propositional devices led to individual use of inner speech and voluntarily controllable mental imagery. Finally, somewhere along this road, the ability must have emerged to control one's own consciousness through the use of internally-generated or socially-generated propositions—the sort of thing we try to teach our children when we want them to do homework rather than play outside. But all of these functions are still just overlaid on the pre-existing global workspace.

Such. then, are the phylogenetic speculations that emerge from this theoretical approach to consciousness.

## SUMMARY AND CONCLUSIONS

We have used an integrative cognitive model of conscious and unconscious functions, explored its neuranatomical basis, and used the results as a basis for some evolutionary speculations. From the point of view presented here, there is no reason to deny some sort of conscious experience to even quite early vertebrates because they seem to have the rudiments of the reticular formation that seems to be the *sine qua non* of conscious experience in mammals and humans. However, the contents and control systems for conscious experience seems to be largely neocortical, and here we find huge differences between humans, early mammals, and ancestral vertebrates.

It is important to point out that have we primarily explored the notion of global broadasting, proposed as a critical property of consciousness by Baars (1983), but not the two other critical properties of conscious coherence and informativeness. It is possible that a detailed evolutionary exploration of these additional properties will show critical differences between humans and other mammals, and between mammals and ancestral vertebrates. Based on the present analysis, however, it is difficult to justify the denial of conscious experience to mammals and even vertebrates in general. If this conclusion stands, it is bound to have major implications: scientific, philosophical, and in the ethics of our dealings with animals.

## ACKNOWLEDGMENTS

Preparation of this chapter was supported in part by the Program on Conscious and Unconscious Mental Processes, Langley Porter Neuropsychiatric Institute, UCSF, funded by the John D. and Catherine T. MacArthur Foundation, whose support is gratefully acknowledged. I would like to thank several people who have contributed to the ideas presented in this chapter, including David Galin (UCSF), Benjamin Libet (UCSF), Paul Rozin (U. Penn.), Michael A. Wapner (CSULA), Theodore Melnechuk (Western Behav. Sci. Inst.), Emil Menzel (SUNY SB), Donald A. Norman (UCSD), and George Mandler (UCSD).

## REFERENCES

Arbib, M. A. (1980). Perceptual structures and distributed motor control. In V. B. Brooks, *Handbook of physiology* (Vol. III). Bethesda, MD: The American Physiological Society.

Baars, B. J. (1983). Conscious contents provide the nervous system with coherent, global information. In R. Davidson, G. Schwartz, & D. Shapiro (Eds.), *Consciousness and self-regulation, Vol. 3*. New York: Plenum.

Baars, B. J. (1985). Can involuntary slips reveal one's state of mind?—with an addendum on the conscious control of speech. In M. Toglia & T. M. Shlechter (Eds.) *New directions in cognitive science*. Norwood, NJ: Ablex.

Baars, B. J. (1986–1987). What is a theory of consciousness a theory of? Empirical constraints on any theory. *Imagination, cognition, and personality, 6*(1), 3–24.

Baars, B. J. (in press-a). What is conscious in the control of action? A modern ideomotor theory of voluntary control. In D. Gorfein & R. R. Hoffmann (Eds.). Hillsdale, NJ: Lawrence Erlbaum Associates.

Baars, B. J. (in press-c). Momentary forgetting as an erasure of a conscious global workspace due to competition between incompatible contexts. In M. J. Horowitz (Ed.), *Conscious and unconscious influences on emotional processes*. Chicago, IL: University of Chicago Press.

Baars, B. J. (in press-c). *A cognitive theory of consciousness*. London: Cambridge University Press.

Baars, B. J., & Mattson, M. E. (1981). Consciousness and intention: A framework and some evidence. *Cognition and Brain Theory, 1981, 4*(3), 247–263.

Baars, B. J., & Kramer, D. (1982). Conscious and unconscious components of intentional control. *Proceedings of the 4th Cognitive Science Conference*, Ann Arbor, MI.

Baddeley, A. D. (1976). *The psychology of memory*. New York: Basic Books.

Bishop, G. H. (1969). The place of cortex in a reticular system. In L. D. Proctor (Ed.), *Biocybernetics of the central nervous system*. Boston, MA: Little, Brown.

Boden, M. (1977). *Artificial intelligence and natural man*. New York: Basic Books.

Broadbent, D. E. (1958). *Perception and communication*. New York: Pergamon Press.

Buchwald, J. S. (1974). Operant conditioning of brain activity—an overview. In M. M. Chase (Ed.), *Operant conditioning of brain activity*. Los Angeles: University of California Press.

Chase, M. H. (Ed.) (1974). *Operant control of brain activity*. Los Angeles Brain nformation Service, Brain Research Institute, UCLA.

Delafresne, J. F., Adrian, E. D., Bremer, F., & Jasper, H. H. (1954). *Brain mechanisms and conscious experience*. Oxford, England: Blackwell.

Dixon, N. F. (1971). *Subliminal perception: The nature of a controversy*. London: McGraw-Hill.

Donchin, E., McCarthy, G., Kutas, M., & Ritter, W. (1983). Event-related potentials in the study of consciousness. In R. J. Davidson, G. Schwartz, D. Shapiro (Eds.), *Consciousness and self-regulation, Vol. 3*. New York: Plenum Press.

Darwin, C. (circa 1838). "Old and Useless Notes". In P. H. Barrett & H. Gruber (Eds.), *Darwin on man: A Psychological study of scientific creativity* (London: Wildwood House, 1974).

Erman, L. D., & Lesser, V. R. (1975). A multi-level organization for problem solving using many, diverse, cooperating sources of knowledge. *Proceedings of the 4th Annual Joint Computer Conference* (pp. 483–490). Georgia: USSR.

Finke, R. (1980). Levels of equivalence in imagery and perception. *Psychological Review, 87*(2), 113–132.

Fodor, J. A. (1983). *The modularity of mind: An essay on faculty psychology*. Cambridge, MA: Bradford/MIT Press.

Geschwind, N. (1979). Specializations of the human brain. *Scientific American, 241*(3), 180–201.

Gould, S. J. (1980). *The panda's thumb: More reflections in natural history*. NY: Norton.

Gregory, R. L. (1966). *Eye and brain: The psychology of seeing*. New York: McGraw-Hill.

Griffin, D. R. (1981). *The question of animal awareness* (2nd Ed.). NYU: Rockefeller University Press.

Grossberg, S. (1982). *Studies of mind and brain*. Boston: Reidel Publishing Co.

Hinton, G. E., & Anderson, J. A. (1981). *Parallel models of associative memory*. Hillsdale, NJ: Lawrence Erlbaum Associates.

Hobson & Brazier, (1982). *The Reticular Formation revisited*.

James, W. (1890). *The principles of psychology*. NY: Holt. (Reprinted by Dovers, NY, 1950).

Kahneman, D. (1973). *Attention and Effort*. Englewood Cliffs, N.J.: Prentice-Hall.

Libet, B. (1977). Neuronal vs. subjective timing for a conscious sensory experience. In P. A. Buser

& A. Rougeul-Buser (Eds.). (1978), *Cerebral correlates of conscious experience*. INSERM Symposium No. 6. Amsterdam: N. Holland/Elsevier.

Libet, B., Alberts, W. W., Wright, E. W., & Feinstein, B. (1967). Responses of human somatosensory cortext to stimuli below threshold for conscious sensation. *Science 158*, 1597–1600.

John, E. R. (1976). A model of consciousness. In G. Schwartz & D. Shapiro (Eds.), *Consciousness and self-regulation*. New York: Plenum press.

LaBerge, D. (1974). Acquisition of automatic processing in perceptual and associative learning. In P. M. A. Rabbitt & S. Dornic (Eds.), *Attention and performance, Vol. 4* London: Academic Press.

Lenneberg, E. H. (1967). *Biological foundations of language*. New York: Wiley.

Magoun, H. W. (1963). *The waking brain* (2nd. Ed.), Springfield, IL: C. C. Thomas.

Mandler, G. A. (1975). *Mind and emotion*. New York: Wiley.

Mandler, G. (1983). *Consciousness: Its function and construction*. Presidential Address to the General Psychology Division of the American Psychological Association.

Marcel, A. J. (1983a). Conscious and unconscious perception: An approach to the relations between phenomenal experience and perceptual processes. *Cognitive Psychology 15*, 238–300.

Marcel, A. J. (1983b). Conscious and unconscious perception: Experiments on visual masking and word recognition. *Cognitive Psychology 15*, 197–237.

McClelland, J. L., & Rumelhart, D. E. (1985). Distributed memory and the representation of general and specific information. *Journal of Experimental Psychology: General, 114*(2), 159–188.

Melnechuk, T. (1980). *Consciousness and brain research*. Paper presented at the conference on Human Consciousness Research, Spring Hill, Minnesota.

Moruzzi, G., & Magoun, H. W. (1949). Brain stem reticular formation and activation of the EEG. *Electroencephalog. clin. Neurophys., 1*, 455–473.

Mountcastle, V. B. (1978). An organizing principle for cerebral function: The unit module and the distributed system. In G. M. Edelman & V. B. Mountcastle (Eds.), *The mindful brain*. Cambridge, MA: The MIT Press.

Neisser, U. (1976). *Cognition and reality*. San Francisco: W. H. Freeman.

Newell, A., & Simon, H. A. (1972). *Human problem solving*. Englewood Cliffs, NJ: Prentice-Hall.

Norman, D. A. (1976). *Memory and attention* (2nd Ed.). New York: Wiley.

Norman, D. A. (1981). *Perspectives on cognitive science*. Norwood, NJ: Ablex.

Posner, M. (1982). Cumulative development of attentional theory. *American Psychologist, 37*(2), 168–179.

Posner, M. I., Klein, R., Summers, J., & Buggie, S. (1973). On the relation of signals. *Memory and Cognition, 1*, 2–12.

Posner, M., & Warren, R. E. (1972). Traces, concepts, and conscious constructions. In A. W. Melton & E. Martin (Eds.), *Coding processes in human memory*. Washington, D.C.: Winston.

Reddy, R., & Newell, A. (1974). Knowledge and its representation in a speech understanding system. In L. W. Gregg (Ed.), *Knowledge and cognition*. Hillsdale, NJ: Lawrence Erlbaum Associates.

Rock, I. (1983). *The logic of perception*. Cambridge, MA: Bradford/MIT Press.

Rozin, P. (1976). The evolution of intelligence and access to the cognitive unconscious. In J. Sprague & A. Epstein, *Progress in psychobiology and physiological psychology*. Orlando, FL: Academic Press.

Scheibel, M. C., & Scheibel, A. B. (1967). Anatomical basis of attentional mechanisms in vertebrate brains. In G. C. Quarton, T. Melnechuk, & F. O. Schmitt (Eds.), *The neurosciences: A study program*. New York: Rockefeller University Press.

Shallice, T. (1972). Dual functions of consciousness. *Psychological Review, 79*(5), 383–393.

Shallice, T. (1976). The dominant action system: An information-processing approach to consciousness. In K. S. Pope & J. L. Singer (Eds.). (1978), *The stream of consciousness: Scientific investigations into the flow of experience*. New York: Plenum.

Shevrin, H., & Dickman, S. (1980). The psychological unconscious: A necessary assumption for all psychological theory. *American Psychologist, 35*(5), 421–434.

Shiffrin, R. M., & Schneider, W. (1977). Controlled and automatic human information processing: II. Perceptual learning, automatic attending, and a general theory. *Psychological Review, 84*, 127–190.

Sokolov, E. N. (1963). *Perception and the orienting reflex*. New York: Macmillan.

Sperling, G. (1960). The information available in brief conscious presentations. *Psychological Monographs, 74* (Whole No. 11).

Swinney, D. A. (1979). Lexical access during sentence comprehension: (Re)consideration of context effects. *Journal of Verbal Learning and Verbal Behavior, 18*, 645–659.

Szentagotai, J., & Arbib, M. A. (1975). *Conceptual models of neural organization. Neurosciences Research Bulletin, 12*, 307–510.

Thatcher, R. W., & John, E. R. (1977). *Foundations of cognitive processes*. Hillsdale, NJ: Lawrence Erlbaum Associates.

Thompson, R. F. (1976). The search for the engram. *American Psychologist, 31*, 209–227.

Underwood, G. (1982). Attention and awareness in cognitive and motor skills. In G. Underwood (Ed.), *Aspects of consciousness, Vol. 3*. London: Academic Press.

# III EPILOGUE

# 13

# Integrative Levels in the Comparative Psychology of Cognition, Language, and Consciousness

Ethel Tobach
*American Museum of Natural History,*
*New York*

## INTRODUCTION

### The Conference Series

The topic for the second conference was chosen because of a heightened interest in the apparent loss of a clear differentiation between humans and other animals. This differentiation has been challenged by a number of experimental, technological, and theoretical developments.

Cognition.  Development in apparently disparate fields such as sophisticated investigations of thinking in the form of artificial intelligence (Simon, 1969) and experiments in complex communication/foraging behavior in invertebrates (Gould & Gould, 1982) are examples of the research contributing to the rapid formation of a "new" interdisciplinary field, *cognitive science*. This contemporary search for proof of the similarity of cognition in all animals, including humans (Griffin, 1981), is a seemingly sophisticated version of the new science of the comparative study of "mental life" of the 19th century projected by Romanes (1889) and Darwin (1981).

Language.  The issue of communication or language as a discriminandum particular for humans had been challenged by von Frisch (1967) to begin with, in his studies of bee communication, and by the more recent "ape-language" investigators (Fouts, this volume; Rumbaugh & Pate, 1984; Savage-Rumbaugh & Sevcik, 1984). The communication of coded information by vervet monkeys has been echoed by continued interest in the use of sound with semantic characteristics by a variety of species (Seyfarth, Cheney, & Marler, 1980).

**Consciousness.** New research with biochemical (Cooper, Bloom, & Roth, 1978), electrophysiological (Hillyard & Kutas, 1983) and immunochemical (Vartanian et al., 1975) techniques has explicated the complexity of the issue of awareness and consciousness. This together with experiments aiming to define some phyletic continuity of the concept of self (Gallup, 1982, 1983), has further sharpened the crisis in understanding and defining the specificity and uniqueness of human consciousness.

This acceleration of technological skills and the resulting increase in the data base for considering these three processes, i.e., cognition, language, and consciousness, assume societal as well as scientific significance. The development of concepts in which humans are "only another species," encouraged by behavioral evolutionists who do not differentiate clearly between human and other species, is nourished further by those who see the vitalistic "life force" as equally present in all living forms. The societal expression of these non-materially based belief systems is seen in the animal rights movements; in animal welfare activism; in the concern with the protection of all contemporary species of non-human life forms, regardless of the societal problems related to their existence; and the return to "natural" ways of life independent of modern technology. The exact historical relationships among these movements and their relationship to advances in technology that threaten the viability of the planet, remain to be elucidated by specialists in the appropriate fields. Similarly, there is a need to examine and analyze the ways in which the societal and the scientific developments act to reinforce each other and effect further research and theory including behavioral evolution.

Those scientists who are bemused by the similarities among the behavioral patterns of humans and other animals, live, however, in a real world, in which certain problems need solution. The first banal reality is that the scientists are studying, writing about, and discussing the other animals. It has been said that the other species may be doing the same, but that people have not been clever enough to discover the records; or, perhaps the animals have not kept records. In terms of species survival value in an evolutionary mode, it is possibly sufficient for non-humans to be able to "control" us systematically, generation by generation. The probabilities are such that, in the long run, the human species may not survive long enough to affect the survival of most of the other species on the planet. (The "cockroach" approach to nuclear war.)

Beyond the banality of this statement lies the serious question: What processes of change are related to the fact that these animals, particularly the primates, have not evolved to carry out behavior patterns similar to those of humans? There appears to be evidence, demonstrated by the complex acts that animals can be trained to perform in controlled laboratory conditions, that the primates and other species have potentialities for far more complex activities than those that thus far have been apparent in their natural habitats.

The second banal reality is that the rules or laws, as we have so far discovered them, that regulate the relationship between animals and their environment are such that, in the long run, non-human animals remain stable as a species in environments that are fit for their survival. Given a relatively stable environment, the activities of the species are not inherently destructive of the species in that enviornment. The human species seems more likely to misuse its resources; there is no indication that there may be a "natural," lawful process that will perpetuate stability of the human species in its relationship with its environment. This is true despite the fact that one of the characteristics of the human species is that it is self-consciously concerned with all other species, as well as with all the circumstances in which its own species has lived, lives now, and will live.

Answers to this apparent conundrum are also forthcoming, primarily from the genetic determinists who put their faith in the genetic imperative to survive despite the pitfalls presented by any particular generation. Although this may be an optimistic approach, the theoretical or logical assurances on which this view is based are not readily forthcoming from experimentally demonstrated information.

The conference was organized so that these apparent incongruities between developments in behavioral science and the daily experiences of the scientist might be examined and some possibilities for their resolution  presented.

## Methodological Considerations of the Concept of Integrative Levels

Accordingly, the organizers of the conference offer a concept that is a theoretically based experimental approach to the analysis of phenomena, to the formulation of questions that are experimentally answerable, and the integration of the resulting data to further develop theory that can be used to explore phenomena that are new or previously observed. The concept of integrative levels of functional and structural organization was presented in Greenberg and Tobach (1985), and in other articles. Because the concept is still in the process of being formulated, tested, and refined, it is used in various ways by different writers, including the four people who organize the conference series. Accordingly, I present here some thoughts about the procedure one might follow in applying the concept, and some definitions of terms so that the reader can have some idea of the ways in which the integrative levels concept is being used in the following analyses and interpretations.

The sequence in which the terms are defined is intended to exemplify the procedure one might use in applying the concept of integrative levels. To begin the analysis necessary to formulate the experimental question, it is assumed that the investigator has a working knowledge of the concept of integrative levels. Therefore, the first item in the glossary is about the concept.

The analysis proceeds by suggestions for defining the category in which the question of integrative levels is to be examined. One may then propose a working formulation of *continuity*. Continuity is used to describe those aspects of the category that might be found to be similar throughout a series of possible levels. Discontinuity in the proposed series develops out of the differences that are found in the comparison of the different levels in the series. Both continuity and discontinuity require continuous monitoring and are amenable to changes in definition as they are tested experimentally. ("Experimental" is used here in the way T. C. Schneirla, 1972a, used it in his article on the similarities and differences of field and laboratory investigations.)

The specification of the levels is the next step, based on operations and experiments to determine whether they satisfy the conditions suggested in the definitions given later. It is clear that in this procedure the types of questions asked may be similar in many respects to the types asked by most scientists. However, by seeking to understand the relationship between levels and the ways in which new levels arise, it is anticipated that new questions will be asked and insights will be gained into the processes of change.

Finally, this procedure should further elucidate the validity of the category used, the relationship between that category and other categories, and the creation of new categories.

The reality of life in the scientific community, however, is that few scientists have the time and opportunity to approach scientific work in that fashion. Most frequently, those who are interested in the concept find themselves applying the concept of integrative levels when a piece of research or a theory seemed deserving of critical analysis. This is the genesis of the earliest statements (Needham, 1943; Novikoff, 1945a, 1945b; Schneirla, 1972b) and some of the contemporary discussants of the concept (Aronson, 1984; Leacock, 1980). In these responses to vitalistic or genetic determinist formulations, through the use of integrative levels, the processes of defining categories, the comparative method, and the definition of levels are apparent.

## ANNOTATED GLOSSARY

### Concept of Integrative Levels

Primarily, the concept of integrative levels is based on the notion that change is an inherent characteristic of matter that is evident throughout the universe and all its parts. A corollary of this concept is that any phenomenon, structural or functional, must have a history. Another corollary is that because of the temporal and spatial characteristics of the history of such change, changes in the structure and function of matter are interrelated and interconnected. Change is studied comparatively in terms of the similarities and differences over time and place of the structure and function of matter. The role of human operations as they effect the change is an integral part of this comparison. The concept of integrative levels is used not only to describe change but also to lay the basis for formulating questions for studying the similarities and differences. The integration of human activity and problem solving by cognitive function (thinking) is basic to the application of the concept of integrative levels. Some examples follow.

A star does not appear *de novo;* it has a history of change in structure and material activity. At the same time, human understanding of a star also has a history. Humans at first could only record the appearance and disappearance of stars but as people travelled and compared their appearances and disappearances, and particularly, the similarities and differences in the positions of the star, it became possible to begin to understand the phenomenon. Use of the stars in navigation and movement over water and land were integral parts of the process of integration of theory and practice. When humans began to use technological aids in studying the stars, and to compare the similarities and differences brought about by the ways in which they operated or acted upon their knowledge about stars (building equipment that could observe stars under different dimensions of time and space) their concept of stars became different from the earliest conceptualizations (i.e., producing a higher level of understanding) and began to approximate the reality of the stars more adequately so that human operations involving stars became more reliable and valid.

When the similarities and differences among members of the same population, or species, or groups could be understood in terms of their reproduction, the possibility of selective breeding for production of animals and plants that were to be used by people became possible. However, the activity of foraging, of learning to plant and harvest, of harnessing the energy of animals, made possible an understanding of the relationships between "natural" reproduction witnessed by people in the course of their activities, and planned breeding to change the characteristics of populations. Increasing technological skills and instruments made it possible to understand the biochemistry and biophysics of molecular configurations that are called *genes* and *amino acids*. This new level of human knowledge and activity makes possible further activities to change or keep relatively unchanged the characteristics of life on this planet. These developments create qualitatively different problems.

At all times, the reality of change and matter are demonstrated by the integration of changing human knowledge with changing human activities.

**Continuity–Discontinuity.**    A corollary yielded by the concept of integrative levels as just described is that interrelatedness of phenomena is explicated in the similarity and dissimilarity of characteristics related to the category chosen. In the evolution of living matter the phenomena that yielded prokaryotes and eukaryotes are interconnected through processes that are not yet clearly understood. The molecular configurations that are described as genes in bacteria (prokaryotes) are similar in some respects to those seen in other types of organisms in which the nuclear organization is different (eukaryotes); that is, there is a continuity, the shared similarities are continuous. At the same time, there are significant differences, or discontinuities. It may be said that the molecular organization known as DNA is a continuity in the category of living systems (using the word "systems" in a common use, or, dictionary sense i.e., "a set or arrangement of things so related or connected as to form a unity an organic whole"; Webster's, 1977). The differences in the organization and function of DNA in different life groups may be termed the *discontinuities*. Each discontinuity may represent a new level of organization and integration, if it can be demonstrated that the preceding level had characteristics that make it possible for a new structural/functional organization to develop. The new level, or the discontinuity, contains within itself some characteristics of the proceeding level to produce a continuity with the preceding level.

In the preceding example, if the category "living systems" is properly defined, and if the continuity (structural/functional organization of DNA) and its discontinuities are properly defined, then levels of organization could come about through differences in such processes as redundancy, mobility of molecules, and other characteristics that are or are not present in prokaryotes. These differences should be seen either as a mesoform (i.e., intermediate form), or at some stages of development in the prokaryotes that would produce a molecular configuration that was more stable in its new form, and included some of the characteristics of the previous form. Some of the little understood phenomena of bacterial and viral reproduction may be evidence of this type of contradictory organization at each integrative level of living systems. The levels sequence might be: virus, mesoform, prokaryotes, mesoform, eukaryotes. By mesoform one may be referring to a structural variation that includes characteristics of both the old and the new form; or one may be referring to a kind of complementarity principle of DNA continuity, in which sometimes the configuration acts in the earlier, or prior, or less complex fashion, and sometimes in the later, more complex mode, but on one integrative level.

**Production of New Levels: Contradiction.**    The previous discussion of the relationship between similarities and differences and continuity–discontinuity suggests the underlying process that brings about the discontinuity, or new level: the concept of contradictory, dialectic, or dynamic structural and functional relationships on any one level. That is, on any one level there are processes/structures/functions that may be dominant, or positive, or forward going (leading to a higher level of complexity) and others that tend to be more resistant to change, inhibitory, regressive, negative, and backward moving (leading to a lower level). The exact explication of this possibility depends on the category of the series of levels being examined.

Thus, in the instance of a metamorphosing insect, the positive forward going contradictory may be the response of the sensory system to the stimulation being received by antennating or licking conspecifics. A resistant, or negative contradictory may be the "drag" on the response brought about by poor temperature conditions in the nest, or other physical conditions that affect the metabolic function of the neural system so that the larva may or may not respond to the stimulation. The response of the sensory system may have neurotrophic effects that promote growth, development, hormonal function, etc. The lack of neural response may permit other metabolic functions to continue (use of energy that maintains thermal state rather than permitting it to fall), and thus inhibit growth, development, etc.

The integration of these systems at one stage of development leads to a new stage in metamorphosis. In the category of development, stages have usually been thought to be equivalent to levels. In the present formulation of levels, there is a significant difference between stages and levels (Tobach, 1981). At each stage, one is dealing with an organism, and the organism itself is a category representing a series of different integrative levels, e.g., biochemical, physiological, behavioral. Stages in development represent changes in the integration of different organismic levels. For example, at the earliest stages of embryonic development, the biochemical/biophysical level of integration is the dominant contradictory in the changing relationship of the biochemical level and the cellular level of integration in the growth and development of the embryo. At mature reproductive stages, the biochemical (hormonal) level has been integrated in new relationships with the physiological level (organismic system, i.e., endocrine and neural) so that the relative dominance of its contradictory character has been altered substantially.

Although the process of contradiction is easier to explicate in development where the integration of levels is expressed in stages, the analysis of levels by defining contradictions may be helpful for other categories. One such category is "cognition" or thinking, which is studied on many integrative levels.

In attempting to understand the relationship between electrophysiological and cognitive processes by studying Event Related Potentials (ERP; that is, changes in cortical electrical activity related to external stimuli), most investigators accept the fact that there is no likelihood of an isomorphic relationship between such biophysical events, or indeed, between biochemical events, and the thinking process and products that are considered "cognitive." Thus, Hillyard and Kutas (1983) say: "Indeed, it is unlikely that the physiological signs of information processing will always bear a one-to-one correspondence with the constructs inferred from behavioral data" (they cite Donchin, 1979). From their review of the literature, it is evident that the actions of the individual whose electrical activity is being recorded is critical: in the selectivity of the stimulation, the importance of the instructions (which may be termed *directions for internal activity*), participation in the social context (importance of language used in the experimental situation).

The remarks of these authors underscore the possible helpfulness of a levels approach. The category, cognition, has several levels that need to be defined. The relationship among the levels also needs to be elucidated, the most difficult task before the investigator. The basic level, the biochemical/biophysical level can be clearly defined in neural function. In the customary description of the organization of levels within an organism, in this case a human, the biochemical/biophysical level (molecular and submolecular), is subsumed in the cellular level (neuronal), and finally in the integration of the physiological systems, in the organismic entity, which functions at the behavioral level. All the other levels continue functioning at all times and are subsumed in succeeding levels of complexity. ERPs that are on the physiological level subsume all the previous levels. In addition, the relationships of the neural system to all other physiological systems are integrated in the expression of neural function, and the function of other systems.

ERPs, being on the physiological level subsume all the previous levels. Therefore, to understand the processes by which this level becomes discontinuous with the next level, the cognitive or psychological or behavioral level, it is necessary to understand the contradictory processes on the physiological level. This requires monitoring other physiological systems, such as motor pathways, respiration, circulation, all of which contribute to the dynamics of the physiological level. Which of these, as they are related to the different organs in the nervous system, and to cortical areas, will represent changing values of dominant or subordinate participation in the ERPs? In this respect, they may produce different cognitive activity, on the next level. At the same time, although the behavioral level integrates all the preceding levels, it has also within it dominant and subordinate processes that make for its change, that is, its own activity on its own level. These processes involve the societal setting (external contradictions), as well as internal contradictions (e.g., the action contingency, the past experience of the individual involved, the goal-directed thinking of the individual, etc). These will affect the activity on the physiological level, but, the phenomena on the psychological/societal level cannot be studied by techniques that are pertinent to the characteristics of the physiological level. There cannot be an isomorphic relationship between the events on different levels, for once the lower level is subsumed by and in the higher level, its relationships to other aspects of the new level became relevant, and the events on the higher level require their own techniques and principles for study.

The questions about studying cognition on different levels address themselves to the relationships among levels. Does the higher, more complex level affect events on the lower, less complex level? Does the function of the lower level change only in response to the dynamics (contradictions, dialetics) of its own level? In what way is the physiological level continuous on the cognitive/behavioral level? In what way is it discontinuous, leading to new types of function and phenomena on the behavioral level? How do these relate to the contradictions on the behavioral level itself?

For example, in trying to understand ERPs, what is the role of the particular period of the activity cycle of the person whose ERPs are being studied? What does the role of the gender and authority of the experimenter play?

The integration of the quantities and qualities of these measurements on many levels may be a formidable task. However, today's technological tools are such that the data may be obtained under sufficiently different conditions in sufficiently different individuals so that the similarities and differences obtained in the measures may be integrated in terms of continuities and discontinuities.

**A Level of Integration and Organization.**    Any one level of integration stands in relationship to other preceding and succeeding levels within a category. Within a category there is an ultimate as well as a base level. Levels preceding the base level of a category, or following the ultimate or highest level of a category, are levels of other categories. Its level in the new category depends on that category.

For example, in the case of ''organism'' as a category, the biochemical/biophysical level, which is the base level in that category, is also a level in the category we call *matter*. In this category, the biophysical/biochemical level is the most complex, or highest level, subsuming levels of inanimate forms of matter.

Individual behavior (psychology/activity), the highest (most complex) level of the category, organism, may become the lowest (least complex) level of the category, social behavior. For example, when the individual organism is passively brought into an aggregation of organisms by an abiotic aspect of its environment, such as current (air, water, electromagnetic energy), it is in the lowest level of social organization. In that aggregation, there are processes that make it possible for the aggregation to become a new level of association, in which individual organisms respond to each other on the basis of sensory configurations that either bring about approach or withdrawal between or among the individuals.

It is also possible for the individual behavioral level to become integrated in a more complex level of organization, such as a family unit in the United States, or a member of an athletic team.

## Category

**Problems of Usage and Definition.**    In the course of presenting examples of various aspects of integrative levels, it was necessary to indicate the category of the series of integrative levels. The problem of categorization as a process in thinking, and in the development of science in philosophical discussions is complex. For most scientists, the term *category* is equivalent to classification or conceptualization. In various systems, there are different types of classification and different kinds of conceptualizations. Sometimes the classification process is included and made a part of conceptualization; sometimes conceptualization is seen as a process prior to classification; sometimes concepts are units of classification or categorization. In other words, the three terms may stand in any combination of relationships.

For example, Bruner, Goodnow, and Austin (1956) state in their book *A Study of Thinking:*

> To categorize is to render discriminably different things equivalent, to group objects and events and people around us into classes, and to respond to them in terms of their class membership rather than their uniqueness. (p. 1)

> When one learns to categorize. . . One is also learning a rule. . . The concept or category is, basically, this 'rule of grouping'. . . in this sense. . . categories are different types of rules. . . for defining the. . . exemplifying instances of a concept. (p. 45)

Categorization and classification appear to be seen as synonymous, whereas conceptualization seems to subsume categorization.

However, Bruner, Goodnow and Austin state later:

> All cognitive activity depends upon a prior placing of events in terms of their category membership. . . A category is simply, a range of discriminably different events that are treated 'as if' equivalent. There is, first of all, the act of concept or category formation—the inventive act by which classes are constructed. (p. 232)

> Regard a concept as a network of sign-significant inferences by which one goes beyond a set of *observed* criterial properties exhibited by an object or event to the *class* (ET, italics) identity of the object or event in question, and thence to additional inferences about other unobserved properties of the object or event. (p. 244)

More recent discussions of categorization in the review by Mervis and Rosch (1981) define category: "A category exists whenever two or more distinguishable objects or events are treated equivalently . . . In this sense, categorization may be considered one of the most basic functions of living creatures" (p. 89). They do not discuss classification as such, but as category is used in this chapter, it differs little from the dictionary definition of classification: to arrange in groups, according to some principle or characteristic (Webster's, 1977).

Throughout this chapter, as in the case of Medin and Smith's (1984) chapter in a later *Annual Review of Psychology,* there is an explicit or implicit use of classification, categorization, and conceptualization interchangeably. For example, Medin and Smith "take *concept* to mean a mental representation of a simple class (i.e., a class denoted by a single word)" (p. 114).

The need to work with the diversity of the processes involved is further evident in the Medin and Smith chapter in their discussion of "concept." Thus, concept is viewed as a simple categorization when it belongs to a complex class.

Many of the investigators of the concepts of conceptualization, classification, and categorization frequently express the necessity to conceptually organize these concepts. This is exemplified in the discussion of "basic level categories and hierarchical levels" (see Medin & Smith, 1984). These behavioral patterns (classification, conceptualization, categorization) occur in a variety of organisms and at early stages of development. They have an obvious significant relationship to thought, or cognition, the most complex human activity (McGaugh, 1973). These considerations emphasize the desirability of some organizing concept to integrate these many aspects of the processes. The integrative levels approach may be used here.

The three processes, classification, conceptualization, and categorization may be seen as three levels of a category, thinking, which has continuity and discontinuity. Thinking itself may be seen as the highest level of another possible category, that is, the integration of organismic experience.

The operational definition of experience by Schneirla (1972c) is useful here: Experience is the integration of adequate stimulation by the organism. Stimulation that changes the organism functionally so that all further changes in function are derived in some part from the stimulation is seen as adequate, and thus constitutes the animal's experience. The relationship between structure and function is such that change in one implies change in the other as well. This view of experience includes "trace" effects of external and internal changes, as for example, phenomena such as "latent learning," or "habituation." Stimulation, that is, external or internal change that becomes temporarily internalized but decays (changes) without the aforementioned effects is not considered "adequate" nor is it part of the organism's experience.

The integration of experience category involves the integration of adequate stimulation effects on various organismic levels (biochemical/biophysical, cellular, tissue, organ, systems). These are integrated at the physiological systems level, and reflected in various processes derived from the relevant relationships among such systems as reproduction, respiration, digestion, neural; etc. Each of these may be viewed as categories as well.

In various organisms, the integration of experience in and by the nervous system specifically (physiological level) becomes identifiable as memory, requiring consideration of a new level in the category, integration of experience. In this new category, neural integration of experience, some processes like habituation, or memory, may be the lowest level. In this category, the psychological/activity/behavioral level of neural integration or experience, which includes the socialization experience of the individual, becomes the highest level, thinking. Thinking becomes sufficiently discontinuous from other bahavioral processes to suggest the need for a new category. In this new category, thinking, classification, conceptualization, and other processes may represent different levels. This possibility requires further work and is not particularly relevant here (see section on "cognition").

The three terms, *classification, conceptualization,* and *categorization,* are discussed at this point because of the proposed definition of *category* that is used in the application of the concept of integrative levels. As this definition of category is not the customary one, it is necessary to clarify its use. By making a distinction among classification, conceptualization, and categorization as levels in the category of thinking, the term *category* is exemplified.

Classification is the lowest level of the category: the defining of individual examples or specimens or things on a comparative basis, according to their similarities and differences. Contained within this level is the possibility of the next higher level. In the process of bringing about the next level, the classifier is also getting at the essence of the things: the characteristics that are essential to the thing as opposed to the characteristics that are variable and related to other essentials. The color of an orange does not make it an orange; rather the color is dependent on the metabolism, climate, growth processes, and development--or to the technological skill of humans who may have picked and colored the oranges. The color is not essential. However, the essence of the orange's color is dependent on the essence of other classifications related to other concepts and categories: fruit is a possible concept; plant development or agricultural product is a possible category. In the act of classification the possibility of the next level becomes a reality: conceptualizations.

Concepts are at a different level of thought organization: from the concrete to the abstract; from the specific to the general; from the observed to the essence mediated by human activity; to the level on which concepts are more specialized tools than classifications. Classifications of living organisms into plant, meso-forms, or animal forms is one level of thinking. The conceptualization of the three classes as levels of integration in which different processes are essential to each other is a higher level than that of classification. The thinking activity that produces units of thought, that is, that creates definitions and relationships among classes and concepts is categorization.

The previous discussion implies that thinking, the activity made possible by this level of integration of neural function and socialization also has some continuity, as classification, conceptualization, and categorization are seen in a variety of animal groups. The discussion was an example of the application of the concept of integrative levels in organizing what Mervis and Rosch (1981) called this area of research: "a kind of experimental epistemology" (p. 109). The category, integration of experience, is continuous over many levels: (a) integration of stimulation among different organismic systems, with varying degrees of neural involvement; (b) storage and retrieval possibilities in the nervous system which makes it preeminent in its relationship to other systems; (c) classification, conceptualization, and categorization are levels in the new, discontinuous category, thinking, produced by the contradictions within the highest level of the new category, neural integration of experience. The relationships among these levels are proposed here and need to be explored further. However, each level is inclusive of the others; each level has within it the possibilities of further development into the next level; and each level is discontinuous as a function of its internal dynamic, as for example, the relations among systems or the organismic level, and as a function of its external dynamic (dialectical) relationships with other categories, such as neural integration and socialization.

Definition of Category.   A working definition of category is proposed specifically for application to the concept of integrative levels.

1. A category is a unit of thought, reflecting human experience in organizing, changing, and planning human relationships with the real world. Categories change with the increasing knowledge and experience of humanity.

2. A category can be defined in terms of its levels of integration and organization; in its relationship to other categories; and its similarities and differences from other categories.

3. The relationship between levels and categories can also be seen in the category of continuity/discontinuity. A category represents a continuity of process (structural/functional) which, changing through quantitative modes, becomes discontinuous and qualitatively different at the next level of integration. The category of continuity/discontinuity is the expression of the relationship between levels and how levels arise.

## Comparative Method

The comparative method is the sine qua non of all scientific operations and the application of the concept of integrative levels is no exception. There are some specializations, however.

The essential characteristics of the entities to be analyzed can be more appropriately identified on the basis of a well-defined category. The similarities and differences of behavior patterns, such as predation and nursing; of different structures, such as skin and feathers; different species, such as rats and ants, need to be organized in terms of the continuity and discontinuity of the category in which they are placed.

Thus, in the case of predation and nursing, the continuity of the category (intake of energy) would be that some form of energy is ingested and transformed. The discontinuities would be at different levels of organization (individual; group) at different stages of development (ontogenetic processes); at different biochemical levels (substances produced by special glands of a conspecific organism versus substance which is another organism or its part i.e., eating grass, eating an insect); different stages, e.g., when nursing disappears and feeding take its place.

The critical characteristic of the comparative method is that it helps to identify the appropriate category, its continuities (similarities) and its differences (discontinuities). It helps to identify how the characteristics (functional and structural) of the lower (less complex) levels contain within themselves the characteristics of the higher (more complex) levels. In the nursing situation, although the substance is produced by the organ of another organism, it is the activity of the nursing organism that plays a significant role in the production of the milk. This activity of the organism in bringing about the production of the ingested material is the dominant contradictory that leads to the organism developing new ways of acting to bring about the ingesting of food. In other words, even at the mother's nipple, the infant mammal begins to associate its activity with consequent changes, which then can affect its further activity.

The continuity in nursing and predation is the contingency aspect of the organism's activity. The discontinuities are many, dependent on other relevant categories, such as social organization. It should be noted, also, that both predation and nursing are discontinuous in the category of energy intake, as are the discontinuous levels of the feeding behavior of sessile invertebrates, and the foraging of bees and ants.

## The Three Categories: Cognition, Language, and Consciousness

Each of the three categories are discussed in terms of the application of the category as it exemplifies the concept. It is difficult to discuss these categories separately, as they are each relevant to each. For example, the category of social organization, and the category of directed activity change and control of the environment in a planned, goal-directed fashion are significant interdependent categories with cognition, language, and consciousness. Accordingly, after relatively brief discussions of each, their interrelationship is examined.

### Cognition

Integrative Levels.    In the previous discussion of cognition, some broad suggestions were made for different levels of integration in thinking. Such activities as association (conditioning); classification (including generalization, abstraction, identifying similarities and differences), and complex problem solutions that may be set for the organism in a human-controlled situation are variously seen in different animal groups and different situations at different stages of development (Chodorow & Manning, 1983). The effect of events paired in a temporal–spatial relationship within the nervous system of the organism (considering that irritable protoplasm as in the case of single-celled animals is the lowest level in the category "nervous system") has been effectively demonstrated in many species. This may be considered a continuity; the discontinuity arises in the storage; retrieval; integration of past and contemporary events; and the integration of past, present and future events as these processes are evident in the nervous system. Thus, there are levels of integration in the "association" category. The efforts to reduce all "thinking" to one or another level of association cannot organize the many complexities and differences as well as the similarities in this category. As another example, the changing threshold in the ganglion neurone of a cockroach when two stimuli are paired in a temporal-spatial fashion, and the free-association test used in psychiatric interviews represent different levels of association, itself a level in the category of cognition.

In his provocative chapter on animal cognition, Premack (1983) states the following:

> As cognition washes belatedly over the shores of animal learning, there is a tendency to 'liberalize' association and to interpret it as cognition. This could bring serious confusion because associative and cognitive processes are not equivalent. They are distinct processes. Found in various degrees in different species, the greatest challenge to understanding them comes from the primate, where both processes are found. (p. 361)

In this chapter, Premack chooses three significant processes for discussion: social cognition, identity, and abstract/imaginal representation. The issue of social cognition is particularly relevant to this discussion.

At the beginning of this chapter, I pointed out that there are some banal facts that need to be dealt with by contemporary theories about higher level mental functions. One of these is the fact that animals seem to be able to do more complex acts in the laboratory than they have been seen to do in their "natural" habitats (what is the "natural" habitat of an animal reared in captivity by humans?). The corollary of this consideration is the fact that we know relatively little of the complexities of the life of animals in habitats other than human ones, that is, about the habitats in which they must fend for themselves. There is a literature on the types of problems animals encounter in foraging, escape from predators, etc. but these are discussed in terms of reproductive fitness primarily. One of the most fertile areas for investigation is that of social behavior, as viewed not in terms of reproductive function primarily, but in terms of its role in development of thinking types of behavior. The subtle, complex, and difficult problems solved by members of a primate group in daily living while foraging, finding suitable places of rest, etc., as indicated by Premack and others, may go a long way toward explicating some of the hypotheses proposed about the relationship between social organization and communication, thinking, and awareness. There have been efforts toward elucidating the behavioral complexities that may exist in the non-human controlled environments of animals by studying patterns derived from human complex behavior. One such behavior pattern that has been studied in the laboratory, is so-called *counting* behavior

(Imada, Shuku, & Moriya, 1983). An examination of counting from an integrative levels approach may be helpful.

To understand counting behavior, the category to which it belongs needs to be defined in terms of continuity and discontinuity. In the life history of an animal, as far as is known, the frequency with which any act is performed (nest building; deposition of eggs; retrieval of food or young to one specific location) is a function of processes on several levels. Each of these behavior patterns may belong to a different category (deposition of eggs, young, building of nests = reproductive, social, parental behavior; food deposition = energy intake). In each case there are processes on the biochemical level that are fundamental to the behavioral end product, a nest and food. In these behavior patterns, the higher behavioral level integrates the lower levels, but the relationship among levels is such that the lower levels change as a result of the behavioral activity. In other words, as the eggs are laid, changes in the sensory-motor pathways in the reproductive system, the behavioral activity effects on the hormonal and neural physiological systems, the adequate stimulation of external, environmental changes, as well as the decrease in the number of eggs internally available all contribute to the number of eggs laid. The number of eggs laid are not a function of a classification process in which the egg-layer compares the number of eggs laid with the number set by a quota system.

In the case of primates, there has, to date, been no evidence of "frequency" or "number" being a factor in the animals' habitat outside of the laboratory. The category of counting behavior, as evidenced in the laboratory, may or may not have any relation to categories that might be used to examine the "real world" behavior of the animals usually studied in the laboratory. And yet, it would appear that certainly primates, and possibly some birds, can respond to the abstraction of "number," although in a limited way.

It has been proposed that one may be witnessing a level of thinking that involves a comparative method, such as might be used in classification; it may be that some level of conceptualization is also involved. In other words, the animal has been trained (has been made to act with goal-directed behavioral organization) to respond upon a signal to one or another classification characteristic, either shape, color, size, or number. The degree of complexity (quantitative and qualitative, or conditional requirements of the task) are at this point not germane to our discussion. The issue is that the animal can respond differentially to similarities and differences in the physical characteristics of a particular stimulus configuration. What has not been clearly demonstrated in this type of training situation is that the animal is going beyond the level of conceptualization. Concepts of shape and relational size have been demonstrated. How is one to determine that the animal has developed a category for directing its behavior in regard to different concepts?

For example, how can we determine that an animal can respond to a problem that is based on predetermined "number" category, rather than a "how many"

concept? For example, Ruby (1984) has raised the question: Is the animal responding to spatial cues rather than a number concept? The explanation of
response by conditioning, whatever type of association is involved is also finding
adherents. The use of operant techniques to direct the animal to the number of
responses required to obtain food is similarly a demonstration of how many,
rather than a *number* concept, or "counting category."

It may be proposed that this type of associative process underlying solution of
a problem involving "how many" is the same process that underlies the human
language category "counting": the stimulus word is "count" but the behavior is
the same whether we are responding to the word or to the signal that has become
equivalent to "how many." The obvious response is that the process of "counting" as a category indeed has the continuity of "how many," but it also has
many discontinuities in human thinking. Thus for humans, counting, is not only
simple addition of 1 (1, 2, 3) but more complex arithmetic operations, algebraic
operations, calculus, statistics, and so on. The level of integration becomes one
that develops its own laws about the concept of "number"—real and imaginary,
negative and positive, prime numbers, zero, and so on.

Therefore, if the category is one that includes "how many" as its base level,
it would be necessary to show how this level contains within itself the possibility
of going onto the next level. It would appear that the "counting" behavior that
humans have demonstrated in some animals is more probably appropriate to the
human category of comparative psychology: that is, what similarities and differences can be found in a certain behavior pattern when animals or different
groups are given tasks to elucidate those differences and similarities.

**Definition of Cognition.**   A synonym for thinking; a process expressed in the
function of that level of integration of nervous system activity in which the
organism stores past experience retrievable in new situations or familiar situations; integrates the experience and organizes the immediate sensory-motor processes for the identification of problems and their solutions; and integrates the
contingency level of behavior (the association of the individual's action with its
consequence) so that planning in a goal-directed fashion can be carried out.

There are different levels of integration in the category of cognition. The
levels in this category require much research and discussion.

### Language

**Integrative Levels.**   Language is within the continuous category, communication. The continuous process in this category is directed activity by one
organism (the director) to another in which the consequences of the activity have
been integrated in the nervous system of the director. This category is clearly
interdepedent with the category of organismic activity, particularly the level of
directed activity (contingency based), as well as the category of social behavioral
organization.

This may be seen to be the lowest level in communication: directed activity in which the consequence in respect to another organism is integrated in the director's behavior. The highest level (most complex) is language. Language integrates this lowest level of communication, but in succeeding levels of integration (which have not yet been elucidated) incorporates the most complex levels of cognitive integration and the most complex levels of consciousness. Language has its own characteristics which require its own type of principles and techniques for study; for example, among those characteristics are syntax, tense, spatio-temporal relationships of symbolic thinking, etc.

Although primates and birds have been trained in the contingency aspect of communication through the use of various forms of signals, and have demonstrated classification and conceptualization behavior through the use of those signs, the issues of syntax, complex levels of semantics, tense, etc. have not yet been demonstrated with acceptance by the scientific community. In the experiments done with the parrot and apes, the factor of socialization has been predominant. The significance of this process in organizing the animals' behavior so that it was goal-directed to problem solution through the use of a specialized communication system has not yet been experimentally elucidated.

The report that animals so trained have been seen to use these systems of communication in conspecific social behavior is not surprising in view of the complex signalling system employed by the apes in their social behavioral organization. The possibility of meaningful sound and gesture productions in the social organization of the animals has been anecdotally described by many animal owners and observers of animal behavior. The sounds made by a nursing female cat in response to the activity of its non-nursing young, and the response of the nursing female to the strong noxious stimulus of a possible predator are common knowledge. These have effects on other animals, but may not be directed. The sounds made by grooming monkeys at the approach of different members of the troup may vary with the relationships of the animals involved. These sounds acquire contingency significance, in the communication category as well as in the social behavior category. Communication is a process on different levels in social organization; it is also an independent category as in this discussion.

Similarly, the finding by Marler and his colleagues (Seyfarth, Cheney, & Marler, 1980) of specialized sound production in different situations is not surprising. What needs to be demonstrated is whether those sounds have acquired or expressed contingency characteristics for the individual making the sounds (in terms of the consequences on the conspecifics and predator), and whether they are directed, and thus represent true communication. The more interesting aspect of the problem that these reports address is the relationship between sound production and language.

The integration of speech and language in the human species suggests that an analysis in terms of levels of integration may yield some interesting guidelines for research with human and non-human species.

Books such as those by Lieberman (1975), in which speech and language are not clearly separated, are typical of most of the discussion of the relations between the two. Noback (1982) reviewed the relationships of sound production, gesture and the evolution of language. In general, there is little consensus as to the relationships among the three. It would seem that the category needs to be clarified. As previously proposed, the category is communication. The use of sound production and gesture are equivalent instruments for directed contingency-based communication. The evolution and development of one set of operations or actions rather than another probably derives from different relationships with dominant environmental and ecological processes. The discontinuities in the evolution of and production of sound or gesture are derived from the effects of external contradictions (ecological environment) on the internal contradictions of the level itself (both gesture and sound being present, but one or the other, the dominant contradictory). So, for example, in the case of the "sound window" in tropical forests (Waser & Brown, 1984), which modifies the effective amplitude of sound, and possibly the effective significance of visual stimulus configuration that would be produced by gesture, the external contradiction of the ecological setting might operate to sharpen the dominant valence of one or the other system, that is sound, or gesture, in the evolution of a communication system in a given population of primates. Similar external and internal contradictions probably played a role in pinneped communication (Schusterman, 1978).

It is interesting to note that in 1934, Vygotsky (1962) saw a relationship between sound production in animals and speech in humans, and that the discontinuity on the human level was the development of language. His formulation may be interpreted as a proposal that language included sound production as a continuity in the evolutionary history of the species. He said that sound production was more related to the expressive patterns of "emotional" behavior and saw that as a continuity in speech. Although this is not a particularly useful dichotomy as viewed in the concept of integrative levels, it did enable him to suggest even then that the way to study linguistic skills in animals was by using the sign-language of hearing–speech disadvantaged humans.

> We should exclude the auditory factor in training the animals in a linguistic skill. Language does not of necessity depend on sound. There are, for instance, the sign language of deafmutes and lip reading, which is also interpretation of movement. . . . In principle, language does not depend on the nature of its material. If it is true that the chimpanzee has the intellect for acquiring something analogous to human language, and the whole trouble lies in his lacking vocal imitativeness, then he should be able, in experiments, to master some conventional gestures whose psychological function would be exactly the same as that of conventional sounds. As Yerkes himself conjectures, the chimpanzee might be trained, for instance, to use manual gestures rather than sounds. The medium is beside the point; what matters is the *functional use of signs*, any signs that could play a role corresponding to that of speech in humans. (p. 38)

Vygotsky arrived at this conclusion based on his views of the relationship between speech and language; Gardner and Gardner (1969) arrived at the same conclusion on the basis of their knowledge of the animals' behavioral repertoire.

It may be that in the case of the category of communication, the inherent characteristics of any of the lower levels (sound production, gesture) was not sufficiently active to bring about new levels of communication without the influence of other categories, which may be said to have been external contradictories to the category of communication. These externally acting categories may have been the interdependence of the category of individual activity to control the environment and the evolution of complex social behavior. The increasing complexity of the relationship between the individual and its activities to promote survival and the individual's dependence on conspecifics for such activity leading to survival (Tobach, 1981) may have been critical in the development or evolution of new levels of communication that eventually were expressed in human language.

Although some writers propose that the use of tools in the socialized control of the environment (tools made to be passed on to others, to be modified and to develop their own increasing levels of complexity) was intimately related to the development of language as a discontinuity in the communication category, there is little consensus in this discussion. The demonstration of complex communication systems in primates that appear in the laboratory but not in their natural environment may be a reflection of a category of specialized environment: socialization with humans and contingency significance of the communication system to solve problems, to control the environment provided by humans—a kind of tool using process.

Experiments in which the relationship between socialization and communication with attendant control over the environment in regard to food, shelter, and other goal-directed activity on the part of the animals, are made pre-eminent may result in a new type of "language" that could be evidenced by a variety of species.

**Definition of Language.**    Language is a socialized means of communication of thinking, using arbitrarily socialized rules of symbolism, referential systems, and expressive of spatial–temporal relationships among individuals, categories and events.

### Consciousness

**Integrative Levels.**    The analysis of the category of consciousness requires consideration of the various categories with which it may be related, as regards similarities or differences. The notion of sentience, that is, functional sensory activity in which the organism is responsive to external changes in the millieu in which it finds itself, is at least one level of consciousness, and is accepted generally as "awareness." In this respect, the continuity of such a category, that is, the category of awareness would permit the arrangement of a series of discontinuities all of which would subsume the fundamental level of sensory responsiveness. This continuity is represented in every living form; it is the *sine qua non* of living matter. In the history of discussions about this category the sensory responsiveness was seen relevant to the organism's ability to direct its activity on the basis of that sensory responsiveness (Romanes, 1889); most commonly, the sensory responsiveness of animals other than humans was seen as different from the consciousness of humans, in whom the awareness of self as such was seen to be a dominant feature. This may be seen as a generally accepted qualitative discontinuity between animals and humans, whether the concept of reflexive response is invoked (James, 1890) or whether the concept is seen as irrelevant and inaccessible for study in biological systems, and only relevant to philosophical discussion (Jennings, 1906).

A more recent statement of consciousness removes the discussion from the consideration of evolutionary issues. For Hilgard (1980) the reference is only human; however, the concern is with the relationship between more complex behavioral states and underlying physiological processes. Here again, the issue of self-consciousness is pre-eminent in regard to delineating the relationship between the behavioral and the physiological levels.

If, as Hilgard (1980) indicates, the category of awareness is to include the most complex of behavioral patterns, consciousness of self, in relation to the societal process that make consciousness accessible for study and discussion; if, as Griffin (1981) proposes, it is to include the relationship of such continuities with the discontinuities among different groups of animals (humans as contrasted with other organisms); and if, as McGaugh (1973) writes, it is to include the intraorganismic levels of function and organization that are usually described as the unconscious, the subconscious and the preconscious, along with states of atypical consciousness produced by pathology or biochemical means; then the category must be clearly differentiated from other categories, or its relationship to other categories must be clearly defined.

As in the case of cognition and language, the intraorganismic levels of awareness may be defined in regard to the fundamental physiological levels that subsume the integration of lower levels of biochemical and biophysical function. The behavioral level integrates these levels as well; however, the level of social organization in which the individual finds itself becomes a significant external contradiction that affects the ways in which the behavioral level of awareness is integrated.

In regard to consciousness, there is one other category besides awareness that is equally continuous as a property of living matter, namely, the category of self-non-self. Every organized living entity is defined by boundaries in which there are energy sources that lie within the boundary of the organism, and energy systems that are external to it. The intake of energy, its transformation and its externalization create the first conditions for self-non-self of every living organism. The immune system is a significant discontinuity in this category, in which the process of comparison of self-non-self is qualitatively more complex, for example, than the simple response of a unicellular organism to the exchange of external energy forms with internal energy forms or the rejection of external matter as sufficiently different from itself to warrant such rejection. Further complex discontinuities arise in the case of organisms that differentiate parts of themselves so that they become non-self and are rejected, as in the cases of appendages of crustacea and fetuses of mammals. Certainly in the case of most organisms, internal changes are identified and responded to appropriately; the awareness of internal processes and their concomitant sensory responsiveness is a continuous process in the category of awareness in animal groups of varying functional and structural complexity, and at all stages of development.

The cognitive process involved in defining the self is, however, more related to the category of socialization. The primate that responds appropriately to members of its group on the basis of past experience (i.e., this one will permit contact, that one will not), is integrating more complex experiences and sensory responsiveness than is the amoeba moving away from another individual, or approaching another amoeba on the basis of immediately acting chemical characteristics. Also, the human cognitive level of categorization of self or non-self is more complex than the behavior evidenced by the primate just described.

Attempts to discover whether other primates or animals are similar to or different from humans in regard to this category of behavior, that is, self-awareness or self-consciousness, have relied primarily on the mirror-behavior technique.

As Gallup (1983) has described in his review article, it would appear that orangs and chimpanzees are able to respond to stimuli on their bodies that can only be visible to them in mirrors, whereas monkeys (Anderson, 1984) and gorillas (Ledbetter & Basen, 1982) cannot.

In two experiments, Epstein, Lanza and Skinner (1980; 1981) have demonstrated that pigeons trained by contingency processes show behavior that appears to be similar to that of the chimpanzee in mirror-behavior (and in social communication). The social behavior of the pigeon, as in the case of the primates, requires the individual animal to be aware of and respond to the behavior of another bird, as in reproduction (see also Pastore, 1984; Poole & Lander, 1971).

In both the primates and in the pigeon, the individual's response based on cues presented by the other animal may be seen as one level of awareness. This level, integrated with the awareness of the consequences of the individual's activity in self-directed activity produces another level of awareness. In other words, the performance of the pigeon and the apes in communication, that is, directed and goal-directed communication is a continuity of self-awareness in both groups of animals.

Further, in both groups of animals, the direction of activity toward self, and the coordination of self-directed behavior in making adjustments such as in preening or self-grooming; in feeding (getting food into the body); or walking over barriers, etc. the animals have a well-developed proprioceptive sense of self and its boundaries.

The problem that is presented for the scientist is to reconcile the reports of these experiments with preconceived notions about the typical progression of behavioral complexity based on morphological taxonomy in which the orang, chimpanzee and gorilla are seen as more or less equivalent (the great apes) and more complex than the pigeon. The fact that monkeys are thought not to be able to demonstrate self-awareness is consonant with the typical progression of behavioral complexity based on taxonomic relationships between ape and monkey. Although there is no inherent reason for some correlation between these morphologically based taxonomic levels of complexity and behavioral levels of complexity, (Aronson, 1984) another possibility is that the behavioral category in which one is trying to arrange the hierarchical relationships among these animals is not appropriate: the behavioral category may not be ''self-awareness.'' If one were to take an operational approach to the experimental situations in which the animals are being observed, it is possible that some insight into a more appropriate category would be obtained.

Several features of the experimental mirror situation point to a category that may involve perceptual problem solving. Looking into a mirror is an ''isomorphic'' perceptual experience. One's right hand is on the right side, that is, the same side as that of the individual seen in the mirror. However, when an organism faces another individual, its right limb is on the side of the other animal's left limb. In the behavioral posturing that is fundamental to the social cues to which animals respond, asymmetry and symmetry are very likely to be important aspects of psychomotor adjustments in interacting with other animals. That is, primates are ''lateralized'' in terms of the probability of one limb or another being used. Animals ''swap'' at each other with a typically-used paw (right or left). It would probably be a more common experience for a mammal, and particularly a primate, to have experience with the cross-referencing of upper and lower limb movement when facing another animal, than to have the animal facing it move the limb on the same side as that which is being used by the actor. Such cross-referencing is probably true for the pigeon in social situations. These possibilities are amenable to observational validation.

The experiences of the animals in their non-laboratory habitats would offer relatively little opportunity for them to see a reflection of themselves. Under certain circumstances, they might see themselves in bodies of water in which the light was fortuitously appropriate. The need for extensive experience with mirrors in order to make the mirror behavior possible indicates that the animals had to develop a clear perceptual relationship between the reflection and their own movements. Important in this problem solving behavior is the contingency aspect: the pairing of the activity of the individual with the consequences of those actions so that some integration in a goal-directed pattern could be developed.

Therefore, we are faced with the familiar problem of understanding the behavior of animals in the laboratory which are being trained or taught to do things that are not necessarily part of their typical repertoire in their natural environment. It appears that we are dealing with a behavioral category in which there is some continuity and discontinuity in the ability of different species to solve a problem presented by the experimenter. The contingencies of their behavior have not always been made clear in the research reports (as goal-directedness based on approval of the experimenter; food; etc.) except in the case of the pigeon where food was the reward. The contingency effect associated with grooming-directed behavior may have been sufficient in the instance of orang and the chimpanzee. What we may be seeing is a behavioral category, chirognosia, in which there are behavioral discontinuities. *Chirognosia* (from the same root as in the word "chirality") is a form of the term "chirognostic sense," meaning the feeling of left and right sidedness. The significance of using "chirality" rather than "laterality" is that a conceptual distinction is being made about "right" and "left" side as in chemistry. *Chiral* is a term used to describe asymmetric molecules that are mirror-images of each other, i.e., they are related to each other optically as right and left hands.

The relationship between chirognosia and the concept of self as seen in mirror-behavior must be elucidated. The levels concept offers some guidelines to the study of this problem. If one defines the appropriate category involved, one begins to find a basis for experimental analysis. Thus, the behavior in the mirror studies may be "self-awareness," a level of integration of great complexity in a series of levels in which the biochemical level (in the immune sense) is the lowest level. One would have to demonstrate how the mirror behavior relates to other levels of self-awareness, such as self-grooming and other motor adjustments that all the animals demonstrate. To demonstrate awareness of right and left side, that is, optic mirror relationships, would appear to be another issue. The literature on concept formation in primates would seem to indicate that all the species mentioned do variably well on "side concept," or "laterality concept". The concept of a mirror relationship between right and left may be another matter.

The issue of the neuroanatomy which might make possible such an integration in problem solving is also not germane. There is agreement by most investigators that there is not likely to be an isomorphism between anatomy and function. However, there is not enough information about functional relationships in the visual system and integrative function in the gorilla, orang, chimpanzee and monkey series especially in regard to chirality. Again, the relationship between morphology and behavior is in the realm of another category; there may or may not be equivalent levels of increasing complexity in function and in neuroanatomy.

Application of the levels of integration concept would seem to indicate that using the mirror technique to arrive at an understanding of self-concept may not be likely to yield a complete answer, because the category may not be self-awareness. The category may be perceptual problem solving in which the animal needs to form the concept of a right/left relationship and when such a discrimination is appropriate.

An important issue in the understanding of consciousness has been whether consciousness should be attributed to animals other than humans. The definition of consciousness given previously would argue against attributing consciousness to species other than humans. According to the levels concept, the appropriate category would seem to be "awareness" in its interconnection with the category of socialization. Crook (1983) came to a similar conclusion in which he presented a concept of five levels of awareness; he formulated the fifth level of awareness in terms of "linguistic self-consciousness" ". . . the insight relating inner feel and agency in behaviour lead(ing, ET) to clear symbolization of self as agent and the use of pronouns in language." Although Crook places the burden of discontinuity on language, there is little in the four preceding levels to indicate the relationship among the five levels which leads to their production as a result of the characteristics of the other levels. In the discussion by Crook (1983), Hilgard (1980), Gallup (1983) and others, there is an obvious need for some criterion or set of criteria to distingish the different complexities of behavior as seen in humans when compared with other organisms.

The category of awareness, and its related category, self-not-self, represent a series of intraorganismic levels in which the inner contradictories in sensory responsiveness are not sufficient to bring about the sharp discontinuity that makes for human consciousness. It is the contradiction between the individual and the social organization in which it finds itself that makes it possible for the new level to arise. Consciousness is the most complex of the three categories of cognition, language, and consciousness, because it is the relationship of the three with each other and with socialization that sharpens the intraindividual processes to produce consciousness, the most complex behavioral category.

**Definition of Consciousness.**    Consciousness is the most complex level of the category, awareness. This level integrates the individual's socialization, including cultural, language, and cognitive experience, to produce a new level of awareness. This subsumes the physiological function of the nervous system with its stored, integrated and retrievable individual and societal history that may be directly and indirectly experienced through stored human knowledge in the form of speech, written language and other types of records (art, drawing, buildings, etc.).

## INTEGRATION OF THE THREE CATEGORIES
## THROUGH THE MEDIATION OF THE CATEGORY OF
## SOCIAL BEHAVIOR

Behind the title of the conference, there is an implicit integrative levels statement about the relationship of the three categories of behavior. Each of the three categories has its evolutionary or comparative continuity of process with discontinuous levels in the world of animal species, and with discontinuous stages in the history of the development of each category. In both phylogeny and ontogeny there is a continuous and discontinuous process that leads to succeeding integrative levels of organization and function of each of the three categories.

All three categories are intraorganismic but as there is no species that develops independently of conspecifics at some stage of its life history, the intraorganismic processes that lead to different levels of complexity (internal contradictions) are interdependent, interconnected and interrelated with extraorganismic processes such as social behavior and ecological relationships with allospecific and conspecific organisms (external contradictions).

The category of social behavior also reflects increasing levels of complexity in the relationships among conspecifics. A significant category that is external to the social behavior and social organization of the individual is the category *environmental control*. The increasing complexity of the relationship between the individual and its group of conspecifics to control the environment in order to ensure individual survival is a dominant factor in two contradictions: one is between the survival of the individual and its relationship to conspecifics; and two, is between the survival of the individual and its relationship to environmental processes. The development of the complexity of interdependence of the individual on the social group, and the group's mastery of the activities that control the environment for survival, are the interrelationships that make possible the intraorganismic development of increasing levels of complexity in communication, awareness and thinking. The most complex levels of thinking, of language and awareness become integrated in the consciousness of humans in which the history of the human species becomes an integral part of the consciousness of the individual. This makes possible the most complex types of categorization and problem solving.

## CONCLUDING STATEMENT

This discussion of the topics of the volume is an attempt to bring out some of the problems posed by attempts to understand cognition, language, and consciousness. The contributors to the volume all had their own conceptualization of the problem. The organizers had equally disparate views, although they were fundamentally united in desiring to test the utility of applying the concept of integrative levels to the issues raised. All four organizers recognize the developing nature of the concept and desire that the scientific community consider the concept as a possible aid to further explorations of the three categories.

Therefore, in my discussion, the literature cited is not exhaustive. Rather, it is an attempt to test how the levels concept may have brought the science further, or how it may be helpful in uncovering weaknesses in approaches that vitiate the robustness of the inferences made from experiments in the three categories. It is also obvious that some pertinent references may have been overlooked, for which the author apologizes. It is also possible that the author uses the material cited in ways which the original writers may find inappropriate to their original intent. This is an issue that can only be resolved by further discussion.

## ACKNOWLEDGMENTS

I am grateful for the many stimulating discussions about the concept of integrative levels that I have had with a number of people in the recent past, particularly, Lester R. Aronson and Gary Greenberg. In addition, the thinking of the following people have no doubt influenced me and I acknowledge their growth-promoting effect, although they are not responsible for the rate of development or stages I have reached: Muriel Hammer; Eleanor Leacock; Erwin Marquit; Sylvia Scribner; Constance Sutton; Samuel Sutton; Roger Thompson and H. R. Topoff.

## REFERENCES

Anderson, M. J. R. (1984). Monkeys with mirrors: Some questions for primate psychology. *International Journal of Primatology, 10,* 163–167.

Aronson, L. R. (1984). Levels of integration and organization: A revaluation of the evolutionary scale. In G. Greenberg & E. Tobach (Eds.), *Behavioral evolution and integrative levels* (pp. 57–81). Hillsdale, NJ: Lawrence Erlbaum Associates.

Bruner, J. S., Goodnow, J. J., & Austin, G. A. (1956). *A study of thinking.* New York: Wiley.

Chodorow, M. S., & Manning, S. K. (1983). Cognition and memory: A bibliographic essay on the history and issues. *Teaching of Psychology, 10,* 163–167.

Cooper, J. R., Bloom, F. E., & Roth, R. H. (1978). *The Biochemical basis of neuropharmacology.* New York: Oxford University Press.

Crook, J. H. (1983). On attributing consciousness to animals. *Nature, 303,* 11–14.

Darwin, C. (1981). The descent of man, and selection in relation to sex. Princeton, NJ: Princeton University Press.

Donchin, E. (1979). Event-related brain potentials: a tool in the study of human information processing. In H. Begleiter (Ed.), *Evoked brain potentials and behavior* (pp. 13–88). New York: Plenum Press.

Epstein, R., Lanza, R. P., & Skinner, B. F. (1981). "Self-awareness" in the pigeon. *Science, 212,* 695–696.

Epstein, R., Lanza, R. P., & Skinner, B. F. (1980). Symbolic communication between two pigeons. *Science, 207,* 543–545.

Frisch, K. V. (1967). *Dance language and orientation in bees.* Cambridge, MA: Harvard University Press.

Gallup, G. G., Jr. (1982). Self-awareness and the emergence of mind in primates. *American Journal of Primatology, 2,* 127–243.

Gallup, G. G., Jr. (1983). Toward a comparative psychology of mind. In R. L. Mellgren (Ed.), *Animal cognition and behavior.* Amsterdam: North Holland.

Gardner, R. A., & Gardner, B. T. (1969). Teaching sign language to a chimpanzee. *Science, 615,* 664–672.

Gould, J. L., & Gould, C. G. (1982). The insect mind: Physics or metaphysics. In D. R. Griffin (Ed.), *Animal mind-human mind* (pp. 269–298). Dahlem Konferenzen, 1982. Berlin: Heidelberg; New York: Springer-Verlag.

Greenberg, G., & Tobach, E. (Eds.). (1984). *Behavioral evolution and integrative levels.* Hillsdale, NJ: Lawrence Erlbaum Associates.

Griffin, D. R. (1981). *The question of animal awareness.* New York: The Rockefeller University Press.

Hilgard, E. R. (1980). Consciousness in contemporary psychology. *Annual Review of Psychology, 31,* 1–26.

Hillyard, S. A., & Kutas, M. (1983). Electrophysiology of cognitive processing. *Annual Review of Psychology, 34,* 33–61.

Imada, H., Shuku, H., & Moriya, M. (1983). Can a rat count? *Animal Learning and Behavior, 11,* 369–400.

James W. (1890). *The principles of psychology.* New York: Holt.

Jennings, H. S. (1906). *Behavior of the lower organisms.* New York: Columbia University Press.

Leacock, E. (1980). Social behavior, biology and the double standard. In G. W. Barlow & J. Silverberg (Eds.), *Sociobiology: Beyond nature/nurture? Reports, definitions and debate* (pp. 465–488). Boulder, CO: Westview Press.

Ledbetter, D. H., & Basen, J. A. (1982). Failure to demonstrate self-recognition in gorillas. *American Journal of Primatology, 2,* 307–310.

Lieberman, P. (1975). *On the origins of language. An introduction to the evolution of human speech.* New York: Macmillan.

McGaugh, J. L. (1973). *Learning and memory. An Introduction.* San Francisco: Albion.

Medin, D. L., & Smith, E. E. (1984). Concepts and concept formation. *Annual Review of Psychology, 35,* 113–128.

Mervis, C. B., & Rosch, E. (1981). Categorization of natural objects. *Annual Review of Psychology, 32,* 89–115.

Needham, J. (1937/1943). *Integrative levels: A revaluation of the idea of progress.* Oxford: Clarendon Press. (Reprinted in J. Needham, *Time: the refreshing river.* London: George Allen & Unwin, 1943.)

Noback, C. R. (1982). Neurobiological aspects in the phylogenetic aquisition of speech. In E. Armstrong & D. Falk (Eds.), *Primate brain evolution.* New York: Plenum.

Novikoff, A. B. (1945a). The concept of integrative levels and biology. *Science, 101.* 405–405.

Novikoff, A. B. (1945b). Continuity and discontinuity in evolution. *Science, 102,* 45–40.

Pastore, M. (1984). Canary before the pigeon. *Nature, 310,* 18.

Poole, J., & Lander, D. G. (1971). The pigeon's concept of pigeon. *Psychonomic Science, 25,* 157–158.

Premack, D. (1983). Animal cognition. *Annual Review of Psychology, 34,* 351–362.

Romanes, G. J. (1889). *Mental evolution in man. Origin of human faculty.* New York: D. Appleton & Co.

Ruby, L. M. (1984). An investigation of number-concept appreciation in a Rhesus monkey. *Primates, 25,* 236–242.

Rumbaugh, D. M., & Pate, J. L. (1984). Primates' learning by levels. In G. Greenberg & E. Tobach (Eds.), *Behavioral evolution and integrative levels* (pp. 221–240). Hillsdale, NJ: Lawrence Erlbaum Associates.

Savage-Rumbaugh, E. S., & Sevcik, R. A. (1984). Levels of communicative competency in the chimpanzee: Pre-representational and representationa. In G. Greenberg & E. Tobach (Eds.), *Behavioral evolution and integrative levels* (pp. 197–219). Hillsdale, NJ: Lawrence Erlbaum Associates.

Schneirla, T. C. (1972a). The relationship between observation and experimentation in the field study of behavior. In L. R. Aronson, E. Tobach, D. S. Lehrman, & J. S. Rosenblatt (Eds.), *Selected writings of T. C. Schneirla*. San Francisco: W. H. Freeman.

Schneirla, T. C. (1972b). The concept of levels in the study of social phenomena. In L. R. Aronson, E. Tobach, D. L. Lehrman, & J. Rosenblatt (Eds.), *Selected writings of T. C. Schneirla*. San Francisco: W. H. Freeman.

Schneirla, T. C. (1972c). Aspects of stimulation and organization in approach/withdrawal processes underlying vertebrate behavioral development. In L. R. Aronson, E. Tobach, D. S. Lehrman, & J. S. Rosenblatt (Eds.), *Selected writings of T. C. Schneirla*. San Francisco: W. H. Freeman.

Schusterman, R. J. (1978). Vocal communication in pinnipeds. In H. Markowitz & V. J. Stevens (Eds.), *Behavior of captive wild animals* (pp. 247–308). Chicago: Nelson-Hall.

Seyfarth, R. M., Cheney, D. L., & Marler, P. (1980). Vervet monkey alarm calls: Semantic communication in a free-ranging primate. *Animal Behaviour, 28,* 1070–1094.

Simon, H. A. (1969). *Sciences of the artificial*. Cambridge, MA: MIT Press.

Tobach, E. (1981). Evolutionary aspects of the activity of the organism and its development. In Lerner, R. M., & N. A. Busch-Rossnagle (Eds.), *Individuals as producers of their development: A lifespan perspective*. Orlando, FL: Academic Press.

Vartanian, M. E., Kolyaskina, G. I., Lozovsky, D. V., Burbaeva, G. Sh., & Ignatov, S. A. (1978). Aspects of humoral and cellular immunity in schizophrenia. In D. Bergsma & A. L. Goldstein (Eds.), *Neurochemical and immunologic components of schizophrenia* (pp. 339–364). New York: Alan R. Liss.

Vygotsky, L. S. (1962). *Thought and language*. Cambridge, MA: MIT Press.

Waser, P. M., & Brown, C. H. (1984). Is there a "window" for primate communication? *Behavioral Ecology and Sociobiology, 15,* 73–76.

*Webster's New Twentienth Century Dictionary of the English Language* (1977). Unabridged, Second Edition. New York: Collins World.

# 14 Some Remarks on Integrative Levels

Lester R. Aronson
*American Museum of Naturally History,*
*New York*

This chapter is introduced by recognizing that the universe and its constitutent parts consist of exceedingly complex systems and, as many scientists and philosophers have observed, the components of most complex systems are hierarchically organized. Numerous hierarchies have been described, and among these descriptions, belongs a particular view, namely, levels of organization and integration, the so-called "levels concept." A distinguishing feature of this concept is its grounding in evolutionary theory and emphasis on the importance of the element of time. It emphasizes continuity in that both the inorganic and organic world are continually changing with a strong trend towards greater complexity in organization and integration. The accumulation of small, quantitative changes lead to transformations into more complex and qualitatively different entities, that is, into higher levels of organization. These changes, described as the transformation of quantity into quality, are recognized as a basic feature in Hegelian dialectics. Moreover, the notion of qualitative change that produces discontinuity is in accord with the punctuational model of evolution strongly advocated by some evolutionists especially by Eldredge and Gould (1972) and Gould and Eldredge (1977).

Levels are thus wholes and at the same time parts of wholes of the next higher level whose properties are now more complex and qualitatively different. In essence, the wholes of one level become parts of the higher one with its unique properties of form and function. Stated in other words, the new level is a system of new, unique and more complex relationships. The laws of the higher level should not contradict the laws of the lower level, and adequate knowledge of preceding levels are clearly needed for a full comprehension of the laws of the higher levels. Nevertheless, the characteristics of the higher level cannot be predicted a priori from the laws of the lower level. For this reason the levels concept is the alternative to reductionistic philosophy which holds that all features of the universe can eventually be reduced to physico-chemical processes.

The transformations also suggest boundaries or discontinuities between levels, but they need not be sharp and exclusive. In fact, mesoforms have been described by several authors at the point of transition and Needham (1937) says that they help to bring out the new features of the higher level. Thus the viruses have been viewed by Novikoff (1945) and Tobach (1981, 1982) as existing between protein crystals (colloidal level) and the level of unicellular organisms where they help in understanding the higher level. One should anticipate important differences in asking questions within levels and in asking questions between levels such as questions about the nature of a mesoform.

Most of the early students of levels of organization and integration took the position that a given phenomenon can be analyzed at one or several appropriate levels, but that the levels do not interact directly. On the other hand Feibelman (1954), Weiss (1969), Schleidt (1981) and others assume complete interaction between all levels, above and below. Eldredge and Salthe (1984) and others take the position that the lower level puts constraints on the next higher level, and that level interacts freely with the next still higher level. To the extent that the lower level provides the material for the upper level it sets certain limitations on this level. However, l maintain that this level is entirely free of influences from still higher levels. To assume that higher levels influence lower levels actually changes the concept in a way that weakens it.

The study of human blood pressure may be used as an example. When taken in the doctor's office or operating room it serves as a very important diagnostic tool, particularly when the interest is in large fluctuations or gross departures from normal. These may be considered analyses at the physiological level. More recently, interest has spread to small fluctuations; to pressures only slightly or moderately above normal. Here it is known that the social setting in which the measurement is taken often affects the pressure. Some would say that the higher social level is influencing the lower physiological level, whereas I maintain that in the latter case we are dealing with a higher level phenomenon, namely the ramifications of the social setting that in this case includes its effect on blood pressure. This can only be studied at the social level.

Several authors have attempted to describe a fundamental or "mainstream hierarchy" of major integrative levels (Needham, 1937; Tobach & Schneirla, 1968; Foskett, 1978; Pettersson, 1978, 1979). A typical example is: fundamental particle, atom, molecule or ion, prokaryotic cell (bacteria or blue green algae), eukaryotic cell, individual animal or plant, family, multifamily society, sovereign state. A still higher level, a union of sovereign states (such as the United Nations) that Needham (1937) looked forward to with great expectation and enthusiasm is still in a very shaky condition and far from forming a higher level or even a mesolevel. Pettersson (1979) recognizes two basic criteria for determining the mainstream hierarchy. First, a compositional criterion which states that a given level is composed (with respect to matter and energy) mainly of members of the level next below. Second, a duality criterion which states that while some members of a level collaborate in the formation of the next higher level, other members do not so collaborate; that is, they are capable of remaining free and independent. Thus, neon and helium tend to remain free while hydrogen and carbon and most other atoms tend to bind readily to form a great variety of molecules. In other hierarchical systems the compositional and duality criteria may not be rigorously applied, or the category may be confounded, as for example the series: gene, organism, local population, species, clade. For clades are assemblies of species, species are assemblies of local populations, local populations are assemblies of organisms, but organisms are much more than assemblies of genes.

Several additional items stem directly from the idea of a mainstream hierarchy. First, Pettersson (1978) showed that there is a continuous acceleration in time in the succession of levels, starting from the beginning of life and becoming very much greater in the three highest levels that reflect social and cultural change. Second, in plotting mass against time using a vertical logarithmic axis for mass and the horizontal axis for time, the evolutionary progression takes the form of a curve tilting upward almost to vertical, indicating acceleration even greater than exponential. The third item is that different disciplines require different hierarchies of integrative levels. For example, in the ecological series modified from Odum (1959) we have: fundamental particles, atoms, molecules or ions, prokaryotic cells, eukaryotic cells, individual animals or plants, populations, communities, ecosystems, biosphere. For those primarily interested in the middle levels we could start with the eukaryotic cell and move to tissues, organs and individual animals or plants. But because tissues and organs do not meet the duality criterion, the latter may be considered items in a secondary hierarchy or possibly mesolevels. There are almost unlimited possibilities for secondary series of integrative levels and with respect to the life sciences most seem to relate, to a greater or lesser degree, to the mainstream hierarchy.

It is important to emphasize that no one level is any better, or more or less deserving of study. It is primarily in the literature on progress in evolution and anagenesis (biological improvement) that we find statements that animals higher in the evolutionary scale are better in some way than those lower in the scale (Rensch, 1959; Yarczower and Hazlett, 1977; Gottlieb, 1984), or are better than lower animals in an engineering sense (Gould, 1976). These ideas, which are based on perceived or imagined human values, could scarcely provide a firm foundation for a scientific doctrine (Aronson, 1984). In contrast to anagenesis and progress, we see complexity as the critical factor, bearing in mind that no usage of this word implies a value judgment.

Four words form the heart of the levels concept. They are levels, organization, integration, and complexity. Levels is very widely used by almost all those who are interested in gradations and hierarchies. It is easily understood and can be described at least in ordinal fashion. Because of the broad usage its meaning has become blurred. Organization and integration can be defined with some difficulty and can hardly be measured, but this does not seem to trouble many people. On the other hand, complexity, which is widely used in discussions of hierarchy and can be defined and measured in various ways, is a constant source of discussion and controversy. Some authors reject complexity as useful in the study of evolution because lower forms can also be very complex and many higher (and seemingly more complex) forms have become extinct. Moreover, evolution is sometimes associated with an apparent reduction in complexity. Levins and Lewontin (1985) point out that processes of increasing complexity and decreasing complexity (which they refer to as simplicity) may occur simultaneously. For example, the skull of higher vertebrates has fewer discrete bones and it may therefore be thought of as being less complex. At the same time, because of large size and the presence of fossa, crests, processes, etc., the skull may be thought of as more complexly organized. If we take as a simple measure of complexity of an object composed of definite parts, as (a) the size of the minimum description of that object (Hinegardner & Engelberg, 1983) or, (b) the length of the shortest possible description of a pattern measured by the number of elementary (structureless) symbols contained in it (Papentin, 1980), or (c) the informational content of the instructions required to build the system (Saunders & Ho, 1981), we see that the large number of very similar flat bones of the skull of lower vertebrates (e.g. fishes) actually requires a much shorter description than the small number of large and intricate bones of a mammalian skull.

Saunders and Ho (1981) note that for many purposes an intuitive understanding of the term complexity is sufficient. If a better definition is required, then the problem is more difficult and a single definition that is suitable for all systems and all problems may not be possible. They refer here to Ashby (1973) who suggests that the degree of complexity can be defined as the quantity of information required to describe the ''vital'' system. Ashby explains the significance of this definition by noting as an example that the brain, which is very complex from the point of view of a neurophysiologist, can be described very simply by a butcher who only has to distinguish it from about 30 other cuts of meat. Saunders and Ho, referring to the butcher (or the equivalent) as the preferred observer, define the complexity of an object as the amount of information required to specify its construction. One must note that a different preferred observer might give a different answer.

This is as far as we can go in this brief excursion into an active and exciting area of scientific philosophy. I hope that I have gone far enough for the reader to appreciate the reality of complexity and that one should not be dissuaded by the negative attitude towards complexity that is frequently encountered.

This still leaves us with the question of what causes the unmistakable trend towards greater and greater complexity in evolution. Saunders and Ho (1976) show that fitness does not increase in evolution and that there are really two separate laws in evolution, namely survival of the fittest and the increase in complexity. But we must still resort to a plethora of words such as laws of growth, biological laws, constraints, biases, tendencies, internally directed or orthogenesis (tendency to vary in a certain direction, Grehan and Ainsworth, 1985) to explain the increase in complexity. However, a fundamental idea that is rarely invoked in such discussions is the Hegelian doctrine that we considered earlier, namely, the transformation of quantity into quality. Note that such transformations most often results in higher, more complex levels. Because more complex entities are likely to favor more complex adaptations, it is the transformations together with natural selection that appear to give directionality in evolution and point the way towards a clearer understanding of the continuous increase in complexity.

Returning now to hierarchies, there are two well recognized classes (Mayr, 1982).

1. Aggregational, in which the higher category includes all of the lower categories. The Linnaean taxonomic system is a good example. Thus the phylum chordata includes all of the classes, orders, families, genera and species of chordate animals.

2. Constitutive, in which there is a structural arrangement or hierarchy and a path of transmission and functional operation. The military ranks are an example. Here the private takes orders from the sergeant, the sergeant takes orders from the lieutenant and so on up to the general. But generals do not include colonels, colonels do not include captains and so on down.

Garland Allen has suggested a third kind of hierarchy that he called a value judgment hierarchy. An example is the great chain of being in which a higher position on the ladder is considered better or an improvement over a lower level and so on up the ladder to perfection (Lovejoy, 1936). The original scale was strictly linear, but modern derivatives of the scale may not be. The current use of the anagenetic scale to explain improvement in biology and psychology is seen as a carryover from the original *scala naturae* (Aronson, 1984). The weakness of this approach has already been mentioned.

The concept of levels of organization and integration represents still another class of hierarchies in which higher levels develop from lower levels (as explained at the beginning of this article). Bearing in mind that this classification of hierarchies is likely to be incomplete, it is important that the several classes of hierarchies be kept distinct for there seems to be much confusion here.

I wish to close with a few historical remarks. Needham (1937) is surely the founder of the concept of levels but he readily acknowledges that several of his major ideas stem directly from the writings of Herbert Spencer, especially the notion that evolution is a necessary progression to higher levels and greater complexity. These ideas are also found in Woodger (1929). Needham's essay (which was a largely unmodified report of a talk given at Oxford University in honor of Spencer) is interrupted by a long discourse on certain shortcomings in the religious dogma of the day and later by several discussions of a new and higher level of organization, a social order based on collectivism. I believe that it is these diversions that discouraged many people in the U.S. who are interested in hierarchies from studying his essay. Some years later Novikoff (1945) further explicated Needham's philosophy in a well-rounded and concise statement of the concept that deserves to be read by all who are interested in the subject. Schneirla (1949, 1951, 1952, 1953) wrote several enthusiastic articles on the application of the concept to social organization but it was not until 1968 in an article with Tobach (Tobach and Schneirla, 1968) that he presented a summary of the concept. Schneirla's articles have been followed by several others by Tobach (1976, 1981, 1982) and Tobach and Greenberg (1984) on the concept of integrative levels and its important application to social problems. Several other authors have contributed to early formulations of the concept, especially Claude Bernard (1957) who was particularly interested in finding an alternative to the highly mechanistic and reductionistic view of the German physiologists of the time.

## SUMMARY

Most of the complex systems in the universe are hierarchically organized. This observation has led to the development of numerous hierarchical systems. Among these is the concept of levels of organization and integration, the so-called "levels concept." The distinguishing feature of this concept is its grounding in evolutionary theory and in dialectic philosophy, especially the transformation of quantity into quality. Thus the accumulation of small quantitative differences lead to abrupt transformations into more complex and qualitatively different entities. These entities that have new, unique and more complex properties are called the higher levels. The relation between levels is the subject of considerable discussion. I take the position that the lower levels must of necessity place limitations on the higher levels, but that higher level processes do not affect those lower down. The overall trend in evolution is to greater and greater complexity. An explanation of this phenomenon is suggested in terms of transformations into higher and more complex levels. Because the more complex levels are likely to favor more complex adaptations, it is the transformations together with natural selection that appear to give directionality to evolution.

## ACKNOWLEDGMENTS

I am greatly indebted to Dr. Ethel Tobach for reading the manuscript and for many helpful discussions of matters considered in this chapter.

# REFERENCES

Aronson, L. R. (1984). Levels of integration and organization: A reevaluation of the evolutionary scale. In G. Greenberg & E. Tobach (Eds.), *Behavioral evolution and integrative levels* (pp. 57–81). Hillsdale, NJ: Lawrence Erlbaum Associates.

Ashby, W. R. (1973). *Cybernetic medicine, 9,* 1.

Bernard, C. (1957). *An introduciion to the study of experimental medicine* (A translation). New York: Dover Publications.

Eldredge, N., & Gould, S. J. (1972). Punctuated equilibria: An alternative to phyletic gradualism. In T. J. M. Schopf (Ed.), *Models in paleobiology.* San Francisco: Freeman, Cooper & Co.

Eldredge, N., & Salthe, S. N. (1984). Hierarchy and evolution. In R. Dawkins & M. Ridley (Eds.), *Oxford Surveys in Evolutionary Biology* (Vol. 1, pp. 184–208). Oxford, England: Oxford University Press.

Feibleman, J. K. (1954). Theory of integrative levels. *British Journal for the Philosophy of Science, 5,* 59–66.

Foskett, D. J. (1978). The theory of integrative levels and its relevance to the design of information systems. *Aslib Proceedings, 30,* 202–208.

Gottlieb, G. (1984). Evolutionary trends and evolutionary origins: Relevance to theory in comparative psychology. *Psychological Review, 91,* 448–456.

Gould, S. J. (1976). Grades and clades revisited. In R. B. Masterton & H. Jerrison (Eds.), *Evolution, brain & behavior: Persistent problems.* Hillsdale, NJ: Lawrence Erlbaum Associates.

Gould, S. J., & Eldredge, N. (1977). Punctuated equilibria: The tempo and mode of evolution reconsidered. *Paleobiology, 3,* 115–151.

Grahman, J. R., & Ainsworth, R. (1985). Orthogenesis and evolution. *Systematic Zoology, 32,* 174–192.

Hinegardner, R., & Engelberg, J. (1983). Biological Complexity. *Journal of Theoretical Biology, 104,* 7–20.

Levins, R., & R. Lewontin (1985). *The dialectical biologist.* Cambridge, MA: Harvard University Press.

Lovejoy, A. O. (1936). *The great chain of being.* Cambridge, MA: Harvard University Press.

Mayr, E. (1982). *The growth of biological thought.* Cambridge, MA: Belknap Press of Harvard University.

Needham, J. (1937). *Integrative levels: A revaluation of the idea of progress.* Oxford: Clarendon Press. (Reprinted in J. Needham, *Time: the refreshing river.* London: George Allen & Unwin, 1943.)

Novikoff, A. B. (1945). The concept of integrative levels and biology. *Science, 101,* 209–215.

Odum, E. (1959). *Fundamentals of ecology,* 2nd Ed. Philadelphia, PA: Saunders.

Papentin, F. (1982). On order and complexity. II. Application to chemical and biochemical structures. *Journal of Theoretical Biology, 95,* 225–245.

Pettersson, M. (1978). Major integrative levels and the *fo-so* series. *Aslib Proceedings, 30,* 215–237.

Pettersson, M. (1979). Vertical taxonomy: for certain social, biological and physical structures. *Journal of Social and Biological Structure, 2,* 255–267.

Rensch, B. (1959). *Evolution above the species level.* London: Methuen.

Saunders, P. T., & Ho, M. W. (1976). On the increase in the complexity in evolution. *Journal of Theoretical Biology, 63,* 375–384.

Saunders, P. T., & Ho, M. W. (1981). On the increase in complexity in evolution. II. The relativity of complexity and the principle of minimum increase. *Journal of Theoretical Biology, 90,* 515–530.

Schleidt, W. M. (1981). The behavior of organisms, as it is linked to genes and populations. In P. P. G. Bateson & P. Klopfer (Eds.), *Perspectives in ethology,* Vol. 4, *Advantages of diversity.* New York: Plenum Press.

Schneirla, T. C. (1949). Levels in the psychological capacities of animals. In R. W. Sellars et al. (Eds.), *Philosophy for the future*. New York: Macmillan.

Schneirla, T. C. (1951). The "levels" concept in the study of social organization in animals. In M. Sherif & J. N. Rohrer (Eds.), *Social psychology at the crossroads*. New York: Harper.

Schneirla, T. C. (1952). A consideration of some conceptual trends in comparative psychology. *Psychological Bulletin, 49,* 559–597.

Schneirla, T. C. (1953). The concept of levels in the study of social phenomenon. In M. Sherif & C. Sherif (Eds.), *Groups in harmony and tension*. New York: Harper.

Tobach, E. (1976). Evolution of behavior and the comparative method. *International Journal of Psychology, II,* 185–201.

Tobach, E. (1981). Evolutionary aspects of the activity of the organism and its development. In R. M. Lerner & N. A. Busch-Rossnagle (Eds.), *Individuals as producers of their development*. Orlando, FL: Academic Press.

Tobach, E. (1982). The synthetic theory of evolution. In G. Tembrock & H. D. Schmidt (Eds.), *Evolution and determination of animal and human behaviour*. Berlin: Vep Deutscher Verlag des Wissenschaften.

Tobach, E., & Greenberg, G. (1984). T. C. Schneirla's contributions to the concept of levels of integration. In G. Greenberg & E. Tobach (Eds.), *Behavioral evolution and integrative levels*. Hillsdale, NJ: Lawrence Erlbaum Associates.

Tobach, E., & Schneirla, T. C. (1968). The biopsychology of social behavior of animals. In R. E. Cooke & S. Levins (Eds.), *Biological basis of pediatric practice*. New York: McGraw-Hill.

Weiss, P. A. (1969). The living system: determinism stratified. In A. Koestler & J. R. S. Smithies (Eds.), *Beyond reductionism. New perspectives in the life sciences*. New York: Macmillan.

Woodger, J. H. (1929). *Biological principles*. London: Routledge & Kegan Paul, Ltd. (Reprinted with new introduction, 1967)

Yarczower, M., & Hazlett, L. (1977). Evolutionary scales and anagenesis. *Psychological Bulletin, 84,* 1088–1097.

# 15 Issues for Continuing Discussion of Integrative Levels

Gary Greenberg
G. Y. Kenyon
*Wichita State University*

## COGNITION

The theme of the second T. C. Schneirla Conference was set to address issues that Schneirla himself was critical of: cognition in non-human animals (Schneirla, 1962), "mentalism" (Schneirla, 1952), and consciousness as a determinant of behavior (Maier & Schneirla, 1935/1964). We were motivated to these themes by the growth of new formulations of cognition in contemporary psychology in general, and comparative psychology in particular. Many point to Neisser's (1967) influential work as the birth of the modern cognitive viewpoint in our discipline and Griffin's (1976) controversial book as the parent of the resurrection of this approach in comparative psychology. That modern psychology has been taken with the cognitive approach is clearly seen in most recent general psychology textbooks. Where psychology was once identified with a behavioral orientation, texts now include extended discussions of cognitive processes (e.g., Zimbardo, 1985). This conference was planned, in part, as a response to the proliferation of the rebirth of "mind" in psychology, a subject discussed at length by Joynson (1972).

Schneirla made it clear that he was not persuaded by "mentalism" in psychology. Thus, in the Introduction to the now classic *Principles of Animal Psychology* (Maier & Schneirla, 1935/1964) appears this caution:

> . . . contemporary psychology has largely discarded the concept "mind" as the basis for a theoretical explanation of the phenomenon of "awareness." Since psychology has not yet reached the stage at which a satisfactory theory of awareness can be formulated . . . there is nothing to be gained from a discussion of

whether given animals are "conscious." To illustrate the point in another way, science has outgrown mystical theories such as "vitalism," because they subordinate the critical treatment of facts to the emotionally biased attitude of the observer, which is all too frequently traceable to an early training in the doctrines of superstition. (p. 6)

It is of some consequence that this important work closed with a similar warning against the infusion of mentalism in psychology:

> The forgoing discussion assumes that conscious states are determining factors in behavior, but this assumption is without foundation. It is therefore necessary to be critical of all experimental approaches which make this assumption. A system of animal psychology must be constructed from behavior data, and complex processes are no exception to this rule. It is therefore our task to develop an objective definition of, as well as objective criteria for, higher processes. (p. 446)

Yet, fifty years after these prescriptions for a scientific psychology, Schneirla's warnings are still unheeded. Remarkably, the most popular and influential approach to cognition in animal psychology, that of Griffin (1976, 1984) is reminiscent of the approach pioneered by Romanes (1899), one of the founders of comparative psychology. One wonders, for example, on what bases Griffin (1984) can make the following statements:

> Perhaps we should be ready to infer conscious thinking whenever any animal shows such ingenious behavior [as the feeding behavior of the assassin bug, or termite fishing of chimpanzees], regardless of its taxonomic group and our preconceived notions about limitations of animal consciousness. (p. 459);

> But within a mutually interdependent social group, an individual can often anticipate a companion's behavior most easily by empathic appreciation of his mental state. (p. 462)

We are somewhat disappointed that the issue of cognition in non-human animals was for the most part unaddressed at the conference. Its growing use in the field (e.g., Gallup, 1983) is alarming to some and suggests that it is clearly a candidate for continued evaluation.

One of the conference participants, N. H. Pronko, did allude to cognitive and conscious phenomena in his presentation, suggesting that we need not adopt such positions in discussing language processes. Pronko would not restrict the use of language to humans; however, it is interesting to note that Schneirla did. This is quite consistent with his use of the levels concept that ascribes to our species unique modes of behavioral interactions (e.g., Tobach & Schneirla, 1968). We believe that his position reflects the fact that Schneirla died before the advent of the research conducted by Roger Fouts reported at the conference on which this volume is based and in other places by Gardner and Gardner (1984) and Savage-

Rumbaugh (Savage-Rumbaugh & Sevcik,1984), Nevertheless, Schneirla did acknowledge the success of one of the earliest forerunners of this research as we will later point out.

## REDUCTIONISM

The Schneirla conference series was conceived as a vehicle to incorporate more fully into contemporary psychology the concept of integrative levels. In more than a passing sense, then, the entire series is about the use of reductionism in psychological theory. What is distressing to us is the persistent dependence in our discipline on physiological reductionism, specifically, the idea that the brain is the organ of behavior. This is the dominant position in psychology today despite a wealth of literature, empirical and philosophical, to the contrary (Greenberg, 1983). Thus, Bunge (1980) was able to define behavior as an *emergent property* of the brain, the allusion to the levels concept in his terminology suggesting that his formulation follows from it. However, Bunge seems to want it both ways:

> We have been preaching the reduction of psychology to neurophysiology, but . . .
> the reductionistic effort should be supplemented by an integrative one. (p. 214)

Not all philosophers, however, share this line of reasoning (Malcolm, 1964). Indeed, neuroscientists are themselves critical of the use of neurological reductionism in understanding behavior (Finger & Stein, 1982).

This issue was reflected in the presentations of Baars and Alland at the conference (this volume) which expressed their theoretical allegience to neurological explanation. Baars identified "consciousness" almost exclusively with the reticular system. Of course, consciousness is an idea, not a thing to be localized somewhere. In fact, some believe consciousness to be merely an "illusion", albeit a necessary one, the result of cultural conditioning (Harnad, 1982; Immergluck, 1964). It is of some comfort to us that an increasing number of neuroscientists are coming to recognize the widespread use of what Durant (1985) has referred to as the "sensationalism of brain science" (p. 27).

Alland, too, turned to the brain, accepting the Chomskian version of language processes, albeit in a modified form. Alland's suggestion is that our capacities for linguistic and artistic behaviors are "brain-based" and, in some sense, genetically encoded. Of course, some have never been satisfied with such an approach to language (Kantor, 1936; Skinner, 1957). Indeed, the viability of Skinner's behavioral understanding of language is reflected in N. H. Pronko's Interbehavioral (i.e., Kantorian) treatment in this volume and in Catania's (1984) very recent discussion of the topic.

## LANGUAGE

It was of some interest to us that the definition of language was not an issue at the conference, especially considering the species represented in the presentations. Some were willing to grant that animals other than humans are capable of true language behavior (Fouts, Epstein, John-Steiner & Panofsky, this volume); this was apparently an acceptable proposition only if infra-human language processes are seen to reflect a different (lower) level of behavioral functioning (Fouts, John-Steiner, & Panofsky, this volume). This view reflects those authors' failures to identify criteria for specifying the presumed levels they refer to. Although, as Barker (1982) has pointed out, there are few guidelines to follow that would enable us to recognize a new level if we saw one.

These authors have aligned themselves with Schneirla's thinking on this point, which suggests that language use by chimpanzees and by humans represents two different levels of linguistic functioning. Thus, Schneirla said, "Man alone has the capacity for systematic codes of language symbols" (1962/1972, p. 77). We are not at all convinced that this appraisal is correct. We tend to agree with the perspective of Gallup & Suarez, (1983) on this point, that many of the precursors to speech and symbolic communication are found in animals other than human beings.

Catania's (1984) appraisal of this situation bears citing:

> But once some features of human language had been demonstrated in chimpanzee behavior, that feature could no longer be regarded as uniquely human; attention then turned to the definition of language rather than to the experimental analysis of its properties. Given these debates, we cannot say with confidence that chimpanzees are or not capable of language; we can certainly say however, that their behavior includes some of its critical components. (p. 249)

That these and other issues concerning language phenomena are of great concern is reflected in the ongoing debate about them (e.g., Harnad, Steklis, & Lancaster, 1976).

Although Schneirla (1949/1972) took great pains to avoid the perspective that identifies absolute differences between chimpanzees and humans, some anthropocentrism, in the Platonic sense, is apparent in his writings. This should not surprise us; the resistance of scientists to change is a familiar story (Barber, 1960). Thus, anthropocentrism is still a potent force in science (Murdy, 1975). As Gould (1977, p. 88) has recognized, "Views long abandoned often continue to exert their influence in subtle ways."

The significance of the idea that we share some form of "language" behavior with chimpanzees is important inasmuch as it reveals our past prejudices about our own place in the animal kingdom. We seem to have perennially tried to establish ourselves as different in kind rather than in degree (Gallup & Suarez,

1983; Gould, 1977). However, the important language studies now being conducted with apes should not lead us to expect to learn anything more about language itself than we could learn from studying our own language development. Nor should we expect this research to reveal any special "intrapsychic" characters unique to chimpanzees. Because it is our language and metaphor system that we are reinforcing in these apes, all that we can expect to get back from this research is what we put into it. If a creationist taught a chimpanzee sign language it would "speak" of its soul and perhaps its mind, and would believe itself created by God some 4 to 6 thousand years ago. A behaviorist-trained chimp would speak a different language indeed, as Epstein makes clear (in this volume). Of course this does not preclude the pursuit of this fascinating avenue of research. We should not, however, overestimate the value of it nor expect more from such studies than they can reveal.

## DEVELOPMENTAL STAGES

Fouts (this volume) attempted to account for cognitive development in a Piagetian sense. Despite the fact that Piaget's theories are still not universally accepted (Catania, 1984; Ezer, 1962; Skinner, 1974), Fouts' use of the levels concept in this context differs from our understanding of how the levels concept is best applied. What Fouts' model proposes is the addition of new developmental stages to Piaget's original five and the use of the term *level* in place of stage. This same proposal was independenty developed by Fischer (1983) who suggested that because developmental sequences show discontinuities (i.e., "stages"), these "developmental discontinuities" are best considered to be new and higher levels "because they do not share some of the characteristics usually associated with the definition of stage" (p. 6). Although both Fischer's and Fouts' formulations are still in preliminary stages of development, we do not believe that their use of levels concept is consistent with the way the concept has grown from the insights of Woodger (1929), Needham (1943), Novikoff (1945) and others. Rather, these expressions seem to reflect "static" Piagetian stage notions that are not part of this stream of thought.

We concur with Gollin (1981) and Toulmin (1981), both of whom believe that development is much more plastic and flexible than the Piagetian model permits. Toulmin's (1981) conclusions are worth citing:

1. We shall have to question the whole familiar scheme of "stages" and "sequences" around which so much recent work has been structured. Rather than one single sequence of stages . . . being accepted as relevant to cultural tasks of all kinds, we should now expect to find different "epigenetic sequences" appropriate to different kinds of tasks. . . .
2. We shall have to make much more allowance for the possibility that different children may arrive at the same specific destinations by alternate routes. . . .

3. We should also set out to develop fresh analytical devices to replace the standard, oversimplified "stage" model. . . . Just as the apparent fixity of organic species has turned out to reflect, at most, a local and temporary stability in the flux of organic populations, so too the apparently static and universal character of developmental stages may be expected to reflect, at most, a statistical dominance of certain kinds of achievement among the children of a given age cohort in the culture concerned. (p. 266)

## LEVELS OF INTEGRATION: CURRENT USAGES AND VARIATIONS

Semantic matters are of no small consequence for science (e.g., Lehrman, 1970), however, they are more important in the theorizing than in the empirical phase where one can point to the phenomena in question for verification. This is one reason for the greater use of operational definitions (Bridgeman, 1927/1961) in science than in philosophy. Some like to think that science means emancipation from philosophy; but science can hardly avoid the philosophic foundations of its enterprise, which often results in unwitting philosophical reformulation.

During the past 100 years we have come to recognize that reductionism and vitalism are inadequate ways for achieving scientific understanding. This is true from the level of particle physics up through the level of the science of culture. As each science has come to generate its own regularities under defined conditions, it eventually comes to appreciate that its data are lawful independently of the laws of the other sciences. This assessment does not imply that they are independent of the phenomena of those sciences; rather, some phenomena (e.g., human social behavior) are sufficiently complex that it is possible to abstract features (laws) out of some events and recognize their lawful independence from other aspects that may interest us but that will not explain that which can be observed scientifically. Thus, $E = mc^2$ even when studying the inking behavior of the marine invertebrate *Aplysia,* although at this level of analysis the implications of that formula are not pertinent or interesting.

A significant alternative to the ideas of reductionism and vitalism is the concept of levels, or hierarchy, of the sciences. As a relatively new way of conceptualizing diverse phenomena, there has not yet developed an acceptable vocabulary that allows for unambiguous discourse. The terms *levels* and *hierarchy* used with others such as organization, integration, complexity, emergence, evolution, epigenesis, stage, etc., are still defined in diverse ways by those who have adopted this newer perspective. Workers in several different disciplines recognize that an improved synthesis of our analytical success is desireable. But whereas these terms and concepts seem to be used with considerable conceptual similarity, there is no common vocabulary. However, use of the same term to refer to different concepts results in confusion whereas the use of different terms to refer to the same concepts (e.g., building, house, edifice, etc.) has merit and is a mark of maturity and understanding. Unfortunately, science and philosophy have not yet reached that level of semantic sophistication. We do not intend here to be normative and legislate the use of terms. We do, however, offer some suggestions about the use of some terms.

## Level

Let us begin with *level*. The term can be used historically (developmentally) or structurally. As an historical concept it can refer to the development or evolution of the cosmos embracing all of the sciences as Darwinian thinking came to be embraced by all the sciences, or it may refer to phylogenesis only. Level may also be used ontogenetically as in embryology or psychological development. It is a term with broad usage that in each case seems to be used to emphasize process and change, as do the terms emergence, evolution, stage, epigenesis, organization, integration, and complexity; hierarchy appears out of place here because it implies stasis.

The term *level* may be used structurally and ahistorically (non developmentally) to indicate the characteristic features of the various sciences that choose different aspects of phenomena as their special study and so generate different laws relevant to their own levels of complexity. We point here to the relative permanence of scientific laws. Note that we are deliberately avoiding the use of "hierarchy" in this context because it connotes subordinate-superior relationships. This is not a useful metaphor unless one thinks that the various sciences are not equal in their worth.

These two different uses of the term *level* are not mutually exclusive. Indeed both are necessary and useful intellectual tools. It is unfortunate that the same term is used to emphasize these different aspects of our understanding; this suggests the use of different terms that would perhaps eliminate some of the babble we often seem to engage in.

## Emergence

One term closely associated with the two uses of *level* is *emergence*. Developmentally or structurally, it has not been difficult to identify the emergence of qualitatively new properties, particularly in the study of increasingly complex events. The concept of emergence may result in the eventual fusion of these two uses of levels. Again, we believe that this possibility is being held back by the absence of an appropriate vocabulary. It is unfortunate that *emergence* carries with it older, vitalistic connotations that will have to fade before the term will be acceptable to the general scientific community.

Clifford Grobstein's (1973) comment, from the perspective of a biologist, clarifies what we mean:

In summary, hierarchical order is characteristic of living systems which tend steadily to enhance it. In the process new properties constantly appear, frequently under circumstances which might suggest some mysterious emergence. In fact, emergence can be understood, at the sacrifice of all of the miracle but little of the fascinations. Formal analysis shows that emergence relates to what may be called set-superset transitions. . . . Hierarchical organization in biological systems thus is characterized by an exquisite array of delicately and intricately interlocked order, steadily increasing in level and complexity and thereby giving rise neogenetically to emergent properties. (p. 46)

A similar assessment was made by the quantum physicist David Bohm (1957):

The concept of relatively autonomous levels has been found to have a rather wide range of application. Thus, even in physics, it has been discovered that beneath the atomic level lies the level of the so-called "elementary particles". . . . In the other direction we have the molecular level (whose laws are studied mainly in chemistry, but partly in physics), the level of living matter (studied mainly in biology) which itself has many levels, as well as still other levels which the reader will easily think of. In all these levels, however, we find the typical relative autonomy of behavior, and the existence of sets of qualities, laws, and relationships which are characteristic of the level in question. (p. 51)

Other illustrations from the (so far) highest level of science, the science of culture, are provided by Leslie White (1949) in his defense of an autonomous level for anthropology:

The development of the symphony or non-Euclidean geometry could not have taken place without the respiratory and digestive processes of composers and mathematicians. But to inject these physiologic processes into a scientific explanation of these cultural processes would not add a single thing to our understanding of them. On the contrary, it would only confuse because of their irrelevance. . . . A culture trait in the form of a sentiment-charged idea will cause a Japanese general to disembowel himself in atonement for disgrace or failure, or an occidental officer to blow out his brains with a pistol. It would, of course, be silly to argue that it was the person, the human organism, that actually does the killing in the examples just cited. Of course it was the human being. But—and this is the point at issue in a scientific analysis of behavior—it was the culture trait, not the human being, that was the *determinant of the behavior,* and hence was the *cause,* scientifically speaking, of the homicides. (p. 97). . . . the individual himself is not irrelevant to the actual culture process. . . . But *the individual is irrelevant to an explanation of the culture process.* (p. 165)

Explanation is presumably one of the things that science is about.

## Biological Reductionism

Reductionism and vitalism have been part of the scientific culture process since Socrates and Plato. It is difficult, as we have just pointed out, to give up old ideas, even in science. On the other hand, the idea of relatively autonomous levels of integration or organization as a recent element in the culture process is an appropriate and timely alternative point of view as Rostand (1959) illustrates:

> Speaking of living organisms, the great Claude Bernard said: "We must not read into them either a chemical retort or a soul: *we must read into them what is there.*" And that excellent epigram contains a criticism of both indolent vitalist theories and of crude mechanistic ones. (p. 29)

Because it is possible to put science and scientific concepts to political use, specious formulations can lead to political decisions that may invade our public lives. This has been the case, for example with biological reductionism expressed as racism and sexism, two current illustrations (Gould, 1981; Lewontin, Rose, & Kamin, 1984). Gould (1977) has recently dealt with these topics although he used the term biological determinism to characterize what others call reductionism. We admire Gould's treatment of the topic but his terminology is unfortunate. Biological experiments lend themselves to causal accounts on their own level of analysis; the notion of biological determinism is thus testimony to successful biological experimentation. However, using biological laws to account for psychological behavior is better called biological reductionism.

## LANGUAGE, COGNITION, CONSCIOUSNESS: THEIR INTEGRATION

As Schneirla (1949/1972) wrote:

> "Mind," ostensibly a term for a generalized functional entity, a very impressive term, actually is only an introductory expression for all of man's intellectual capacities and attainments considered as a system. It is only in a relative and not at all an absolute sense that the processes denoted by terms such as reasoning, thinking, imagining, knowing, perceiving, anticipating, learning, and attitudinizing constitute a unitary and integral system. (p. 225)

Schneirla was one of the few psychologists who saw the discipline mature enough to develop its own "psychological way of thinking." Thus, his system reflects theorizing about behavior at its own level, understanding the necessity for appreciation of the influence of physiological, biochemical, and biological events, but not overly emphasizing those events. Schneirla's understanding of the origins of behavior was an epigenetic one, although we must realize that such thinking is not monistic (Kitchener, 1978). All behavior, including what we call cognitive behavior can be traced back to the organism's experiences during its course of development. This is true of human awareness as it is of all other animal behavior. As Schneirla (1949/1972) stated:

> The comparative study of man in the various sciences, from biology to psychology and anthropology, assuredly does not mark human beings off as different from lower animals in absolute ways. The differences are of course striking and outstanding. . . . There is one capacity in particular, man's facility in the technique of articulate language, which seems to be prerequisite to his superior attainments. Yet this qualitative distinction is not an absolute or complete one in this respect, since the most essential characteristic of language, the formulation and delivery of symbols in directive, purposive ways has been demonstrated in the lower primates (Crawford, 1937). Furthermore, man is not absolutely different from lower animals in his capacity for thinking and reasoning, because levels of difference have been demonstrated among lower mammals. . . . (p. 229–230).

This conference helped demonstrate that the concept of integrative levels and levels of organization make possible a non-reductionistic, non-spiritual, objective, behavioral analysis of even the most inaccessible and private behaviors: language, cognition, and consciousness.

## REFERENCES

Barber, D. (1960). Resistance by scientists to scientific discovery. *Scientific Manpower Bulletin,* 36–47.

Barker, M. (1982). Biology and ideology: The uses of reductionism. In S. Rose (Ed.), *Against biological determinism* (pp. 9–29). London: Allison & Busby.

Bernard, C. (1865/1957). *An introduction to the study of experimental medicine.* New York: Dover.

Bohm, D. (1957/1971). *Causality and chance in modern physics.* Philadelphia: University of Pennsylvania Press.

Bridgeman, P. W. (1927/1961). *The logic of modern physics.* New York: Macmillan.

Bunge, M. (1980). *The mind-body problem.* Oxford: Pergamon Press.

Catania, A. C. (1984). *Learning* (2nd Ed.). Englewood Cliffs, NJ: Prentice Hall.

Durant, J. R. (1985). The science of sentiment: The problem of the cerebral localization of emotion. in P. P. G. Bateson & P. H. Klopfer (Eds.), *Perspectives in ethology, Vol. 6: Mechanisms* (pp. 1–31). New York: Plenum.

Ezer, M. (1962). The effect of religion upon children's responses to questions involving physical causality. In J. F. Rosenblith & W. Allinsmith (Eds.), *The causes of behavior* (pp. 481–487). Boston: Allyn and Bacon.

Finger, S. & Stein, D. G. (1982). *Brain damage and recovery.* Orlando, FL: Academic Press.

Fischer, K. W. (1983). Developmental levels as periods of discontinuity. In K. W. Fischer (Ed.), *Levels and transitions in children's development* (pp. 5–20). San Francisco: Jossey-Bass.

Gallup, G. G. (1983). Toward a comparative psychology of mind. In R. Mellgren (Ed.), *Animal cognition and behavior* (pp. 473–510). Amsterdam: North Holland.

Gallup, G. G. Jr. & Suarez, S. D. (1983). Overcoming our resistance to animal research: Man in comparative perspective. In D. W. Rajecki (Ed.), *Comparing behavior: Studying man studying animals* (pp. 5–26). Hillsdale, NJ: Lawrence Erlbaum Associates.

Gardner, R. A., & Gardner, B. T. (1984). A vocabulary test for chimpanzees (*Pan troglodytes*). *Journal of Comparative Psychology, 98,* 381–404.

Gollin, E. (1981). Development and plasticity. In E. S. Gollin (Ed.), *Developmental plasticity* (pp. 231–251). Orlando, FL: Academic Press.

Gould, S. J. (1977). *Ever since Darwin.* New York: Norton.

Gould, S. J. (1981). *The mismeasure of man.* New York: Norton.

Greenberg, G. (1983). Psychology without the brain. *Psychological Record, 33,* 49–58.

Griffin, D. R. (1976). *The question of animal awareness.* New York: Rockefeller University Press.

Griffin, D. R. (1984). Animal thinking. *American Scientist, 72,* 456–464.

Grobstein, C. (1973). Hierarchical order and neogenesis. In H. H. Pattee (Ed.), *Hierarchy theory* (pp. 29–47). New York: George Braziller.

Harnad, S. (1982). Consciousness: An afterthought. *Cognition and Brain Theory, 5,* 29–47.

Harnad, S. R., Steklis, H. D., & Lancaster, J. (Eds.). (1976). *Origins and evolution of language and speech. Annals of the New York Academy of Science, 280.*

Immergluck, L. (1964). Determinism-freedom in contemporary psychology: an ancient problem revisited. *American Psychologist, 19,* 270–281.

Joynson, R. B. (1972). The return of mind. *Bulletin of the British Psychological Society, 25,* 1–10.

Kantor, J. R. (1936). *An objective psychology of grammar.* Chicago: Principia Press.

Kitchener, R. F. (1978). Epigenesis: The role of biological models in developmental psychology. *Human Development, 21,* 141–160.

Lehrman, D. S. (1970). Semantic and conceptual issues in the nature-nurture problem. In L. R. Aronson, E. Tobach, D. S. Lehrman, & J. S. Rosenblatt (Eds.), *Development and evolution of behavior* (pp. 17–52). San Francisco: Freeman.

Lewontin, R. C., Rose, S., & Kamin, L. J. (1984). *Not in our genes.* New York: Pantheon Books.

Maier, N. R. F. & Schneirla, T. C. (1935/1964). *Principles of animal psychology.* New York: Dover.

Malcolm, N. (1964). Scientific materialism and the identity theory. *Dialogue, 3,* 115–125.

Murdy, W. H. (1975). Anthropcentrism: A modern version. *Science, 187,* 1168–1172.

Needham, J. (1943). *Time: The refreshing river.* London: Allen & Unwin.

Neisser, U. (1967). *Cognitive psychology.* New York: Appleton-Century-Crofts.

Novikoff, A. (1945). The concept of integrative levels and biology. *Science, 101,* 209–215.

Romanes, G. J. (1899). *Animal intelligence.* New York: D. Appleton.

Rostand, J. (1959). *Can man be modified?* New York: Basic Books.

Savage-Rumbaugh, S. & Sevcik, R. A. (1984). Levels of communicative competency in the chimpanzee: Prerepresentational and representational. In G. Greenberg & E. Tobach (Eds.), *Behavioral evolution and integrative levels.* Hillsdale, NJ: Lawrence Erlbaum Associates.

Schneirla, T. C. (1949). Levels in the psychological capacities of animals. In R. W. Sellars, V. J. McGill, & M. Farber (Eds.), *Philosophy for the future* (pp. 243–286). New York: Macmillan. (Reprinted in L. R. Aronson, E. Tobach, D. S. Lehrman, & J. S. Rosenblatt (Eds.) (1972). (pp. 199–237). *Selected writings of T. C. Schneirla* (pp. 199–237). San Francisco: Freeman.)

Schneirla, T. C. (1952). A consideration of some conceptual trends in comparative psychology. *Psychological Bulletin, 49,* 559–597. (Reprinted in L. R. Aronson, E. Tobach, D. S. Lehrman, & J. S. Rosenblatt (Eds.) (1972). (pp. 887–925). *Selected writings of T. C. Schneirla.* San Francisco: Freeman.)

Schneirla, T. C. (1962). Psychology, Comparative. *Encyclopedia Britannica, Vol. 18,* 690Q–703. (Reprinted in L. R. Aronson, E. Tobach, D. S. Lehrman, & J. S. Rosenblatt (Eds.) (1972). *Selected writings of T. C. Schneirla* (pp. 30–85). San Francisco: Freeman.)

Skinner, B. F. (1957). *Verbal behavior.* New York: Appleton-Century-Crofts.

Skinner, B. F. (1974). *About behaviorism.* New York: Knopf.

Tobach, E. & Schneirla, T. C. (1968). The biopsychology of social behavior of animals. In R. E. Cooke (Ed.), *The biological basis of pediatric practice* (pp. 68–82). New York: McGraw-Hill.

Toulmin, S. (1981). Epistemology and developmental psychology. In E. S. Gollin (Ed.), *Developmental plasticity* (pp. 253–267). Orlando, FL: Academic Press.

White, L. A. (1949). *The science of culture.* New York: Grove Press.

Woodger, J. H. (1929). *Biological principles.* London: Routledge & Kegan Paul.

Zimbardo, P. G. (1985). *Psychology and life.* Glenview, IL: Scott, Foresman.

# Author Index

*Numbers in italics indicate pages with complete bibliographic information.*

## A

Adams, R. M., 126, 127, *134*
Ainsworth, R., 273, *275*
Alberts, W. W., 226, *235*
Alland, A., 179, *183*
Altmann, S. A., 32, *50, 52*
Amarnek, W. S., 76, 78, *83*
Ames, L. B., 79, *83*
Anderson, J. A., 217, *234*
Anderson, M. J. R., 260, *265*
Arbib, M. A., 217, 219, 225, 229, 231, *233, 236*
Arlin, P. K., 78, *82*
Aronson, L. R., 185, *206*, 242, 261, *265*, 271, 273, *275*
Ashby, W. R., 272, *275*
Atherton, M., 34, *50*
Austin, G. A., 248, *265*

## B

Baars, B. J., 209, 210, 211, 213, 215, 216, 231, *233, 234*
Baddeley, A. D., 214, *234*
Bahn, A. K., 110, 112, *116*
Bain, B., 86, *96*
Bandura, A., 37, *50*
Barber, D., 280, *286*

Barker, M., 280, *286*
Barlow, D. H., 108, *116*
Basen, J. A., 260, *266*
Bateson, P. P. G., 33, *50*
Bauer, H. R., 34, *60*
Bauman, R., 109, *115*
Beer, C. G., 32, 34, *50*
Bellugi, V., 62, *83*
Benson, F. B., 101, 102, 107, *115*
Bentley, A. F., 128, 131, *134*
Bergmann, G., 20, *28*
Berk, L. E., 93, *96*
Berko-Gleason, J., 45, *50*
Bernard, C., 274, *275, 286*
Bever, T. G., 59, 62, 70, *83*
Bishop, G. H., 227, *234*
Black, M., 121, 122, 123, 124, *134*
Bloom, F. E., 240, *265*
Bloom, L., 44, *50*
Boal, L. M., 34, *53*
Boden, M., 218, *234*
Bohannon, J. N., III, 45, *50*
Bohm, D., 284, *286*
Boysen, S., 34, *55*, 69, *83*
Brazier, D. Q., 223, *234*
Bridgeman, P. W., 282, *286*
Broadbent, D. E., 214, *234*
Brodal, A., 100, *115*
Brooks-Gunn, J., 24, *29*
Brown, C. H., 257, *267*

289

# Subject Index

*Page numbers followed by n indicate footnotes.*

## A

Activity
  as form of reflection, 199–200
  human, labour and, 200–201
Adaptation, appropriation versus, 204–205
Aggregational hierarchy, 273
Analogue models, 122
Animal(s), *see also specific animal*
  abilities of, interspecies communication and, 33–35, *see also* Interspecies communication
  psychological settings of, 3–7
  thinking in, 19–28, *see also* Cognition, in animals
Animal consciousness
  materialism and reductionism in, 137–160
    Griffin's *Question of Animal Awareness* and, 138–142
    mechanistic errors and dialectical potential in, 151–157
    mechanistic versus dialectical philosophy and, 143–151
    socio-political context and, 157–160
*Animal Thinking,* 25
Anomic aphasia, 107
Anthropocentrism argument, 140
Aphasia, 99–115
  classifications of, 101–110
  definitions of, 101–104
  levels concept applied to, 101, 110–114

Appropriation, adaptation versus, 204–205
*Artistic Animal, The,* 179
Avian intelligence, 35n, *see also* Interspecies communication, with African Grey parrot
Awareness, *see* Consciousness

## B

Behavior
  purpose and, 24–25
  social, integrative levels and, 264
  variables controlling, 22, 23–24
Behavioral evolution, human, *see* Human behavioral evolution
Behavioral sciences, dichotomization in, 75
Behaviorism
  myopic focusing of, 75–76
  nativism versus, 85–86
  praxics versus, 19–21
Biological alchemy model, of emergent development, 71–81
Biological reductionism, *see* Reductionism
Bipedalism, evoltuion of, 192–193
Birds, *see also* Interspecies communication, with African Grey parrot
  comparative intelligence of, 35n
Brain
  evolution of, 190–192
  global-workspace theory of consciousness and, 223–230